T A

CW00531868

THE RABKA FOUR
INSTRUMENTS OF GENOCIDE AND GRAND LARCENY

A Warning from History

Robin O'Neil

The Rabka Four: A Warning from History

All Rights Reserved. Copyright © 2011 Robin O'Neil

No part of this book may be reproduced or transmitted in any form or by any means, graphic, electronic, or mechanical, including photocopying, recording, taping or by any information storage or retrieval system, without the permission in writing from the copyright holder.

The right of Robin O'Neil to be identified as the author of this work has been asserted in accordance with the Copyright, Designs and Patents Act 1988 sections 77 and 78.

Spiderwize
Office 404, 4th Floor
Albany House
324/326 Regent Street
London
W1B 3HH
UK

www.spiderwize.com

The views expressed in this work are solely those of the author and do not necessarily reflect the views of the publisher, and the publisher hereby disclaims any responsibility for them.

The author would like to thank all those who have given permission to include extracts or images in this book. The author has made every endeavor to trace the copyright owners of each extract/image. There is, however, a small number of images for which the source is unknown to the author and publisher. We apologise for this and would be glad to hear from the copyright owners of these extracts/images so that due acknowledgement can be made in all future editions or removal of the extract/image.

ISBN: 978-1-908128-15-7

Other Publications by the author:

Belzec: Stepping Stone to Genocide: Published by the Museum of Jewish Heritage: wshalewitz@mjhnyc.org; NY, 2008

Oskar Schindler: Stepping Stone to Life: Published by Susaneking.com NY, 2010

Frontispiece: Sipo-SD School, Rabka, Poland:
by kind permission of Yad Vashem Photographic Archives

Note (Original photograph (1942). Translation: 'The School of the Commander-in-Chief of the Security Police and Security Services'). Displayed at the top of the building.

...it must all be recorded with not a single fact omitted... and when the time comes...as it surely will—let the world read and know what the murderers have done.'

'Yidn, shreibt un farschreib'[1]

For the families Künstlich (Kynst—Australia) and Galle—(USA)... wherever they are!

In Memory

Mojżesz and Rachel Künstlich (Neé Scheer)
Both murdered at the Sipo-SD Police School,
Rabka, Poland—1942.

Figure 1: circa 1926:
With their three sons:
Eleizer, Benjamin and Efraim.

****

And
2nd Lieutenant Americo S. Galle (USAF) Awarded: Air Medal
With 3 Oak Leaf Clusters, Purple Heart
Murdered by SS Security Forces at Enschede, Holland, 21st November 1944

****

To all flyers who failed to return home as the result of the
Kugel Erlass ('Bullet Decree')

****

*'Old men forget: yet all shall be forgot, But they'll remember with advantages
what feats they did that day'*
Shakespeare Henry V. 1V. 3

TABLE OF CONTENTS

Historical Background; The Police state; Evolving Security Apparatus: Sipo-SD; Functions of the SD; Genocidal Policies; Architects, Planners, Perpetrators; Security Amalgamations; Police in German Society; Ideological Differences; Idiosyncratic Language of the SS.

Emerging Conflict and Collusion: Ukrainian Auxiliaries and Helpers!

Security Services; Nowy Targ Actions;

Soviet-German Occupation; Poland is sliced in Half; Operation Barbarossa 22nd June 1941; Rabka Four Join the Hunting Party; Women and Children – Gender Killing Policy? Jews for Labour

Background to Events; The Leadership of zbV; Ominous beginnings; Entry into Lvov; Eye Witness Accounts; Persons Murdered on 4th July; Wulecki Hills; Courtyard Murders Hostel Ambramowicze; Murders 12th July; Murders 26th July; Dr Schoengarth's Shooting Seminar; Hans Krueger moves to Stanislawow.

Appendices:

Acknowledgements

N o work of this nature would be possible without the full support of Historical Archives. I am indebted to the Yad Vashem Archives, Israel; the United States Holocaust Memorial Museum; the George C Browder Archive; the National Archives at Kew and the British Library; The Directors Villa Hoge Boekel, Holland. To personally thank the many individuals who have helped and contributed to my research over many years was an impossible task. To close friends, survivors of the Holocaust, Archivists, and Academia in general, I pay due acknowledgment.

However, special mention must go to Darren Jelley, Museum Director 493rd Bomb Group Archives, Debach, Suffolk; the United States Embassy, London; to Krystyna Kynst, Melbourne, Australia; Sara Schon, Israel; Pastor Werner Oder, Bournmouth, Dieter Pohl, Germany; the Authors: Malcolm MacPherson and Hans Knoop who brought the Podhorodze catastrophe to notice of the general public and finally; to my long suffering mentors: Professor Michael Berkowitz, Sir Martin Gilbert and the late John Klier, who have born their duties with some endurance and fortitude. Finally, special thanks are extended to my long term editor, friend and mentor, Professor of the English language (USA) Joyce Field who I first met in the old East Galician town of Lvov many years ago when the search for justice began.

Postscript:

The very day that I received this book from the publishers I also received, after many years searching, photographs and family connections of 2nd Lt. Americo S. Galle (murdered by the SS 21 November 1944) and his flight colleague, Merle Auerbach (now aged 86 years). This presented many problems for me but without hesitation I contacted my editor and publishing assistant Joanne Moore who arranged, even at this very late stage, for these photographs to be inserted: See pages 179-80. I therefore further acknowledge and extend my thanks to Craig Galle; Candace (Galle) D'Addario (nephew and niece of Americo Galle); Jim and Bill Auerbach (sons of Merle Auerbach).

Note by the Author

I WAS MOTIVATED to write this account some twenty years ago when several Jewish survivors of the German Security Services Training School at Rabka related their stories to me. At that time I had no idea where this would lead but as my investigations proceeded I was drawn further and further into a black hole, an unbelievable pit of horror and deprivation. It soon became apparent that under the cloak of war—personal vendetta, corruption, robbery and murder—this criminal virus spread out to other places and was now endemic among the SS leadership and their associates. When the war finished our protagonists, for a time, escaped immediate attention, but as the evidence emerged they were, one by one, tracked down and dealt with according to the law.

This kind of work and, indeed, this small book gives me no pleasure and in many respects grinds one down and makes one ponder whether it was all worthwhile, or indeed, necessary after all these years. On reflection I concluded that it was right for two reasons: to expose the suffering of the individual victims and bring some comfort and justice to those left behind; and secondly, by this research providing the details and circumstances of Americo S. Galle's untimely, violent and unnecessary death. Lieutenant Galle was a single man, a Latin Scholar and devout Catholic. Americo's father, Vincenzo Poggiogalle was born in Tagliacozzo, Italy, a small town in the province of Abruzzo. He was an immigrant from Italy and changed his name to Galle on arrival at Ellis Island in 1912. Americo's mother, Margaret, was born outside of Naples, Italy. She met. Vincenzo in New York where they married. Vincenzo, like most immigrants from Tagliacozzo settled in Yonkers, New York where Americo, his brothers' Irving, Salvatore and Vincent Jr. were born and raised. Unfortunately, at this time, despite the assistance of the American Embassy I have been unable to trace his family or dependants, but the search goes on. Lieutenant Galle initially lay in an unmarked and unidentified grave in a foreign field but is now safely among his friends in an American War Cemetery.

One plus that survives and rises above all else in this misery is the individual bravery of Mojżesz and Rachel Künstlich and that of Lt. Americo Galle. These were exceptional cases where evidence of their conduct and bravery is corroborated by the very men who executed them.

For the first time I am able to show the world what happened to Lt Galle after leaving his damaged aircraft on that fateful day. Not only does the record show that he was killed in action but now, by this research, the circumstances surrounding his death.

One minus, alas—in spite of my best efforts and intentions to set out the day-today barbarity of these times, I doubt if it has been possible accurately to convey to the reader the realities. It was exceedingly difficult to describe truthfully, and with some clarity, the enormities of these crimes that quantitatively and qualitatively exceed human imagination.

There is more:

Having already included in the appendices a discussion programme regarding Pastor Werner Oder, I thought it was the best I could do in the circumstances and left it at that. However, on the day that I finalised this manuscript I received a telephone call from Pastor Werner requesting to see me to talk over his father's (Wilhelm) duties in the Police School.

We met and had an open, frank and friendly discussion which in many ways corroborated my own research: that his father was the SS 'execution' instructor at the school setting up mock and real situations using Jews who been brought into the School for this purpose. It was on these occasions I suggested, that his father had perfected 'shot in the neck' method, (*'Genickschuss Experte'*)? This operational exercise was subsequentely practiced in the entire Reich and occupied territories. It was the method that had killed my airman, 2nd Lieutenant *Americo S. Galle* in 1944. When I discussed this and the murder of *Mojżesz and Rachel Künstlich* who had been executed at the School, Werner agreed that in all probability his father would have been supervising these incidents: '*that was his job*', said Werner. Below: A photograph of a real life execution at Vinnitsa Ukraine in 1942 which had previousy appeared in a magazine co-written by Pastor Werner depicting the *'Genickschuss Experte'* in action.

Robin O'Neil
Hon. Research Fellow,
University College London,
Salisbury, UK—2011

Vinnitsa Ukraine in 1942

THE RABKA FOUR

INSTRUMENTS OF GENOCIDE AND GRAND LARCENY

A Warning from History

Sipo-SD

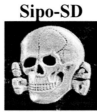

SCHOOL

Befehlshaber der Sicherheitspolizei und des SD im GG Schule des Sicherheitspolizei

Figure 3: Left to Right 1-4

1 SS – Brigadierfuehrer Dr. Karl Eberhard Schoengarth
2 SS – Untersturmfuehrer Wilhelm Karl Johannes Rosenbaum
3. SS – Schafuehrer Pieter Menten 'the Dutchman'
4. SS – Hauptsturmfuehrer Hans Krueger

Photographs Acknowledgements

PHOTOGRAPHS AND DOCUMENTS come from the author's own collection (A), the Jewish Historical Institute in Warsaw (HIW); United States Holocaust Memorial Museum (USHMM); the Yad Vashem Institute of National Remembrance (YV); Villa Hoge Boekel (VH); Robson Books (RB); Sir Martin Gilbert (A. MG); Salisbury Journal (SJ); National Archives (NA): Littman Library (LM): Debach Museum (DM); Wikipedia Resources; Chris Webb & Carmelo Lisciotto Archival Resources: New Statesman (NS): Krystyna Kynst (KK)[2]

Figures:

1. Mojżesz and Rachel Künstlich: (KK)

2. SD Uniform insignia: (A)

    2a. Add: 2a: Vinnitsa, Ukraine, 1942 (YV)

3. Rabka Four: (YV)

4. Map: Generalgouvernement 1942: (A. MG)

5. Map: East and West Galicia: (A. MG)

6. SS-Brigadier Karl Eberhard Schoengarth: (HEART)

7. SS-Major Wilhelm Rosenbaum: (YV)

8. SS-Captain Hans Krueger: (YV)

9. SS-Sonderfuehrer Pieter Menten 1935: (ANP)

10. Pieter Menten 1941: (De Telegraf)

11. SS: Heinrich Himmler (YV)

12. SS Reinhard Heydrich (USHMM)
13. Figure Partition of Poland 1939: (A. MG)

14. Sipo-SD School and Gestapo Interrogation Centre, Zakopane: (HIW)

15. SS Hauptsturmfuehrer Wilhelm Rosenbaum: (YV)

16. Map: Barbarossa 1941: (A. MG)

Note on Language

THE SS AND THE STATE BUREAUCRACY employed elaborate titles and designations which can be confusing to anyone but the specialist. As far as possible these designations have been simplified and wherever possible the German original has been used followed by the English translation in parentheses.

Terminology was a crucial device of the Nazis. As Raul Hilberg writes: their policy was: 'never utter the words appropriate to the action'.[3] The euphemistic language spoken within the Nazi Police State conveyed a climate of 'order' and 'intention'. This is the language of deception that helped shape the pattern of society, pertinently explored by Hans Paechter[4] and Viktor Klemperer.[5] The Nazis thought up new terms and used old words contrary to their original meaning. By euphemistic presentation, they misled their enemies, victims, and those hovering on the periphery, to divert and obscure the most hideous of crimes.[6]

It is very easy to be drawn into the Nazi code of euphemistic language. Indeed, it is difficult to avoid it and mean what we say. This double meaning was introduced as the system of genocide was perfected, thus, from October 1941 onwards, we find: *Judenaussiedlung* (emigration of Jews), *Judenumsiedlung* (Jewish resettlement) and *Judenevakuierung* (evacuation)—all synonyms for mass murder. When Eichmann defined his purpose we find: *Aussiedling* (evacuation); *Verwertung der Arbeiterscharft* (utilisation of labour); *Sachverwertung* (seizure and utilisation of personal belongings); and *Einbringung verborgener Werte und Immobilien* (confiscation of hidden assets and real estate).

When the instruments of murder moved from the euthanasia programme and concentration camps we find *abspritzen* (to spray—administering a lethal injection), or *Totbaden* (death baths). The euphemistic bureaucratic terminology was perfected by the SD as the persecution progressed: *Actionen* (operations), *Säuberung* (cleansing), *Sonderbehandlung* (special treatment), *Ausschaltung* (elimination), or *Exekutivmassnahme* (executive measure). After each mass execution in Auschwitz, camp commandant Rudolf Hoess submitted a report to the RSHA in a disguised formula:... *so und so viel Personen gesondert untergebracht worden seien* (...such and such a number of people separated, or segregated). These terms create the illusion of a bureaucratic paper chase, not genocide, where euphemistic 'double-speak' was an essential ingredient in the Nazi war against the Jews. The illusion of 'plain speak' contaminated, and indeed indoctrinated, the minor functionaries caught-up in State racial persecution policies.[7] Any sense of moral perspective was abandoned to conceal the true meaning of the word employed.

Another aspect of this was the euphemistic jargon of the concentration camp guards, police and male psychiatric nurses. They used such terms as '*not worth keeping*', '*treat*' the child, '*processed*', '*authorisation*' '*put on the grill*', which all simply meant 'to kill'. All those so engaged at every level of mass murder became used to communicating in this 'sanitised' language. Although it might appear a minor point, it had immense relevance in smoothing the day-to-day working in both the euthanasia institutions and the death camps.[8]

The euphemistic language was constantly being refined. When Eichmann's office was relieved of the task of compiling statistical reports pertaining to *Reinhardt*, these duties were passed over to Dr. Richard Korherr, the SS Chief statistician, who drafted a report for Himmler on the progress of the 'Final Solution'. He noted that 1,449,692 Polish Jews had already received *Sonderbehandlung* ('special treatment').[9] Himmler returned the document and demanded a more appropriate phrase, *durchgeschleust* (passed through), thereby suggesting that the numbers of Jews referred to in the report simply and safely passed through transit camps).[10]

Himmler was a past master of euphemistic language and used it continually. The only time he appears to have dropped this camouflage was in his speech in Posen in October 1943, when he spoke directly to his SS in a protected environment.[11] Historians too have differed over the exact terminology appropriate to defining the Jewish catastrophe.

Geographic Aspects

Area of the Generalgouvernement incorporating East and West Galicia 1942

Generalgouvernement Area

1942 - 1943 GENERAL GOVERNMENT

FORMERLY POLAND

MINSK •

MALY
TROSTENETS KZ

• BIALYSTOCK

TREBLINKA
900,000 MURDERED

WARSAW

150,000 MURDERED

CHELMNO

LODZ

SOBIBOR
250,000 MURDERED

REICHS COMMISSARIAT UKRAINE

GREATER GERMANY

LUBLIN

CHELM

MAJDANEK KZ

KRASNYSTAW   PIASCI

ZAMOSC

BELZEC
500,000 MURDERED

VOLHYNIA

AUSCHWITZ
1.25 Mil MURDERED

KRAKOW

PLASZOW KZ

JANOWSKA 100,00 MURDERED   TARNAPOL

RABKA SIPO-SD
SCHOOL

2,000 MURDERED

WEST GALICIA   LVOV

PODHORODZE

STRYJ

EAST GALICIA

SLOVAKIA

STANISLAWOW

KOLOMYJA •

0 10 20 30 40 50 MILES

0 20 40 60 80 KILOMETRES

HUNGARY

ROMANIA

DEATH CAMPS

R. O'NEIL 2011

Figure 4: The Generalgouvernement 1941- 1943

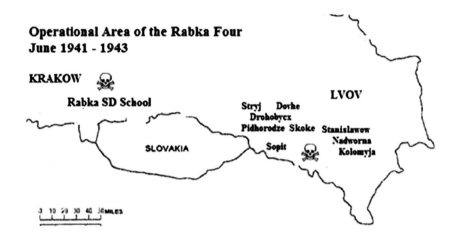

Figure 5: East and West Galicia

T HE AUSTRIANS originally referred to Galicia as 'Galicia-Lodomeria' after they expropriated that territory from the Polish-Lithuanian Commonwealth during the First Partition of Poland in 1772. Over the years, the borders varied slightly, especially during the Napoleonic Wars, following which Krakow and the surrounding lands were eventually added to Galicia. Galicia became the largest province of the Austro-Hungarian Empire, and bordered Moravia in the west and the Ottoman Empire to the south. For a time, Bukovina was included in Galicia; however, this area today forms a part of Romania. Galicia was returned to Poland when the Polish Republic was re-established after the First World War.

Today, the eastern half of Galicia is part of the Republic of the Ukraine, while the Western half lies in the Polish Republic. The term Galicia therefore no longer describes an administrative or political region in either country. By far the largest proportion of the rural population in agricultural eastern pre-war Galicia was of Ukrainian nationality, followed by Poles and Jews, the latter dominating commerce and trade.

It was not until the German invasion of the Soviet Union that east Galicia was integrated into the Generalgouvernement, an area where all manner of experiments directed at the Jewish population took place.[12] It was also the area where the most affluent Jews and the poorest lived alongside the wise men and the simple, the intelligentsia, artisans, beggars, and bankers alongside the Hasidim. Regardless of their social standing and circumstances, they all found their final resting places in Belzec, Sobibor and Treblinka. The region was a centre and spiritual home of the Diaspora, which was to have its heart torn out in the gas chambers of Belzec. Largely annihilated, the Jews of Galicia and their culture never recovered.

Introduction

THIS RESEARCH FOCUSES on the murderous activities of senior officers of the German Security Services who, at the outbreak of war in 1939, were brought together at the newly established Sipo-SD School at Zakopane and later Bad Rabka, Poland. In June 1941, all education facilities of the School were suspended in preparation for the war against Russia when the School leadership were dispatched to other duties. Their activities continued in the provincial districts of east Galicia, where their unprecedented murderous actions wiped out the intellectual base of the Polish intelligentsia and Jewish community towns.

The Sipo-SD School, between 1941 and 1944, was where the Nazis turned a girls' school into a centre for training the *Einzatsgruppen* (death squads) and Special Agents operating throughout Eastern Europe. They rounded up Jews and Poles and shot them in the woods behind the School. Children were used as live targets for machine-gun practice. It was here that SS-Major Rosenbaum and his staff perfected and developed the *Genickschuss* method of shooting victims in the nape of the neck—considered the most efficient means of execution other than the gas chambers. In 1944, this method also became known as the *Kugel Erlass* ('Bullet Decree'), which was widely adopted on Hitler's orders to deal with Allied airmen who parachuted to safety over occupied territory.

For the duration of the war, the 'Rabka Four', in some way or other, used the facilities of the establishment of the Sipo-SD School as a centre for their unlawful activities. All four protagonists remained in contact even after the war. Each is ultimately subjected to war crimes investigations and is appropriately dealt with within the War Crimes Judicial System.

Finally, as the result of the 'Rabka Four's' activities, a high percentage of Jews within the East and West Galicia were deported to the Belzec death damp never to return. Very few escaped from the camp to inform the world of the happenings within. One such escapee, Rudol Reder, published his memoir *Belzec* in Krakow, 1947. This personal account is attached as an appendix.

A brief introduction to our 'Rabka Four' opens with a brief summary of their beginnings and unfolds further with the passage of time. This was an exceptional period in our history and clearly, the very stuff of life was precariously balanced on the edge, for both sides.

1. SS - Brigadier Dr. Karl Eberhard Schoengarth.

Figure 6: SS - Brigadier Dr. Karl Eberhard Schoengarth.

Promotions

- SS-Untersturmfuehrer – November 9, 1936
- SS-Obersturmfuehrer – January 30, 1938
- SS-Hauptsturmfuehrer – April 20, 1938
- SS-Sturmbannfuehrer – August 1, 1938
- SS-Obersturmbannfuehrer – September 10, 1939
- SS-Standartenfuehrer – January 1, 1940
- SS-Oberfuehrer – January 30, 1941
- SS-Brigadefuehrer und Generalmajor der Polizei – January 30, 1943

Notable decorations

- War Merit Cross First Class with Swords
- War Merit Cross Second Class with Swords
- SS-Ehrenring
- Reichs Sport Badge
- Honour Sword of Reichsfuehrer SS

EBERHARD KARL SCHOENGARTH was born in Leipzig on 22nd April 1903. He studied law, achieved a doctorate and first joined the Nazi Party in 1922 but left the same year. After serving in the army during 1924 he worked as a university professor in Leibnitz. He rejoined the NSDAP in 1933 and joined the SS on 1st March 1933 as well as the Prussian Gestapo in 1935. From November 1935 to 1936 he was assigned to the press section in the Berlin Gestapo and during the first half of that year also acted as a political lawyer.

He was in charge of the Gestapo office in Arnsberg from May 1936 through 1937 and was commissioned as an SS-Untersturmfuehrer on 9th November 1936 when he was assigned to the SD Hauptamt (later the RSHA), from November 1936 to October 1939. He was promoted to SS-Obersturmfuehrer on the 30th January 1938, to SS-Hauptsturmfuehrer on the 20th April 1938 and to SS-Sturmbannfuehrer on the 1st August 1938. Four weeks later he was promoted to SS-Obersturmbannfuehrer on Himmler's orders. Dr. Schoengarth headed a number of Gestapo offices in Bielefeld during 1937-1938, then Dortmund in the first quarter of 1938 and Munster. He was the Senior Inspector of the Sipo and SD in Dresden from early October 1939 until he went to the Generalgouvernement in January 1941 and to supervise the newly re-constructed Sipo-SD School at Bad Rabka.

Dr. Schoengarth was promoted to SS-Colonel on the 1st January 1940 and was also made an Oberst der Polizei on the 1st March 1941, based in Krakow where he was Senior Commander of the Sipo and SD until mid-June 1943. In July 1941, Dr. Schoengarth led an Einsatzgruppen in Poland which saw service in Eastern Poland and Western Belorussia. In total, his command was responsible for murdering approximately over 17,000 victims at the time it was disbanded in the autumn of 1941, when he returned to Krakow to head the security police and direct operations in the reorganisation of the Sipo-SD School at Rabka. He was one of the top five SS commanders who worked very closely with Himmler and Heydrich and was a leading contributor at the Wannsee Conference on 20th January 1942, concerned with the Jewish Question.

2. SS-Untersturmfuehrer Wilhelm Karl Johannes Rosenbaum

Figure 7: SS-Untersturmfuehrer Wilhelm Karl Johannes Rosenbaum [13]

WILHELM ROSENBAUM was born on the 27th April, 1915 in Prenzlauer Berg, Berlin. His father, Peter Rosenbaum was a municipal worker at the central covered market at the Alexanderplatz. His mother died when Wilhelm was just one year old. The father re-married which brought forth the stepbrother of Wilhelm, Franz, born in 1910. He has been listed as missing since the Second World War. The second marriage was dissolved after three years.

On his 18th birthday, the 27th April, 1933, he was admitted to the NSDAP; and applied for work with the German Work Front and was accepted on the 5th August, 1933; he dealt with the postal dispatch office and other menial tasks. From the 1st November, 1934, until September, 1935, he served voluntarily with the 'Reichswhr', namely the 12th infantry-regiment Dessaue-Halberstadt. He has unpleasant memories of this period. The training was hard and the soldiers were often harassed and excessively put through the mill. He left the 'Reichswehre' as a Lance Corporal.

With the assistance of the SA, Wilhelm found a job as clerk at the SS-Head Office. Again he was given menial tasks, probably just within his capabilities. He remained there until the spring of 1936. On advice he applied for, and was accepted by the Head Office of the 'Staatspolzei', Berlin. He worked for Department 1, (Management and Law) as a police office clerk where he registered reports of weaponry and confiscation issues. He had no decision-making authority.

SS-Career Commences 1936

Based upon his employment at the head Office of the security police, Wilhelm was taken on temporarily (on probation) by the SS on the 1st July, 1936, a critical time at the onset of Security Services amalgamations. Wilhelm had married Hedwig Bober in August, 1937; on the 22nd June, 1938, their daughter Ellen was born. The marriage was not a success and they were divorced in 1940 by mutual consent.

With the outbreak of war against Poland, Rosenbaum, as a member of the SS, was transferred to the Inspector of the Security Police in Oppein. He was issued with a grey SS-uniform of the 'Oberschafuehrer' rank and joined the 'Dr Schafer' task force which consisted of some 60-80 men. This task force was commanded by SS-Obersturmbannfuehrer' Sens. This unit was to fight partisans and find 'insurgents' and render them harmless. After a short stay in Oppein, the task force operated in Tschenstochau and then moved to Krakow. In Krakow Rosenbaum was transferred to Sipo-SD squad that had to shoot enemies of the Reich who had been condemned by court martial. The officer in charge was Sipo-SD SS-Hauptsturmfuehrer Hans Krueger.[14] Krueger, a ruthless and brutal man, obsessed with national-socialist ideas, made an immediate impression on the 24-year-old Rosenbaum.

In early November, 1939, Rosenbaum was moved to the department of the Commander-in-Chief of the Security Police and Sipo-SD (BdS) in Krakow, whose leader was SS-Obergruppenfuehrer Dr. Karl Eberhard Schoengarth. Under the direct leadership of Hans Krueger (Schoengarth's deputy), Rosenbaum and his squad were mobilised to force their way into Jewish homes to collect money and 'contributions' from the Jews of Krakow.

In December, 1939, Rosenbaum was commissioned to take over the re-organisation of a School of the Commander-in-Chief of the Security Police

(Sipo-SD) in Zakopane as 'Wirtschaftsfuehrer' (economic leader). The commandant of this School was the aforementioned Hans Krueger.

In July, 1940, Rosenbaum was at that time on holiday. The School was transferred from Zakopane to Bad Rabka. He received orders to terminate his leave and go direct to Bad Rabka to take over duties of SS-Untersturmfuehrer and Police Secretary to the newly located School. He was now deputy to Hans Krueger. The Rosenbaum-Krueger administration was short lived. Transfers, promotions and sideways moves were numerous. Krueger was seconded to the office of Dr. Schoengarth in Krakow, and Rosenbaum took his place though without promotion.

Rosenbaum was like a rabbit caught in the headlights of a car when he was in the presence of Dr. Schoengarth.[15] Rosenbaum idolised him and became literally absorbed by him, as he had Hans Krueger; this may have been a result of his unlucky childhood from which sprang a longing for authority and a role model. Dr. Schoengarth quickly turned into his Fuehrer—a father figure to whom he submitted himself blindly and unconditionally. Therefore, he carried out his orders and directions, so to speak, automatically and without any forethought; on top of this, he had the tendency to interpret every move, every remark and comment of Dr. Schoengarth as an order. He made a diligent effort to receive a 'good mark' and deserve the high estimation of his Commander-in-Chief. His efforts to win the favour of Dr. Schoengarth led to effeminate subservience. He readily responded to each wish from his superior's mouth, hanging onto every word, serving him blindly and zealously as soon as he came back to Bad Rabka.

Rosenbaum did not always receive the appreciation and recognition he sought. In spite of everything, he remained, in the eyes of Dr. Schoengarth, the 'foolish kid' and 'bootjack'. Whenever Dr. Schoengarth showed his dissatisfaction with him, e.g., criticised loudly that the served food was not enjoyable, the Schnapps too warm etc., Rosenbaum was deeply hurt and became depressed. When criticised, Rosenbaum always felt this to be an outrageous insult, had a self-pitying reaction and immediately broke out in tears whenever Dr. Schoengarth criticised him. The situation even sank to the level of perversion in the sense that Rosenbaum considered it an honour when Dr. Schoengarth treated him in this manner.[16]

After a bizarre incident, when Rosenbaum presented Dr. Schoengarth with a brace of geese in order to please him, there were terrible repercussions. Rosenbaum had mistakenly taken the geese from property belonging to the

Higher SS Police Fuehrer, F.W. Krueger (not Hans Krueger) who was informed of the incident. Rosenbaum received a 'tongue lashing' from Dr. Schoengarth over the incident and as a result sank into further depths of depression and cried on the shoulders of a comrade, SS-Unterscharfuehrer Kluck.

All these humiliations did not result in Rosenbaum's breaking away from his inner fixations on Dr. Schoengarth as role model and father figure. His idolatry would remain intact, until reasons led to the separation of the roads of destiny that each man travelled. To outsiders, Rosenbaum, the small Untersturmfuehrer, became someone respectable, as a personal confidant and indispensable aid and organiser. Dr. Schoengarth, the big benefactor, had inadvertently turned him into a little god while despising him at the same time.

Oskar Schindler joins the throng

In April, 1941, Rosenbaum and his immediate staff were withdrawn from the School and seconded to Dr. Schoengarth's office in Krakow. Rosenbaum was given the task of organising an officers' club. It was at the officers' club that he came into contact with the art expert Pieter Menten ('the Dutchman') which was the start of a lasting friendship. Another welcome associate who frequented the club was the Krakow factory owner, Oskar Schindler. Rosenbaum remained in Krakow until receiving orders in June, 1941, to join the 'Einsatzcommando' zbV of Dr. Schoengarth with whom he remained, seeing service in Galicia, returning to take charge of the Sipo-SD School in Rabka in the autumn of 1941.

3. SS Captain Hans Krueger

Figure 8: Hans Krueger[17]

SS-CAPTAIN HANS KRUEGER was undoubtedly the right man for the job: he had joined the SA in 1929 at the age of twenty and was thus a seasoned 'alter Kaempfer (Old Soldier).' While growing up in his hometown of Poznan, he had seen the German-Polish 'cultural struggle' first-hand; together with his parents, he had been expelled by Poles in 1918. Krueger rose rapidly in the SA ranks. Instead of working in agriculture, for which he had specific training, he took over as leader of a SA 'Stormtrooper unit'. Shortly after the Nazis seized power in January 1933, Krueger was soon active in 'combating adversaries', having been appointed head of the Political Section in the Oranienburg concentration camp. After the Roehm Purge in June 1934, and the subsequent disarming of the SA, he was also demoted, ending up as a section head in a labour office.

Krueger did not return to the Nazi apparatus of repression until 1939, joining the Gestapo as an official in his native Posen and then in Krakow. Here, too, his Nazi fanaticism and brutal ruthlessness did not go unnoticed, and the Krakow KdS named him director of the Sipo-SD School in the town of Zakopane. There he trained Ukrainians and others as future Sipo-SD personnel, men whom he would later command in Stanislawow. Krueger's big chance came with the attack on the Soviet Union on the 22nd June, 1941, when he joined the zbV Commando unit as deputy to Dr. Schoengarth on their drive into Lvov.

4. Pieter Nicolaas Menten

Figure:9: Pieter Nicolaas Menten (right) with the Villagers pre war

O N THE 22ND MAY, 1976, Holland's biggest newspaper, *De Telegraf*, described a remarkable venture planned by the art-auctioneers Sotherby-Mak van Way. **Pieter Nicholaas Menten**, one of the richest men in Holland, was selling his Amsterdam apartment. He had to dispose of 425 pictures and other objets d'art for which there was no room in his country house already crammed with other treasures.

Menten was quoted as saying that his fortune had first been acquired in pre-war Poland; he had been ruined by the Nazi occupation, but had restored his finances, and his art collection. What Menten didn't say was that before the war he was working as an agent for the German Sipo-SD-*Abwehr* in Southern Poland and Galicia.

Pieter Nicloaas Menten was born on the 26 May 1899, in Amsterdam into a wealthy Amsterdam family. He claimed descent from the founders of Van den Bergh's (Unilever), claiming that his father had been in Royal Dutch Petroleum but broke away after the Shell take-over. The truth was not to become apparent until well after the war. In 1980 at the conclusion of a protracted War Crimes Trial, it was disclosed that his predecessors had never had anything to do with Shell or Unilever.

His father had been a dealer in rags and waste paper, the company was named Menten and Stark and his grandfather had been a butcher's assistant. Pieter had a brother Dirk, two years younger, who had joined the family's waste paper business.

On his father's death in 1922, Menten broke away from the family empire and established a business in Danzig under the name 'Menten and Stark.' With his business activities and deals of a dubious nature, he became a millionaire overnight, and the largest timber trader between Holland and Eastern Europe. Most of his acquired wealth in Danzig was the result of fraudulent activities and as a result he fled with his wife to Lvov where they occupied a small flat.

Pieter Menten soon developed an extensive export trade in Dutch products to Poland. He moved to East Galicia in 1923 (then in Poland and later part of Soviet-Ukraine), where he became a wealthy landowner and businessman. Described as mild-mannered and quiet, he developed a deep grudge against a prominent neighbouring Jewish family over a business dispute.

In Lvov, Menten was introduced to the Jew Isaac Pistiner who had two large estates that he had purchased from Princess Maria Lubomirska. Both men went into partnership, Menten renting from Pistiner the timber rights and the hunting lodge of the Sopot estate and almost immediately acquired the stance of benefactor and employer of the local peasants. The 'Dutchman' or 'Petro Menten' as he was known throughout the Stryj valley, became 'family' to Frieda and Isaac Pistiner and their eight children. This fatherly figure extended to relatives of the Pistiners, in particular to a young boy named Lieber (Bibi) Krumholz.

Figure 10: The Dutchman: Pieter Nicolaas Menten:
Art Expert 'V' Agent working for the German Security Services 1934 – 1943

Krumholz had been born in Lvov, now the Western Ukraine which used to be Eastern Galicia in pre-war Poland. His uncle, Isaac Pistiner, an industrialist who owned large forests in the Carpathian foothills, had a county house at Podhorodze—a village inhabited by Ukrainian peasants and Jews, where the Poles were the policemen, officials and foresters.

Pieter Menten befriended the young impressionable 'Bibi' Krumholz and they would often be seen together in their walks around the woods and fields in the Stryj valley. The Dutchman and Bibi Krumholz had become inseparable and remained so until Bibi Krumholz left Podhorodze for Palestine on the 24 October 1935. Bibi Krumholz took the name Chaviv Kanaan and kept in touch with his family by letter, also with postcards to his uncle Pieter Menten. A regular correspondence was maintained for years, and the dialogue ended when Poland was partitioned in 1939.

In 1935, Poland's hyper-inflation was nearly as bad as Germany's and provided rich opportunities for anyone with ready Dutch guilders. Pistiner, now sorely pressed for cash, was obliged to sell the Sopot estate to his partner Pieter Menten. Pieter Menten and his wife had become prominent among the Polish landowners and Jewish timber merchants around Lvov, and did many deals, some of a dubious nature with the Jew Isaac Pistiner. But also in 1935 Menten and Pistiner quarrelled, this time the basis of the dispute being a shady land and property fraud on Menten's holdings in the Stryj valley allegedly committed by Pistiner on Menten.

A bitter legal fight between the two men ensued and never abated. Meanwhile Menten had established his position in Lvov society. He became a naturalised Pole and also the honorary Dutch consul for Krakow. It was in this capacity he met Princess Juliana of the Netherlands, arriving in 1937 for a Carpathian honeymoon with her German husband Prince Bernhard. From 1936, the Sipo-SD and the Abwehr had been penetrating and recruiting sympathisers of the OUN movement.

The Menten case reflects the procedures adopted by the SD when recruiting 'V'-agents. Pieter Menten is pertinent to this study for the following reasons: it discloses the methods of counterespionage operating by Sipo-SD and Abwehr on the borderlands of the Reich. As all agents have to undergo training at some stage, we may presume that Sipo-SD training establishments in Germany (probably Berlin Greenwald) had some impute to field officers so engaged.

With the occupation of Poland, Sipo-SD were very quick to set up other training establishments of excellence, i.e., Zakopane and Rabka.

The above four individuals had come together in June 1941, at the commencement of the German-Russo-war where, in the ensuing months and years, they would cause havoc: pillaging, robbing and mass murder. Their subsequent background will emerge as we progress.

Uniformed and Non-uniformed German Police Ranks and Equivalent

Ranks in the SS and the U.S. Army

Security Police	Uniformed Police (Orpo)	SS	U.S. Army
Kriminalassistent	Zugwachmeister	Oberscharfuehrer	Staff sergeant
Kriminaloberassistent	Hauptwachtmeister	Hauptscharfuehrer	Technical sergeant
Kriminalsekretär	Meister	Sturmscharfuehrer	Master sergeant
Kriminalobersekretär	Leutnant	Untersturmfuehrer	Second lieutenant
Kriminalinspektor	Oberleutnant	Obersturmfuehrer	First lieutenant
Kriminalkommissar	Hauptmann	Hauptsturmfuehrer	Captain
Regierungs- und Kriminalrat	Major	Sturmbannfuehrer	Major
Oberregierungs- und Kriminalrat	Oberstleutnant	Obersturmbannfuehrer	Lieutenant colonel
Regierungs- und Kriminaldirektor	Oberst Oberfuehrer	Standartenfuehrer;	Colonel
Kriminaldirigent	Generalmajor	Brigadefuehrer	Brigadier general
Reichskriminaldirektor	Generalleutnant	Gruppenfuehrer	Major general

Chapter 1

The Nazi State and Blueprint of the Security Services

Figure: 11: Heinrich Himmler

Fig 12 Reinhardt Heydrich

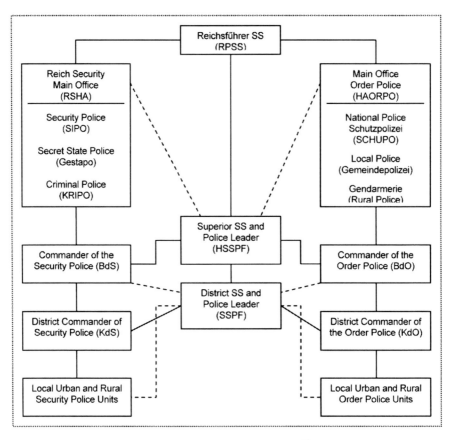

German Police Organization[18]

THE POWER BASE OF GENOCIDE

Historical Background:

WITH THE DEFEAT OF GERMANY in 1918, a fully-fledged democratic society was introduced and the Weimar Constitution[19] protected minorities against discrimination and fully enshrined human and civil rights. This did not completely satisfy the masses, as they felt their defeat greatly heightened their sense of paranoia. Many Germans simply refused to accept that their country had been defeated on the battlefield and preferred to believe that it had been brought about by internal enemies: pacifists, socialists and Jews. It was this situation that was the breeding ground of Nazism. Even before 1914, it was considered by many, the anti-Semites, that German Jewry would gradually disappear by natural wastage. German Jewry was more assimilated and sophisticated than their brethren in the east, and as such had small families and trends were towards even greater assimilation, secularisation, conversion and intermarriage.

It wasn't until the years between 1929 and 1933, when the rise of National Socialism took hold of the masses, that the seeds of the racial state were sown. The question arises, but will not be dealt with here, is why so many Germans voted for Hitler and his movement and put them into power? What we do know is that it resulted in the most catastrophic failure of democracy this century. Once in power, Hitler and his cohorts were able to bemuse the electorate with fuddled policies that camouflaged their real intent. It could be all things to all men. Parties of the left could not understand this Nazi phenomenon and retreated in panic, closing their doors behind them and sealing their fate. The middle Liberal middle classes were no better off; having endured war and defeat, the hyperinflation of 1923, and the Great Depression, they were confused and impotent to resist the unknown swirl of power that was contrary to the world as they saw it.

In the early 1920s Hitler had peddled his volkish racialist ideas accompanied with physical and verbal violence and anti-Semitism. In 1933 his racial theories were damped down as they served no useful purpose in the course of indoctrinating the people to his qualities as a serious leader and not an extreme revolutionary. With his charismatic personality he was able to mesmerise and lead the masses down the path of National Socialism and to the Nazi Police state that was to engulf a nation.[20]

The Police State

National Socialism was entirely indifferent towards the notion of a constitution. Germany was a state built on the Fuehrer principle: it was a Fuehrerstaat— Fuehrer state. It is ironic, but this same principle was applied to the leadership in the Jewish ghettos.

The Fuehrer consciously refused to give the Third Reich a written constitution. It already had a new constitution in the sense that there was a political organisation of the German people in the Third Reich. This, however, found expression not in the charter, but in a series of fundamental laws, and above all in the fundamental concepts that had already acquired the force of common law.[21]

This One-Party and One-Man State was encapsulated in the slogan: One Nation, One People, and One Leader *('Ein Reich, ein Volk, ein Fuehrer')*—the Leader's will is supreme law (*'der Wille des Fuehrers ist oberstes Gesetz'*). This was National Socialist law, which Goering defined as responsibility of the subordinate to the superior; authority from the superior to the subordinate.[22]

This dictum clearly emphasised that NS did not want to deprive the people of its right to self-determination; but believed that the will of the people was better represented by its own selection of its leaders. To this end, the NSP introduced many decrees, the most important of which was the suppression of all other parties.[23]

Central to this dictatorship in 1933 was the demolition of civil and human rights and the rule of law, and the materialisation of the *'Volksgemeinschaft'* (the 'people's community'). Germans were no longer citizens but *'Volksgenossen'* (national comrades) to which the Jews were excluded.[24] Hitler and his national socialists executed the disbanding of legislative acts and taking over unlimited discretionary powers in the order of the *'Fuehrerbefel'*, culminating in combining the High Offices of State for his own personal use within the principle of 'Fuerhrerprinzship', the leader principle on which all NS organisations were built.[25] The Fuehrerbefel became the instrument of government by which most of the criminal activities of the later stages of the Third Reich were carried out.

Undisciplined behaviour of the SS in the mistreating of Jews and political agitators caused early friction between the police and party officials: Himmler, Rohm and Dr. Hans Frank. Once this local difficulty had been overcome, it paved the way for more open abuse and murder in the Dachau concentration camp on the outskirts of Munich.[26]

Himmler was to make good use of this procedure in dealing with 'asocial elements' in 1937/8 by virtue of the authority given to him by Hitler.[27] The Euthanasia campaign rested on authority given by Hitler as Head of the SS and Security Services which, as it materialised, was a dress rehearsal for a solution to the 'Jewish Question'. This ideological model for Genocide was based on the murder of mental patients and handicapped people regarded by the state as genetically flawed.[28]

The Jews were already second-class citizens by dint of the Nuremberg Laws of 1935, which became the genesis of serious anti-Semitic attitudes. The principle of unequal citizenship was declared in the Second Nuremberg Law: '*Gesetz zur Regelung von Reichsburgerscahft und Staatszugehorigkeit*' (9/15/1935).[29] It gave people of German blood and political reliability the status of full citizenship (*Reichsburger*), whereas subjects of non-German blood are '*Staatsangehorig*' who have no right to vote, to bear arms, or to acquire landed property. In practice, the law was of little consequence; anti-Semitic measures were never based on it.[30]

The Evolving Security Apparatus: Sipo-SD

The abbreviation '*Nazi*,' the acronym '*Gestapo*,' and the initials '*SS*,' are well known to us today. We ponder when we hear '*SD*' and are even less uncertain when we hear the combination of '*Sipo-SD*', even though Sipo-SD was at the centre of the National Socialist police state.

SD was not a police organization and it did not belong to a uniform police system or have police functions. It concerned itself only with discovering what public opinion was and although it reported the intentions of hostile factions within the state, it took no executive action. Any executive action against treasonable groups concerned the Gestapo. The SD as such was a Party organization and served the Party and the State in equal proportion. The Party, however, lacked confidence in the SD and the State did not issue orders to it. Within the Party Organization SD agents kept the Gauleiters (Civic Leaders) informed of the state of affairs but they were not actual members of their staffs.

The function, for instance, of their office was to ascertain the moods and reactions of the people towards measures taken by the Government. It received no orders from the Party leaders.

THE SD may be divided into several sections which give a general overview of its compilation and purpose:

1. The SD was a party information agency developed to report on the morale, opinions and conditions of the people in all their 'spheres of life', (Amt 111). It reported foreign intelligence (Amt 6) and carried out various forms of research (Amt 7).

2. The SD was not a police force. It grew up and worked independently of the SS and the Gestapo. It had in general no executive powers and no powers of arrest.

3. It only dealt with Jewish problems in an advisory and research capacity. Its function as far as the Einsatzgruppen and concentration camps are concerned was similar. It carried out investigations on religious questions but played no part in the persecution of the Church.

4. Both in Germany and in occupied territory the term 'SD' was used in a very general sense to denote other departments, such as the RSHA and the Gestapo and Security Police. A considerable number of people who were really members of the SS and other organizations wore SD on their uniforms and were called 'SD men'. Consequently, many of the crimes with which the SD proper is charged were really committed by other groups.

5. The number of persons belonging to the SD who could have known about the Eichmann program, about Einsatzgruppen or about concentration camps was extremely small.

6. About half the agents employed by the SD were volunteers and half were paid as regular agents. It is within this category that our 'Dutchman', Pieter Menten, and Oskar Schindler were operating in Poland before and during the war period.

The functions of the SD can be further subdivided:

(1)   'General Information' which literally covered everything, as noted in official SD documents—the 'Lebensgebiete' or spheres vital to the Nazi government, all government offices, and social circles in Germany.

(2)   'Special Functions' referring to the elaboration of special files and lists of certain persons, primarily in countries which were to be invaded (See reference to the '88' list when zbV enter Lvov). The filing cards and lists held names of people who were to be subjected to the 'special regime', namely either to be physically destroyed or confined to concentration camps.

(3)   The function of supplying personnel for the special criminal organisations directly concerned with the realisation of German plans for the annihilation of the politically undesirable elements and intellectuals in the occupied territories, and for conducting savage 'executions' and 'actions'. [31]

In addition the SD was primarily charged with solving (not hands on) the 'Jewish Question'.

The SD always retained its character as a Party organisation, as distinguished from the Gestapo, which was a State organisation. The 'Jewish Question' and all that came to surround it, was unequivocally in the hands of the SD. This is powerfully illustrated by the fact that the SD was the organisation that created the *Einsatzgruppen* (Operational Groups), the mobile killing squads which roamed the rear areas behind the advancing Wehrmacht, murdering over one million victims on the Eastern front by shootings. Later, when the policy changed, the victims were deported to the death camps, which paved the way for the near total destruction of the Jews of mainland Europe.

By 1939, with the police amalgamations, the SD made great strides in establishing its credentials as the foremost security service in the Reich. After the outbreak of war the SD quickly moved into Poland to help widen security operations in the occupied areas.

The Himmler-Heydrich-Executive (HHE) set up a Training School in Zakopane, and later at Bad Rabka,[32] with the unwieldy title of *Befehlshaber der Sicherheitspolizei und des SD im GG Schule des Sicherheitspolizei.* By the outbreak of the German-Soviet war in 1941, the Sipo-SD had become an *élite* security and thoroughly politicised organisation.

The SD had its own organisation with an independent headquarters and posts established throughout the Reich and occupied territories. A membership of 3-4,000 professionals assisted by thousands of honorary members, known as 'V'-men (*'Vertrauensmänner'* = confidential agent/informer like Pieter Menten and Oskar Schindler), and by spies in other countries. The *Abwehr*, headed by Admiral Wilhelm Canaris, was the military intelligence branch and did not become amalgamated with the SD until near the end of the war when Canaris was arrested and immediately executed for allegedly being involved in the 20th July 1944 bomb plot against Hitler.

The SD always managed to keep ahead of their military partners, as the transfer and general movement of their members within the Reich were relatively infrequent, whereas the turnover of troops and administrative officers in the military was more rapid. This was policy within the SD; wherever possible SD leaders remained in the same location. As a result, the SD was significantly better organised than everyone else, with knowledge and information about local situations and particular individuals. Following Operation Barbarossa (the invasion of the Soviet Union), it was the only stable arm of the military in the Generalgouvernement.

The relationship between the Gestapo and the SD was sometimes ambiguous as measures in the Reich were carried out under the direction of the Gestapo assisted by the SD. Measures in the occupied regions were always under the leadership of the SD which was the most important link in the SS police machinery. It was a unique espionage and intelligence organisation spread over the entire territory, both in the 'Old Reich', as well as throughout occupied regions and countries.

Sipo: The term originated in the early years of the Nazi power in Germany. Germany, as a federal state, had a myriad of local and centralised police agencies, which often were un-coordinated and had overlapping jurisdictions. Himmler and Heydrich's grand plan was to fully absorb all the police and security apparatus into the structure of the SS. To this end, Himmler took command first of the Gestapo (itself developed from the Prussian Secret Police) and later of all the regular and criminal investigation police, assuming the title *Chef der Deutschen Polizei* (Chief of the German Police). As such he was nominally subordinate to Interior Minister Wilhelm Frick, but in practice Himmler answered to no-one but Hitler.

In 1936, the state security police were consolidated and placed under the central command of Reinhard Heydrich, already chief of the party Sicherheitsdienst (SD), and named jointly Sicherheitspolizei. The idea was to fully identify the party agency (SD) with the state agency (Sipo). Most of the Sipo members were encouraged or volunteered to become members of the SS and many held a rank in both organisations. In practice, however, the Sipo–SD frequently came into jurisdictional and operational conflict with each other, due in large part to the fact that the Gestapo and Kripo had many experienced, professional policemen and investigators that considered the SD as an organisation of amateurs and often thought the SD a rather incompetent agency.

Furthermore, in 1936, the state police agencies in Germany were statutorily divided into the *Ordnungspolizei* (regular or order police) and the *Sicherheitspolizei* (state security police). The two police branches were commonly known as the Orpo and Sipo (Kripo and Gestapo combined), respectively.

In September 1939, with the founding of the SS's RSHA (*Reichssicherheitshauptamt*), the Sicherheitspolizei as a functioning state agency ceased to exist as they were merged into the RSHA as separate departments. However, its terms survived in common usage within Nazi Germany.

Inspektor des Sicherheitspolizei und SD was used by local security force commanders in charge of SD, Gestapo, Kripo, and Orpo units. The Inspectors of the Security Police answered to both the RSHA and to local SS and Police Leaders. The term *Sipo* was also used figuratively to describe any security police forces of the RSHA.

Opposition Forces: Church and State

We now come to the heart of this racial state in dealing with all those outsiders who were opposed to it. Opposition was not to be tolerated and the machinery of the state had to be formed in dealing with those people labelled '*asocial*' or '*racially unhygienic*'. To these ends, the Nazi Regime turned to the 'Himmler-Heydrich-Executive' (HHE) and the forces at their disposal.

When the Nazis came to power in 1933 they fully intended to create a police state, the foundations of which had already been laid which they accomplished, surprisingly enough, with the acquiescence of the German people. The most pressing opposition, and the one most feared, was the Church. The conflict between Church and State was political rather than dogmatic. Hitler and other Nazi leaders had frequently declared that they were not interested in religious affairs. The Churches were deprived of political and social influence: institutions not connected with the service and ministerial duties were abolished and all YMCA buildings were taken over by Nazi welfare organisations.

On the whole, however, the Churches suffered less persecution than other independent organisations. By their co-operation in the co-ordination of German souls they remained generally unharmed. Despite the alienation of the Church, the government continued to collect taxes and pay minister's salaries, and the Roman Catholic Church concluded a concordat with the Nazi government. In truth, the Nazi government, once they had frightened the Churches into passive submission, more or less let them do their own thing as long as it suited them. Officers of the SS Security Services were barred from belonging to any church.[33]

Nazi policy favoured the *'Deutsche Christen'* denomination, which satisfied the requirements of the totalitarian State. This denomination denied the Old Testament's equal standing with the New Testament. It rejected the baptism of Jews, and maintained that each race understood divinity in its own way and rejected any international authority in matters of faith.[34] To the opposers of this new State, the term *'Neuheiden'* (new heathens) was coined to denote the various sects of religious new Order, including the German Race Movement, whose founder Ludendorff, author of the slogan *'Erlosung von Jesus Christus'* (deliver us from Jesus Christ) who claimed: 'The experiencing of God according to our race character and the German approach to God, springing from racial heritage, keep the race soul healthy'[35]

One sect, Rosenberg's German Faith Movement, was influential in the beginnings of the Nazi regime, due to the fact that socialist free-thinkers sought refuge in this organisation after their own communities had been suppressed. Removal of the radical leaders, however, deprived this movement of all importance in the new Police State of the Reich.[36]

There was a subtle difference between a Police State and the SS-Nazi Police State (NPS) that was later to prevail under the leadership of the 'HHE'.[37] It became clearly apparent from the coming to power of the Nazis in 1933, that a tightening of the rules of law and order must be re-defined for the benefit of the 'New Order'.

Genocidal Policies

The examination of the police detectives, other civil servants, and employees drawn into the Gestapo and the Kripo has revealed the complexity of the Security Police, Sipo. A few were indeed the sadistic sociopaths of popular imagery. The vast majority, however, were not. After several years of transformations, however, these more or less 'normal' men would manifest behaviour that made it difficult for their victims to distinguish them from the stereotype. Furthermore, all contributed in some way significantly to the horrors of the Third Reich.[38]

'Industrialised' mass murder integral to the Final Solution was instigated and supervised by a relatively small group of politically motivated state and security functionaries. Although ultimately accomplished by a combination of expertise, there was a clear delineation of function and its progression may be divided into two quite separate elements. The first was in the euthanasia programme where the methodology for the extermination of groups of people was first perfected, and the perpetrators thereafter retained for subsequent duty within Action Reinhardt. The second element was the delegation of authority by the KdF (Hitler's Chancellery) to the RSHA to implement genocidal policies in areas outside of the death camps.

The Nazi *'New Order'* with its visionary concepts was generally conducted openly and was answerable to the protocols of government. However, Action Reinhardt was an exception. This distinction is important for a basic understanding of the integral parts of the RSHA machine.

The catastrophic consequences of the Final Solution are of such a magnitude that it is difficult to comprehend how it was possible for such a small group of men to implement it so successfully. Of course, in the wider sense, a multitude of sympathetic or apathetic government personnel were also essential to its implementation, and indeed many were eager to rally around the Nazi flag.

Architects, Planners, Organisers and Perpetrators:

Architects and Planners: Fuehrer's Chancellery (KdF): Reichsfuehrer-SS Heinrich Himmler and SS-Lieutenant General Reinhardt Heydrich and associates: Himmler – Heydrich – Executive.
Organisers: Sipo-und SD (Gestapo/Kripo and working SD).
Perpetrators: Police Leadership – Globocnik's Reinhardt Organisation – Ukrainian Guard Units.

Security Amalgamation[39]

With the reconstruction of the security services in 1936 as we have discussed, there were all manner of difficulties to overcome. In the early days, the SD had to contend with an identity crisis involving their image and acceptance by the public; it was a somewhat ramshackle organisation with no budget, borrowed typewriters, cardboard boxes for files and very few personnel.[40] Winds of change were sweeping across Germany and many officials of all ranks who were considered to be politically unreliable were being purged. Others, who had shown their loyalty and commitment, were accepted for inclusion in the 'New Order'. In general, it was predictable that the Nazi State would adopt radical measures to improve the operational efficiency of the police and security agencies that were so central to its programme.[41] High on the agenda of this radical thinking was the dispersal of 'old wood'—officers who did not measure up—to the outer reaches, bringing in convinced Nazis to replace them.[42]

To most people, the SD was the guardian of Nazi policy and a despised and hated section of the security services, often referred to as the 'black power'. In occupied Poland and the Ukraine, the SD had become an unyielding octopus, with tentacles reaching to the outermost parts of the occupied territories. No one liked the SD; the Wehrmacht commanders cursed it and civilian government officials wrote poison-pen letters to Berlin about it. Yet, the SD was all-powerful. It is not known that anyone ever prevailed against it in the Generalgouvernement, or elsewhere. The Jewish Question and all that surrounded it, was emphatically in the hands of the SD.[43]

Police in German Society

It is a generally agreed, under Western democratic principles, that a police force can only operate in a free society with the consent of the people. Prior to the ascent of the Nazis, the German police force was no exception to this principle and had remained a fully professional and proud service from its inception. Throughout the Weimar Republic until the arrival of National Socialism in 1933, and the major reconstruction of all security services in 1936, the police strove to retain their independence as the guardians of civil law and public order. Yet a large majority of Schupo and Kripo officers secretly backed the Nazis long before 1933; they saw Nazism as the only authoritarian way of getting rid of the 'red menace' (communists) and solving Germany's internal problems and they welcomed the Nazi seizure of power.

To ensure both the police and public accepted the 'New Order', the State hierarchy formulated its own rules and regulations, which broke down many of the traditional boundaries of police and judicial power. To a hard-pressed police service, there were distinct advantages in these increased powers. For a start, it untied their hands from cumbersome ethics when negotiating the intricacies of criminal law and procedure. Search warrants, judges' rules for the interrogation of suspects and applications for bail were dispensed with—complaints against the police were prohibited. Instead, executive search orders, and orders for arrest and detention without any proper legal grounds were introduced and freely applied; statutory appearances before the courts were replaced by orders for committal to the newly established concentration camps for indefinite periods. Consequently, the police were now outside the very law they had previously sworn to uphold and were overtly encouraged by Heydrich to act ruthlessly.

This new turn of events may not have been completely acceptable to every police officer, but the camaraderie and the subculture of the police service held them together through these initial draconian changes. Eventually, by gradual involvement, the police found themselves so deeply involved in their work for the Nazi state that there was little opportunity of escape. They found themselves caught up in events that they had no power to change. One has a clear view of the difficulties facing the professional police officer from interviews conducted in 1971 by Gitta Sereny with Franz Stangl, the former commandant of Sobibor and Treblinka death camps.[44] Stangl, a native Austrian, exemplifies the pressure brought to bear on waverers.

Ideological Differences

The Sipo-SD, in its role as the main security service, was now the effective defender of the Party and State, and it was impressed on them that the Party was the State and the State the Party. Some disaffected career detectives did not welcome this all-embracing security system[45] and consequently suffered from a crisis of image and identity. They found themselves on the receiving end of SD penetration into their hitherto closely-guarded police culture, and struggled to resist Nazification and retain their professionalism and self-esteem. According to the Himmler dictum, the transfers between the SS, and Sipo-SD, were essential for an integrated Reich Security Service.

To the immense annoyance of long-established career detectives, the Gestapo, which they considered an inferior branch of the police service, plundered the ranks of the Kripo of its finest men. Further resentment was caused by the transfer of 'inadequate and inexperienced' officers from the Gestapo to normal detective duties in the Kripo; these were usually the poorly trained elements considered unfit even for Gestapo service. Such was the concern within the Kripo that these Gestapo misfits were not permitted to enter the service with the same rank. However, the Kripo were more receptive to Gestapo officers who had been rejected as 'politically unreliable'. The overall impression formed by the majority of Kripo officers was that these rejects from the Gestapo were arrogant and tended to lord it over fellow officers, considering themselves untouchable. As far as the Kripo were concerned, such men were fundamentally unsuitable for normal detective work.

The reorganisation resulted in many police officers becoming disillusioned and frustrated, and consequently seeking transfer or retirement rather than serve under the HHE 'umbrella'. This is perhaps the reason why several of the Kripo were encouraged to transfer to other agencies, one of which was the euthanasia programme (T4). These misgivings were fully understood by Heydrich who appreciated that his ideas would only be fully accepted by future generations of security personnel. Only later, when his policies had time to become established, would his vision of a fully integrated security apparatus be accomplished.

The era of the career detective was almost over with the introduction of career civil servants and academics of the higher social order—the officer class, appointed from outside to senior command posts in the security services and police. The majority of Sipo-SD personnel who filled the lower ranks were of a lower social status and had a lower standard of education.[46] Considerable emphasis was therefore placed on education and training which would continue throughout a candidate's career. Officer training lasted many months during which time the candidate would serve in all sections of the security offices, including Abwehr, Sipo-SD and Kripo, to obtain the necessary experience, earn the entitlement to wear the uniform and gain the respect of their subordinates.[47]

The HHE maintained a tight control of Sipo-SD recruitment. A distinct disadvantage to joining or remaining in the Sipo-SD was Catholicism whose adherents were continually being purged. In the Sereny-Stangl interviews, it is interesting to note Stangl's observations on this point. Known to be a Catholic and of suspect loyalty to the Nazis, Stangl was targeted for demotion. After the police re-organisation of 1939, when he moved to Gestapo headquarters in Linz, he was re-designated from Kriminalbeamter (established Detective and Civil Servant with pension rights) to Kriminalassistent (temporary appointment with no pension rights). Stangl successfully challenged this realignment of rank and was reinstated with the rank of Kriminaloberassistent.

Having tried and failed to downgrade him, the establishment then attacked his religious views. As it was known that he was a regular churchgoer, Stangl was served with an official document to sign which confirmed that he was a '*Gottgläubiger*' ('of no religious affiliation'), and that he had relinquished his religion and all further contacts with the Catholic Church.[48] After some misgivings—or so he claims—Stangl signed as directed. By thus surrendering his religious principles to the Nazi creed, Stangl had compromised himself and was set on a slippery slope.[49]

With the plundering of related agencies for recruits to the security services, it was initially accepted that some candidates would compromise the philosophy of the Sipo-SD. These elements, such as the rowdy uneducated members of the SA as well as the 'Old Guard', were therefore purged. To maintain the momentum of the recruitment drive, those who were physically sub-standard physically or unmilitary in demeanour were not automatically excluded from membership of the Sipo-SD. To emphasize the obsession with the notion of a pure German Volk, Himmler set genealogical requirements: Sipo SD non-commissioned officers and their wives were required to supply certified details of family blood lines going back to 1750. Refusal to comply or unacceptable results meant dismissal.[50]

There was such a degree of overlap between the SS, SD and Sipo that it was often difficult to establish the difference; for example, although Eichmann was a Gestapo officer, he wore the SD uniform. Gestapo officers serving in Germany tended to wear civilian clothes while those serving in the occupied territories usually wore the SD uniform. With few differences, the colour of the uniforms was the regulation Wehrmacht 'Feldgrau'—field-grey, the same as the Waffen-SS. The shirt was yellowish to indicate Nazi Party affiliation. A telltale sign of a

Sipo-SD officer was the high-brimmed field-grey cap with a black band bearing the silver 'Totenkopf', or Death's Head insignia.

Most of the personnel serving in the Einsatzgruppen, regardless of whether or not they were members of the SD, wore the full service uniform of the SS. Those who were actually SD men wore a small black diamond-shaped insignia, containing the letters 'SD' embroidered in silver, on the left sleeve. Those who had served in the Gestapo wore similar badges, but with a silver cord edging. The Sipo-SD held the mantle of leadership in the Einsatzgruppen in Poland and Russia, and in many wartime photographs of executions it is often difficult to differentiate between uniforms.[51]

The Sipo-SD of the HHE would, at the end of the day, be the main arm responsible for the mass extermination of the Jewish people—men, women and children. Many of these Jews would come from the towns and villages in Germany, where they had been part of the country's foundation. They had been resident for over a thousand years and their contribution to German life is immeasurable, especially in the aftermath of the First World War. Their contribution rebutted by the Nazi State, they were now to suffer ignominy of exclusion because of the 'Enabling Act', which not only excluded them from schools and universities, but also labelled them as foreigners within their own country.[52] Jealously guarding their German culture, these Jews strove to contribute to the well-being of that nation and failed in the effort. 'The ordinary men' of Hitler's executioners, excelled.

The Idiosyncratic Language of the SS

Finally, to the outsider, of which I partly include myself; the German security service rank structure is not easy to fully grasp. I am prompted to conjure up some kind of example of comprehending the idiosyncratic difficulties:

> 'Within the police state, two men sit across a table in the same office. One man (Herr Smith) is the director of the company and pays the wages. The other man, Herr Brown, is a lowly office clerk with the same company. Both men are members of the SS. However, Herr Smith (the boss), holds the SS rank of SS-Scharfuehrer (Sergeant). Herr Brown, on the other hand, holds the rank of SS-Obersturmbannfuehrer (Lieutenant colonel). This anomaly may present some internal difficulties in any acrimonious exchange over future disputed office policy. Could be tricky!'

Chapter 2

Soviet-German Occupation
and Ukrainian Collaboration

A **T THE OUTBREAK** of the Second World War the Germans and their neighbours, the Soviet Union, conspired to share the proceeds in the occupation of Poland: The Molotov–Ribbentrop Pact, named after the Soviet foreign minister, Vyacheslav Molotov, and the German foreign minister, Joachim von Ribbentrop. This pact was an agreement officially titled The Treaty of Non-Aggression between Germany and the Soviet Union and signed in Moscow in the late hours of 23rd August 1939. It was a non-aggression pact under which the Soviet Union and Nazi Germany each pledged to remain neutral in the event that either nation were attacked by a third party. It remained in effect until 22nd June 1941, when Germany invaded the Soviet Union.

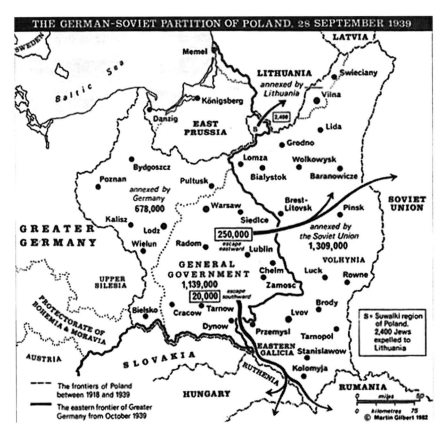

Figure 13: Partition of Poland.

The demarcation line for the partition was along the River Bug. By the time some refugees reached the German-Soviet demarcation line they found the border closed and heavily guarded. Some refugees attempted to cross, often at great risk and if caught, were arrested and brutally treated. Those refugees who were accepted and agreed to accept Soviet citizenship were safe. The rest faced deportation. Between 1940 and 1941, the Soviet secret police arrested and deported as 'unreliable elements' hundreds of thousands of residents from Poland to Siberia, Central Asia and other locations in the hinterland of the Soviet Union. Lvov remained secure until Barbarossa, June 22 1941.[53]

Emerging Conflict and Collusion

Once the Germans had established their presence in Poland (mid-1940), draconian measures were taken to reduce the country to a non-state, annexing parts to the Reich, and the setting up of administrative regions under the auspices of a regional network of Generalgouvernement administration which closely paralleled the regional machinery in the Reich.

The principle means of carrying out this policy was the mass evacuation of all classes of people to the 'Generalgouvernement' and confiscation of all movable and immovable property. The repatriation of internees in Hungary and Rumania, near the frontiers of Poland, was encouraged by the Germans for the following reasons:

1   Anti-German propaganda in Hungary and Rumania on the part of the refugees.
2   To prevent internees joining the Polish Army abroad, and
3   To obtain labour and recruits in annexed territory.

Administration in occupied Poland was solely in German hands and was carried out according to a German pattern. German laws and even Party N.S.D.A.P. decrees were introduced. All Poles were excluded from the Civil Service and also from leading positions in economic life; education was tightly controlled, and all universities were closed. The Poles, as a Slav race, had become second-class citizens and treated accordingly. The Germans had introduced a hierarchy of races: The Nordic peoples were at the apex, while the mixed Western Europeans, southern Europeans, the inferior Slavs, Asians, the Blacks, the mentally ill, and the Jews and Gypsies, were considered as non-human and beyond moral law (*untermensch*).

Ukrainian Auxiliaries and Helpers

The alliance of German-Ukrainian collaboration was now to be tested. In the '*Action Reinhardt*' camps (from March 1941) and many others in the occupied territories, the reports made by survivors identify the auxiliaries as their most cruel tormentors. These auxiliaries were identifiable by a special identity card that was issued at the Ukrainian training establishments at Trawniki, Furstenberg, and Zakopane/Rabka. These Ukrainian cadres were more tolerated than welcomed and were never permitted to bear full arms as the general German military or Security personnel. They were rarely issued with field grey Waffen SS/Sipo-SD uniforms, but issued with obsolete pre-war, black Allgemeine-SS (General SS) service dress, altered by the addition of light-green or light-blue facings to the collar and cuffs. In its short and murderous history, the Third Reich did not enjoy the advantage of more devoted hirelings and henchmen than it found within the Ukrainian Nationalist movement. Approximately 30,000 Ukrainian Nationals defected from the Western region of the Ukraine and collaborated with the Nazis. These collaborators were the recruits for the infamous '*Nachtgil*' and '*Roland*' battalions.

Ukrainian Nationalist 'patriots' served their Nazi masters long before the outbreak of World War II. In the 1930's (and earlier), The OUN had close connections with the Nazi Abwehr in Berlin (Sipo-SD). Espionage information provided by the OUN network in the Western Ukraine was utilised by the Third Reich to its best advantage when it invaded the Soviet Union. The Nazis made great use of the V-Agent network of Nazi Agents to establish and co-ordinate the Sipo-SD in the early 1930s. The activities of the Dutchman, Pieter Menten, are well recorded, acting as a 'V' agent for the German Abwehr.

The Nazi control of information was total and well rehearsed, and it arrived in Ukraine on many levels. The mainstay of propaganda decimation to the Ukrainians was of course the SD, Gestapo and Abwehr, which had been well rehearsed and filtered to the masses by radio, under the auspices of the Anti-Comintern Bureau.

The propaganda personnel within Ukraine were in the main Germans, Volksdeutsche (Polish/Ukrainian) and Ukrainians. The most insidious of the propagandists was a group of the so-called *Sonderfuhrers* (V-men as the Dutchman Pieter Menten), consisting partly of Ukrainian officers who, after the Soviet occupation, had sought refuge in Germany and occupied Poland. In May 1941 the Nazis assembled about 300 Ukrainian officers and Polish collaborators in the occupied territories and gave them various military units as '*Sonderfuhrers*'. It was for this purpose that the Zakopane/Rabka Sipo-SD Schools were formed and used to train these men. They were issued with German military uniforms, and instructed by Ukrainian/Polish speaking Sipo-SD instructors. Certainly, National Socialist ideology was high on the agenda, but as already stated, the implementation of mass killings within the training establishments or elsewhere may have been inferred and not spoken about.

In Soviet occupied Ukraine proper, at the outbreak of Barbarossa, the indigenous Ukrainians experienced their first doses of anti-Semitism through the broadcasts from Berlin, which commenced with the deafening sounds of marching music. The marching songs and cries of '*Sieg Heil*' continued for 15 minutes or so, followed by a brief pause. Then an announcement came: 'Radio Berlin, here is Berlin. An important speech will follow soon.' Partnership with German Fascism was their only means of achieving Ukrainian statehood. If Ukrainian statehood was to be at the expense of the annihilation of the Jews, then so be it. Both church and state administrators of the Ukraine looked to their own advantage at the expense of a select band of their population—the Jews.

The butchery of Ukrainian and Polish Jewry, even as early as the 4th July, 1941, cannot have gone unnoticed. The annihilation of Ukrainian Jewry to the fall of Kiev (Babi Yar) in late August, 1941, can only confirm the complicity (by inaction) of both Church and State.

The Nazis had no intention of acquiescing to the aspirations of the Ukrainians, but at the same time, depended on their co-operation until the difficulties of invasion and security control had subsided

Lvov was to become one the chief killing grounds as we shall see, which was taken on the 29/30th June, 1941: its first entrants after the Wehrmacht being the '*Nachtigal*' battalion, commanded by Professor Dr Theodore Oberlaender (Wehrmacht) and included Stephen Bandera and numerous members of his Organisation of Ukrainian Nationalists (OUN). Amorality linked Bandera and the Nazis, in spite of Hitler's express intention to clear all Slavs from the Ukraine: OUN's members accepted a 'Decalogue' specifying (among other things) that 'none would hesitate to commit the greatest crimes'.

Dr Oberlaender, a veteran of Hitler's abortive 1923 putsch, was assigned to exploit nationalism inside conquered territory, and the '*Nachtigal*' began at once a classic Ukrainian pogrom of Jews, Poles and political opponents.

The close collaboration between German and Ukrainian Nationalists in the Nazi-occupied territories during World War II was very extensive. In the entire region under Nazi rule the Ukrainians collaborated in the expectation of mutual respect and ideals—or so they thought.

By the 6th July, 1941, when '*Nachtigal*' marched on, some 7,000 of 160,000 Jewish men, women and children had been shot, beaten or tortured to death—not, of course, without assistance.

As is now known, many Ukrainian Nationalists served as guards in slave labour camps, extermination camps, and Jewish Ghettos. Tens of thousands of Ukrainians also served as Hiwis (helpers) in the Wehrmacht, while others accepted arms and fought alongside the Nazis in numerous special action and anti-partisan battalions, as well as in the larger formation, SS-Division Galicia.

Some of the eastern volunteers who fought in front-line combat units of the Waffen-SS and Wehrmacht did so with great gallantry and distinction, and would be justified in feeling proud of their military record. Unfortunately, the records of many were those who fought in the SS, who controlled auxiliary police units, and were distinguished not by gallantry but by atrocity. Indeed, after using them to assist in anti-Jewish atrocities, the Einsatzcommandos often also murdered their own auxiliaries, to ensure any witnesses did not survive

If the Einsatzcommandos were happy to use the services of the auxiliary police units to carry out some of their 'dirty work,' the concentration camp guard units were even more willing to enlist such aid in the dirtiest work in guarding the camps. From special training camps, such as the one in Trawniki near Lublin, the SD School at Berlin Grunwald (German recruits), Berlin Furstenberg (for Latvian recruits) and the SD School in Zakopane/Rabka (Ukrainian, Polish and German), came some of the most brutal criminals in history, whose behaviour towards the inmates matched the worst excesses of their German counterparts. We must remind ourselves, contrary to popular belief, that it was the Sipo-SD and not the *Allemeine-Schutzstaffeln* (General SS) that were responsible for Jewish murder. In addition to the abovenamed training academies, many others sprang up all over the occupied territories. In the small villages of Vught in the south of Holland, the Sipo-SD operated a training establishment called Ellerkom where Jews were brought in for treatment. The premier Schooling for these tasks were the Sipo-SD, experts in torture training, training other Sipo-SD in the finer points of their trade within the compounds of the Rabka Sipo-SD School. Many hundreds of Jews suffered and were killed in this establishment. Those that survived treatment were sent to the Sobibor or Belzec extermination camps.

How and why did these Ukrainian, and to a lesser extent, Polish citizens, engage in this complicity of genocide, directed to the entire extermination of the Jews— an entire ethnic-national group—and at the same time despise their 'Masters'? Accepting German dominance over them was a *fete a comple'e*. Why did these 'assistants to murder and cruelty' vehemently and enthusiastically carry out, with hatred, their duties to such a sadistic excess and at the same time translate their racist, anti-Semitic aggression, ignorance and hate-filled ideology into the language of extermination? Did 'other nationalities' under German domination and control engage in a like manner? We know more about the German perpetrators, and yet still yield to incomprehensible understanding why this phenomenon occurred. In the context of this paper, there is an overwhelming urge to give some explanation, particularly with regard to the Ukrainian and Polish Nationals engaged in pro-German activity during the Holocaust.

We have two interesting documents which expose the Nazi-Ukrainian collaboration in their oppressive conduct towards the enemy (Jews, communists, commissars, activists, anti Nazi partisans and others), and their overwhelming confidence that the war with Russia was all but won. It is tempting to review the whole aspect of 'anti-Semitism' throughout several decades in Russia and Eastern Europe. However, it is accepted by most scholars, that within the period of the Holocaust, the important groups that were engaged in the complicity of genocide against the Jews, were the Poles, Ukrainians, Latvians, and Lithuanians who were inherently anti-Semitic and to the present day, the Jews continue to be an anathema to the majority of these states.

As a further gesture of friendship and favour, the German military was ordered to show special preference to Ukrainians when releasing Soviet POWs. German military documents demonstrate that by the end of January, 1942, 280,108 Soviet POWs had been released. Of this number of discharges (*Entlassungen*), not a single soldier was Russian, but an astonishing total of 270,095 were Ukrainians. Of these a great majority (235,466) had been captured or surrendered in Ukraine itself. These ex-POWs were very much utilised to form the core of the auxiliary police (*Hilfspolizie*), although some were employed in a variety of jobs, such as farm work. Those Ukrainians who came from Galicia were very nationalistic, hated the Russians, and even more so the Jews. They had long memories of their treatment in the civil war of 1918-20, and more recently from the brutal occupation by Soviet troops in 1940, which followed the division of territory in Eastern Europe according to the secret protocols of the Molotov-Ribbentrop Pact of August 23, 1939.

The ethnic Russian POW's were not so fortunate. The campaign against the U.S.S.R was not just war between states and armies but a contest of ideologies, namely between National Socialism and Bolshevism, and it was to be fought to the death with no quarter taken. The draconian steps taken against the Russians prisoners were instigated by Heydrich and his Security Service (Sipo-SD of the *Einsatzgruppen*). The measures taken were the introduction of a 'screening service' of all ethnic Russian prisoners, including Jews. The Jews in particular were segregated and used for mine clearing operations and army labour. The Sixth Army at Kiev ordered the Jews from the Dulag (transit camps) at Khorol, where there were no latrines, to pick up the dirt with their hands and drop it into barrels. In Army District 10, the camp commander immediately shot all Jews and Communists.

From the Jewish collecting point of the 11th Army, Jewish soldiers were handed over to the Sipo-SD every month, around the clock. Einsatzgruppen report of group Sondercommando 4a reports the number of executions carried out had increased to 55,432, the larger part again being Jews, and a considerable part of these were again Jewish POW's who had been handed over to the Wehrmacht. At Borispol, at the request of the Commander of the Borispol POW camp, a platoon of Sondercommando 4a, shot 752 Jewish POWs on the 14th October, 1941, and 357 Jewish POWs on the 10th October, 1941. Executive activity continued: a sample monthly report shows 1,116 shot and 111 handed over to the Sipo-SD. The returning Ukrainians to their homeland also underwent screening, but for an entirely different purpose.

It was these Nationalist groups from which the Nazis selected the men to be indoctrinated and trained in the Sipo-SD School at Zakopane and Rabka. However, the Nazis were very careful not to entrust power and responsibility to them. According to the German view, the Ukrainians showed themselves to be unreliable as translators for the German Army as they violated secrecy rules. In the Belzec death camp two Ukrainian guards who were off duty drinking in a local bar were thrown into the gas chambers for bragging to other customers about the work.

The relationship between Ukrainian Nationalists and the Germans was starting to wear very thin. The hopes and dreams of the O.U.N. started to dissipate, and bed partners were falling out throughout the occupied areas. The Germans, who had had their hands full with the 'Jewish Question', were now confronted with increasing resentment from the Ukrainians who had new bedfellows in the *Armia Krajowa* (Polish resistance). The new centre of this Ukrainian opposition was in the Stanislawow region. By November-December, 1942, as we shall find out, SS Captain Hans Krueger had been very successful in dealing with the Jews and partially successful in the suppression of the main armed Polish underground. With the upsurge of Ukrainian opposition and now with the combined forces of the remnants of the largely dissipated *Armia Krajowa* in the Lvov-Stanislawow region, Krueger set about the brutal action to destroy all opposition, executing many communist sympathisers in the district

Again, Hans Kruger was successful and managed to contain this upsurge until the autumn of 1943, when the newly organised Ukrainian Army Rebellion

(UPA) mounted concerted offensives against the German occupational forces. During this phase, the initiative slipped from the Nazis, and from then on they never recovered.

By 1945, Jewish-Polish-Ukrainian relations had come full circle. Old accounts had been settled. The Ukrainians had risen from an under-class to a position of some consequence under their German patrons, only to be ditched when the tide of war turned. The Poles had side-stepped the indignity of a non-nation status and had survived and regained some measure of stability in their adjusted borders. The losers, of course, were the Jews who had been the subject of genocide, instigated by all three caretakers. Ukrainian-Polish anti-Semitism did not begin with Hitler's Third Reich, and it didn't end with it. It is there today as it has always been.

Chapter 3

The Sipo SD School and Gestapo
Interrogation Centre, Zakopane

Figure 14: 'The Palace' Hotel Stammery Gestapo Headquarters 1940-1944

Security Services[54]

DURING THE FIRST MONTHS after the occupation of Poland, the Commander-in-Chief of the Security Police (BdS) SS-Brigadier-Fuehrer Steckelbach [55] and then Dr Schoengarth founded the Sipo-SD School close by the Slovak border in Zakopane, a winter resort at the bottom of the high Tatra. The purpose of the School was to train selected candidates of Sipo-SD, Ukrainian Nazi sympathisers, Polish Police Officers and other Sipo-SD personnel ('V'-Agents) under the leadership of the Commandant, Hans Krueger. These agents were employed by the SD to collect information, and were known as V-men. These confidence men were unpaid and acted from unselfish motives and only in the interests of the State. Their work was not particularly secret and their existence was known to the whole nation. They did, however, use 'cover names'. They were drawn from all walks of life and some of the people recruited were those who took a critical attitude towards National Socialism. This was because the SD wished to get the reactions of the whole population and not

26

merely of party members. It would appear that at the end of the war about fifty per cent of these confidence men were regularly employed and paid and the remainder were volunteers. They were *not* allowed to resign.   The main curriculum at the School at this time was as follows: lecturer and course co-ordinator, Sipo-SD, Robert Weissmann—Criminal Law and Procedure in respect of those laws applicable to German Reich Law; Emergency laws and decrees drafted and initiated RSHA, Berlin.

Zakopane was turned into an entertainment centre for senior officers of the SS/Sipo-SD and the German army.   All Jews were supposed to have been removed from the district by the end of November, 1939, but two years later (according to the Ben-Ami report on the activities of the Zakopane Judenrat) 47 Jews were still in the area.[56] The Nazis had set them to work uncovering hidden Jewish 'treasures' in the town.[57] Some 200 documents relating to the three years of the activity of the Judenrat in Zakopane have survived.[58] Immediately after the Nazi take-over, Zakopane's largest hotel, the Palace, was converted into the headquarters of the Gestapo. Part of it served as the 'labour bureau', where Jews were sent to register for forced labour. The cellar at the hotel served as an interrogation centre and prison for Jews accused of disobeying Nazi laws. According to a number of Jewish witnesses who survived the war, as many as 300 Jews were murdered at this centre, many of them women and children. The head of the Gestapo was Robert Weissmann, and his deputy, Richard Samish.[59] The main hall on the first floor was reserved for dances and entertainment for the Nazi officers. The hotel was known to the local population as 'Death's Head Resort'[60].

In late 1939, on the outskirts Zakopane the Sipo-SD School, alongside the Gestapo headquarters, was established in the hotel 'Stamary'.

**Figure 15: SS-Oberscharfuehrer Wilhelm Rosenbaum Police
School Secretary 1940**

On the 20th April, 1940 Rosenbaum was appointed Police secretary at the School, and deputy to the Commandant (Hans Kruger). His duties were more of a matronly nature, arranging board and lodging, salaries, welfare of conscripts and general administrative duties. Among other permanent staff were the brothers, Oberscharfuehrers Wilhelm and Johann Mauer. The brothers, once officers in the Polish army and who spoke Ukrainian, were enlisted to train and instruct the Ukrainian personnel.[61] Their sister, Lisa Schumacher, nee Kaufmann, did the office work. The kitchen and feeding arrangements were organised by local Polish personnel.

Nowy Targ.

Closely associated to the happenings in Zakopane, and before Rabka, was the town of Nowy Targ, situated half way between Rabka and Zakopane. Like most Jews in Poland, those in Nowy Targ refused to believe that Hitler would dare attack Poland, in view of guarantees given to the latter by France and Great Britain. The Jews preferred to believe General Ridj-Shmigli, the Polish Chief of Staff, when he boasted that the prowess of the Polish Army would halt the Nazis in their tracks.[62]

Nowy Targ was in a precarious position because, only six months earlier (March, 1939), Slovakia had proclaimed its independence, under the aegis of Nazi

Germany. Nowy Targ's proximity the border made it a prime and vulnerable target. And, indeed, the Germans entered Nowy Targ on the first day of the war. The Polish troops retreated in disorder, commandeering all the vehicles in the area and leaving the population stranded to face the German forces.

Organised Nazi activity began with the arrival of the newly organised '*Einsatzgruppe*'. This 2,700-man unit, commanded by Gruppenfuehrer Bruno Steckelbach, set about with their prepared lists to round up the Polish intelligentsia and dispatch them immediately to forced labour and open graves. Having overcome all resistance, Nowy Targ was assigned to the Third Company, commanded by Dr E. Hasselberger. The main force of this Einsatzgruppe moved on to Jaroslav.[63]

Anti-Jewish measures were then set in place. All Jewish enterprises were taken over and handed over to the *Volksdeutsch* (German-speaking Poles). The other businesses were liquidated and their merchandise sent to Germany; all Jewish assets, business and personal, had to be declared; every Jew above the age of 10 had to wear the Jewish Star on an armband on the left sleeve; every Jew and Jewess had the name 'Israel' or 'Sarah' added in the town registry; Jews were forbidden to walk on the main streets and only allowed to shop at certain hours; the men were to cut off their beards and earlocks; Polish shops were closed to the Jews who were forced to bargain with the local Polish population for food; Jews were forced to sell all their belongings at a fraction of their worth. On the 12th November, 1939, all Jews were placed under the supervision of the Gestapo.[64]

The Germans wanted to clear the Podhala district of all its Jewish population, and Nowy Targ was selected as the site to which all Jews would be sent. Because Nowy Targ had no closed ghetto, no Jewish police force (*Ordnungsdienst*) was set up.[65]

The Jewish suffering was heightened by the behaviour of the Poles, who brought up fictitious accusations against any Jew they wanted out of the way. Their accusations were sufficient for the Gestapo to send the Jews to the Palace Hotel, Zakopane, where they were brutally tortured and murdered. While there were no organised roundups of Jews in Nowy Targ until 1942, the SS had the right to kill on the spot. As in Rabka, which I will refer to later, if you were a Jew and had the same name as the German commander (Rosenbaum), this was an added disadvantage, and your life was forfeited immediately.[66] The unfortunate Jew named Weissmann and his family were shot because they bore the same name as the Chief of the Gestapo in Zakopane, Robert Weissmann.[67]

The curriculum and training at the School underwent a number changes according to the progress of the war. Selective recruitment of German Sipo-SD, Ukrainian and Polish candidates were selected and trained in intelligence and counterintelligence activities.[68]

In Zakopane, through the intermediary of the Jewish Council, Oberscharfuehrer Rosenbaum took male and female workers from the Jewish population for maintenance and cleaning work, care of the garden and all other rough work. The Jew, Paul Beck, was appointed overseer of the Jewish workers. With his experience in practical things and a good portion of deceitfulness, Beck who spoke a number of languages[69] knew how to conduct himself and mediate between the 'Jew workers' and the SD. Rosenbaum always addressed himself to Beck, who knew his way around, whenever he wanted foodstuffs or other 'particular' goods. When, in July, 1940, the School and its permanent staff were about to be moved from Zakopane to Bad Rabka, [70] a number of Jewish workers (including Beck) were selected.

Bad Rabka was a small health resort located on both sides of the Raba River and halfway between Krakow and Zakopane. At the outbreak of war there were approximately 7,000 inhabitants in town. The Jewish population was about 1500, which increased during the early part of the war. Relatives and friends of the local Jews moved from the larger towns to the area less exposed to persecution elsewhere. This was an age-old custom of the Jews who sought protection and comfort in numbers in times of stress.

Institutions and offices of the Reich and Wehrmacht as well as other organisations established themselves in Bad Rabka. Apart from the local Commander's office and the government departments, there was a military convalescent home, children's homes and a German guest house. Bad Rabka had all the trappings of a small town, served well by both road and rail. The adjoining railway station of Chabowka, a central junction for the larger towns in Poland, also served Bad Rabka.

The School initially occupied premises of a requisitioned Jewish religious institution for children, situated near the Chabowka railway station. In the late autumn the School moved to new and much larger premises to the 'Theresianeum'—also called 'Thereska', a high School for girls. The four-story building was located in the northern part of the town called Slonna, on a tree-covered slope alongside the Slonna River which flowed into the Raba River.

Hans Kruger remained at the School until July, 1940, when he was recalled to Krakow to take up the duties of deputy to Dr Schoengarth. For a short period SS Hauptsturmfuehrer Rudolf Voigtlander took over, but within a few weeks Wilhelm Rosenbaum was appointed Commandant of the School, where he remained until April, 1941, when he was also recalled to Schoengarth's office for preparatory work for the implementation of 'Barbarossa'.[71] The School activities were suspended but retained a small staff to caretake the premises. The Sipo-SD School did not recommence activities until November, 1941, when both Rosenbaum and Schoengarth returned from Lvov.[72]

Chapter 4

Barbarossa: East Galicia Part 1[73]

O PERATION BARBAROSSA was the code name for Germany's invasion of the Soviet Union during World War II that began on 22 June 1941. Over 4.5 million troops of the Axis powers invaded the USSR along a 2,900 km (1,800 miles) front. In addition to the large number of troops, it also involved 600,000 motor vehicles and 750,000 horses. Planning for Operation Barbarossa started on 18 December 1940; the secret preparations and the military operation itself lasted almost a year, from spring to winter 1941. The Red Army repelled the Wehrmacht's strongest blow, and Adolf Hitler had not achieved the expected victory, but the Soviet Union's situation remained dire. Tactically, the Germans had won some resounding victories and occupied some of the most important economic areas of the country, mainly in Ukraine. Despite these successes, the Germans were pushed back from Moscow and could never mount an offensive simultaneously along the entire strategic Soviet-German front again.

Operation Barbarossa was the largest military operation in human history in both manpower and casualties. Its failure was a turning point in the Third Reich's fortunes. Most important, Operation Barbarossa opened up the Eastern Front, to which more forces were committed than in any other theatre of war in world history. Operation Barbarossa and the areas that fell under it became the site of some of the largest battles, deadliest atrocities, highest casualties, and most horrific conditions for Soviets and Germans alike, all of which influenced the course of both World War II and 20th century history.

During the Soviet occupation of East Galicia, the mainly Polish-Ukrainians (including Jews) had been subjected to Soviet style oppression in many forms. Like the Germans who were shortly to replace them, the Soviets installed their own style of government with devastating effect. Politically led by the NKVD, their first priority was (like the Germans) to rid themselves of the educated classes. Although the policies of both occupiers were similar in all respects, that is, by removing the threatening classes, there was one subtle difference. Under Soviet occupation, the intelligentsia (Polish/Ukrainian/Jews) were simply removed to the Gulags of the Soviet interior. If you were a Jew and should you be able to survive the labour camps and the harsh conditions - you lived. The Soviets deported over one million persons from this district during their period of occupation. Only a few weeks before the Germans arrived in Stanislawow, in June 1941, several transports had left Stanislawow on this long journey to deportation. Under German administration, the same tactics applied, but if you were Jewish - you died.[74]

Figure: 16 Map Barbarossa

The SS was convinced that it could by mass executions on the spot 'solve' the Jewish Question in Russia, by murdering all the Jews it could catch. No family was to be spared, nor were any resources to be wasted in setting-up ghettos, nor in the deportations of Jews to distant camps or murder sites. The killing was to be done in the towns and villages at the moment of military victory.

The Rabka Four Join the Hunting Party.

Units of *Einsatzcommandos* were established for this purpose by Heinrich Himmler. These units, led by high-ranking SS and police officers, were to follow the army; arrest prominent individuals according to the beforehand prepared proscription lists, and shoot them. Himmler warned that actions performed by these special units were not subject of control either by prosecutors or courts of law and that any attempt at interfering with these activities would be decisively punished.

A major conference held on the 21st May, 1941, between Heydrich and the Army Command (OKH), reviewed the security forces needed for the impending attack on the Soviet Union. The main principle to emerge, was an agreement with OKH of the defined responsibilities of the *Verfugungstruppe* (Emergency Troops/Einsatzgruppen) and the duties of the security units which would operate independently from, or alongside, the *Einsatzgruppen* against civilian populations, enemies of the state.[75]

In June 1941, the HHE decided to raise further emergency troops to deal with 'purification' duties behind Einsatzgruppe 'B' (shortly to be adjusted to 'C') on the Polish-Soviet borders into East Galicia. This direction was given to the *Einsatzgruppen zur besonderen Verwendung*, or zbV, a group of Sipo-SD personnel, commanded by the Commander-in-Chief of the Security Police BdS-Krakow, SS-Lieutenant General Dr Karl Eberhard Schoengarth (professor of Law) who organised three small Commandos.[76] Dr Schoengarth was an officer privy to the inner decision-making policies and was personally favoured by the HHE. His brief for the ensuing action was given to him personally by Himmler and before 'Barbarossa'.[77]

Initially, zbV were to act as a follow-up support unit to the main force of EG 'C' (commanded by SS-Gruppenfuehrer Otto Rasch), the Wehrmacht and units of the collaborating OUN (Ukrainian militia). The overall purpose of zbV was to tidy-up the rear areas by eradicating and crushing all political adversaries. To this end, Dr Schoengarth established a further six commando units which would act independently from his own command (zbV), which were designated to the areas of Slutsk, Pinsk, Brest-Litvosk, Bialystok, Vilna, Minsk and Rovno.[78] Dr Schoengarth reserved his own commando (including Krueger, Rosenbaum and Menten) for actions in and around Lvov, and then dispersed his commando to the major towns and cities in East Galicia where 'Special Offices for Jewish Affairs' (*Judenreferent*) were to be established.[79] We may define this period of operations up until the end of July 1941.

Although by the time these groups had been organised (end of June), many thousands of Jews had already been murdered in the Russian occupied territories, but there was no talk of a wholesale destruction policy. There was also no talk of permanent Jewish 'resettlement' (*Umsiedlung*), 'evacuation' (*Aussiedlung*) and 'death camps' (*Mortlager*). However, there seems little doubt that in the background, there was something going on as Dr Schoengarth carried with him orders for some kind of possible ultimate 'solution' to the 'Jewish question'.[80] Dr Schoengarth was a central Figure: with regard to 'Jewish affairs', which is endorsed by his presence at Wannsee on the 20th January 1942, when the final seal of approval for the codified mass expulsion of European Jewry to the death camps was finalised.[81] Although this decision was made on this date, we must appreciate that the Belzec death camp was already built and was undergoing tests. It is clearly apparent that there was a conspiracy by the SS to involve other government departments so that they, the SS, could not be in isolation as the deciders should the tide of war turn.

Figure 17: List of attendees at Wannsee   Dr Schoengarth line 3 – 3rd from right

From the evidence shown in post-war German testimonies and documents, we may deduce that the orders for the mass slaughter of Jews in the occupied Soviet territory of East Galicia had already been given.[82] We have confirmation of this as set out in the order from Heydrich of 2nd July 1941. Heydrich instructed the higher SS and police chiefs to brief the Einsatzgruppen commanders of how the war was to be conducted: to establish order and to liquidate the ruling elite of Bolshevik Russia (particularly Jews), as in other occupied regions. These orders dealt with Jews among the Russian prisoners of war—the summarily execution of all Jews in Party and State positions. Also attached to this order (Operational Order Number 8), sent out by the Chief of the Security Police and SD (and carried by zbV) was the 'German Research Book': 88 list, which contained lists of addresses of the Polish intelligentsia and a 'special Research Book' for the USSR, in which were entered all the names of dissidents considered dangerous and a threat to German aspirations.   To assist in carrying out these orders, were the collaborating Ukrainians and Poles who had all been specifically trained for this purpose in the SD School at Zakopane and Rabka.

In May 1941, in the preparation of Barbarossa, the Nazis had assembled about 300 Ukrainian officers and Polish collaborators in the occupied territories and designated them various military units as *'Sonderfuehrer'* ('interpreters' and advisers).   It was for this purpose, that the Zakopane/Rabka Sipo-SD School (as we shall see) were formed and used to train these men which were issued with German military uniforms, and instructed by Ukrainian/Polish speaking Sipo-SD instructors.   Certainly, National Socialist ideology was high on the agenda, but the implementation of mass killings in East Galicia may have been inferred but was not spoken about.   Schoengarth's secondment of Pieter Menten to zbV for dubious purposes was made under this provision.

Women and Children: Gender Killing Policy?

It is generally accepted that orders given to the Einsatzgruppen immediately before the Russian war, were to implement murder of all the Jewish Bolshevik leadership and intelligentsia, or any person who was, or likely to be, a threat to the Nazi state.   Whether this order was to include women and children is contentious. There appears to be no argument that the 'all gender' policy was certainly being carried out after mid-August 1941.   In the rural areas of Lithuania this practice had been endorsed even earlier (end of July), when the German civil authorities were murdering all Jews.[83]   It is in the opening weeks that we have conflicting views.

Certainly, in the first wave of killings, many thousands of Jewish men and communists of military age had been slaughtered, but the women and children detained in the round-ups were released.[84]   This is the debatable point.   Dr Otto Ohlendorf, Commander of Einsatzgruppen D: *'Himmler stated that an important part of our task consisted of the murder of Jews—women, men and children.   I was informed about this about four weeks before the advance'.*[85]

In Brest on 10th July 1941, over 6,000 Jews, men, women and children were shot into pits by the EG, which is recorded in the state archive of Brest.[86].   In the Tarnopol region, several hundred women and children were killed out of a total of 5,000 Jews, between the 4th and 11th July, 1941.[87] This all-gender policy was clearly understood by Dr. Ohlendorf.

These early all-gender killings appear to be corroborated by events occurring a thousand miles away in Lithuania. On 24th June 1941, in the border village of Gargzdai, the SD and auxiliary police, under the direction of Dr Walther Stahecker, shot 201 Jews, including women and children. Dr Stahecker claimed that he also had received orders (he claims from Heydrich) to kill all Jews regardless of gender. On 23rd June 1941, Dr Stahecker continued this order in the town of Tilsit where the local police shot Jews of all genders.[88]

Further evidence that there was such an order of 'total genocide order', including women and children, comes from SS-Captain Hans Krueger and that this order was given by Schoengarth just prior to him returning to Krakow at the end of July. So between the end of July and mid-August there was a definite policy. The high-powered Goring conference (Hitler, Goering, Lammers, Rosenberg and Keitel) on 16th July 1941, and Goering's subsequent order ('all necessary measures etc.') of 31st July 1941, seem to confirm this.[89] This 'order' by Goering has been the bedrock by historians for interpretation of a 'final solution'. Although this Goering order still stands, there is now further evidence of an earlier note recently found in the Moscow Special Archive that is dated 26th March 1941. This gives perhaps a wider interpretation and should not be underestimated and sends a clear message: that the final Chapter of the Holocaust has yet to be written, and that major contributory factors may yet be found in Russia. Researcher Goetz Aly (Berlin) has interpreted this information:

'In this document he commissioned Heydrich to submit a comprehensive blueprint of the organisational subject-related and material preparatory measures for the execution of the intended "final solution" of the Jewish Question'. Aly concludes that this note of 26th March 1941 must be understood as a confirmation, possibly an extension of an assignment for the 'final solution' of the 'Jewish Question'.[90]

We get some indication of the position from Hans Krueger:

'Among other things...I'd been given the order (from Dr Schoengarth) to clean the area of Jews. Initially, that meant deporting the Jewish population or concentrating them in ghettos. A bit later (he doesn't say exactly when), a directive from the RSHA gave the order to render the area judenfrei, a new interpretation: their liquidation'. [91]

In fact, it wasn't until the 14th August 1941, that there was some confirmation and clarification, when Himmler issued a confirmative directive to the Higher SS and Police Leaders (HSSPF) in the occupied Soviet territories, ordering them to murder all Jews irrespective of gender and age.[92]

An interesting point arises from these zbV actions, particularly the Podhorodze action of 7th July 1941, as we shall see later with the release of the Jewish women and children.[93] Were the standing orders of the day for East Galicia different from Lithuania? Only Jewish males over the age of 15 years were to be slaughtered. In zbV's second visit to the murder scene on 27th August 1941, they rounded up the women and children and murdered them.[94] By this action it would seem to confirm Himmler's Order of 14th August, 1941. One counter argument to this action at Podhorodze was that Pieter Menten was personally leading this massacre for personal reasons which may not count for 'lawful orders'.

We have a further contradictory explanation. At about this time (mid-July) there was a massive build up of reserve security forces to back up the Einsatzgruppen.[95] However, police auxiliaries report that the order to kill women and children did not come until the end of August 1941.[96] The probable answer is that (as we know), some women and children were being killed from the very commencement of 'Barbarossa' as Ohlendorf and Staheckler have stated. With the euphoria of success in the East, it was only a minor adjustment to spread this all-gender killing to East Galicia.

The evidence is both conflicting and confusing. We must remember that some of the leadership were expounding defensive explanations on a morally heated issue. There are two points (among others), which in my view, tend to confirm an all-out gender killing policy was instigated from the beginning: the general honesty of Ohlendorf which comes over in trial transcripts, and the evidence from a much lower ranking officer, SS-Unterfuehrer Krumbach who was engaged in Jewish slaughter in Tilsit, Lithuania (June 1941). In answer to the question 'were women and children also discussed?' he answered, 'According to an order from the Fuehrer, the whole of Eastern Jewry had to be exterminated so that there would be no longer Jewish blood available there to maintain a world Jewry'.[97]

So, from very early on, women and children were being killed in increasing numbers, but by mid-August it had become official policy. Before then, it very much depended on the whim and authority of individual commanders.

On 16th July 1941, Hitler authorised East Galicia to be incorporated into the Generalgouvnement (official decree 1st August 1941) in order to spike OUN aspirations of statehood. What makes this interesting is that East Galicia was now within the Reich jurisdiction (under Reich Law) with an added bonus of half a million Jews.[98] With no clear direction from above, the SD leadership were making the decisions and exercising their own initiatives and acting on their own responsibility (as encouraged by Heydrich) in dealing with this added problem—shooting them as exemplified by Hans Krueger in Nadworna and Stanislawow in early August 1941. By late August 1941, when Pieter Menten and zbV returned to Podhorodze, it didn't matter anymore.

Jews for Labour

It is clear that there was a consensus between the SS and the different departments of the local administration about the mission to kill Jews. This is documented in the statements of SS men such as Krueger and Katzmann, but also in the eager compliance of civilian officials. Kreishauptmann (local official) Heinz Albrecht, an official of the internal-affairs administration who had previously held a similar post in Konskie, was a committed National Socialist and dedicated anti-Semite, as reflected in his inaugural speech delivered in the town of Rohatyn on 28th September, 1941, and re-confirmed in testimony given in 1962: '*As a National Socialist, I believed then that the Jews were the cause of all our misfortune.*'

When the Higher SS and Police Leader, Frederich Wilhelm Krueger intervened in the Jewish question on 10th November, 1942, a Police Order was issued for the introduction of Jewish quarters as 254, 989 Jews had already been evacuated or resettled. Since the Higher SS and Police Leader gave further instructions to accelerate the total evacuation of the Jews, further considerable work was necessary in order to catch those Jews who were, for the time being, to be left in the armaments factories. These remaining Jews were declared labour prisoners of the Higher SS and Police Leader and held either in the factories themselves or in camps erected for this purpose. For Lvov itself a large camp was erected on the outskirts, which held 8,000 Jewish labour prisoners at the present time.

The agreement made with the Wehrmacht concerning employment and treatment of the labour prisoners was set down in writing: SS-Lieutenant General Katzmann's report, a vital piece of evidence on several levels. It uses the terms '*special treatment*' and '*resettlement*' in a context where it is undeniable that the terms meant killing. It lists the belongings of dead Jews and connects their fate specifically with *Action Reinhardt*. It demonstrates beyond question that forced labourers were not intended to remain alive after their labour had been completed (nor were the SS reluctant to shoot even those who were desperately needed for such labour). It also confirms that the SS were willing to override civilian authorities and employers in their ideological determination to make Galicia *'judenfrei'*. We have some evidence of these intentions, later witnessed by the late Dr Marek Redner:

'I was successful in gathering, from reliable witnesses, detailed accounts describing the liquidation of Lvov's Ghetto. The details reported are similar to scenes reported by others, relating the liquidation of Warsaw Ghetto during the April uprising. Same atrocities, mass shooting on-sight of people attempting to escape burning houses, throwing of grenades and incendiary explosives into hiding places and cellars. Children escaping the flames were driven right back by the Gestapo or grabbed by their feet, smashed against telephone poles and light posts. Those jumping from the windows were finished off with the weapon butts.

The streets and the pavement were literally flooding in streams of blood. Over ten thousand women with their children, that obediently followed the first orders to voluntarily evacuate their apartments, were marched by the Ukrainian Militia to the Janowski Camp, and were liquidated there in one day. This mass killing, in groups of 100 to 200 victims, was carried out in the hills of Kleparow suburbs. The victims were forced to undress and run to the bottom of a precipice, and killed in a hail of machine-gun fire, literally chopping up mothers with their children hugging together.

The screams of the victims were dampened by the roar of truck engines intentionally left running, but it was not possible to hide streams of blood seeping for several days down the valley toward the village of Kleparow. The inhabitants of Kleparow described these facts with tears in their eyes, and showed the piles of bones and ashes remaining in the valley after burning the corpses.'

The men were first moved to the Janowski Camp, employed in German factories and later suffered the same fate, when the front started to move closer. Lvov was finally empty of Jews, becoming *'Judenfrei'*. This was the news greeting the first survivors returning to Lvov, free of Jews. [99]

Chapter 5

Murder of the Lvov Professors[100]

Background

PRIOR TO SEPTEMBER 1939 and the joint Nazi-Soviet invasion of Poland, Lvov, then in the Second Polish Republic, had 318,000 inhabitants of different ethnic groups and religions, 60% of whom were Poles, 30% Jews and about 10% Ukrainians and Germans. The city was one of the most important cultural centres of pre-war Poland, housing Lvov University and Lvov Polytechnic. It was the home for many Polish and Jewish intellectuals, medical fraternities, political and cultural activists, scientists and members of Poland's interwar elite.

After Lvov was occupied by the Soviets in September 1939, Lvov University was renamed in honour of Ivan Franko, a Ukrainian hero, and the language of instruction was changed from Polish to Ukrainian. Lvov was captured by German forces on 30th June, after the German invasion of the Soviet Union in June 1941. Along with the German Wehrmacht units, a number of Abwehr and SS formations entered the city.

Ominous Beginnings:

On 29th June, the city of Lvov fell to the Germans, which was the trigger for Dr Schoengarth to initiate his move towards Lvov with his specialist officers of zbV and to set up the framework of ensuing Nazi policies in the districts of East Galicia.[101] Elsewhere, the Jewish communities were being subjected to atrocious brutality and trembled with thoughts of more to come.

On July 1st, 1941, as the fast-advancing German army entered the City, and only two days later, by order and with the encouragement of the Field Komandanture, Lvov's Ukrainians organized a systematic, unusually bloody and beastly pogrom of the City's Jews. The action

41

started July 3rd about 10 a.m. and lasted till 6 a.m., with German uncompromising punctuality.

Thousands of Ukrainian rioters, mostly young peasants between 14 and 30 years old, armed with heavy wooden sticks and steel bars, appeared from nowhere, simultaneously in all the Jewish neighbourhood streets. In groups of a dozen or more, they broke into one house after another, and then into individual apartments, beating every Jew they found in a heinous manner, frequently to kill. Crowds of followers, men and women, kept them company, and avidly lent a helping hand in beating or murdering the victims, and grabbing everything in sight in large bags brought along especially for this purpose. These hoodlums did not spare anyone—sick, handicapped, old people, women, even pregnant women, or children. In some houses they were throwing Jews, beaten unconscious, from balconies down to the streets or patios, to their death. Then they gathered groups of victims in the prisons near Zamarstynowska and Kazimierzowska streets (called Brygidki), where a pile of prisoners' bodies murdered the night of June 30, immediately prior to the entry of the Germans, was found by militias. The Germans and Ukrainians spread rumours implying that retreating Bolsheviks perpetrated the murders. They blamed the Jews, acting as 'prison guards and prison heads', and consequently directed the revenge toward all Jews, in accordance with their concept of collective responsibility, avenging the Jewish cooperation with the Soviet authorities.

Their revenge was atrocious. The Jews assembled in the prison yard were undressed, and subjected to tortures impossible to describe. They were beaten with wood and steel bars, suffering broken bones, torn beards, were forced to drink urine, to perform dancing and walking on nails, to mutually beat each other. Amidst screams and insults they were ordered to clean and bury the murdered prisoners in a common grave. All these activities were performed in the presence of German officers, observing with a smile the sadistic performance of Ukrainian hooligans, giving them encouragement. They also kept taking photographs, which was indeed, their preferred activity.[102]

Entry into Lvov

Dr Schoengarth, with 230 men of Commando zbV, marched into Lvov on the heels of 'EG' 'C' in the afternoon of the 2nd July, and immediately began to fulfil their orders, to arrest and execute all members of the Polish intelligentsia and prominent Jews.[103] Over 3,000 Ukrainian politicals had already either been murdered by the NKVD or left in the prisons.[104] As soon as the Russians had withdrawn, Ukrainian nationalists (OUN) turned on the Jews in the city, murdering up to 10,000 in the wake of the German occupation.[105] One other task, which had been delegated to zbV, was the seizure of art objects and documents. For these purposes and taken along for the ride, the expertise of a civilian foreign Dutch national and art expert, Pieter Menten, was given the title of *Sonderfuehrer* and the bogus rank of *SS-Scharfuehrer*.[106]

The Leadership of zbV:

SS-Brigadier Dr Schoengarth[107]	Commander-in-Chief BdS and zbV.
SS-Captain Hans Krueger[108]	Regional Commander KdS East Galicia
SS-Lieutenant Colonel Heim[109]	Deputy to Schoengarth
SS-Major Helmut Tanzmann	Personnel
SS-2nd Lt. Wilhelm Rosenbaum[110]	Logistics
SS-Sonderfuehrer Pieter Menten[111]	Interpreter
SS-2nd Lt. Oskar Brandt	Specialist Jewish Affairs
SS-2nd Lt. Kuch	Specialist Jewish Affairs
SS-2nd Lt. Grothjan	Specialist Jewish Affairs
SS-2nd Lt. Otsch Kiptka[112]	Specialist Jewish Affairs
SS-Scharfuehrer Horst Waldenburger	Specialist Jewish Affairs
SS-Captain Dr Walther Kutschmann	Specialist Jewish Affairs
SS-Scharfuehrer s[113]	

Officers from zbV, now in possession of the '88' list of prominent members of Lvov society, began to comb the area.[114] The first victim to succumb to the work of zbV was an ex-Polish prime minister, Kazimierz Bartel, who was immediately shot.[115] Professor Groer, of Lvov Medical Institute, and a witness, escaped death by chance and lived to testify to the Soviet Special Commission who investigated the crime after the war.[116]

During the night of 3/4th July, 23 Professors from the two Lvov Universities were arrested with their families and taken to the interrogation centre of 'Bursa Abragamovichev House', the headquarters of zbV. Some of the first victims were: Professor Tadeuz Ostrowski, a noted surgeon and art-collector; Professor Jan Grek, an internal medicine expert, also an art-collector. Among those killed by the zbV team during the next few days was every member of the Grek and Ostrawoski families. During that night, a firing squad was detailed consisting of five ethnic German SD, and two Ukrainian police auxiliaries.[117]

At 5 a.m. on the morning of 4th July, officers of zbV took the arrested professors and their families in trucks to the Wulecka hills where two Ukrainians had prepared a pit. All twenty-three professors and their families were then executed. The two Ukrainians were also executed and thrown on top of the other dead bodies.[118]   A witness to these murders was a resident from Lvov, named Golzmann, who also gave evidence to the 'Soviet Special Commission': he had seen 20 persons, including four professors, lawyers and doctors, brought into the yard of 8, Arciszewski Street and soon thereafter removed together under guard.[119] These murders were carefully concealed from the outside and repeated enquiries from relatives and friends were ignored. It wasn't until the first week in October 1943, when the Blobel Commando 1005 exhumed a number bodies at Wulecka and burned them, that the fate of the professors were known and confirmed.[120]   In addition to the recollections of the escaped Jewish prisoner Leon Wells,[121] the 'Soviet Special Commission' and two further witnesses, whose names were Mundel and Korn, corroborated the findings.[122] What part Hans Krueger played in these murders cannot be ascertained. After the war, Krueger was closely questioned about these murders but declined to give any further information.[123] We do know that the whole episode was conducted under the direct orders and supervision of Dr Schoengarth.[124]

Pieter Menten is prominent when delving into the facts surrounding the 'professors' murder. According to Simon Wiesenthal, in a letter to the author, 'it's not at all unlikely that Menten played some role in those professors' murders'.[125] For sure, the Lvov neighbours of the Ostrowsky's confirmed that Menten became their neighbour just hours after the murder, and immediately had men working to remove the art collection to a warehouse near the railway station.[126]

In the house of Dr Tadeusz Ostrowsky, which was situated at 3 Slowackiego Street, (now called Saskasangsko), had been used as a safe house for fellow art collectors of the Lvov intelligentsia society whose art collection was said to be worth millions.[127] On the night of the 3/4th July, it was Menten who had selected this venue from the '88 list'. In the company of Horst Wallenberger (the identity of this officer is debatable), Menten removed the occupants from the apartment and took them to the zbV headquarters for interrogation. The following morning, Menten alone, returned to the apartment and requisitioned it.   He also requisitioned the apartment of Jan Grek. Pieter Menten personally took possession of some of the most valuable art collections from these premises. After the professor's murder, Menten organised the removal of this valuable collection to a warehouse near the railway station and from there to Krakow. As was the case in these times, only a proportion of this property was dealt within the regulations and sent on to Berlin for cataloguing and disposal. A few selected items, no doubt of exceptional value, found their way to a secluded warehouse at the rear of the Sipo-SD Rabka School.[128]

One curious aspect of the Professors' murder, was how they were able to remain in Lvov under Soviet control, when it was clearly their principle to deport all such intellectuals to the outer regions? How were these academics, from the highest of Lvov cultural and literary society, able to operate under the eyes of the NKVD (later KGB)? It is not a question that can be fully answered here, but it is enough to say, that some selected members of the Polish elite were being protected by the Soviets for political reasons, perhaps to play the 'Polish Card' at some indeterminate time.[129]

Eyewitness Accounts:

The first genocidal action that the Nazis carried out in Galicia was the murder of the Lvov professors in the first week of July 1941. This was described by Polish historian Zygmunt Albert:[130]

Here is what the sole survivor, Professor Groer, stated:

'We were taken to the Abrahamowicz dormitory. The car was driven into the courtyard; brutally pushed we were crammed into the building and told to stand facing the wall. There were already many professors there. We were ordered to lower our heads. If someone moved he was hit with a rifle butt or his head was struck with fists. Once, when a new group of captured men was brought in, I tried to turn my head but was immediately hit with a rifle butt and, henceforth, I refrained from such attempts. It was probably half an hour past midnight, and I stood motionless until 2 a.m. More victims were brought in and told to stand against the wall. Every ten minutes or so we heard screams from the cellar and sounds of shots commented by one of the Germans: 'Einer weniger' (one less), which at that time I considered to be an attempt of terrorizing us. Every few minutes the name of a professor was called and the man was led to a room on the left. I remember well that Prof.

Ostrowski was called; afterwards I was the tenth or perhaps twelfth to go as the next. I found myself in a room where there were two officers, a younger one who arrested me and another one of a higher rank, a large, portly man. He immediately shouted at me: "You dog, you are a German and have betrayed your German country! You served the Bolsheviks! Why didn't you, when it was possible, depart with all the other Germans to the West?" I began to explain, at first quietly and then louder, as the officer raised his voice, that although I was of German descent I considered myself a Pole. Secondly, even had I intended to go west, the Soviet authorities would not have permitted it because of my high social position as University Professor and well-known clinician—they considered me indispensable? I was then asked to explain the meaning of the visiting cards of British consuls found in my possession. I replied that I was married to a titled English lady and we were often visited by British consuls. He grew quieter, and apparently impressed he said: "I'll have to speak to my boss, we shall see what can yet be done for you" and hurriedly left the room.

The younger officer who remained with me said quickly: "That really depends only on him, since he has got no superior here. Tell him you have made an important medical discovery, which may be useful to the German Army. This could save you." At that moment the other officer returned. There was no time to say a word because they ordered me out of the room. I was taken to the opposite, i.e., left side of the corridor, allowed to sit down and smoke a cigarette. I was even given a glass of water. Beside me there were standing professors Solowij and Rencki. After a while one of the Gestapo men asked them how old they were. I think they said 73 and 76. I was certain that due to their age they would be set free. I also thought that my case was not quite hopeless. The officer who interrogated me came and told me to go into the yard and walk, adding: "Behave as though you were never arrested." I began to walk round the yard smoking one cigarette after another. I kept my hands in my pockets. Some time went by. All at once two Gestapo men entered the yard from the street. The building and the yard were of course guarded. The two saw me, rushed at me, slapped my face shouting furiously what business I had in the yard strolling with my hands in my pockets. I said I was told to behave as a non-arrested person. They grunted something, lost interest in me and entered the building.

It was perhaps four o'clock in the morning when a group of 15 to 20 professors was led out of the building. The group was headed by four professors: Nowicki, Pilat, Ostrowski and, I think, Stozek who carried the bleeding body of young Ruff. They were followed among others by Witkiewicz. When they passed the gate and disappeared on the Abrahamowicz Street, the Gestapo ordered Mrs Ostrowska and perhaps also Mrs Grek to wash the blood off the stairs.

Twenty minutes later I heard some shots from the direction of the Wulecki Heights. Shortly afterwards a group of 20 to 30 persons was led into the yard through the same back door of the building and was told to stand in two-three rows facing the wall. Among them I recognized only Assistant Professor Mlczewski. Some time later the Germans led out of the building Dobrzaniecki's service staff, Ostrowski's cook and a younger female servant, Grek's cook and domestic servant and the English teacher who stayed with the Ostrowski family. The Gestapo chief, who had earlier interrogated me, asked them if they all belonged to the domestic service. Only the teacher replied negatively stating who she was. The German, obviously annoyed, ordered her to join at once the group facing the wall and told his comrade loudly that those (standing at the wall) were to be taken to prison, while those others (indicating the servants and me) are to go free. I noticed that the servants talked with the Gestapo man and a civilian agent. The Gestapo man told the servants to return home, take their belongings and go wherever they wanted. They may look for work. All would be well now, no more Poland or Soviets, henceforth there would be only Germany forever.

When I was about to leave I went up to a Gestapo men and asked him if I could get back my photo camera. He pointed to a room where another German arranged all the plunder. Being afraid they may remember the 20 dollars I had, I gave these to the Gestapo man and he returned my belongings. As I was leaving the room he rushed out saying: "Listen, give us your address because another unit may come and take you in again. We shall make a note here, so you will be left alone and not bothered again." He wrote down my address in his notebook, I left the building and went home. Later, the same morning, on my way to the clinic, I met near Prof. Ostrowski's apartment the Gestapo officer, who had arrested me on the previous night. Smiling he said: "You were very lucky." Several days later I was visited by two German officers who were present at my arrest. They wanted to buy my photo camera and carpets. During their visit I found out their names, one was Hacke, the other Keller or Kohler. In the following two or three months, despite evicting me from my apartment, the Germans came several times, beguiling me out of various valuable objects, for instance, photo cameras which I have been collecting. Once I ventured to ask Keller what happened to the other professors. Waving his hand he said: "They all were shot that night."'

Further witnesses come forward

Tadeusz Gumowski, an engineer, who lived with his family at Nabielak Street 53. During the night from July 3 to 4, 1941, they were woken up by the Germans and Ukrainians who demanded to see their registration papers. He described the events:

'[...] I spent some time sitting in the garden. At the first light of the day I saw soldiers digging a hole on the slope of Wulecki Heights. Feeling apprehensive, I called my family and we watched the Germans through the window. The pit was dug in about 30 minutes. The prisoners were brought in batches of four from the direction of the "Abrahamow buildings" (this was their name if I remember correctly) and made to stand in line facing us along the edge of the pit. The firing squad stood on the opposite side of the grave. A volley rang out and almost all fell into the pit. Prof. Witkiewicz crossed himself and collapsed. The men were not handcuffed. We counted the groups of four. If I remember correctly there were about five such groups. I think there were also three women. The whole action did not take long and other batches of four persons waited nearby. After the execution the ditch (grave) was quickly filled up, the earth stomped down. This was done by German soldiers. We, myself, my father, wife and sister, watched the execution in turn through field-glasses. At present my sister lives abroad, the other members of my family are dead. We watched from the same room and the same window. I recognized no one besides Prof. Witkiewicz. But the others recognized several persons including Professor Stozek and his sons, Professor Ostrowski and his wife, Professor Longchamps and probably his wife, and others. One of the ladies wore a blue shawl. There were probably three women. One of them, unable to walk, was dragged by two soldiers. My sister Zofia Nowak-Przygodzka lives now in Paris VII, 31 rue Rousselet. Approximately twenty persons were shot that night. None of them received a "coup de grace" after the volley. It is quite probable that some were buried alive. On the second or third day after the execution, I, my sister and my wife went towards the grave. It was rather indistinguishable and we found it only because we knew the exact spot. A bunch of flowers was on it and this may have been an indication to the Germans that the grave site was known; so, several days later, they excavated the bodies and took them away. I did not see the exhumation. We assumed it took place, because we noticed that the grave was dug up [...]'.

Gumowski's sister, Dr. Zofia Nowak-Przygodzka, who moved to Paris after the war, stated:

'[...] In Lvov I lived in a villa at 53 Nabielak street, next to the condominium of professors from the Institute of Technology, and also Prof. Witkiewicz. Our villa stood on a 12-meter high embankment, several hundred meters from the Wulecki Heights, where the Abrahamowicz Educational Institution and the House of Technicians were.

That critical night I got up as usual to take a look at my little children. As always I went up to the window to look around. We have been living in constant fear because of German searches and arrests. Two nights before, they sought Prof. Witkiewicz in my house. He was arrested the same night together with two other professors from the Institute of Technology.

I noticed some unusual movement on the Wulecki Heights: several men were digging. I woke my parents and we began to watch, but taking care not to be seen.

After some time we saw people coming down on the left side of the hill in a file along a pathless tract. I noticed soldiers in German uniforms and a dozen or so civilians. Some women (perhaps three) were at the end of the column. One wore a shawl, which was well visible because it undulated in the breeze. The soldiers helped some persons to walk down. Several persons were then lined up along the pit, which just had been dug. We heard dry cracks (shots), and the persons dropped from the row into the pit.

Another group followed the first to be executed. Distinguished among them was a grey-haired man who crossed himself. The women were in the rear. The pit was filled up. Watching the execution we had no idea what it was all about. There was no mention about it anywhere next day. We knew that to have witnessed it was dangerous to us. The execution was also watched from the neighbouring houses and it became known that professors were murdered.

Weeks later I ventured to go up the Wulecki Heights as though taking my children for a walk. I found the place of the execution. It hardly differed from the surroundings; the soil was slightly depressed, and grass grew as everywhere. I would not have found it had I not known the area well. I was told later that the Germans secretly exhumed the bodies.'

This is how Mrs Lomnicka described the execution after her husband was arrested:

'[...] sleep became impossible. I stood at the window for hours waiting for daybreak, wishing to go out and find out more about the raid. At dawn I saw from the window of our third floor apartment some movement on the Wulecki Heights. Silhouettes appeared, a group separated from the others who remained near the Abrahamowicz Institution, went down the slope and disappeared from sight behind the house of Dr Nowak-Przygodzki. I sat on the couch wondering what was going on at such an early hour (4 a.m.). At this moment I heard the first shots and all became clear. I rushed to the staircase where the window looked out to the right and made a better observation possible. I saw that those who came down the hill stopped midway in a small dale. I recognized German soldiers and men in civilian suits. There were also women; one figure gave the impression of being a priest in a cassock. One of the men wore a grey suit. He looked like my husband, but I quickly rejected the gruesome thought. They led up groups of five at a time and I saw how they collapsed after each volley of shots. I stood there "frozen to the floor", semi-conscious, watching the ghastly spectacle. Two ladies from the neighbourhood were with me: Mrs Janina Wieckowska, later to become the wife of judge Zenek in Kracow, and Mrs Solecka, wife of a secondary-school professor in Lvov at Kazimierzowska Street. Were those people the professors arrested that night? Was my husband among them? It was impossible to be certain because of the distance [...]'.

Maria ZaLeska, an artist who also lived at Nabielak Street, stated:

'[...] those to be executed were brought down the hill in pairs. The place of execution was not directly in front of us but slightly to the right. It was a small depression among the trees. I saw three of them standing on the embankment. One group after another came down the hill. If I remember correctly, one person was dressed in black—it could have been a woman or a priest. My son, with whom I shared the field-glasses, watched other groups. I saw at the rear a slowly walking, lone woman. In our field of vision there were three soldiers from a special squad. The area was so narrow and steep that it is doubtful whether there were more than six. If I remember correctly, the men I saw were hatless. I did not recognize anybody. We thought in horror that they might be executing Jews. Soon after the execution we were told that the grave was watched. I was there in winter or early summer, 1959. I knew nothing of the exhumation and was surprised that there was a depression where the grave was supposed to be and no embankment nearby. During that tragic night the events were also watched by my son—he was executed in Stutthof in 1944. In my opinion, most information could be obtained from Prof. Witkiewicz's tenant and Dr Ostrowski's housemaids—but who knows where they are?

Here is some hearsay evidence: 'the last to be shot was Mrs Ostrowska who could barely walk suffering from a leg ailment. A woman with a bright scarf was seen. Prof. Witkiewicz, easily recognized by his neighbours, was hatless. It was said that the Germans made the arrests assisted by Ukrainians, and that the list of those to be seized must have been prepared some time ago, because they also came to arrest Professor Dr Leszczynski who had died already some time ago, as a victim of Soviets.'

Zofia Orlinska-Skowronowa related:

'[...] we lived in a villa with a small garden at 55 Nabielak Street, facing Wulecka Street and, for this reason, could see the Wulecki Heights from the window of my room on the second floor. On the tragic day I was awoken by a volley of shots from the direction of Wulecki Heights.

Approaching the window I saw a group of persons, about 36, walking in a file from Abrahamowicz Institution in groups of five or six, assisted by a German, towards the foot of the hill. They stopped on the flat part of the slope, a clearing, stood in a row with their backs to Wulecka Street, facing the Abrahamowicz Institution. My attention was drawn to the firing squad consisting of about ten soldiers in grey-green uniforms, who shot those standing in front using automatic weapons. As the bodies that collapsed could not be seen on the surface, it was obvious that a pit had been dug, but I do not know when and by whom.

I have also noticed that at the left side of the pit there was a small group of military men. They may have been German officers. The execution described above was repeated until all prisoners, including one woman, were killed. I recognized Professor Wlodzimierz Stozek and his son Emanuel (called Mulek) among those executed. Concerning Emanuel, I remember a horrible moment: after the volley all persons except Mulek Stozek fell into the pit. He remained standing, but soon a single shot threw him into the common grave. He was dressed in a tobacco-brown coat and grey trousers. Prof. Stozek wore a dark overcoat. I watched the execution through binoculars from about 3:30 to 4 a.m. Shortly afterwards, several soldiers—they may have been either from the firing squad or from the group standing nearby—filled the pit up [...]'.

But the most detailed statement describing the execution was made by Karol Cieszkowski, an engineer:

'[...] during the night from July 3 to 4, about 10 p.m. I heard violent knocking on the door of the neighbouring house at 53c Nabielak Street, where Prof. Witkiewicz lived. Because no one opened the door, the intruders—I was told later—shot into the lock. At about thirty minutes past midnight the Germans came to our house and took away Professor Stozek—who lived on the ground floor—and his two sons. I do not know whether they went by car or were led away on foot. As I was very upset I could not sleep all night.

At 4 a.m.—I remember the time well because I was just checking my pulse by means of a phosphorescent watch. I heard some shots from the direction of Wulecki Heights. The day dawned. On the slope of the Wulecki Heights, well seen from the window of my corner room extending to the north, I saw some scores of civilians standing in a row and at a distance; right and left of them there were several smartly, one could say elegantly dressed German officers with revolvers in their hands. I did not count the civilians; there may have been about 40 to 50 persons. Somewhere in the middle of the slope I saw on the edge of an excavated pit four civilians facing the slope with their backs to me. Behind them were four German soldiers armed with rifles. An officer was nearby. Probably at his command, the soldiers fired simultaneously and the four persons fell into the pit. Another batch of four was led down the path and the action was repeated. This went on until all civilians were brought down and murdered. The last to be shot down was an elderly woman in a long black dress. She was alone and walked staggering. As she was led to the edge of the pit filled with corpses she reeled and was held up by an officer. A soldier shot her and she fell into the common grave.

As regards details of this execution, I recognized some persons with certainty, not only because I watched the proceedings through binoculars but some of them I knew very well and even with the naked eye I recognized their suits, characteristic movements, etc. I distinguished Prof. Stozek beyond question. He stood at the pit in his characteristic pose with his hands clasped behind his back. But I failed to see the professors Lomnicki, Pilat and Witkiewicz. I did not see or recognize professors Weigl and Krukowski. But I failed to see the execution of the first victims because I approached the window after the first shots were fired. Nor did I see any more women in addition to the one killed at the end.

I distinctly remember that four of the condemned came down the slope carrying an unconscious man. Another group of four came down slowly because one of them visibly limped. I suppose it might have been Prof. Bartel, but I failed to recognize him. I remember that when one of the groups of four stood at the edge of the pit, with their backs to the soldiers, one of the condemned turned to the killers and holding his hat in his hands (all condemned men took off their hats probably by order) began to remonstrate animatedly gesticulating. An officer standing at the side made a gesture as though telling him to turn round, and when the man obeyed, the soldiers shot him down.

I remember other details. A second before the order to 'fire' was given, one of the victims jumped into the pit, probably to save himself, and tried to get out immediately after the volley, but a soldier shot him; the man staggered and fell into the grave.

The pit was rectangular, divided by a non-excavated strip of earth, so that the victims standing on it fell, after being shot, forwards or backwards always into the pit. It happened only once that one of Prof. Stozek's sons standing on this narrow strip at the end of the line of four did not—after the volley—fall into the pit, but his body was pushed down by soldiers.

After the execution the squad led by an officer remained at the pit. The soldiers took off their coats, rolled up their sleeves, picked up spades and began to fill up the grave. At first, they proceeded carefully because the earth was spattered with blood, which I saw as large red patches. From time to time the soldiers interrupted their work and listened to the officer who seemed to talk to them or explain something.

The execution was watched from my window by my father, my sister and a tenant. They all came to my room because being farthest to the north, it was nearest towards the Wulecki Heights. Watching the murders, my father did not say a word and afterwards never talked to me about them. But my sister and the tenant recognizing individual persons (for instance when Prof. Stozek's sons were led to the pit) cried: "Oh, they are leading Mulek!"'

Persons Murdered 4th July 1941: Wulecki Hills

1. Prof. Dr Antoni Cieszynski, age 59 Chairman of Stomatology, UJK
2. Prof. Dr Wladyslaw Dobrzaniecki, age 44, head of Surgery, PSP
3. Prof. Dr Jan Grek, age 66, Chairman of. Internal Diseases, UJK
4. Maria Grekowa, age 57, wife of prof. Grek
5. Doc. Dr Jerzy Grzedzielski, age 40, Chairman of Ophtalmology UJK
6. Prof. Dr Edward Hamerski, age 43, Chairman of Internal Diseases, AWL
7. Prof. Dr Henryk Hilarowicz, age 51, Chairman of Surgery, UJK
8. Priest Dr Teol Wladyslaw Komornicki, age 29, relative of Mrs Ostrowska
9. Eugeniusz Kostecki, age 36, husband of prof. Dobrzaniecki's housekeeper

10. Prof. Dr Wlodzimierz Krukowski, age 53, Chairman of Electrical Measurements, PL

11. Prof. Dr Roman Longchamps de Berier, age 59 Chairman of Civil Law, UJK

12. Bronislaw Longchamps de Berier, age 25, PL-graduate, son of professor

13. Zygmunt Longchamps de Berier, age 23, PL-graduate, son of professor

14. Kazimierz Longchamps de Berier, age 18, Secondary School-graduate, son of professor

15. Prof. Dr Antoni Lomnicki, age 60, Chairman of Mathematics, PL

16. Adam Miesowicz, age 19, HighSchool graduate, grandson of professor Solowij

17. Prof. Dr Witold Nowicki, age 63, Chairman of Pathological Anatomy, UJK

18. Dr med. Jerzy Nowicki, age 27, senior assistant of the Chair Hygiene, UJK, son of professor

19. Prof. Dr Tadeusz Ostrowski, age 60, Chairman of Surgery, UJK

20. Jadwiga Ostrowska, age 59, wife of prof. Ostrowski

21. Prof. Dr Stanislaw Pilat, age 60, Chairman of Petrol and Earth-Gas Technology, PL

22. Prof. Dr Stanislaw Progulski, age 67, Chairman of Pediatrics UJK

23. Ing. Andrzej Progulski, age 29, son of professor

24. Prof. Dr Roman Rencki, age 67, Chairman of Internal Diseases, UJK

25. Dr med. Stanislaw Ruff, age 69, Chairman of Surgery, Jewish Hospital taken from prof. Ostrowski's flat with his family

26. Anna Ruffowa, age 55, wife of dr Ruff

27. Ing. Adam Ruff, age 30, son of dr Ruff

28. Prof. Dr Wlodzimierz Sieradzki, age 70, Chairman of Forensic Medicine, UJK

29. Prof. Dr Adam Solowij, age 82, ret, Chairman of Obsterics and Gynaecology, PSP

30. Prof. Dr Wlodzimierz Stozek, age 57, Chairman of Mathematics PL

31. Ing. Eustachy Stozek, age 29, ass. PL, son of professor

32. Emanuel Stozek, age 24, PL-graduate, son of professor

33. Dr Iur. Tadeusz Tapkowski, age 44, taken from professor Dobrzaniecki's flat

34. Prof. Dr Kazimierz Vetulani, age 52, Chairman of Theoretical Mechanics PL

35. Prof. Dr Kasper Weigel, age 61, Chairman of Measurements PL

36. Mgr iur. Jozef Weigel, age 33, son of professor

37. Prof. Dr Roman Witkiewicz, age 61, Chairman of Mechanical Measurements PL
38. Prof. Dr Tadeusz Boy-Zelenski, age 66, writer, Chairman of French Literature at the University, arrested in prof. Grek's flat

Persons murdered in the courtyard of the hostel of Abramowicze:

1. Katarzyna Demko, age 34, teacher of English, taken from apartment of Prof. Ostrowski
2. Doc. Dr Stanislaw Maczewski, age 49, Chairman of Obsterics and Gynaecology, PSP
3. Maria Reymanowa, age 40, nurse taken from apartment of Prof. Ostrowski
4. Wolisch, age 40-45, businessman taken from prof. Sieradzki's flat

Persons murdered on 12th July 1941:

1. Prof. Dr Henryk Korowicz, age 53, Chairman of Economics, AHZ
2. Prof. Dr Stanislaw Ruziewicz, age 53, Chairman of Mathematics, AHZ

Person murdered in prison on 24th July 1941:

1. Prof. Dr Kazimierz Bartel, age 59, Chairman of Design Geometry, PL, former prime minister of Polish Republic (three terms of office), who has been arrested already on 2nd July 1941.

After World War II the leadership of the Soviet Union made attempts to diminish the Polish cultural and historic legacy of Lvov. Crimes committed east of the Curzon line could not be prosecuted by Polish courts. Information on the atrocities that took place in Lvov was restricted.

In 1960 Dr Helena Krukowska, the widow of Prof. Dr Włodzimierz Krukowski, launched an appeal to the court in Hamburg. After five years the German court closed the judicial proceedings. Public prosecutor von Beelow argued that the people responsible for the crime were already dead. This however was not true since at the same time SS-Hauptsturmfuehrer Hans Krueger, commander of the Gestapo unit supervising the massacres in Lvov in 1941, was being held in Hamburg prison (he was sentenced to life imprisonment for the mass murder of Jews and Poles in Stanislawow, committed several weeks after his unit was transferred from Lvov). As a result no person has ever been held responsible for this atrocity. In the 1970s Abrahamowicz Street in Lvov was renamed Tadeusz Boy-Zelenski Street. Various Polish organisations have made deputations to remember the victims of the atrocity with a monument or a symbolic grave in Lvov. These requests have been so-far rejected.

Medical Practioners Targated by zbV[131]

Figure 18: Dr. Marek Redner

The first doctor who perished at the hand of German murderers, starting the bloody chain of nightmares, was Dr Perec Gleich. On that morning, he left his house at Kollataja Street. A few hours later he was executed by a German firing squad in the yard of Brigidki, together with the rabbi, Dr Lewin, and the newspaper editor, Henryk Hescheles.

The second victim, although not killed, was Dr Ascher Izrael, who was dragged to the yard of the Zamarstynowski prison, where he was terribly beaten, his face transformed into bleeding rags and his body covered with open bleeding lacerations. The third victim was Dr Mejbaum, a surgeon, also heavily lacerated to a point that he never recovered and was unable to return to work. He was killed in an action at a later date. On that day several hundred Jews were killed, and over 2000 were severely wounded. The next day the situation was quiet and we started the work, caring for the victims of the pogrom. The Jewish neighbourhoods had the appearance of a battlefield, covered with traces of the terrible butchery. Most houses were full of victims of beating, calling desperately for help and assistance.

The next Action followed on July 25[th,] (directly after the prison murders) and was directed specifically by zbV against the Jewish intelligencia, including a group of most prominent doctors. This pogrom was called the '*Petlura Action*', since it was carried out following a list prepared by the Ukrainians cooperating with the German authorities. They were taken in the middle of the night from their beds, and given orders to take a blanket and change of underwear, under the pretext of being taken to a field hospital. They were taken to the police station and never seen or heard of again. Some unconfirmed reports were received later that they were deported to one of many extermination camps near Lvov. During this Action, approximately 2000 Lvov Jews, mostly prominent citizens distinguished by their social and professional position, perished. Among them were 20 doctors, including Dr Mauryc Pensias, an outstanding radiologist; Dr Schneider, president of the Medical Union; Dr Marek Wollner, laryngologist; Dr Bernard Sonnenschein-Swiatlowski, Dr Kornelia Graf, wife of Dr Natan Graf, president of T.O.Z (*Towazystwo Ochrony Zdrowia,*) and many others.[132]

It was a sad reality of the times when German doctors, both military and civilian, quietly looked on while Jewish doctors were murdered and tortured. They observed the tortures and bestialities inflicted on their colleagues without a single word of protest and without any sympathetic reaction. They participated actively in actions, with willing zeal. They derived personal profits, exploiting the hopeless situation of Jews, blackmailing whenever possible, extorting gifts in exchange for worthless 'Ausweis', armbands, certificates, 'iron lists' or similar 'protective' devices. They frequently evicted their fellow Jewish doctors literally on to the street, occupying their fully furnished apartments.

The German doctors, in committing these felonies and crimes, used their own initiative and zeal, not necessarily imposed by the regime, but rather flowing directly from their own anti-Semitic instincts. There is abundant evidence of this: Immediately following these actions, in front of the Jewish hospital on Alembek Street, Dr Doppheide, principal physician of 'District Galicien', arrived in his car with his staff. After emptying all the halls and evicting all the patients, he stole, with great deal of effort, all the expensive instruments left by the departing Jewish doctors, delighted with his looting.[133]

The days following these events brought an avalanche of new directives and orders, following each other at a lightning pace, not giving the battered community time to breathe or recover. The orders to surrender radios and telephones were followed by prohibition of employment of a Jew in workplaces, then interdiction of employment of Aryans by Jews, the immediate release of

Christian domestic helpers, interdiction of school attendance by Jewish children, forbidding the Jews entrance to movies, theatres, public parks, restaurants, coffee shops, etc. Then, buying food in markets, use of public transportation, such as streetcars or railways were prohibited. Shortly afterwards, the closing of synagogues was followed by the burning of the Temple on Zolkiewska Street, and finally the order to wear a white armband on the left arm with an embroidered star of David.

At the same time, Jewish assets were confiscated including businesses, retail stores, warehouses, real estate. Farms were confiscated and taken over by so-called German '*Treuhanders*'. In order to dig out hidden assets and jewellery, huge 'contributions' were imposed. With these powerful blows, the Germans, in a very short time, eliminated all advances and gains of the emancipated Jewish community. Jews were removed from the protection of law, becoming free game for every Aryan without a hunting permit, totally unprotected. An active hunt could even result in a reward and recognition by the German authorities, while hiding or helping a Jew was punishable by death.[134]

Dr Mark Redner:

'Now, let's review some numbers. The number of Jewish doctors annihilated in Lvov by the Germans cannot be established accurately. When the Red Army occupied Lvov in September of 1939, they found many doctors, refugees from Western Poland, who fled at the time the war started from Hitler's advancing armies and found in Lvov a warm welcome, hospitality, and jobs, thanks to the help and friendly attitude of the Jewish and non-Jewish population. At the very end, they did not escape their tragic destiny, when they fell back into the hands of their German executioners, with the exception of those few that the Soviets deported deep into Eastern Soviet Union. As a result of these complications, it is impossible to account exactly for the number of Jewish doctors remaining in the city on July 1st 1941, which is the day of the occupation of the city by the Germans. Also, we cannot establish exactly the number of colleagues that survived the annihilation. Many escaped the city and survived using 'Aryan' papers, changing their names and religions, staying in Poland, and perhaps till today retaining their assumed identity. Many of them, after the war, broke ties with the Jewish community as a result of the loss of their families and of the persecution they suffered. One thing is certain, that the Jewish medical community, so rich and remarkably excellent, was completely annihilated and simply ceased to exist.

The expulsion of Jews from their apartments located in the Aryan neighbourhoods started soon after the invasion by German troops. In the beginning, it was a sporadic and random action affecting mostly the largest and most beautiful apartments of doctors and other wealthy Jews. After a while, the Germans started to clean up whole streets, or city blocks of the newest and most modern houses, assigning them to dignitaries, members of the N.S.D.A.P, military authorities, and civilians assigned on the basis of '*Raumungabefehland,*', issued by Stadthauptman's office. It was also a daily occurrence to see an arbitrary expulsion of a doctor by a Hitlerite, with typical brutality. It would be perpetrated by a Gestapo bureaucrat, or by another German kicking in the door, with loud screams, requesting the owner to vacate the house within hours. It was not uncommon to see the expulsion carried on with a whip, chasing people from their home straight onto the street, and not allowing them to carry any belongings. More than one doctor suddenly found himself under the blue skies, sometimes with a sick child in his hand… In a very few exceptional cases Germans returned some items, such as bedding and clothing to the owner. The medical instruments, X-ray equipment, and other medical tools were confiscated, if not saved previously by donation to a Jewish Hospital or institution.

The local Ukrainians also took an active part in the expulsion of Jewish doctors. In a few instances, Poles, including professionals and neighbours (till recently "good friends") participated in the plunder, with the help of Gestapo friends or acting with a formal allocation from the Stadthauptman's office. A classic case of this type was the expulsion of Dr Nadel by Dr Reinc, a Volksdeutsch, in an extremely brutal manner, without any warning.'

Dr Schoengarth's Shooting Seminar.

A matter of hours after the professors' murder, Dr Schoengarth gathered his officers and proceeded to lecture them on their forthcoming duties. His senior officers, including Krueger, Rosenbaum and Kutschmann, were taken to the Lvov prison where they were shown the thousands of dead prisoners the Soviets had left behind. It was emphasised that they had been killed by the Soviets at the instigation of the Jews.[135]

The shooting of the prisoners found in the three prisons in Lvov, were committed by the NKVD prior to the Russians' withdrawal from the city and on the orders of the Soviet 'Special Courts'. From the prison, the SD entourage was taken to a previously prepared pit on the outskirts of the town where shooting of Jews had already commenced. Dr Schoengarth lectured his men on the exact way that these pits were to be prepared. According to Hans Krueger's testament after the war, Schoengarth pointed out the precise Berlin-designated dimensions, transport, security, the varieties of execution, the placement of the bodies in the graves, and the *coup de grace*:[136] '*Schoengarth stood at the pit edge while the executions were going on. Ukrainians were in the pit arranging the dead bodies. Men and women were driven up in trucks. They stood at the edge of the pit and were then shot. They had remained clothed. The Ukrainians were then ordered into the pit to arrange the bodies*'.[137]

Other reports of the Dr Schoengarth seminar suggest that he instructed all his commanders to personally engage in the killing.[138] Evidence was given of Jewish men and women being brought to the pit and made to undress, robbed of their possessions and made to kneel or stand at the edge of the pit.[139] Each commander took it in turn to shoot at least one Jew. SS Scharfuehrer Wallenberg (noted chief executioner of zbV) and Dr Schoengarth demonstrated to those present how this was to be done. Wallenberg selected his Jew and shot him in the nape of the neck. He then called the next officer to repeat the action with another victim and so it went on.[140]

Hans Krueger describes events:

'Schoengarth ordered his commanders to shoot Jews during these actions. On the evening after the Lvov demonstration, Schoengarth gathered together all SS staff. Rosenbaum and Menten were there. Schoengarth made a speech. He said, "You saw how it was done. Every man should join in the shooting. I will shoot anyone who doesn't agree. I will back up every SS Fuehrer who shoots a man for not obeying my order."[141] We all felt it was horrible but necessary to deal with any sissies.

Two SS men who refused to kill Jews were driven to commit suicide by Schoengarth: some SS men went into the woods near Lvov in search of partisans. An SS Fuehrer shot himself there. The other SS men reported that partisans had shot him. In fact this man had shot himself on orders from Schoengarth because he did not wish to kill Jews.

Schoengarth gave him the opportunity to kill himself so that his wife would receive a pension, which she wouldn't have done if the officer had appeared in an SS Court.[142] In Warsaw, an SS Fuehrer refused to kill Jews and was imprisoned. Schoengarth had arranged for a pistol to be put in his cell and the man shot himself.'[143]

Krueger's remarks are interesting. In most war crimes trials the accused continually put up the defence of 'Acting under orders'. 'If I refused to obey an order, I could be shot.' Prosecution at these trials invariably challenged this assumption. Many historians today assert that there is no evidence where a German officer was disciplined for refusing to shoot Jews. The evidence that no German was ever killed or incarcerated for having refused to kill Jews is conclusive. The officer was given other duties or transferred.[144] We have in Krueger's testimony a direct contradiction (if true). I would suggest that repercussions for refusal very much depended on the Commanding Officer of the day. Dr Schoengarth was not one of those officers who adhered to leniency. We will see later where seven of the SS-garrison in Belzec were acquitted of mass murder, citing their defence: 'If we disobeyed orders, our lives and our families lives were in danger.'[145] We will also review the suicide by shooting of two SS-Sharfuehrer s in the 'Reinhardt' camps brought about by fear of Commandant Wirth.

Hans Kreuger moves to Stanislawow

Dr Schoengarth sent Hans Krueger, no stranger to executions, to Stanislawow as a forward unit of Sipo-SD where, in October 1941, he would instigate one of the biggest mass murders in the history of the Holocaust and pave the way for the resettlement transports to Belzec. In my view, this was a defining moment that set in motion the entire destruction policy of European Jewry.

Stanislawow was in south-east Galicia and had been occupied by the Hungarians before the Nazis' arrival. The first killing action in the city was overseen by Krueger on August 2nd and resulted in the murder of approximately 500 male Jews and 99 Poles in the forest near Pawelce. This was documented at Krueger's trial after the war.

These killings still came within the scope of the so-called 'Intelligenz-Action': killing the intelligentsia. An escalation of killing to include normal civilian men, women and children occurred in September, and was prompted by the decision of the new Lvov chief, SS-Major Tanzmann, to set up a ghetto in Stanslawow that was too small to hold all the Jews. Krueger gave a candid account of this process in his pre-trial interrogation of 26th June, 1962. One small area where Krueger would not have to concern himself with, were the lost villages in the Stryj valley, where a splinter group of zbV (BdS) were about to make a visit.[146]

Dr Schoengarth (taking with him Wilhelm Rosenbaum) had now returned to security duties in Krakow, probably to supervise the oncoming Jewish resettlement in the Generalgouvnement and the re-commissioning of the Sipo-SD School at Bad Rabka. SS Captain Hans Krueger after the initial settling of accounts in Lvov now commanded his own SD unit in Stanislawow where he was engaged in setting standards for Jewish destruction. Krueger co-ordinated mass slaughter of the Jews and supervised rounding-up techniques for deportations to the Belzec death camp and Pieter Menten went his own way.

Dr Schoengarth's zbV final report to Himmler would detail that their Einsatzgruppe could be credited with 17,887 victims up until September 1941, not including the four Pieter Menten massacres in the Stryj Valley.

Chapter 6

The Leadership Return to the School

WITHIN DAYS OF THE RABKA SCHOOL becoming operational again, a large black flag and a swastika was prominently mounted on the roof, and in large black letters, the following was displayed across the top floor of the building: *'Befehlshaber der Sicherheitspolizei und des SD im GG Schule des Sicherheitspolizei.'*

Figure 19: Sipo-SD School Rabka 1942

Figure 20: School for disabled children 1998

Figure: 21 Wilhelm Rosenbaum (L) Rabka c.1942

General Administration

Within a few months after the commencement of Barbarossa (June 1941), the German hierarchy realised that the war would be long and protracted, with the result that there was no more emphasis on political and military training requirements. Final decisions had been made with regard to the 'Jewish Question', and these requirements would be reflected in the new courses about to commence at Bad Rabka.

Figure 22: Sipo-SD Students School 1942

In occupied Poland, although the German police and security personnel were thin on the ground, they resisted taking into their confidence the indigenous population. Generally speaking the Polish police, although used for law and order purposes in the Generalgouvnement, were rarely given full access to the SS/SD security services in Jewish actions. Paradoxically it was local Jewish collaborating cadres who were preferred to Poles when Jewish actions were contemplated In German eyes, the Poles were only just above the Jews in the pecking order of 'untermenschen'. Only those Poles fully vetted and considered loyal collaborators, usually of some years standing as V-Agents, were favoured for further training in the SD establishment.

To encounter their military move into the east, the School curriculum was updated to reflect their foreseen duties. Selected candidates for the re-established School were nominated and recruited from a wider range of sources, but mainly from German security establishments, Waffen SS, and the Civil Service (Polish and German) throughout the Reich. Pro-Nazi Poles and Ukrainians were also open for selection for police training and V-Agents (spies). The Rabka School, since its establishment in Zakopane, had introduced specialist Ukrainian instructors, namely, the Mauer brothers (Johann and Wilhelm who had remained behind with Hans Krueger in Stanislawow), and the Ukrainian SS- Scharfuehrer s Wosdolowicz, Jaworski and Vasilko were all transferred to the SD School at Rabka to take charge of the Ukrainian and Polish recruits.[147] The Ukrainians were in a slightly more favoured situation having welcomed the Germans into the Ukraine proper and were now considered trusted friends of the Reich. The carrot for them was the prize of Ukrainian independence, a prize they were never to achieve.

Organisation: Academic Chart of the RSHA 1941 – 1943:

Chief of the Sipo – SD and overlord of Training Establishment at Rabka: the Befehlshaber der Sicherheitspolizei und des SD (BdS) of the General gouvernment, SS-Oberfuehrer Schoengarth (Krakow)

Divisions of Exam Study and the engagement of lecturers under the Direction of SS-Lt Rosenbaum:

1. Organisation and Law
    A. Legislation
    B. Indemnification
    C. Reich Defence
    D. Confiscations
    E. Passports
    F. Budgets
    G. Technical matters

2. SD – Inland
    A. Legal Practice
    B. Ethnos (Volktum)
    C. Culture
    D. Economy

3 Gestapo
    A. Border Police
    B. Enemies
    C. Communism
    D. Sabotage
    E. Liberalism
    F. Assassinations

G. Sects
H. Catholicism
I.   Protestantism
J.   Freemasonry
K. Evacuations and Jews
L. Card Files (See '88' List)
M. Spheres of Influence
N. Counter intelligence
O. Treason

4. Kripo

A. Policy
B. Crimes (Einsatz)
C. Identification
D. Krimminal Institute

5. SD – Foreign

A.General
German-Italian sphere
Russo-Japanese sphere
West
Investigation
Technical Matters

6. Ideology

A. Evaluation—Jews

Visiting lecturers to the School were drawn from specialist offices in the Generalgouvnement. Many of the teaching staff, in addition to the established instructors, came on secondment from Berlin and were specialists in their field, e.g., SS-Captain Heinrich Vopel was an expert on 'Free Masonry' and questions of 'World View', SS-Obersturmbannfuehrer George Schaepel, Head of section V (Criminal Investigation), BdS Krakow, took the Polish Police courses for Criminal Law and Procedure during the wartime emergency.[148]

Prospective candidates for non-commission courses were required to be healthy men between the ages of eighteen and thirty-five, were ranked and segregated according to their standard of education. Not all recruits were successful. Johann Bornholt, an ethnic German was inducted into the School but was soon found to be below the educational standard required. Bornholt was transferred to the prison establishment at Nowy Sacz where he was made a prison guard in the SD security detention block.[149]

Figure 23: Staff in lecture hall and Ukrainian Students 1942 SD School 1942.

Since November, 1941, there had been a steady stream of Polish, Ukrainian and German military conscripts passing through the training courses of the Rabka School. This was in addition to the Senior and Intermediate Command courses that were continually going on. The length of the courses fluctuated, but usually they were for a month for the non-commissioned personnel and between 3 and 6 months for the senior commanders. During the Barbarossa campaign emergency courses were the practice, but once the initial phase of the destruction of the Jewish population were realised, the School settled down to a more conventional syllabus, and continued in this manner until 1944, when it was transferred to Berlin due to the Russian advance

There were specially designed courses for those doing emergency service, i.e., the armed SS. SS- Unterscharfuehrer Wilhelm Oder was in charge of this course. Although Oder was on Rosenbaum's staff, he was directly answerable to Dr Schoengarth. He was at the Rabka School from the autumn 1941 until March, 1943 when Rosenbaum left. Oder did much of the killing by way of example to his student conscripts. He was an expert in the 'shot in the neck' method. He would show his students how to do this, using his pistol, a Walther PPK, calibre 765, shooting Jews at a distance of 10-20 centimetres. Also used were a various assortments of machine-pistols. (See appendices re Werner Oder.)

SS-Hauptscharfuhrer Walter Proch[150] was also one of the main instructors at the school and like Oder he trained the conscripts in the art of killing and torture. He personally shot many individual Jews in the School. He shot a Jew in the street of Rabka just because he had a beard. Proch shot many people single handed during operations witnessed by the Jews. Aszer and Grossbarth Blatt were witnesses to the following:

> 'SS-Hauptscharfuhrer Walter Proch—1942-3 Gestapo officer at the Rabka School—shot 6 people for no reason. In 1942, the transport of Jew-workers from Nowy Sachs (Neu-Sandez): he shot 6 Jews while they were washing, and a further 2 for no reason. On the same day he shot up to 50 Jews in a Rabka action. Blatt personally saw Proch hang a Jewish family who were U.S. citizens in the woods at a School execution action.'

Also on the teaching staff: SS-Hauptscharfuehrer/Kriminalassistents Alois Bohnert and Schuppler had been on the permanent staff since November, 1940. SS-Scharfuehrer Bandura was the School driver, Dziuba was clerical officer. These officers from the Waffen SS were brought in to train emergency conscripts and the lower ranks of the Sipo-SD. The female contracted staff (and witnesses) were Meta Kuck (nee Speck), Personal Secretary to Rosenbaum (41-42), Schindler (nee Hendriks), and Engelmann who were also secretaries to Rosenbaum and senior staff. As many as 200-500 Ukrainians, non-commissioned Poles and Germans passed out of the School each month after 6-8 week courses. Students of officer rank on the command courses were of between 3 and 6 months duration.

In addition to the basic recruits, Sipo-SD officers of the senior command structure were sent to the School for refresher courses of shorter duration and personal assessments prior to promotions or change of duty before returning to the war zone. As early as November, 1941, there is photographic evidence of senior Sipo-SD officers from various districts of the Generalgouvnement in the classroom, being lectured by Dr Schoengarth.[151] There is no way of knowing what was subject under discussion, but in view of the circumstances at that time, we may assume with some probability, that engagement of war and the 'Jewish Question' were high on the agenda. Lecturers at the School came from the elite of the Nazi hierarchy: Dr Hans Frank (GG); Globocnik and Hoefle (Lublin); F.W.Krueger, Scherner, Muller, Grosskopf, Schoengarth, Dr Neiding (Krakow); Katzmann, Tanzmann and Hans Krueger (Lvov).

The Soap Rumour

Dr Schoengarth would often chair these lectures and meetings before retiring with his students to the casino for refreshment. Dr Kurt Neiding, a sitting Judge of the SS/SD Court in Krakow, remembers one such lecture given by an SS-Fuehrer (probably Hoefle) from the office of Odilo Globocnik, SS-Lieutenant General, Lublin and the overall officer in charge of '*Action Reinhardt*' in the Generalgouvnement':

> I once took part in a commanders' meeting in Bad Rabka, which was chaired by Dr Schoengarth. An SS-Fuehrer, who was stationed in Lublin, brought a piece of soap with him. It was an experiment which on the orders of Polizeifuehrer Globocnik, had been made out of Jewish corpses. There were obviously attempts being made to use the Jewish corpses to make soap.[152]

In the same trial the statement of the Jew Goodrich who dug the graves in the woods of the Rabka SD School is recorded; he was present when a family was brought to the school for execution. When the family were standing naked, one SS executioner remarked, '*the girl is so fat that soap could be made out of her.*'

Domestic Arrangements

Figure 24: Lucia Schon (Centre) Rosenbaume's domestic worker and witness to the activities at the School.
(March 2011: Lucia Schon celebrates her 90th birthday in Israel).

Accommodation for Rosenbaum, his guests and lecturers was located in the villa 'Margrabianka', known as the '*Fuehrerheim*' situated on the other side of the

Slonka river closely guarded by Ukrainian sentries at all times. The Casino was also available for the SS-Leaders and visiting Security Service personnel. A recreation place for the general SS was established in the villa '*Haus Annemie*'. Rosenbaum's fiancée, Annemarie Bachus, was managing the establishment.

Shortly after Rosenbaum's return to the School with Dr Schoengarth from Lvov he appointed auxiliary staff to open up and prepare the School for the first intake of students in the third week of November, 1941. In the School premises he had installed a variety of workshops: tailor's shop, shoemaker, saddlery and a hairdresser's shop, which were all manned by Jewish workmen under the direct supervision of a few Ukrainians; the brothers Czarnowicki and the Jew Herman Gold belonged to the Jewish tailors, the Jew Zelinger worked in the saddlery, the Jew Trieger was the gardener, and Michael Ettinger was locksmith and driver whose domain was based in the School garage, and as such, was in a position to observe the School activities on a daily basis. The Jewess Hela Bauman had been brought from Zakopane to work in the laundry.[153] The Jewesses Sara Schon (Nee Louisa Goldfinger) and Ada Rawicz (Nee Ada Peller) were cleaners and worked in the 'Margrabianka'. The Jewess Schon also worked as a maid and nanny in the households of Krueger, SS-Schuppler Proch, and finally Rosenbaum. Overseer of the Jews and personal interpreter to Rosenbaum, and very much central to this investigation, was the Jew Paul Beck who lived on the School premises with his son.

Construction of the Shooting Range

Based on the employment of the Jews, Rosenbaum constructed more buildings in the School grounds. He also laid out a sports ground and shooting range in the small woods behind the School. Building materials for this construction work came from Jewish cemeteries in the district. From the Jewish cemetery of Nowy Targ, the smooth granite and marble stones were shipped to the Rabka School and used in the construction of the shooting range and the paved area at the front of the School.[154]

Rosenbaum obtained additional Jewish workers from the responsible Employment Office in Nowy Targ. Later on, from May 1942, Jews from other neighbouring towns were transported to the School based upon his needs. When these Jews had outlived their usefulness, they were simply killed off and replaced by others. Arthur Kuhnreich recalls his time in the School:

Figure: 25 Arthur Kuhnreich[155]

'On September 1, 1939, war broke out between Poland and Germany.

When the war started, I was 16 years old. I had a beautiful family: a sister, Hessa who was 18 years old and parents. Father's name was Eliasz, mother's was Braindl. We had a lumber export business, chemical farm fertilizers and building materials. We were considered well off and respected by the townspeople. The Germans confiscated everything they could lay their hands on. We found ourselves stripped of all our possessions and for food had to barter clothing, linen, etc. At times, local farmers who knew us brought some potatoes and bread. A Judenrat (Jewish Council) was established in Makow at the order of the Gestapo. They nominated an Obmann (Chairman), Beno Pastor. Asked to join, my father categorically refused. Every day, the Germans gave orders to the Judenrat demanding money, jewellery, furs, furniture, works of art and free labour. Every Jew in town from 16 to 60 was obligated work, without pay, of course. Makow had a population of approximately 5,000, of which 500 were Jews. All Jews had to wear a white armband with a blue Star of David.

In 1941, the Jewish population was about 450. This was a resort town, near Rabka and Zakopane. For some reason, our town was lucky; there were no killings as yet. All this changed drastically with the start of war with Russia in 1941.

At that time, the Gestapo took over the villa Marysin and made it their headquarters. The chief was named Schmidt. Every day, someone was beaten, arrested or shot. The first one to be murdered was the Shochet of

Makow, Mr Mann, for ritually killing a chicken. A short time later, an elderly couple, Eliezer and Liba Grubner were murdered for selling yard goods in exchange for food. They raided a farm house in Bialka on the outskirts of town, wiping out the entire family of Artur Edelstein, an attorney, his wife, son and daughter. Everyone was very fearful.

In the first week of December 1941, the Gestapo demanded twenty men to be sent to Auschwitz concentration camp for work. Father was arrested, but released. We were so happy they let him go, we could hardly believe it. My father said, "I don't trust them. It must be a trick." The next day, early in the morning, all of us, men, uncles, cousins, seven in all, went into hiding at the farm of Polish friends, Salapatek, who helped us many times. That same day, two Gestapo men showed up at our house asking for me. My mother told them that I was at work. They said very politely to report to them in the evening and bring all my documents to be checked. My mother asked innocently if there was anything wrong. They said, "No, just checking." Naturally, I stayed in hiding, never slept or ate at the same place, afraid of being caught. Of the twenty men arrested and sent to Auschwitz, nobody survived. All were dead within two weeks' time and their ashes were returned to their families for which they had to pay.

In Rabka Zdroj, a similar situation existed, but on an even more cruel and much larger scale. In 1940, the Gestapo confiscated a large building, St. Teresa School, and a couple of villas near a forest. This place became a training School for SS Gestapo (Sicherheitpolizei) in occupied Poland. The sole purpose of this School was to teach how to torture and kill people. From here, murderers were sent out to other places to torture and kill. Chief of this 'college' was Wilhelm Rosenbaum. In 1942, at age 25, he held the fate of thousands of Jews in his hands. In Rabka, he murdered around 1,000 Jews. Nearby, Nowy Targ had another murderer, Heinrich Hamann, who butchered hundreds of Jewish people.

In Makow, we lived in fear, not knowing whose turn would be next. On the 28th April, 1942, large contingents of Gestapo arrived early in the morning in towns of southern Poland: Rabka, Nowy Targ, Nowy Sacz, Makow, etc. They took Jewish people out of bed to the Gestapo, where they were shot. Being on the list of hostages, they came to get me. I made the mistake of sleeping at home that night. They knocked on the door and shouted, 'Aufmachen!' ('Open up!') Thinking that they were probably looking for men, my sister pushed me toward the window and urged me to jump out and escape. My father also jumped out and we hid in the cellar. When they opened the door, my mother was too stunned to answer, but my sister spoke up, saying that she did not know our whereabouts. They told her to get dressed and to come along. She was taken to the villa Marysin, which housed the Gestapo. After it quieted down upstairs, we came out of the cellar. Upon learning that my sister was arrested, I went to surrender myself so that she is freed. My parents were against that. My father made a notation in a Holy Book, saying that his daughter was arrested and he hoped that she would not be harmed, that perhaps she will only be sent off to work. On my way to surrender myself, I met a former Polish policeman, who asked me where I was going. I told him. He said that it was already too late; all hostages, including my sister, were shot immediately against the wall of the Gestapo building, ten men and two women. He said that if I went there, they would do the same to me. I went home, very sad and depressed, but kept quiet, not being able to relay such terrible news to my parents. The Polish neighbours knew and also kept quiet. About three weeks later, my father found out from a Volksdeutch, who worked for the Gestapo. How my parents took this is very hard for me to describe. Father made another notation in the Holy Book, giving the date and describing what happened. In case someone survived, Kaddish (Memorial Prayer) could be said for my sister. The Holy Book was found after the war by a friend of mine, and because it had our business seal with the name on it, he knew it belonged to us. He found me and mailed it to me.

In 1941, the Gestapo raided the house of Warenhaupt, who was a barber in town. He had four sons, one of whom, Dolek, lost his life on the front in 1939. Three were active in the Underground. One day, while visiting their parents in Makow, the Gestapo came to arrest them. They jumped the two Gestapo men, banging their heads together, thereby knocking them out. They escaped. Two of them, Kuba and Heniek, survived the war. Maniek was recognized in Katowice, in late 1942, while cutting hair in a barber shop. That same Volksdeutch who told my father the "news" about my sister, recognized Maniek Warenhaupt and shot him on the spot. Sometime later, the brothers Kuba and Heniek, together with partisan friends, came to Makow. They took this murderer out in the middle of the night, read him the Underground death sentence and shot him for the murder of their brother.

The weather in the months of May, June and July 1942 was beautiful. All was in bloom. But at the same time, ominous clouds were gathering over the Jewish people. Everyone felt that something terrible was about to happen. During that summer, my father and I were on a list of employees at a brush factory, supposedly employed. The owner, Mr Emil Pierog, was my father's friend from School. This used to be a brick factory and the tall chimney served to hide the antenna of the Polish Underground radio transmitter. Mr Pierog was a leader in the Underground, but we did not know it at that time.

I was afraid to go home, staying away to avoid capture. One day, on the 1st, 1942, there was a commotion near our house. Noticing a local unarmed policeman, I asked him what was going on. He told me that my mother was arrested and held at the prison, the reason being that the Gestapo had me on their list of three men who were needed in Rabka. I told him, "You can take me with you, but make sure my mother is freed." He kept his promise. Mother cried and was very upset about my surrender. I told her not to worry, it might be safer for me in Rabka and it was only for work. That same policeman escorted me to Rabka camp. Before boarding the train, my aunt, Kaila Kuhnreich Lebron, her husband Jonas, son Romek, and daughter Henia, who had come to stay with us to avoid going to the Cracow ghetto, gave me postcards, with instructions that I should write when I arrived, so that my parents would not worry. It was strictly forbidden to do that, but the policeman mailed it for me. On the 2nd of August, 1942, I found myself together with one hundred young men between 18 and 28 in the Rabka camp. We had to be ready for work at six o'clock in the morning. Breakfast consisted of dark warm water, nothing else. At noontime, there was soup and one slice of bread which had to last the entire day. We were building a sports complex and to work 14-15 hours a day at a fast pace, seven days a week. Armed guards watched us and beat us for no reason at all. They told us how much had to be accomplished every day; if not, ten of us would be shot. If they thought that you worked too slowly, you were shot on the spot. At times, the Gestapo brought large transports of Jews from nearby towns to be executed in the forest. We were forced to dig the ditches, and then bury the victims. We were forced to watch a hanging of ten innocent people. This was part of Wilhelm Rosenbnaum's entertainment. Besides being exhausted, desperate and horrified, we were also starved all the time. Some of our people could not take it and committed suicide. Many were on the brink of it. When leaving for Rabka, I had promised my cousin, Henia Lebron, that I would write another card to the address of our Polish neighbour, Mr. Kokot, and that I would tell how it was at the camp. I wrote that it would have been better for me to have gone where my sister Hessa was. They understood my message. I received two food packages from home; at the time, I did not know that it had been smuggled in by Mrs Genowefa Pierog, who risked her life doing it. She was the wife of my father's friend, Mr Emil Pierog. Mrs. Pierog, with her two daughters, survived the war, but her husband, Emil, was arrested in the summer of 1944, sent to Zakopane, tortured, and then executed in the Montelupich prison in Cracow for Underground activities.

The other two men from Makow, besides me, sent to Rabka, were Feingold and Fischer. Rumours began circulating that any day now, the whole southern part of Poland would become *Judenfrei* (free of Jews). The feared end came on a sunny Sunday, the 1st September, 1942.

Wilhelm Rosenbaum and his cohorts assembled all Jews from Rabka at our camp. He also removed from the camp anyone with red hair, which he especially hated, those who wore glasses, and, in general, anyone who did not pass his scrutiny. They were all herded off on a freight train to their final destination, Belzec. One of the three from Makow, Feingold, was among those taken, because he happened to have red hair. That same day, the Jews of Makow, about 160 in number, were packed into freight cars after being ordered by SS Officer Heinrich Karhof to assemble at the railroad station. Among them was Szmuel Zainwel Beer, the Rabbi of Makow. All were sent to the crematorium in Belzec. Out of 600,000, not one person survived.

About 92 Jews escaped into the surrounding villages. They could not hide out for very long. They were captured and gathered up at the villa Marysin, the Gestapo headquarters. They were kept in the cellar under inhuman conditions for two to three weeks, and then taken out into the yard, one at a time, and shot. All were killed and buried right there. The Obman of the Makow Judenrat, Beno Pastor, shot himself. One Jewish woman was saved by the stationmaster of Makow. He received a medal from Yad Vashem in Jerusalem after the war. Jewish workers in Zakopane were all executed on that fateful day of September, 1942, among them, my cousin, Romek Lebron.

I was one of 100 men left in the Rabka camp for the time being. The atmosphere among us was that of hopelessness. We knew that the past had been destroyed forever and we did not see any future. Even the Gestapo looked depressed, for there were no more Jews to be killed. Here and there, some were dragged out of hiding, from bunkers, but very few in comparison to the past, and that made the SS unhappy. Also, they did not relish the idea of going to fight at the front. Three of us, Unterberger, Schiff and I, were assigned as gardeners for Rosenbaums' girlfriend, Ann Marie Bachus.

A villa belonging to a rich Pole was confiscated for their love nest. It had a big orchard. We were to work, doing gardening, picking and storing the fruit in the basement. Every morning, we were escorted by an armed guard to work and back. The three of us wanted some apples, but all were afraid, until I got careless and before leaving work, I stuffed some into my knickers' legs down in the basement. It seems the guard must have noticed and promptly reported me. Rosenbaum and his girlfriend, with other SS, were having a dinner party upstairs. One SS came down to check it out. He ordered me to open my knickers and the apples fell out. Seeing the crime, he punched me hard in the jaw a couple of times and said not to do this ever again. Next time, just ask. Of course, I never did. After a while, we thought that this episode had been forgotten. Rosenbaum did not. One evening, after 9:00 p.m., armed guards came to tell the three of use and seven others who must have sinned, that Rosenbaum wanted to see us in his office. We cried, said goodbye to our friends and thought that this must be the end. The guards took the ten of us to the Gestapo building. We waited in the hallway in utter terror. We saw Polish prisoners brought in for interrogation and heard their screams; they looked awful. Around midnight, Rosenbaum showed up with a cane in his hand. We were lined up in a row; each one was hit with the cane over the head, once forward and once back. Two huge bumps swelled up on each head. I had one bump, being at the end of the line. It was painful and we had swollen heads, but were glad to be left alive. We returned to the camp and went to work the next day as usual. This was a first in the history of this camp. We still worked on the sports complex which was carved out of a forest.

In the middle of February 1943, the camp was ordered to be divided in half. Fifty workers were sent to the Plaszow concentration camp. I even volunteered, thinking about escape. There was no chance at all.'

Accommodation for Jews

The mobilised Jews who, like all Jews in the Generalgouvnement, had to wear an arm band with a blue Star of David as identification were able to stay in their houses. Outside Jew-workers were accommodated in the proximity of the School in three houses on Slonna Street (now called Ulica Poniatonskiego), which had become a mini-camp surrounded by barbed wire and guarded by armed Ukrainians. Each day these Jews were marched under escort into the School for work and returned under guard in the evening. Gradually, the Jewish population from Bad Rabka were massed together there. The Jews of Rabka fared better than many other communities in the district, not only retaining 200 workers in full employment (without pay) but they managed to stay alive. [156] Many of these Jews had been personally selected by Rosenbaum from Jews in the immediate town or brought in from outside the area. The camp kitchen was under the supervision of the Jewess Alicja Nogala.

Appearance of Rosenbaum

Rosenbaum made sure of showing himself regularly in his impeccable smart uniform during his service and free time. According to the dress regulations, he was wearing 'roebuck leather' or grey gloves. On his blue uniform shirt, he was wearing, apart from the gold H-J sign (Hitler Jugen), the Reich-sports sign, the SA-sports sign and later the war merit cross with swords and other decorations.[157] Within the Sipo-SD-Fuehrer-corps, he was looked upon as a sharp, dynamic and well-educated Sipo-SD-Fuehrer. Rosenbaum, in the first place considered himself an SS-Fuehrer above his loyalty to Party. He was proud of being promoted SS-Fuehrer at the age of 25, and being the youngest SS-Fuehrer in the Krakow District.

Conduct of Subordinates

Friends of the same rank considered Rosenbaum to be arrogant and a man where the 'Fuehrer went to his head': others considered him friendly in their official and private relationship. The Sipo-SD-staff under him, knew to respect him Rosenbaum appeared to others as a superior who was used to giving orders and being obeyed without question. Nobody dared not to execute his orders, nor act without his orders for important things. Rosenbaum was correct and polite towards female employees of his office. They considered him to be a lively and cheerful Sipo-SD-Fuehrer.[158]

Conduct towards Jews

Rosenbaum exercised power with a despotic cruelty over his Jewish-workers. He tortured them physically, psychologically, mentally and hurt their religious feelings. From their point of view, he was the 'master over life and death', 'the horror of the camp', a 'God'. He put the Jews working in the School in constant fear of death. Each worker avoided him. His appearance in the places of work meant corporal punishment, or the possibility of being shot. Almost daily, Rosenbaum appeared on foot or horseback at the building sites in the School area, shooting range, sports grounds, and stables. Among the workers, everyone became restless; working faster, not to attract attention. Rosenbaum urged on the frightened people: *'Shovel, Shovel, fill the carts and run!'*, *'Shovel, shovel, shovel you Jews, I will show you how to work!'*, *'Go, go, on the double!'* were his commands. If a worker drew attention for no reason, he received a lash with a whip covered by a metal piece at its end, which Rosenbaum always carried with him. The lash was given in such a way that the metal end of the whip would hit the victim from the back towards the front in the face, in the proximity of the eyes causing swelling and bruising of the eye socket. Rosenbaum also used other objects and his bare fist to maltreat his workers with the slightest excuse.[159] He used every possible opportunity to hurt the Jews in their human dignity—the 'foolish kid' of Dr Schoengarth was making his presence felt with unprecedented power.[160]

There was a catalogue of violence and abuse against his Jew workers, that would pale into insignificance when placed alongside the catalogue of murder that was about to break out in the Rabka School.

Training Students

Of particular significance, was the 'on-site' practical training using 'live bait'!—Jews: men, women and children specifically selected from the locality and held in captivity in the School grounds, were brought out of their confinement when required for shooting practice seminars, as happened with the young mothers and children from the Jordanow 'action' on the 30th August, 1942. The practice of shooting babies in the air, which was practised in the School, was a preferred method and adopted mostly by the Ukrainians. The ostensible reason was to avoid ricocheting bullets which were a danger to the shooter, and were well documented in occurrences in the Generalgouvrnement. The dominant motivation was to show their total disdain for the Jews and show off their expertise.[161]

Gravesites in the School

Another practice introduced during training was the digging and preparation of graves at the sites of execution. Under supervision of SS-Scharfuehrer Bohnert, these graves were dug by the Jewish staff in the presence of the instructors and students. The graves or pits were of exact Berlin manual dimensions of shape and size, but may be varied according to soil construction. At Belzec where the ground was all sand, pits (between 10m. x 10m. x 6m. deep and the largest 65m. x 25m. x 6m deep) were dug by hand with straight sharp edges. Later a machine was brought in to do the excavating. In these isolated execution sites (like Rabka) small and large pits (5m. x 5m. x 3m. deep), the digging was all done by hand. Initially, the Jews were told that this work was for 'air raid defence', but they were never fooled and there was always one spare pit held over for unexpected arrivals[162]. When Hans Krueger organised the mass killing of 12,000 Jews on 'Bloody Sunday' (12.10. 1941) in Stanislawow, he preferred to have the pits 'V' shaped so that body fluids settled below the corpses. Another addition practised at the School and elsewhere, was the plank over the pit method used by in the villages in the Stryj valley. Alternatively, the plank was placed on the pit edge. In both these cases the victims were ordered to stand on the plank; in one case they fell into the pit when shot, in the other, the victim was propelled forward into the pit. The idea of executing Jews in the woods near the SD School appealed to the Gestapo for its exclusiveness.

Methodology of Murder

Initially throughout the GG, the Jewish victims were shot clothed, but this changed when orders came from the RSHA that all Jews were to be shot naked, the clothes cleaned and sent directly to the KdS in Krakow.[163] The method of shooting and the selection of weapons were also displayed at the School. Rosenbaum preferred to shoot his victims in the back of the neck with a pistol, a practice he had learnt from Dr Schoengarth in Lvov, but the instructors used all manner of weaponry depending on circumstances. For running targets across the School shooting range carbines were used. Throughout the Generalgouvnement and occupied areas, particularly on Soviet territory, the Einsatzgruppen initially executed their victims with more or less standard execution procedures using rifles, two shooters to a victim or properly convened execution squads with man to man, woman or child! There were no such considerations or niceties in Bad Rabka.

Supply and Demand

To fit in with training schedules, Jews were often snatched off the streets in towns and villages and bussed into the School from a wide area: Nowy Sacz, Lvov, Tarnow, Krakow, etc.[164]   Several witnesses declared that Rosenbaum hacked hands and feet off Jewish children, then ordered the children tied to trees, and then proceeded to shoot these atrociously tortured human targets himself.[165]

Figure: 26 (circa. 1950). Sent to the author by Krystyna Kynst. On the back of the photograph was written:
'Silver fir tree next to where people were shot. It was hit by so many bullets that its sap ran like tears.' [166]

During his quieter moments, Rosenbaum would take pot-shots at Jews from his office window, from his horse carriage, while on horseback, or just walking the grounds. In one of his more enlightened exhibitions, Rosenbaum called on one of his instructors to demonstrate to a gathered audience the School's torture techniques which had become a daily occurrence. The selected victim had an iron rod placed across his neck. The instructor balanced his full weight on the rod, rocking from side to side until he had crushed the man's neck until he died. Another victim was brought forward and the exercise was repeated with variations.

It wasn't just the Jews who were subjected to this inhuman behaviour as there are many recorded instances of similar atrocities committed against POWs under German control, particularly the Russians: some were tortured with bars of red-hot iron; their eyes gouged out, their stomachs ripped open; their feet, hands, fingers, ears, and noses hacked off.[167]   During the Barbarossa campaign two Russians, political and military personnel, were found nailed to a stake with a five-point star carved on their bodies. Another Russian soldier found nearby was burned and his ears cut off.[168]

All forms of murder and torture were carried out here at Bad Rabka: shooting, hanging and beatings. It is estimated that over 2000 Jews from 30 neighbouring villages were held and the victims executed in the School grounds. It was in many cases murder by appointment.

Further evidence came from the local official named Grimmlinger. He exposed the Weissmann, Hamann and Rosenbaum murder conspiracy. Grimmlinger's office supplied goods to the School from Neu Markt and was a regular visitor to the School and was present when executions were taking place. He remembers on one occasion over 100 Jews were being prepared to be shot at the shooting range. He was also privy to the shooting of Beck at a later date. Grimmlinger stated that there were many murders of 'picked-up' Jews by the Border Police. It was an accepted procedure for a phone call to be made to the School just to arrange a grave. The SS would just turn up, murder the victims and leave until the next time. It was only necessary to inform Rosenbaum or Bohnert by phone. No records were kept. See also Rosenbaum statement 9th August, 1962, 993/69, the witness Dattner.[169]

Pious Jews brought into the School were received with particular satisfaction as it gave the reception cadre the opportunity to extend their anti-Semitic cruelty even more intently, which also provided entertainment. These unfortunates were made to run the gauntlet of the SS and Ukrainians, who beat them mercilessly before being imprisoned in the specially prepared cells in the stables and pigsties which had been adapted for this purpose.[170]   Kept imprisoned, without food or water in filthy conditions, they waited for selection at the whim of the Commandant.

Again, to fit in with schedules and the curriculum of daily instruction, a selected number of these pious Jews were brought out of the cells to be humiliated and ridiculed before being marched to the pits that had been prepared in the woods. Stripped naked, their scrolls cut into shreds, they fell or walked the plank before being shot into the pit crying 'Shema Yisrael!' (the Jewish prayer to be repeated at death). These actions were all staged managed performances in the presence of V.I.Ps, senior and junior SS ranks candidates from all over the Generalgouvnement. To cover up their murder, Rosenbaum ordered the Rabka Town Clerk, Cheslav Tribowski, to register the deaths as 'victims of heart attack'.[171]

Further Actions within the School[172]

In addition to the recognised form of static targets, Jews were brought to the School specifically to be used as 'running targets' across the shooting range. For training on the shooting range, buses laden with children came from Auschwitz, and were released like 'Hares' to be shot as moving targets.[173] These incidents were widely known and were not isolated or unusual occurrences. We also have corroborated reports in the camps and ghettos, of Jews rounded up for liquidation, who were sent running and used as target practice.[174] We have other corroboration and confirmed reports from a number of locations where Jews were used for shooting targets at the whim of the perpetrator, particularly in the Janowska and Plaszow camps. In the town of Makov Podhalanski, near Zakopane, Jews were taken to the Gestapo headquarters at the Marishia Hotel, where they were tortured by recruits from the Rabka Sipo School, then taken to the courtyard one by one and used for target practice.[175] In the village of Bely Rast, Krasnaya Polyana district, a 12-year-old boy was placed on the porch of a house where he was used as target practice by the SS who then moved around the village taking pot-shots at other children running in the streets.[176] In the village of Voskresenskoye, Dubinin district, a three-year-old boy was selected for target practice and shot with machine-gun fire.[177] In the village of Basmanova, Glinka district, 200 schoolchildren working in the fields were rounded up and used for target practice.[178] In the village of Vinnitsa over 500 Jews had been rounded up in the market place where they tore up their paper money. The children, and there were many, made a run for it across the square only to be picked off by the marksmen: 'I saw children being shot as though they were hares and you could see a number of children's bodies lying in the street.'[179]

It wasn't only the students of national-socialism that underwent instruction. The Jews had to undergo courses of instruction, but of a very different nature, as explained by the Jew Michael Ettinger:

'Selected Capos of the Jewish prisoners were regularly ordered by Scharfuehrer Bohnert to attend instruction classes which were usually arranged early in the morning. We were taken to the fields behind the School where we were given instructions as to how to conduct ourselves when called upon to dig pits. We were not stupid and knew that people were being shot in the woods. At first they told us that the pits were for anti-aircraft purposes, but this lie had no meaning to us.

After a time, even the Germans knew these lies were not practical. The pit had to be dug to precise measurements which would be given at the time. On arrival of the Commandant we had to make ourselves scarce and hide in the bushes with our backs to the pit. On the sound of a whistle we would return to the pit and work to instructions, which meant arranging the dead bodies, and then filling in the pits to a level. Of course, some of us looked at what was going on: groups of people were brought to the edge of the pit and made to undress. Then they were positioned at the edge and shot in the back of the head. The shouts, pleas and screams were terrible.'[180]

It was Ettinger that brought to notice that the Dutchman, Pieter Menten, was a regular visitor to the School when he would back his car up to the garage and unload the most magnificent paintings you have seen in your life.[181]

Rosenbaum gave the orders for all executions, and was present at all the following ascertained actions. These actions of both mass shootings and individual shootings were carried out according to a specific plan based upon trained shooting practices in the Generalgouvnement in which Rosenbaum was personally engaged. Only cases where there was direct evidence against Rosenbaum were the subject of later trials. There were certainly many other incidents that we will never know about.

In the case of mass executions, the Jews that were to be shot were accommodated during the day in the bunker next to the School, which was guarded by Ukrainians. Where smaller groups were concerned, which was frequently the case in executions of 'picked up' Jews, the victims were locked up in the so-called 'clinks' (cells).[182] One of these was the cellar under the pigsty where the victims were made to lie face down on earth floors.[183] According to the size of the group, a number of Jew-workers were ordered by Scharfuehrer Bohnert to dig the graves hard and fast so as to be ready on the day of execution. By the afternoon, the work of digging the grave always had to be finished ready for the executions which usually took place early evening. Small groups of 3-5 people, sometimes more, were taken out of the bunkers to the graves and executed.

The gravediggers had to come out of the graves as soon as they saw the victims arrive in order not to be shot themselves. The Jews had improvised their own method based on their experience to avoid being stuck in the pit: from a depth of 3 metres, the workers built steps into the side of the pit which enabled them to climb out in a hurry. It was frequently the case that the victims brought to the grave had already been beaten up and were ordered to undress and stand as directed. During this time, the gravediggers were either sent back to the School or had to hide in the undergrowth or amongst the trees in the woods some 20 metres from the graveside depending on circumstances. If ordered to hide nearby, they were instructed to turn away from the shooting until ordered to return and then seal the grave.

At the time of these executions, Rosenbaum would appear with his SS Party. Sometimes terrible scenes took place. The victims screamed in Yiddish for fear of death and begged for their lives. Mothers were imploring the SS to shoot them first, before shooting their children. Women refused to undress and their clothes were ripped off by force from their bodies. Then these chosen Jews were ordered, by force if necessary, to stand at the edge of the graves or sit around the graveside. They were killed by a single shot in the nape of the neck (as per training). The bodies fell into the grave or were given a kick by their executioner right after the shot. Other methods were also used: the plank was placed across the pit, and the victim was invited to walk across the plank to the centre when they were shot.[184] (This procedure was exactly the same adopted by Pieter Menten and zbV in their flurries into the villages in the Stryj Valley.)

The grave was a horrifying sight: the bodies were lying in total disorder, one on top of the other and covered in blood. The Jewish workers were called, usually with the blow of a whistle, and were sent into the graves to arrange the bodies. Often they would notice that some of the Jews were not dead. Rosenbaum or other executioners would fire additional shots to finish them off. After the shootings the bodies were covered with lime and then with earth. The execution site was then sealed over. The clothes of the victims were collected by the Jewish workers, taken to the School where they were cleaned and repaired, removing Jewish Stars etc., then either sent to Krakow or re-used locally.[185]

On the 20th May, 1942, Rosenbaum ordered through the Judenrat at least 45 old and disabled Jews from Rabka (those that he had previously noted) to come to the School. Among them there was the mother of the Jewess Nogala (Mrs Paster), as well as the grandmother of the Jewess Schon (Mrs Ernestine Kranz), and her uncle (Chaim Beim). The grandson of Mrs Kranz, Mark Goldfinger, 11 years, remembers the day his grandmother (Mrs Kranz) was taken away by the local Polish policeman and a representative of the SS:

> 'When the Polish Police and SS called at our house they asked for Ernestine Kranz. My mother told them she wasn't at home, to which the SS man said my mother should come instead. My grandmother must have heard the conversation as she suddenly appeared and identified herself. She was taken away to the SS School.
>
> On the next day I took some sandwiches to the School, hoping to give them to grandmother. I approached the School from the rear and when I reached the clearing by the woods I saw that a grave was being prepared. I was watching from behind a bush when suddenly a Ukrainian guard saw me and told me to clear off as fast as possible.
>
> That same evening, my grandmother was among a number of Jews who were shot into the grave. We heard the shots as we lived close to the School. My sister Sarah, who worked for Rosenbaum, told me later that Rosenbaum had come to her and regretted that her grandmother had to be shot, but assured her that he hadn't allowed her to suffer.'

The Jews concerned: the ones Rosenbaum had marked with a cross in his lists came during the day to the School, not expecting the worse. After their arrival, the Jews were locked in the bunker next to the School building and guarded by Ukrainians. They had to lie flat down, with their faces towards the earth floor. (See appendices re Mark Goldfinger and Werner Oder.)

That same day, Jewish workers had started to dig a grave at the execution site behind the School. SS-Scharfuehrer Bohnert had chosen about 20-25 Jewish workers to do this work. At 5 p.m., the locked up victims in the stalls were taken in small groups by the Ukrainian guards, who were beating them and urging them on to the execution area. The gravediggers were concealed in the bushes nearby, facing away from the execution site. The Jewish victims were ordered to undress and then to stand or sit around the grave. One Jewess who refused to undress had her clothes ripped off her body. Simultaneously, Rosenbaum arrived with a posse of Sipo-SD and immediately started the action. Rosenbaum personally shot at least 6 Jews with his pistol in the back of the neck. Sipo-SD - Bohnert, Oder, Bandura, and the Ukrainian Wosdolowski all shot Jews into the grave. The bodies were arranged and the graves treated as generally described above.[186]

Rosenbaum believed the Jewish workers from Bad Rabka to be insufficient for the work to be carried out at the School. He requested more workers to complete the projects he had in mind. The Employment Office of Nowy Sacz was the Central Employment Agency for Jewish labour, so he made a number of requests for more labour. Between May and July, 1942, at least three working transports were sent to Bad Rabka from Nowy Sacz, on the confirmation order of the Commander-in-Chief of the Security Police (Dr Schoengarth).[187]

Nowy Sacz Actions (1)

In late 1940, Nowy Sacz had become a centre for a Jewish labour pool which was drawn from towns and villages in the surrounding area. The camp was established in the Carpathian Mountains in the village of Lipie near the town of Koluszowa. Here the Jews were put to useless work breaking up rocks and transferring the debris from place to place. Not far from Koluszowa and near the town of Debica, was the labour camp Pustkow where the Jews from the Lipie camp were often sent to join hard labour gangs building roads. This was a cruel camp whose Commandant, Schmidt, hanged Jews on a regular basis.[188]

The Gestapo Chief, in Nowy Sacz (1941-1943), was SS-Obersturmfuehrer Heinrich Hamann, (who was no less efficient than Rosenbaum) as he had already shot 881 Jews in the nearby Mishana Dolne,[189] and shot his own deputy SS-Untersturmfuehrer Koster in a drunken brawl following celebrations in the Casino after the shooting of 300 Jews in the town cemetery. Hamann was the organiser of this transport to Rabka, and later to the final clearing and murder all the Jews in the big ghetto in August, 1942.[190] Nowy Sacz was adjacent to Rabka and was the main supplier of Jewish labour to the SD School. A separate prison block of 12 large, 6 medium and 3 single cells had been set aside for Jews supervised by the SD School reject Bornholt.[191]

Prison Guard Bornholt gives us an interesting view as to the attitude to the shooting of Jews:

'Members of the Grenzpolizeikommissariat, Krakow (Nowy Sacz), were, with very few exceptions, quite happy to take part in shooting Jews. They had a ball! Obviously they can't say that today! Nobody failed to turn up... I want to repeat that people today give a false impression when they say that the actions against Jews were carried out unwillingly. There was great hatred against the Jews; it was revenge, and they wanted money and gold. Don't let's kid ourselves; there was always something up for grabs during the Jewish actions. Everywhere you went there was always something for the taking. The poor Jews were brought in, the rich Jews were fetched and their homes were scoured.'[192]

Nowy Sacz Actions (2)

In May 1942, the first transport was organised from Nowy Sacz by Herr Swoboda, Head of the Employment Department for Jewish workers.[193] The Judenrat kept a file of all fit Jews available for transport. Those unfit for work were not registered and taken to the cemetery to be shot. When a registered Jew died, the card was marked with a cross in the files and then destroyed.[194]

A call went out from the Judenrat to the Jewish Police to round up male Jews between the age of 15 and 40, and bring them to the former 'Maccabi' clubhouse. After a short fitness inspection by the Employment Office a selection was made. At least 60, probably 80, healthy and fit Jewish men of the required age group were selected and ordered to present themselves with their luggage in a few days at the Jewish Employment Office in Nowy Sacz. On the 9th May, 1942, the transport with the Jew-workers left by train for Bad Rabka.[195] The transport was received in the afternoon by the Rabka Judenrat, Paul Beck (from the School), and Scharfuehrer Bohnert. The transport escort handed over a list of names to Beck who brought the Jews to the local baths where they were shaven. Beck then allocated them accommodation in one of the three houses in the work-camp.

The following morning the newcomers were brought to the School and received by Scharfuehrer Bohnert who checked the transport list. Rosenbaum arrived in a horsedrawn carriage. Beck informed the Jews: '*Here comes "Leutnant" Rosenbaum!*' Rosenbaum made a speech and expressed with sharp words that one had to work and work again. Whoever did not work was 'dealt with'. Accompanied by Bohnert, Rosenbaum inspected the Jewish workers. The Jews were divided into 4 or 5 groups and each group had a Kapo who was chosen from the ranks. The Kapos selected were the Jews Farber, Sammy Frolich, Lonker, Hennek, Grossbard and Joseph Grossbard. The Jewish workers were sent to their places of work in the School. Separate groups were set to work levelling the terrain around the School, while other groups had to build a cellar under the Pigsties—later to be the prison bunker for the prisoners—and the biggest building project, the installation of the shooting range, which was planned a few hundred metres behind the School in the woods. In order to make clear the lines of fire on this range, considerable earth masses had to be removed.[196]

Already, Rosenbaum and Bohnert, during their inspection walks, had made notes of individual Jews. Rosenbaum had a list of 8 Jews in his notebook. He would approach a work-group and say to a Jew, '*What's your name?*' This selection was entirely random. In no way did it concern weaklings or Jews unfit for work. It may have been because the Jew wore glasses, or looked in a particular way. Among the 'noted' Jews was the fit and healthy butcher called Wieldstein who happened to have a scar on his face.

For the time being these 'noted' 8 Jews were ignored. Then on 26th May 1942, very shortly after, these 'noted' Jews were separated from their work groups and brought to the bunkers and imprisoned. A large posse of Jewish gravediggers supervised by SS-Scharfuehrer Bohnert and Ukrainian guards went to the woods and prepared a mass grave. That same day, the 8 Jews were paraded before an assembled class and shot by Rosenbaum in the back of the neck. Among them was the gravedigger Schermer who probably was not part of the chosen victims, but was in the grave to arrange the corpses and had failed to get out in time.[197]

On the same day, in the evening, 60 Jews were brought to the execution site. Supervised personally by Rosenbaum who demonstrated to the assembled class how each Jew was to be shot, the Jews were made to undress which brought laughter from Rosenbaum because they couldn't undress quickly enough, then in small groups were made to face the pit and shot in the presence of the other waiting Jews. The witnesses to all this were the Jewish gravediggers hiding in the nearby bushes waiting for the 'whistle order' from Bohnert to cover the bodies and fill the grave.[198]

Nowy Sacz Actions (3) [199]

In June, 1942, a further transport of Jewish workers from Nowy Sacz arrived at the railway station to be picked up by Beck, SS-Scharfuehrers Bohnert and

Proch. Several of the Jews from this transport were shot en route to the School.
The others were dealt with in the normal way.

At the end of July, 1942, in the early afternoon, another transport of Jewish
workers arrived from Nowy Sacz. Some of the 100-strong group were orthodox
Jews with '*pajes*', beards and dressed in traditional clothing: some of them were
carrying holy books and Torah Scrolls. The Jewish workers were young, fit and
healthy to be employed on the terrain or building sites in the School. The Jews
were met by Beck, the Sipo-SD and Ukrainians and taken to the baths as
described above. On the march to the School, between 5 and 10 Jews from this
transport were shot by the escort. Some of the corpses were buried on the spot at
the side of the road, others collected later by lorry and taken to the School to be
buried with other actions of the day.[200]

When these Jews arrived at the School, Sipo-SD and Ukrainians organised
games. The Jews were driven back and forth in wheelbarrows, the elder Jews
had to sit in the wheelbarrows and the younger Jews had to push them through
dirt and water pools until the wheelbarrows turned over. The Torah Scrolls
taken from the religious Jews were destroyed or kept back to allow these Jews to
take them to the graves. This was not a consideration but an added torment as it
produced laughter among the SS. Dogs were let loose on the Jews to frighten
them, for fun. Their tormentors also beat them with sticks. Rosenbaum took part
in this scene by whipping the Jews and screaming to these anguished people:
'*Where is your God now, you damned Jews?*'[201]

During the day, about 20 Jewish workers had excavated a large grave in the
woods. The pit measured 20m. X 4m. and 3m. (Deep) About 12-15 Jews were
picked out from the newly arrived transport and separated from the others. That
evening at least 59 Jews were executed in the woods. Rosenbaum personally
directed the execution in the presence of eager onlookers and was carried out by
the Sipo-SD and Ukrainian Instructors as described above.

Action against Picked-Up Jews (1)

Approximately one month before the deportation en-bloc of the Rabka Jews to
Belzec (end of August), Rosenbaum ordered 5 Jewish workers to dig a grave in
the woods.[202] The digging was supervised by the Ukrainian guard Jawoski. The
Jewish workers had to hurry-up in order to finish on time. Some diversion
brought Jawoski to say the following: '*Let's go, hurry up, if Rosenbaum finds
you still working, he will kill you all!*' All of a sudden, Jawoski ordered: '*Get*

out of the hole and disappear 10 metres in the vicinity; when you hear a whistle, show yourselves again!' The Jew-workers hid in the surrounding bushes and trees. Directly after that, Rosenbaum, whose voice could already be heard, appeared with SS-Scharfuehrer Bohnert. A family: father, mother and a 20 – year-old daughter with their grandchild were brought to the graveside. They were 'picked up' Jews, namely the kind that was either caught with Aryan papers, denounced, or had moved outside of their residential area.[203] The victims first realised what was about to happen when they saw the pit and started to scream. They were forced to undress and stand on the edge of the pit. The mother of the grandchild begged Rosenbaum to shoot her before the child. Rosenbaum shot the child first and then the mother. After the execution of this family, the Jew-workers appeared on the command of a whistle. The Jew Susskind was ordered to get into the pit and arrange the bodies. When Susskind touched the child, he almost fainted. Rosenbaum yelled and cursed: *'You dog, if you do not turn these people around, I will shoot you!'* The Jew Form took his working colleague out of the pit and took his place in the pit. During this time, Rosenbaum was standing at the edge of the pit and was watching the Jew Form working who was now covered in blood. Subsequently, the grave, as usual, was closed and levelled.[204]

Murder by Appointment

At about the same time as the 'group' hanging at the School was organised by Rosenbaum, the Zakopane Gestapo team led by SS-Captain Weissmann and SS-Scharfuehrer Bottcher, brought to the School a large group of people and placed them in the detention block. It is not know if they were Jews or Poles. The Rabka Jews, supervised by SS-Scharfuehrer Bohnert, prepared a very large grave in the woods. In the late afternoon the prisoners were brought out in small groups to the execution site where they were individually shot into the pit.[205]

About two days later, the Zakopane Gestapo team returned with a single Polish prisoner and took him directly to the stable block where he was hanged with rope supplied by Bohnert. The Jewish workers took the body to the woods for burial. Some days after this hanging, the Zakopane Gestapo brought a family of American Jews (named Falk or Feig) to the School. They had attempted to cross the border into Slovakia but were caught. The family were taken to the woods in the usual way where they were individually shot by Proch.[206]

Group Hanging

A few days before Sunday the 30th August, 1942, when the deportations took place in both Bad Rabka and Neu Markt to Belzec, a new type of execution took place, deviating from the now practised methods. News about a forthcoming deportation had filtered through to the Jewish population. Some of the Jews who belonged to the permanent staff at the School decided to escape. Two of the escapees, the brothers Czarnowicki, both of whom worked in the tailor's shop, managed to reach Krakow. More Jews escaped when they started to close off the accommodation of the Jewish workers, whose 3 houses were below the School premises right on the Slonnka River. Based on this development, Rosenbaum decided to put a plan to the test, in order to avoid further escapes.

Immediately after work, the Jewish workers were ordered to gather for a roll call on open space behind the School. Not less than 150 Jews paraded. In a barn type shed on the building site, at the back of the School, preparations were made for a hanging. Ropes were placed or attached with hooks on horizontal beams. Underneath there were boxes or barrels covered by boards. Apart from the Jewish workers, Rosenbaum, SS-Bohnert, Oder, Badura, Paul Beck (Jewish foreman), the Ukrainians instructors and students were present. Ten Jews were brought to the spot, among them being the young boy Edek Liebenheimer who was Rosenbaum's 'boot boy'. All the victims had been locked in the 'clink' (cells). Also among these chosen Jews was one member of the Judenrat, Simon Zollmann. The 10 Jews were placed on the prepared barrels and boards. The ropes were put around their necks. Rosenbaum yelled to the gathered mass that workers had escaped and therefore these Jews would hang as a deterrent. The gathered Jews were ordered to look in the direction of the execution place. The boards were pushed from under the victims' feet so they fell; the ropes tightened and strangled the victims. It didn't all go according to plan. The Jew Liebenheimer's noose ripped or he slid through the noose of the rope and fell on the ground. Liebenheimer tried to escape. When the Sipo-SD was about to shoot him, Rosenbaum yelled in wild excitement: '*Do not shoot, hang again!*' Liebenheimer begged Rosenbaum: '*Mr Untersrurmfuehrer, please shoot me!*' Rosenbaum yelled at him: '*You dog, for you I am not a 2nd Lieutenant anymore, you will be hanged!*' He was hanged a second time. This time, the noose also ripped and he again fell to the ground. The third attempt was successful.[207]

The victims were taken by the Jew-workers to the grave in the woods. One living victim, carried by the Jew Kalfus, was shot on the way. Shots were fired in the grave to make sure all were dead. Rosenbaum stayed at the execution place until the end of the hanging action.

Eyewitness Statements:

Hirsch Schiffeldrin

On Yom Kippur Eve, 1942, many Jews were rounded-up for failing to report for a deportation (to Belzec). Hirsch Schiffeldrin recalled:

> 'There was no way out; the Gestapo was making ready to deport the Jews. I had to return to the labour camp. At the railway station I presented my travel pass, but the Polish policeman ignored it and took me to the gathering area in Rabka. I saw my family there, along with the others we were divided up by Rosenbaum. I found myself in a special group of four, a man named Shaut a tinsmith, Yehiel Tirk a mechanic, Finkelstein a locksmith; I, an electrician, was the fourth. We were put to work on maintenance of the target practice range.

> On Yom Kippur Eve 1942, the four of us were taken to a spot where 30 Jews were to be executed for failing to report for the deportation. The Germans shot them. Next to the pit stood a barrel of lime. The four of us were ordered to pour lime on the corpses and cover the pit with earth. All the possessions of the Jews were taken to a large warehouse for sorting and refurbishing.'

Dr David Yacobovitz:

> 'Untersturmfuehrer Willhelm Rosenbaum was the worst of all the Gestapo men in the Rabka district. The others tried to hide their barbaric acts by committing them some distance outside the town. Rosenbaum and Heinrich Hamann, head of the Gestapo in Nowy Targ, committed the atrocities in broad daylight for all to see.

> Rosenbaum's favourite place for executions was the densely populated Salona quarter. The doctors in the sanatoriums complained that the cries and shootings disturbed their patients, but Rosenbaum paid the complaints not the slightest heed. Hamann selected Mishana Dolna for his executions. He demanded that the Judenrat collect an exorbitant amount of money, supposedly to pay for the deportation of the Jews.

When the Judenrat could not come up with the payment, Hamann gathered 800 Jews in the square and murdered them.'[208]

Frania Tiger:

We Jews of Rabka were only 1500 souls, in a population of 10,000. On the 31st August, 1942, all the Jews were rounded up and later sent to their death in Belzec. The Poles were warned not to help Jews,[209] nor conceal information about them, under pain of death. Many Jews were shot wherever they were found. Those who tried to escape were hanged. The common graves dug for the victims in the woods at the Rabka School contained seven times as many corpses as there were Jewish inhabitants in Rabka before the war

Eight days before the deportation, my mother and I hid in an attic. My father was working for the Germans in Nowy Targ. Our hiding place was not discovered because the attic had a secret access. We survived the war due to the help of a Polish neighbour, Mrs Wagner.[210]

On Yom Kippur Eve, 1942, many Jews were rounded-up for failing to report for a deportation (to Belzec).

The end of August, beginning of September, 1942, (a few days after the hanging) the widow of Simon Zollmann (one of the hanged) was 'picked up' with one of their two sons. The Jewess Zollmann and her son were locked up in the bunker and the pigsty with other Jews including a certain Stern.

The Jew Gold, with others, was ordered to dig a grave in the woods—the usual procedure—the locked up Jews were brought to the graveside, including the Jewess Zollmann with her son. Zollmann begged Rosenbaum for mercy and implored Rosenbaum to keep her son alive, as he 'doesn't know he is a Jew'. Rosenbaum shot the child and then the mother. The grave was covered in the usual way.

Picked-Up Jews (2)

A woman, man and young girl aged 18-19 years—most probably a family—were 'picked up' and brought to the School. The Jew-workers Kalfus and two others from the Neu Markt transport, Bier and Grunspan, were ordered to dig a grave in the woods. The victims were ordered to undress and face the pit. One of the SS who was watching said that the girl was so fat that soap could be made out of her. Rosenbaum executed the family in the usual way.[211]

Picked-Up Jews (3)

Towards the end of 1942 when the ground was already frozen, the Jew-workers Form and Stammberger were ordered to dig a grave in the woods in the usual way. In the afternoon, at least 15 Jews from the bunker were brought to the graveside. While passing the bunker, the Jew-workers heard yelling and screaming through the grated windows. The prisoners were hungry and wanted food and water. Among the Jews who were walking towards the wood, was a father, mother and a 4-year-old child who was being carried in the father's arms. When the group knew what was about to happen, they hugged and kissed each other. Among the group was a girl in her teens. She was approaching the grave cheerfully and pleased in protest. One of the Sipo-SD guards, or maybe it was Rosenbaum, went to the girl and yelled: 'Do you not know where this is leading to?' The young girl answered: 'I want to show you how a Polish girl faces death!' Rosenbaum led this execution in the usual way.[212]

Shooting of the family Rosenbaum (7)

In Bad Rabka, there was a Jewish family who had the same name as the School Commandant (Rosenbaum). There was a mother, father, and a 15-year-old daughter and son, who was about 10 years old. Before the war, the mother's side of the family owned a haberdashery shop near the railway station. Until the German occupation, the father was a 'driver'; he took care of all the affairs in Bad Rabka, travelling to other cities and to the countryside. As soon as the School of the Commander-in-Chief of the Security Police (BdS) was settled in Rabka, he became a Jewish worker in the School; he worked on the small farm and guarded the sheep. Only when the Jewish population had to present themselves in the School, in the spring of 1942, SS-Rosenbaum noticed that there was a Jewish family in Bad Rabka with his name. He could not stand the thought of this. Rosenbaum realised he had a name with a Jewish sound and therefore, he had previously filed an application before the war to change his name, which was never taken care of. It was a standing joke amongst the School staff and they would talk about 2nd Lieutenant Beck (the Jew) and the Jew Rosenbaum (the Commandant).[213] This was also the basis for his being so shocked and infuriated: that the Jewish origin of his name was confirmed by this family Rosenbaum from Rabka.

On one occasion, in the summer of 1942, quite a while before the general deportation of the Rabka community to Belzec, Rosenbaum killed the family Rosenbaum. In a late afternoon, they—father, mother, daughter and son—were brought to the School. Whether all the family members were brought together or father and son, who worked in the quarry, were brought later, cannot be ascertained.   After the family had been assembled in the School yard, Rosenbaum appeared and rushed at the father, cursing: 'You damned Jew, by what right are you carrying my good name!'   He then beat the father. Rosenbaum called for SS-Scharfuehrer Bohnert and ordered him to shoot the family there and then, on his responsibility, on the School premises.   Bohnert drew his pistol and shot the family in Rosenbaum's presence.   The news of the shooting quickly spread throughout the community and resulted in an increase of outrage, fear and terror among the Jews.[214]

Simon Wiesenthal reflects on the shooting of the Rosenbaum family which he passed on to the author 1990:

Figure:27 : Simon Wiesenthal

'I first heard of Sammy Rosenbaum in 1965, when a Mrs Rawicz from Rabka came into my office in Vienna to testify at a War Crimes trial. Mrs Rawicz remembered Sammy Rosenbaum as "a frail boy, with a pale, thin face and big, dark eyes, who looked much older than his age—as did many children who learned too early about life." Sammy was nine-years-old in 1939 when the Germans entered Rabka and made life a nightmare.

Sammy's father was a tailor who lived in two musty rooms and a tiny kitchen in an old house. But they were happy and religious. Every Friday night Sammy went with his father to the synagogue, after his mother and sister lit the Shabbat candles.

In 1940 the SS set up a training centre in a former Polish Army barracks near Rabka. In the early phase of the war, the SS platoons shot their victims; fifty, a hundred, even a hundred and fifty people a day.

The SS men were being hardened at Rabka so they would become insensitive to blood, to the agonizing cries of women and children. The job must be done with a minimum of fuss and maximum of efficiency. That was a Fuhrerbefehl—the Fuhrer's order.

The school commander was SS Untersturmfuehrer Wilhelm Rosenbaum from Hamburg. Cynical and brutal, he walked around with a riding crop. "His appearance frightened us," the woman from Rabka remembered.

Early in 1942, SS Rosenbaum ordered all Rabka's Jews to appear at the local school to "register." The sick and the elderly would be deported, and the others would labour for the Wehrmacht.

Toward the end of the registration, SS Fuhrer Rosenbaum appeared, accompanied by two deputies, SS-Oberscharfuehrer Wilhelm Oder and Walter Proch. SS Fuhrer Rosenbaum read through the list of names. "Suddenly, he beat his riding crop hard on the table," the woman from Rabka told me. "We each winced as if we had been whipped." SS man Rosenbaum shouted: "What's this? Rosenbaum? Jews! How dare these verdammte Juden have my good German name?"

He threw the list on the table and strode out. We knew the Rosenbaums would be killed; it was only a matter of time. People would be executed because their name was Rosenberg, or if their first name happened to be Adolf or Hermann.

The Police school practiced executions in a clearing in the woods. SS students shot Jews and Poles rounded up by the Gestapo, while SS Fuhrer Rosenbaum observed students' reactions with clinical detachment. If a student flinched, he was removed from the execution squad and sent to the front.

After the registration, Mrs Rawicz worked in the police school as a charwoman. "When the SS men came back from the clearing in the woods I had to clean their boots covered with blood." It was a Friday morning in June 1942. Two SS men escorted "the Jew Rosenbaum," his wife, and their fifteen-year-old daughter Paula. Behind them came SS Fuhrer Rosenbaum.

"The woman and the girl were marched around the schoolhouse and then I heard some shots," the witness said. "I saw SS man Rosenbaum beat our Rosenbaum with his riding crop, shouting: 'You dirty Jews, I'll teach you a lesson for having my German name!' Then the SS man took his revolver and shot Rosenbaum the tailor two or three times. Then the SS sent an unarmed kapo (Jewish policeman) to the quarry to get Sammy."

He went to Zakryty in a horsedrawn cart. He stopped and waved at Sammy Rosenbaum. Everybody in the quarry stared—the Jewish labourers and the SS guards. Sammy put the stone in his hands on the truck, and walked toward the cart.

Sammy looked up at the kapo. "Where are they?" he asked—"Father, Mother, and Paula. Where?" The kapo just shook his head.

Sammy understood. "They're dead," he muttered, and spoke matter-of-factly: "Our name is Rosenbaum, and now you've come for me." He stepped up and sat down next to the kapo.

The policeman had expected the boy to cry, perhaps run away. Riding out to Zakryty, the policeman wondered how he might have forewarned the boy; allow him to disappear in the woods, where the Polish underground might help him? Now it was too late. The SS guards were watching.

The kapo told Sammy what had happened that morning. Sammy asked if they could stop for a moment at his house. When they got there, he stepped down and walked into the front room, leaving the door open. He looked over the table with the half-filled teacups left from breakfast. He looked at the clock. It was half past three. Father, Mother and Paula were already buried, and no one had lit a candle for them. Slowly, methodically, Sammy cleaned off the table and put the candlesticks on it.

"I could see Sammy from the outside," the kapo told Mrs Rawicz. "He put on his skullcap, and lit the candles. Two for his father, two for his mother, two for his sister. And he prayed. I saw his lips moving. He said Kaddish for them." Kaddish is the prayer for the dead. Father Rosenbaum always said Kaddish for his dead parents, and had shown Sammy the prayer. Now he was the only one left in his family. He stood quietly, looking at the six candles.

The Jewish policeman outside saw Sammy slowly shaking his head, as though he suddenly remembered something. Then Sammy placed two more candles on the table, took a match and lit them, and prayed.

"The boy knew he was already dead," the policeman said later. "He lit the candles and said Kaddish for himself."

Sammy came out, and sat down near the kapo, who was crying. The boy didn't cry. The kapo wiped away his tears with the back of his hand and pulled the reins, but the tears kept coming. The boy didn't say a word. He gently touched the older man's arm, to comfort him—to forgive him for taking him away.

They rode to the clearing in the woods, where SS Fuhrer Rosenbaum and his students waited.

'About time!' screamed the SS man.

No tombstone bears Sammy Rosenbaum's name. No one might have remembered him if the woman from Rabka had not come into my office. But every year, one day in June, I light two candles for him and say Kaddish.'

The Jews of Jordanow

Jordanow's location near the Slovakian border also led to its early occupation by German forces. Like Nowy Targ, the Jews were immediately subjected to the now familiar restrictions. A Judenrat had been formed and the Jews ordered to register for labour. The young were sent to work as forced labourers in the stone quarries where, like the Jews in Nowy Targ, they were made to break up rocks for no apparent reason. The women cleaned the streets and other menial tasks at the whim of the Germans. In 1940, the Jewish Quarter was placed under curfew and the arm band regulations introduced. In 1941, all Jewish property was confiscated. Jews from the town of Sluptza in the Posnan district were cleared and sent to Jordanow where the Judenrat had to arrange accommodation for them in the dilapidated Jewish Quarter.

At the beginning of 1942, the Nazi destruction machinery commenced with the introduction of a census to be conducted by the Judenrat to list all Jews in the town. Unachievable ransom levies were demanded from the Judenrat. The Judenrat, who were unable to pay such large sums, went to their community for help. Great efforts were made to meet these quotas, many of the Jews removing their gold teeth as a donation to the cause.

On the 30th August, 1942, on the same day as the Nowy Targ liquidations, instructors and recruits from the Rabka Sipo School, led by Rosenbaum, assisted by the SS/SD from Nowy Targ, carried out a brutal action in the town of Jordanow The Jews of Jordanow were rounded up and taken to the town square where they were assembled. For some unknown reason at that time, mothers and small children were separated from those assembled and marched off separately Specially prepared pits had already been dug in the lawns of the Jewish cemetery bordering the square. Local Poles, who needed no invitation, assisted the SS in guarding the Jews, and when the Jews were ordered to remove their clothing and shoes, the Poles took it away for their own use.

Rosenbaum, who had taken personal charge of this 'action', had sent a team under the supervision of SS-Scharfuehrer Proch to prepare the pits in the Jordanow cemetery. Apart from the mothers and children, every Jew in Jordanow was shot into the pits using the 'plank and walk' technique perfected by Proch. Many were not killed outright but no 'mercy' shot was given. The pit was filled in, burying many half dead Jews. Reports that the ground was heaving are not exaggerated. The Ukrainians and Poles who were guarding the grave site had to stamp the ground to even out the heaving earth.[215]

On checking their lists, the action squad discovered that some Jews were not accounted for and still at large. All houses in the town and surrounding villages were searched ferreting out those they could find who were immediately shot on the spot. Some Jews escaped into the nearby forest and tried to cross into Slovakia. The local Polish peasants assisted in the search that then extorted from the Jews their last valuables before handing them over to the Gestapo, who killed them on the spot. Local farmers with their wagons collected the corpses and took them to the horse cemetery at Ushlatz. That day there was a great celebration at the Rabka School for a job 'well done'.[216]

Late in the afternoon, directly after the slaughter, horsedrawn wagons arrived in Rabka, fully laden with young mothers and very small children (babies and 3—4-year-olds). The local Jewish community did not know about the massacre, and were perplexed at the arrival of these wagons and their distressed cargo. The SS had killed every Jew in Jordanow, with the exception of these young mothers and children. The mothers from Jordanow were in shock after seeing their families shot in the cemetery. On Rosenbaum's orders, the mothers were taken to the Judenrat who were ordered to house and feed them.[217]

Figure 28: c. 1942 'Selection'

Mark Goldfinger, who was then 11 years of age, was with his mother when this dreadful sight entered the town. Mark remembers going with his mother to collect clothes, food and blankets for the unfortunate women of Jordanow. The Jewish community could not understand why the women and children had been spared by the SS. They knew enough not to expect humanitarian considerations. A few weeks later, on a date unknown, all became clear:

The arrival of these women was the first indication of what had happened in Jordanow, that every Jew, with the exception of the women and children, had been murdered. The explanation for the spared selection did not take long to emerge. A few weeks later, all the women and children were rounded up and taken into the School. They were imprisoned in the stables and bunkers where previous prisoners had been held. The mothers and children were used in small batches of 3 and 4 at a time and used as examples by the SS staff at the School to show the new recruits how, and the best way, to murder women and children when engaged on Ghetto-clearing duties and other actions.   Recruits who showed dissatisfaction after these exercises were carefully noted and removed from the School. After the completion of these exercises, the bodies of the women and children were disposed of in the usual way in the woods.[218]

It was at about this time that Dr Schoengarth became aware of an SS investigation into corruption and theft of the Krakow and Lvov Sipo-SD which was instigated at the highest level. There was now a damage limitation exercise by Dr Schoengarth and a hurried covering of tracks began. The first action was the shooting dead of the Jew Beck at the Rabka School.[219] Beck had been privy to every known murder in the Rabka School. As a Jew, he was in possession of very sensitive information of the personal activities of Commandant Rosenbaum, his senior members of Staff and their murdering activities. Beck must have known that he was only tolerated for his expertise, and that after all a 'Jew is a Jew', and anathema to the Reich Masters. Beck had witnessed the huge warehouse in the School packed with beautiful paintings, he had helped to carry the property to Rosenbaum's villa, and had assisted Pieter Menten (who we shall deal with later) to reverse his trailer and helped unload the goods. The Jew beck was the man who knew too much about the black market deals of his Nazi bosses that had been played out before his very eyes. Dr Schoengarth sent an immediate order to Rosenbaum to have Beck shot.

Within hours of that order, SS-Unterscharfuehrer Bohnert had taken Beck to the woods and shot him dead. [220] There was panic in the School among the Jewish staff. There were escapes in all directions, many ending up voluntarily in the confines of the Plaszow Lager. The Jew Ettinger, who, like Beck, was just as privy to the goings on in the School, had escaped to Krakow and found his way into the clothing factory of Julias Madritsch.[221] Ettinger met his brother Henryk there, and together they were taken out of Plaszow with the Oskar Schindler transport to Brunnlitz in Czechoslovakia, and survived to tell the tale of the Rabka happenings.[222] The important point is that these Jews somehow survived, and in the final analysis, were able to give evidence at later war crimes trials.

Once the initial phase of the destruction of the Jewish population were realised, the School settled down to a more conventional syllabus, and continued in this manner until January 1945, when it was transferred to Berlin due to the Russian advance.

One of the most curious aspects of the Rabka School murders was the secrecy Rosenbaum was able to maintain. When Rosenbaum gave evidence at his trial in Hamburg in 1968, he agreed that he had done his utmost to conceal the murders from the domestic staff at the School. That is why most executions were committed in the evening time, when all the general office and domestic staff had finished work and gone home. To this extent he was successful. While the witnesses Meta Kuck, Kathe Engelmann and Adela Schmitt (non-Jews)—all employed in the offices of the School in 1942—were quite ignorant, the witness Elfrieda Bohnert—wife of SS-Scharfuehrer Bohnert—noticed the places during her walks in the woods where graves were located. She had overheard the kitchen staff that Jews were killed. However, she considered questions about this were inappropriate. The Jewess, Lucia Schon, in her special relationship with Rosenbaum and the senior SS staff, mentions that the SS wives climbed onto the roof to view the killings when they were taking place in the woods.

However, this is not the end of the story. The conspiracy of associations between our protagonists steps up a gear, as we shall see!

Chapter 7

Hans Krueger in Stanislawow, Kolomyja and District[223]

'Among other things...I'd been given the order to clear the area of Jews. Initially, that meant deporting the Jewish population or concentrating them in ghettos. A bit later, a directive from the RSHA gave the order to render the area judenfrei, a new interpretation... "their liquidation."

Hans Krueger.

Hans Krueger establishes the Sipo-SD in Stanislawow.

DR SCHOENGARTH remained in Lvov with Wilhelm Rosenbaum to organise the setting up of Sipo-SD regional offices, while dispersing his personal commando units to other locations. Oskar Brandt, a brutal Gestapo officer who had served as a 'special officer for Jewish affairs' with the Security Police in the Krakow District, was sent with six men to Stanislawow. He was joined a week later by Hans Krueger[224] who was ordered to set up a branch office of the Regional Command of Sipo-SD in Stanislawow. The Sipo consisted of the Gestapo and Criminal Police and was a part of the SD.[225] The SD personnel, who had set out from Krakow with zbV, were now dispersed throughout East Galicia. After disbandment of zbV in mid-July, these officers were sent to the major towns in East Galicia to organise and prepare for further Jewish actions and the later, as it turned out, Jewish resettlements to Belzec:[226]

The majority of these men were experienced 'Jewish Affairs' Officers [227] selected personally by Dr Schoengarth from many districts in the Generalgouvnement specifically to carry out his task. By the very nature of their geographical postings, they covered all of East Galicia under the command of the SS and Police Leader, Fritz Katzmann[228] and SS-Captain Hans Krueger. The inclusion of the SD in the 'Jewish Affairs' portfolio reinforces the prominence of this select bunch of zbV and their designated purpose. These instruments of the HHE were vehemently and brutally anti-Semitic and the ideological representative bureaucrats of death and destruction in East Galicia.[229]

105

The roaming and movable task force of zbV had now changed into a stationary, external office Commanded by Major General Katzmann in Lvov and SS-Oberstumbannfuehrer Dr Tanzmann (Department 1V Jewish Dept) in Lvov. Hans Krueger's KdS office in Stanislawow, which had evolved from the initial zbV, was now operational with additional branches spread over east Galicia. [230]

After the 22nd June, 1942, the Russians had immediately evacuated Stanislawow. A week later the town was occupied by the Hungarian Army, who despite the arrival of the German Werhmacht and the Einsatzgruppen, held on to the civil and military administration. Within weeks, hundreds of weak and hungry Jews who had been deported from the Hungarian-Ruthenian border into Galicia were arriving at the railway station in the town. Here Jews were brutally beaten and marched to a holding prison known as Rudolf Mill, a flour mill situated in Halitzka Street.[231] It soon became common knowledge among the Hungarian government administrators that it was the intention of the Germans to kill all the Jews.[232]

On about the 10th July, 1941, forward detachments of zbV, led by SS 2nd Lieutenant Oskar Brandt, arrived in Stanslawow and set up office in the former NKVD building.[233] Brandt was shortly followed by Krueger on the 20th July, 1941, who took overall command of the Security Services.[234] It is also probable that Krueger carried with him orders to liquidate the Jewish and Polish intelligentsia in Stanislawow and extend his orders to other districts by the process of staged elimination.

The war against the partisans was utilised by Hitler not only as a mask for mass murder, but also as a way to build a broad consensus of all the Nazi forces operating in the occupied areas with regard to the murder of Jews The Jews were portrayed by the Nazis as partisans or potential partisans, both as a group and as individuals, and as such were targets not only for the security services, but also the military and civil administration. By camouflaging the murder of the Jews as a war against partisans, Krueger lent to it a different dimension. Under the banner of fighting the enemy behind the front lines he murdered Jewish children, women and men. In the context of the overall war situation, the 'Jewish Question' was but a side-line, effectively being carried out by a select minority within the German sphere of influence.[235]

What was Krueger's specific contribution to the course of the 'Final Solution' in the area under his control? Due to the fragmentary state of the sources, we can only venture a partial answer. Krueger was the first to organize mass murders in the region while it was still under Hungarian occupation. In the fall of 1941, seizing the initiative before the other Gestapo leaders, he proceeded to execute Jews in legally unclear situations, e.g., Jews or half-Jews apprehended without the obligatory armband. Elsewhere at that time such offenses were still being penalized by fines. A murder order was issued by Krueger for just such an offence:

'I was informed confidentially that the Jew H.S. was walking around without the mandatory Jewish armband. I had him arrested on October 10, 1941 and confined in the local jail here. In reply to why he was not wearing the obligatory armband, he stated that he didn't know that he, as a baptized Jew, was also required to wear the band. It is my recommendation that the Jew H.S. be liquidated as a consequence of his failure to adhere to the German regulations.

Lange   SS-Sergeant   Security   Police   Stanislau,   16th   October, 1941/Galicia/Order

1. The Jew H.S. is to be liquidated.
2. Prepare a record card. /done La. /
3. SS-Sergeant Hehemann should complete the E [execution]-list.
4. File it away.
                    Krueger'[236]

Emergeance of Genocide

On 15th July, 1941, announcements were posted on walls throughout Stanislawow with the 'armband' decree. Every Jew, including Catholics whose Jewish ancestry could be traced back to the third generation, was required to wear a 'Jewish armband' on the right sleeve—a Star of David painted blue on white fabric. The marking of Jews was an open invitation to Poles and Ukrainians to rob them in the streets, with the knowledge that little or no complaint would be made to the German authorities.[237] In other towns in the Generalgovenment, it was the practice that a Jew caught without 'the Star' paid a fine and that was it. In Stanislawow and other towns in German occupied Galicia the matter had taken a decisive turn of a more sinister nature.

At the beginning of August, 1941, the Stanislawow region was still under Hungarian sovereignty.[238] There was not quite a meeting of minds between the

Hungarian military and Krueger's Commando. In Operation Report USSR No. 23, the following is reported:

> Einsatzgruppen C: 'Former Polish officers and Jews play an important part in the Honved (Hungarian) Army. The translators are almost without exception either Jews or scoundrels. All the leading military Hungarian circles sympathise with the Poles, most of them also with the Jews. Poles were preferred in Zaleschiki and Stanislawow. The Hungarian Feld gendarmerie is apparently favouring the setting up of Polish units.

> In the area of Zaleschiki, the Poles co-operate with Soviet Russian gangs who are still hiding in the forests. Hungarian circles deny knowing of Polish activities in connection with Bolsheviks.

> All the intelligence officers are either Jews or under Jewish influence. I personally had dealings with six officers in the area who were undoubtedly Jews. A Polish officer, Dabrowski, holds a leading position. Isolated actions against Jews were carried out by the militia (Ukrainian). As a consequence, the Hungarian Army intervened immediately. One could see leading officers together with many Jews in the restaurant Kiev.'[239]

Galicia as the 5th District

A number of important changes were now taking place in east Galicia. On 1st August, 1941, after a high level conference in Lvov attended by Dr Hans Frank, Dr Karl Lasch and SS-Major General Katzmann, it was decided to incorporate east Galicia into the Generalgouvnement as the Fifth District. Katzmann was immediately appointed as SS-Major General, the highest police authority in Galicia. Dr Karl Lasch was transferred from Radom district and appointed Governor in Lvov. Katzmann and Lasch were old friends who had served together in Radom 1939-41, with no apparent friction. They now had the task to subdue and organise their new territory.

The HSSPF, F.W. Krueger in Krakow had been subordinate to Frank in 1940, but was now carrying out police duties without reference to Dr Frank, taking his orders directly from Himmler. Krueger thus side-stepped Frank so as not to involve the Governor-General with police and security matters. Frank was not at all pleased with the situation and made it known. Another quirk in this obscure chain of command was the SSPF in Krakow, (Scherner), who was receiving his orders direct from the SSPF in Lublin (Globocnik) on all Jewish matters.

Katzmann had many tasks to fulfil and not just the 'Jewish Question'. Many thousands of Poles had to be screened and transported to Germany for voluntary or compulsory agricultural work. The oil refineries had to produce twice as much oil (in the oil fields of Boryslaw and Drohobycz) for war-use in Poland and for the Russian Front, so that the refineries had to work day and night with Jewish, Christian and Ukrainian workers supervised by German engineers, technicians and plant directors. The whole economic base of skilled labour and raw materials had been badly neglected, and was made worse by demands on labour for service in the I.G. Farben industrial complexes at Auschwitz. In addition to this, Katzmann had to keep the Ukrainian Nationalists on his side, which was proving very difficult. Elsewhere, now that zbV had disbanded, the SD moved into other parts of east Galicia and were making up their own minds on economic and political priorities and were very much working to their own agenda..

Mass Killings Emerge as a Solution

To make a point and to set precedence Krueger organised a mass shooting in Stanislawow on the 2nd August, 1941, under the guise of 'registering the wealthier class.'[240] 800 Jews reported to the police. Of these, 200 skilled workers were sent back home. The rest, the intelligentsia, the cream of the Jewish community, were transported the following day to the forest near Pawelce where they were secretly executed by the security police.[241] Among them was Dr Boleslaw Fell, who had practised in Warsaw before the war; Ernestyn Fach, a graduate of the University of Nantes; and her sister, Dr Klara Fach.[242] This is another example of how a centrally agreed solution had been reached to lure selected Jews to destruction, as the same deception and procedures were occurring in many locations, thousands of miles apart, by different cadres.

Preparations for the 'Final Solution of the Jewish Question' in the Galician District (and elsewhere) appear to have been officially initiated in September, 1941, According to Krueger's statement, the corresponding orders had been issued by Schoengarth before he left Lvov that Jews unfit or unqualified for work were to be shot, and the remainder detained in concentration camps. Krueger makes no reference to women and children who he was slaughtering daily.[243] The 1st September, 1941, was a defining moment, with the establishment of permanent District Government with its power base in Lvov. It is about this time that Schoengarth and Rosenbaum returned to Krakow, leaving Menten to pursue his activities confiscating seizure of art under the umbrella of the seizure order 'Rosenberg'.[244]

One of the first priorities to be sorted was the influx of refugees now appearing on the borders. On 25th August, 1941, at a conference of the Wehrmacht, representatives of the newly formed East Ministry met at the General Quarteriermeister-OKH.[245] Thousands of Hungarian Jews were congregating in the area of Kamenets-Podolsky, having been expelled by the Hungarians. The HSSPF in this district, Lieutenant General Jeckeln, reported that this problem would be solved by 1 September, 1941.[246] A unit of Schoengarth's Einsatzgruppen, which had reached Tarnopol, reported having turned back 1000 Jews who had been deported by the Hungarian 10th Pursuit Battalion across the Dniester River.[247] Hans Krueger solved the problem of the Hungarian Jews by removing them to the Stanislawow Ghetto (Rudolf Mill) where the majority received on-going 'special treatment'.[248] To the Germans, the Hungarian government were playing a curious game that was not appreciated by the Wehrmacht, and even less so by Hans Krueger.

Jews drafted into war

The Hungarians were also operating to their own agenda when it came to Jewish labour. They had formed their own Jewish forced labour system where Jews were liable to be drafted into the Hungarian army for 'auxiliary service' where they were used for mine-clearing operations and construction work. With the entry of Hungary into the war on the German side, these Jewish labour battalions fought at the front (behind the Hungarian and German lines) well into 1943. A report from a Foreign Office official in Krakow in November, 1943, reported that a Hungarian Jewish labour battalion was stationed in Stanislawow (well after the final deportations) and were wearing Hungarian uniforms.[249] Other reports of Jewish labour battalion activities were reported at the battle of Kursk salient and Brest-Litovsk.[250]

These kinds of activities by the Hungarians were in complete contrast to the view that was being spelled out by Katzmann at a meeting of the Lvov District government on 21st October, 1941, where he stressed that the leadership of the SD and Polizei interests in Galicia is guaranteed. What Katzmann meant is shown by comments made by Dr Hans Frank on 16th October, 1941, in Krakow in front of government members:[251]

'I will say to you quite openly, we must get rid of the Jews—So as far as Jews are concerned I expect them to disappear. They must go. Gentlemen, I must ask you to be forearmed against any feelings of compassion; we must exterminate the Jews wherever we find them. Of course this will be achieved by methods different to those that Amtschef Dr Hummel spoke about. The Jews are for us too extremely harmful pigs/eaters.

We now have in the Generalgouvnement 3.5 million Jews. We can't shoot 3.5 million Jews, we can't poison them, but we will have to take steps that will somehow lead to an "extermination successes". The Generalgouvnement must be as Jew free as the German Reich. Where and how this happens is a matter for the authorities that we are setting up here...'

Out of this conference came the Order from the Commander of the Order Police (BdO) that all Jews encountered on country roads were to be shot on sight. The special courts that were to deal with relatively minor infringements by the Jews, were working too slowly,[252] and it was agreed that something had to be done. Frank's speech gave the answer and was welcomed as a solution to the problem. The only Commander who was not impressed was Hans Krueger in Stanislawow—he had been carrying out his own solutions since the 1st September, 1941. These actions by Krueger in the regions of east Galicia set the precedent, and I believe influenced the decisions of the Krakow conference on 16th December that was to extend to all the regions of the Generalgouvnement. Krueger agreed at his trial that there was no special jurisdiction in Galicia and that he was acting within the norms of German law at the time.[253]

Prelude to bloody Sunday

Over 16 months between 1941 and 1943, Krueger, with a small squad of men sometimes numbering as few as 25, organized and implemented the shooting of some 70,000 Jews and the deportation of another 12,000 to death camps in this part of Galicia.

There may have been several key reasons why Krueger selected the districts around Stanislawow for his personal contribution to the Holocaust. First they were located on the border with Ruthenia (Carpo-Ukraine), annexed by Hungary from Czechoslovakia in November, 1938 and March 1939. Since July, the Hungarians had been deporting thousands of non-resident Jews from this territory across the border into eastern Galicia. Those deportees from Hungarian-occupied Ruthenia (some of whom were imprisoned in Rudolf Mill) became the victims of the largest massacre of the 'Final Solution' up until that time, which was perpetrated in Kamenets-Podolsk on 27-28th August, 1941. Sturmbannfuehrer Tanzmann also ordered that all Galician Jews who had been captured by Hungarian border guards while attempting to flee and were sent back over the border should be shot. Secondly, a ghetto was to be set up in Stanislawow, to be kept as small as possible. Several witnesses, including Krueger, concur in citing this motive for the mass murder:[254]

> 'When the heads of the various branch offices were installed by the new commander in Lvov, Tanzmann specified areas were assigned, and then the guidelines for work were set down. Jews not suitable for deployment as labourers were to be shot. Since they realised that such shooting could not be organised overnight, the plan was that the residential area set aside for the Jews should be progressively reduced. The result was that a certain number of Jews had to be shot on a regular basis, because space was no longer available.'

In Stanislawow, Krueger and his small team of Gestapo, Kripo, and SD,[255] carried out some of the most brutal actions of the Holocaust with the minimum of resources. He was fighting on two fronts: (1) the liquidation of the Jews until the autumn of 1942, and (2) Polish Armia Krajowa, and Ukrainian Nationalists at the end of 1942. In addition to this, he had the border passes of Tatarow and Wyszkow to contend with.[256] He utilised local auxiliaries of Polish and Ukrainian Kripo (CID) officers to supplement his skeleton staff of ethnic German security personnel.[257]

For the major 'Jewish Actions', and this was normal practice in the Generalgouvnement and other areas of occupation, all manner of departments were called upon to help to cleanse the area of Jews. In the area of operations the civil authorities[258] backed up these actions, railway staff were called upon, even the local inhabitants, including scouts and the 'Hitler Jugend' were used in the security dragnet to get the job done.

Auxiliary Security Forces

Much more important was the additional personnel supplied by the Ordnungspolizei (Orpo). In August, 1941, a contingent of the Schutzpolizei (sub-division of Orpo), was brought into the district from Vienna.[259] Even larger than the Schupo contingent on special duty, were units of the Waffen SS and Reserve Police Battalion 133, whose 1st and 2nd company was stationed in Stanislawow.[260] All these extra security troops had only one duty to perform: to assist the SD in rounding up Jews for the forest pits and Belzec.

The weekly reports of Police Reserve Battalion 133, (First Company), from the 25th July to 12 December, 1942, show a complete disregard for human life—780 Jews killed in mopping-up operations. Operating in the Stanislawow District of eastern Galicia, PRB 133 wreaked havoc amongst the impoverished Jews. The man-hunt for Jews was unyielding in its ferocity and purpose. Detailed reports sent back to their headquarters show exact numbers and categories of Jews killed. Between the 1st November, and 12 December, 1942, 481 Jews are reported killed, justifying the slaughter by pernicious explanation: thieves, beggars, vagabonds—banditry, partisans, etc. The real purpose was because they were 'Jews' which was, in itself, sufficient reason.[261] In comparison, the Stanislawow killings set new standards for PRB 133 in the overall genocide.

'Bloody Sunday' and after...

By 1st October,[262]1941, plans for the extermination of the Jews were ready. Krueger had made extensive preparations for his first big action. He chose Nadworna, a small town to the south of Stanislawow to try out his men and procedures—a dress rehearsal for the destruction of East European Jewry.

In the planning and carrying out of the Nadworna 'action' Krueger adopted his own blueprint of extermination which he had devised at the BdS office in Krakow and would later lecture on at the Rabka SD School. For the benefit of his subordinates, Nadworna was to be a seminar for ghetto clearing and extermination. On 6[th]October, 1941, all the Nadworna Jews were ordered to assemble in the market place where the town's Judenrat and their families were separated from the rest. The remainder of the Jews, nearly 2000, were marched under guard to nearby woods, stripped and shot into previously prepared pits.

For the Stanislawow 'action' (Bloody Sunday) a week later, the operation was divided into manageable parts, appointing a specialist in each part (usually of SS-Scharfuehrer rank) to study the area and draw up plans for implementation: A few days before the action, the ghetto area was reduced in size. On the morning of the action Jewish Sondercommandos were brought to the town cemetery and ordered to dig a number of pits appropriate to the numbers of victims. Each pit was dug like an inverted pyramid. Either step would be dug in the side for the victims to walk down and then lay down face forward on top of other victims, or in the case of the Stanislawow murders, wooden boards were placed directly in front of the pit for the victims to stand on. Sometimes a plank would be placed across the pit for the victims to walk across the plank to the centre; they would be shot on orders of the officer in charge, usually a preselected Scharfuehrer of the execution squad. The weapons preferred were the Russian machine- pistol which held a clip of 50 rounds of ammunition and could be fired singly or automatically.[263]

By the 10th October, 1941, Krueger had completed his plans. He gathered together all personnel at his disposal, including RPB (Reserve Police Battalion) 133, under the command of Gustav Englisch, Civil administration, and Railway police. The first task of Krueger was to reduce the size of the Ghetto perimeter which was completed by the 11th October 1941, when Krueger held a final conference with his commanders and issued his orders for the following day's events. At 0600 hours on the 12th October, 1941, the mayhem began. The SD lead auxiliaries into the Jewish houses and drove them onto the streets to a holding point. Depending on the numbers, the Jews were led off in groups at short intervals by the Order police.

The Jews were marched in columns to the edge of town where they entered an ever-reducing funnel of guards directly into the Jewish cemetery. In batches of fifty, the Jews were pressed forward to the undressing and handing over of property area. Then, naked, men, women and children were led to the open pits. Two large pits measuring 20m. x 20m. x 6m. Deep, had been prepared in the cemetery which was surrounded by a high wall—there was no way of escape. The boards before the pit[264] method was used and the Jews were lined up to take their turn. The executioners were mainly Sipo men, including Krueger, Orpo, Railway Police; all had a go at shooting the Jews.[265] Many Jews pushed past others to the head of the line, as they had had enough and wanted to get it over with. Those executioners resting from fatigue were drinking and taking photographs of the proceedings:[266]

'On Sunday 12th October, 1941, the unthinkable happened. The day of Hoshanah Rabba (The seventh day of the holiday, Succoth) became the blackest day in the history of the Jews of Stanislawow. Early in the morning the streets were choked with German and Ukrainian police. A large number of canvas covered trucks were going up and down the main street and turning off at the corners. Outside we could hear shouts, screams, bursts of rifle and machine gun fire. The police were going from house to house, yelling "Juden Heraus! Juden zu Arbeit!" (Jews get out! Jews to work!). All our family went to separate hiding places. After it was over, my mother was missing and we learnt that she had been taken to the cemetery. A neighbour who returned later that day told us that mother was at the cemetery standing with her back to the crowd. When the shooting started, mother ran to the front and never came back. They had tried to kill all of us, the entire Jewish community of Stanislawow, in a single day.

The cemetery was surrounded by Ukrainian militia, who stood, guns drawn inside and outside the walls. Germans were posted with machine guns at several locations. On the fortress-like, square building inside the cemetery, several Gestapo men manning machine guns were stationed as guards and observers. One operated a movie camera. A row of machine guns stood at one end of the cemetery, on one side of a row of several long deep pits, with mounds of earth piled alongside. In front of the pits were boards, forming a crude platform. Truck after truck unloaded the Jews. As they came off the trucks, the Jews were ordered to put their hands behind their heads and march to the back of the cemetery and line up.

Krueger was now pacing in front of the battery of machine guns. He had sent a group of young Jewish girls to collect the valuables from the lines of people in the cemetery. The girls returned again and again with baskets filled with watches, jewellery, gold coins, and various personal objected. While the collecting of valuables went on, German and Ukrainian guards prodded the people in the first row, using their rifle butts, forcing them to line up on the boards in front of the first pit. They were then made to take off their clothes, which were piled up to one side. A hush fell upon the cemetery. Even the babies stopped screaming and now whimpered softly. All about people mumbled prayers. Then a shot was heard. It was Krueger. He shot the Jew standing directly in front of him. That was the signal. The machine guns began to rattle. The blood bath had begun.

The machine gunning continued for several hours. The gunners did not stop even to eat: food was brought to them; they ate and continued shooting. The girls who were collecting valuables were sent back for more, and as they turned, Krueger shot them all. Row after row fell into the pits; more were brought to take their places. Many who fell into the pit were not dead. Some lay for hours before they died. A few managed to extricate themselves and while this massacre was in progress, Krueger was entertaining his friends. It was now getting dark. The drizzle had turned to rain mixed with snow. Krueger gave the order to stop firing. A voice was heard shouting, *"Wer lebt gruesst mit dem Ruf 'Heil Hitler!—Whoever is alive yell 'Heil Hitler!'"* Then a moment later, *"Wer lebt kann gehen!—Whoever is alive can go!"* A wild stampede ensued. In the rush to escape people fell upon each other. Many were trampled. 12000 perished in the cemetery. My mother, many relatives, and entire families had lived in Stanislawow for generations, their lives all snuffed out in that one day.

The entire operation was overseen by Hans Krueger, Chief of the Gestapo, and a tall blond German in his mid-thirties. At the gates of the cemetery Krueger was approached by Dr Teitelbaum, who served as a liaison between the Judenrat and the Gestapo. When Dr Teitelbaum told Krueger that he was going to join his people and die with them, Krueger took out his pistol and shot Dr Teitelbaum in the head and ordered his men to throw him in the pit.'

Another witness to this action was the grand-daughter of the Jew Yosef Duner, the landlord of David Kahane whose sources are shown in these footnotes; Duner recalled the events in the Stanislawow Ghetto under the command of Hans Krueger:

'Almost all the Jews in the town were shot. Once the Stanislawow ghetto had been emptied of its residents, the Germans started bringing Jews in from the surrounding townships and villages until there were no Jews left in the entire district. The Jewish graveyard in Stanislawow turned into a huge mass grave. Several thousand Jews were brought to the cemetery to be killed. The men of the Gestapo execution squads were dead drunk. As usual, such drama unfolded in perfect order. The unfortunates waited for their death lined up in long columns. One unit kept order among the columns, while the other unit positioned itself behind the column on the edge of the pit and did the shooting. The victims fell straight into the pit. (The notorious, well rehearsed, and characteristic shot, aimed to the neck perfected by Krueger worked instantly.)

A woman reported that on this occasion "The drunken Gestapo men lost control of the crowd and their shaking hands failed to aim accurately. Many Jews fell into the pits still alive and then covered with earth. The next morning (she noticed from her window) that the mound of earth stirred."[267]

That same morning this woman witnessed the shooting of her husband together with other Jews as the slaughter continued. She removed her armband, sneaked out of the ghetto and escaped to Lvov.'

The Jewish concentration in Stanislawow is recorded in a 1931 census as 24,800 (51% of the population)[268]; subsequent estimates, with the influx of outsiders, from Hungary and other towns in the district, far exceed this. 'Bloody Sunday' was just the start—Krueger and his crew still had another 20,000 to deal with—he was setting a precedent; having murdered the 12,000[269] and sent the remainder back into the Ghetto, he was still left with an over-crowded ghetto. It was his practice to firstly expel the Jews, then kill them, and then replenish the ghetto with other Jews from outside in that order.

Krueger would go on devising new tactics and so refine the system of killing, and set new examples and records as time went on.[270] On 16th October, 1941, Ernst Varmin from the Border Police in Tatarow, together with the 3rd Company of PRB 133, began the slaughter of Jews in Delatyn and Jaremcze, the most southern Jewish communities in the region. On 29-30 October, a Sipo unit from Stanislawow shot several hundred Jews in Bolechow. There were further mass shootings in the towns of Rohatyn, Kalusz and Dolina. In December, 1941, there was a temporary halt to the killings as the ground was frozen and it had become difficult to dig the murder pits.[271]

Belzec Resettlement—Rudolf Mill

In March, 1942, Krueger got to hear that the Jews in the areas around Rohatyn, to the north of the Dniester River, were destined for the Belzec extermination camp. Not to be outdone, Krueger sent his men to Rohatyn and murdered some 2,300 Jews in the freezing cold.[272]

The Stanislawow town massacres continued. A comprehensive alphabetical list of his Jews was compiled by the Judenrat, and there was a further reduction of the Ghetto perimeter. Security personnel were again put on alert. Another shooting took place in March, followed by a Ghetto fire that lasted three weeks.[273]   On 31st March, (Passover eve), several thousand Jews were arrested and weeded out.   The Jews were then marched to the railway station and deported to Belzec on the1st April, 1942.   There were no survivors.[274]   The blood-letting continued when Krueger ordered the Stanislawow Labour Office to make further selections, and thousands more were selected and murdered.[275] With the culling of the Stanislawow Ghetto, Jews from other towns and villages were brought into the Ghetto and the whole procedure repeated itself.

At the end of June, 1942, the situation in the ghetto declined further.   The SD was now in charge of all Jewish work establishments and immediately began to liquidate these groups.   The Judenrat were summoned to Gestapo Headquarters where they were all arrested and taken to the forest pits.[276]   Also at this time, Rudolf Mill was purged for the last time.   The several hundred Jews in the Mill were all taken to the Jewish cemetery and shot into pits.   One Jew of note among the victims was Jewish police commander, Zigo Weiss.   Weiss had been collaborating with the Germans for many months as administrator of Rudolf Mill.[277]

Mass Hangings in Stanislawow

After the June liquidations, a new Judenrat was formed.   Goldstein, who had been spared the pits, was now appointed Head, very much against his will.[278] With the influx of new victims other tricks were tried.   The Germans, alleging that a Ukrainian had been shot by a Jew, ordered the Judenrat to supply 1,000 men within 3 days.   During this period, a large pit was dug on Blodarska Street and a gallows erected adjacent to the police building.   The Judenrat refused to nominate the 1,000 men as requested with the expected results.

Immediately the ghetto was sealed and all the occupants were turned out in a bloody furore and taken to Blodarska Street.   In a systematic selection, Jews were lined up and shot into the pit. Children were just thrown in to save ammunition. The Judenrat were lined up and forced to watch these proceedings. SS-Captain Hans Krueger ordered the President of the Judenrat, Goldstein (Golsztain) to fetch a rope which was the signal to proceed with hangings. Goldstein, (the heaviest) was the first, but the rope broke. He was finished off with Ukrainian rifle butts. Next, 20 Jewish policeman were selected and hanged on the lamp posts on Badarska Street and remained there for three days; the local non-Jews were issued tickets to enter the ghetto to view the scene.   Over 1,000 Jews died that day.   Some were more fortunate, being kept over in their work places by sympathetic employers. The views and recollections of the witnesses vary, but capture the essence of the 'action'.

Amalie Salsitz:

> 'A young Jew named Yusek attacked a Ukrainian and beat him with his own rifle. Yusek then went into hiding. The Germans summoned Mordecai Goldstein, the President of the Judenrat, and ordered him to arrest Yusek within 24 hours. This he was unable to do. Hans Krueger rode into the Ghetto on his white horse, surrounded by a heavy guard. He summoned Goldstein, all the other Judenrat members and the Jewish police force. Krueger dismounted and walked over to Goldstein and demanded Yusek, or "else you will be the first of a 100 Jews to hang. Make the list!" Goldstein replied that he was not God and refused to make the list. Krueger ordered all those present to be arrested and then sent for fifty yards of rope.

> Every tenth Jewish policeman was singled out and guarded, with his hands tied behind his back. The rope was cut into lengths and the Jews, led by Goldstein, were hanged from the lamp posts in the street. Several of the ropes snapped, some Jews were then shot; one Jew managed to escape and survive the war. The hanging continued until the next day. About a hundred Jews were hanged and their bodies left there dangling for a week.'[279]

This witness, Amelie Salsitz, made her escape from the Ghetto with the help of Edmund Abrahamovitch, a Karaite who had been spared by the Germans and lived in the town of Halitz.[280]

Clearing Operations

Now it was the turn of the Jewish communities of Dolina, west of Stanislawow in the Kalusz District. Rudolf Muller from the Border Police at Wyszkow Pass commanded a unit that rounded up the 3,500 Jews of Dolina. After a selection in the Market place, 2,000 Jews were taken to the local cemetery and shot in the usual way.

On 28th August, 1942, the 4th, 9th, and 26th of September, and 3rd October, several hundred Jews were shot each day in the courtyard of the SD headquarters in Stanislawow. Also at this time was the bloody clearing of a hospital and (according to reports heard by a German agricultural official) a procession of Jews moving to the train station on their knees.[281] There were still 11,000 Jews in Stanislawow at this time. The selections and deportations continued until the final liquidation on 15th, 17th September, 1942. By the 15th October, 1942, the Jewish community in Stanislawow was largely annihilated.[282]

In December, 1942, all Jews had been evacuated from the country districts or transferred into the Stanislawow Ghetto. The Ghettos in the towns of Tlumacz and Nadworna had been liquidated. Several of the Jewish employers set up safe havens for their workers:[283] the head of the army barracks protected 140 Jews, the austbahn 100 Jews, the army transport division 120 Jews; the Margushes factory,[284] the carpentry shop on Piast Street, the Vatzk wagon factory, [285] the weapon purchase department, the rubbish collection service, several sawmills, were safe havens. Small numbers of Jews were also hidden by Poles in the districts of Meizli and Gorki. Those Jews who couldn't find safety and were fit for work, were now housed in a new camp on Milanaraska Street, in the former meat plant and hospital where they were closely supervised. Each Jews was issued with a new identification badge.

Destruction of the Ghetto

For the Jews now ghettoed in Stanislawow, the end was near. In January, 1943, mass murders and selections continued unabated. On 24/25th January, a 1,000 Jews were shot who had no work permits, and a further 2,000 were deported to the Janowska camp in Lvov. Finally, on 22 February 1943, the Ghetto was surrounded: all residents were arrested. Only a few hundred workers employed in scrap reclamation, and workers at the eastern railroad and supply depot were selected out; all others were shot. There is a single report dated 9 March, 1943, in which the security patrol reports the murder of a Jew discovered in the former ghetto area.

Stanislawow was liberated by the Soviet army on 27th July, 1944. Only about 1,500 of its pre-war Jewish population remained alive. About 100 were saved by hiding in the city, with the assistance of sympathetic Aryans.

The Katzmann Report

The whole area of East Galicia was being systematically 'resettled' under the Generalgouvernement administration of SS-Brigadier Katzmann. This was the National-Socialist answer for dealing with the 'Jewish Question' which was outlined in his report in 1943. This report is one of the most important testimonies relating to the Holocaust in Poland and extermination of Polish Jews. It is a report of SS-Gruppenfuehrer Fritz Katzmann, Commander of the German SS and Police in the District of Galicia, entitled 'Loesung der Judenfrage im District Galizien' (The Solution of the Jewish Question in the District of Galicia) submitted on 30th June, 1943 to the SS and police chief Friedrich Wilhelm Krueger in Krakow. After the war the Public Prosecutor of Stuttgart (1965) sent forty-six volumes of evidence in respect of fourteen accused arraigned on 295 indictments in respect of atrocities committed in Lvov and east Galicia between 1941-1943.

The Katzmann Report was published in German and Polish. A Polish translation of the report had already been published in the 1950s, but with the censors taking out references on the communist underground, and without a scholarly edition that came with the contemporary edition. A full uncensored text of the 'Katzman report' was published in 2009. The recent edition by the Institute of National Remembrance is furnished with a scholarly introduction and extensive footnotes.

One further matter of some interest is the deportation to Belzec of the Jew Rudolf Reder. Reder was one of many thousands of Jews deported to the Belzec extermination camp from Lvov (Lemberg) in late August 1942. Reder escaped from the death camp and survived the war to tell his story. Reder speaks for all those Jews who did not survive to bear witness. Reder's account is included to this account as Appendix 5.

Chapter 8

Enter 'the Dutchman' Pieter Menten[286]

Figure 29: SS Sonderfuehrer Pieter Nocolaas Menten 1941

When he first appeared in Lvov, the Pistiners said that he epitomised Western culture—he smoked Egyptian cigarettes, carried a silver-topped walking stick, and spoke with an enduring accent; his wife possessed a beauty 'off a movie screen'. In the uniform of the Sicherheitsdienst and with the rank of SS-Hauptscahrfuehrer, Menten supervised the killing in Pistiner's garden, suggesting an actor in the wings of a theatre, about to enter onto the stage. [287]

General background and Introduction

PIETER MENTEN used the Sipo-SD School at Rabka as a storehouse for art and other collectables seized from Jewish homes. He was the Third Reich's principal 'roving collector' who toured the museums and art galleries seizing valuables on behalf of the Reichsfuehrer SS Himmler and Reichsmarschall Herman Goering...and provided self-service to the Rabka Four.

When Hitler invaded Poland on the 1st September, 1939, Pieter Menten and his wife Meta took refuge on their estate in Sopot near the town of Stryj, where they had expected the imminent arrival of German troops. Unknown to the Mentens, the Nazi-Soviet Pact provided for east Galicia's absorption into the USSR, and on the 17th September, 1939, the Soviets arrived in East Galicia and immediately began confiscating Polish estates and distributing them to the Ukranian peasants and deporting the owners to labour camps.

Pieter Menten had been operating in the area as a spy (V-Agent) for the Sipo-SD-Abwehr in Berlin for some time[288] which had been well known to Soviet Ukrainian sympathisers. It wasn't long before he was arrested by the NKVD and detained in the Stryj jail when Samuel Schiff, a Jew from Podhorodze, somehow extricated him. With the help of Samuel Schiff, a Podhorodze Jew, he escaped with his wife to Lvov where they sought the assistance of the Dutch Consul, Jacob Jan Broen, to get back to German occupied Poland[289]:

'Till the end of 1939 I was consul of the Netherlands in Lvov (Lvov), as a successor to Dr Witkovsky. Because of the war activities in Poland I had to leave Lvov towards the end of December 1939. Shortly before my departure, P.N. Menten came to see me, asking me in my function as consul for a Dutch passport. Although I wasn't quite sure whether Menten still possessed Dutch nationality—this on the basis of a note in my files on Menten, written by my predecessor—I decided to issue him with a passport, mainly from considerations of humanity. Our party left Lvov on December 27, along with Mr and Mrs Menten, Menten's mother, and another Dutchman by the name of Jan Huig and wife. Our destination was the Netherlands, but our papers were only valid to Krakow. We were to get new travel documents there. Each member of our party was allowed no more that about 150 pounds of luggage. Mr Menten, too, could only take limited luggage. He had already told me before, weeping, that he'd lost everything, that his estate had been plundered but the Russians, and his house burned. When we arrived in Krakow, it soon became apparent that Menten was on good terms with the Germans. He was really getting thick with them, and saluting in the Nazi German way. And very soon afterwards he came to tell me he wasn't going on with us to the Netherlands, but had decided to stay in Krakow to try to earn back at least part of the fortune he had so recently lost.

I do not know that Mr Menten owned a house in Lvov before 1940. I do know, however, that from September 1939 to December of that year he resided in a very small room in Lvov; he lived in such small quarters that mother Menten had to share the couple's bedroom.'

On the 27th December, 1939, the Mentens arrived in Krakow, the centre of Germany's colonial rule over Western Poland, and the hub of Nazi activity. Pieter Menten immediately reported to the Sipo-SD Security Office and offered his services. This office controlled both the SD (Security Service, including the Gestapo) and the Sipo (Security Police) commanded by SS Oberfuehrer Bruno Streckenbach, who was almost immediately replaced by Dr Eberhard Schoengarth, and it seems likely that Menten was able to gain access to Streckenbach because of his previous service with Nazi intelligence as a 'V' Agent.

The city which attracted Menten had just become the focus of Germany's colonial rule over Western Poland, and a centre for the deliberate genocide which during the next six years was to make Poland into the death factory of European Jewry and cause the deaths of three million 'Aryan' Poles. Krakow's Jewish population had been swollen to 80,000 by refugees from Nazi terror elsewhere.

Krakow was not a large city, so it was easier for the Germans to create a German majority. All undesirable Polish elements had been removed, and only those Poles who showed allegiance to the Reich and who had been carefully vetted, remained as officials in the administration. The Germans had made considerable efforts to restoring the facades and maintenance of the infrastructure which was being resolved to everyone's satisfaction. This would explain why a few days after his arrival in Krakow, Menten was seen in uniform with the rank of SS Hauptscharfuehrer. As the Germans settled into ruling Poland, Jewish property was seized in operations enabling Menten to serve both the Germans and himself. He became administrator for Jewish antiques and art-collections under Streckenbach, then Schoengarth. Menten in 1940 (according to family testimony) knew very little about art, but he knew how to pick brains, particularly those of Joseph Stieglitz, a Jewish art dealer who had owned galleries in Krakow and Lvov, and with whose aid he tracked down numerous treasurers for the benefit of the Reich. [290]

Just before the Wehrmacht invaded the USSR on the 22nd June 1941, Menten enabled Stieglitz to escape to Hungary—from which he reached Palestine, returning many years later to Holland to help Menten stave off prosecution. The Barbarossa campaign had sparked Menten's deep commitment to something altogether darker than legalised art-robbery and treachery to his naturalisation: namely to Hitler's 'Final Solution'.

The Naturalisation of Menten in the 1930s as a Polish citizen is contentious.[291] There appears to be some credence to this, as in 1951, the Polish government were still smarting because the Dutch government had not responded to their requests for extradition, and had taken the unusual steps of informing the Dutch press on the grounds 'that Menten during the German occupation of the province of Lvov had, as a functionary of the German Sicherheitspolizei, participated in the murdering of citizens who were being persecuted because of their race; notably that on the 27th August, 1941, in Urycz (District of Stryj), he, with the assistance of two members of the German Sicherheitspolizei, had executed about 180 people of Jewish origin; they were shot in a specially prepared pit and also buried there; among them were four sisters of a man called Michael Mirski (Michael Hauptmann)...'

A second point stressed in the Polish bulletin was that Menten during the same period had been a functionary of the German SS, and that as *Verwalter* (trustee or administrator) he carried out the administration over 'former Jewish firms' in the province of Lvov and Krakow. Also, that Menten had appropriated the household goods of Dr Ostrowsky (a professor at the Jan Kazimierz University in Lvov) right after he had been shot by the Germans. The furnishings of the house were later transported by Menten to the Netherlands (via the Rabka School?).[292]

The Unfolding Story

The central pivotal point of the Menten story is undoubtedly the tenacious investigation by the Dutch journalist Hans Knoop. In 1976, Knoop received information from an informant that a big story was about to be broken in the Israel Press about a Dutch resident who had been a German collaborator in the last war. Following this, the Amsterdam daily *De Telegraaf,* acting on further information, interviewed Mr Menten and confirmed that he would be auctioning some of his art works. This publicity alerted the public to further rumours that Pieter Menten had been involved in Nazi atrocities in the Ukraine.

On the 29th May, 1976, Knoop, by appointment, visited Menten at his residence and when entering the property found a showplace of riches, a veritable museum. The walls were covered with paintings and Gobelin tapestries. Pieter Menten received the journalist politely and when Knoop put to him the nature of the information which was about to be published in the Israeli newspaper *Ha'aretz,* that he, Menten, as part of an SS extermination squad into the village of Podhorodze and several neighbouring villages, personally had selected various villagers and had killed them: revenge was his motive, for he had quarrelled with a business partner, Isaac Pistiner, a Jew. Menten denied any knowledge or association with the facts as set out. Knoop left, dismayed, and set on a course which would lead him to the inner wilderness of the Stryj Valley, Ukraine, and many years of a bitter fight to establish the truth.

It would appear that the information had come, in the first instant, from an Israeli journalist, Chaviv Kanaan, who was personally involved. After the war Kanaan had changed his name from Lieber Krumholz to Chaviv Kanaan and was now telling the world about his early life as a 15-year-old boy in the Village of Podhorodze in the Stryj Valley, East Galicia (at the time Poland but now Ukraine). The boy Krumholz worked on his uncle's farm where he came into daily contact with the owner of an adjacent estate, Pieter Menten. There was a close business association with his uncle's family (the Pistiners) and the Menten estate. The association was that close that the young Kanaan referred to the owner as 'Uncle Pieter'. In 1935, young Lieber Krumholz left his home village and emigrated to Palestine where he started a new life. Contact with his family in Podhorodze was maintained until the beginning of the Second World War when Poland was partitioned between the Soviets and Germany, when all contact ceased until 1944.[293]

Krumholz, now Kanaan, met Jacob Loebel, a family friend, who had recently arrived in Palestine from Eastern Europe. Loebel brought bad news about the boy's family to the effect that they had all been murdered in a terrible onslaught and the man behind the murders was the family friend Pieter Menten. Loebel described Menten as a Gestapo Agent and that the background to these events was over bad business deals with his uncle, Isaac Pistiner.

Hans Knoop and Chaviv Kanaan eventually came together and set about building the evidence to support government action into the activities of Pieter Menten during the Nazi occupation of Poland and the atrocities committed in the Stryj Valley.

The Dutchman revisits old friends in the Villages of the Stryj Valley: Podhorodze. [294]

Peter Menten (na prawo) jako oficer S.S.

Figure 30: The Dutchman (R) 1941, Podhorodze

Very soon after zbV arrived in Lvov and had dealt with the University professors, Pieter Menten went on a shopping spree looking for major works of art for the benefit of his new clients—the senior Nazi command. Many journeys were made to and from the Sipo-SD School where he stored his loot under the watchful eye of the retained care-taking staff. In between his visits he was out to settle old scores in the suburbs of the city and the Stryj Valley for times gone by. To assist him he was supplied with a team of Ukrainian militia and SD personnel from the Rabka School.

On the 6th July, several Sipo-SD non-commissioned officers and Ukrainian militiamen (Banderovtsy—OUN), led by the Dutchman Pieter Menten[295] from zbV, arrived at Podhorodze, a small village in the Stryj Valley.[296] Immediately, local Ukrainians with shovels were ordered by Pieter Menten to go to the residence of Isaac Pistiner. On directions from Menten a pit, measuring 16 x 11 x

10.8 feet deep was excavated near the rose garden. The Execution squad: SS Sonderfuehrer Pieter Menten; Phillip Muller, Volksdeutsch supervisor; and a specialist executioner (Holz Apfel) seconded from the Rabka SD School prepared their lists for the following day.

On the 7 July, all local male Ukrainian 'politicals' were rounded up and forced to the graveside. The remaining villagers were assembled and forced to watch as groups of prisoners were made to walk a plank and then shot into the grave on orders of Menten.[297] The remainder, the Jewish men of the village, were brought out one by one. Each walked the plank and each was shot into the pit. In less than 5 minutes, 23 Jewish men had been murdered for no other reason than that they were Jews and by personal vendetta.[298] All the Jewish women and children were released.[299] The local villagers threw Kreutzers and Kopecks into the pit as homage to the dead. This coinage was later recovered from the pit when the bodies were exhumed by the Soviets well after the war.[300]

Non Jewish victims resident in Podhorodze: Alexander Nowicki; Bronislaw Nowicki; Alfred Stephan (Bronislaw's brother); Vladimir Pistolak; Petro Starzinsky.

The Jewish Victims resident in Podhorodze.: Benzion Nauman—carpenter; Josel Nass—schoolteacher; Moshe Halpern—postman; Uzik—dentist; Shabtai Katz; Alfred Favel; Mendel Yeckel—butcher; Mordechai Londner; Voit Heller; Pinchas Bernstein; Mr Greenberg; Geiwel Hellmar; Chaim Jacov; Schlossberg; Schleitter; Zuckerman; Phillip Wecker; plus 6 others. Women and children were spared and ordered back to their homes.

On the 27th August 1941, a small unit (again led my Menten) of zbV officers returned to the villages in the Stryj Valley and completed their unresolved business in the slaughter of 180 Jews (of all genders and age) in the village of Urycz, near Podhorodze, employing the 'pit-and-plank' technique.[301] Witnesses to these events were local villagers Michael Hauptmann and his cousin Abe Pollak, Polish-born Jews who vividly remember those horrible events of Aug. 27, 1941. Both Pollak and Hauptmann ran from the scene and managed to escape the massacre that befell their families and their Jewish neighbours. Also escaping were the Schleiffers. These witnesses hid in a house a short distance from where the action was happening and recorded the events that would be the basis of Menten's trial well after the war. In this action, two hundred Jews had been herded together and in groups were ordered to walk over a long plank where, after a few paces, Menten ordered them to be shot. Abe Pollack:

'Armed Ukrainians were herding other Jews in our direction. Some had locked themselves in their houses and the doors had to be broken down and the people dragged out kicking and screaming. I recognized Pieter Menten in a German uniform, along with two other Gestapo agents. They had mounted machine guns in front of them. I saw Ukrainians digging a pit some 15 yards from the guns. You could hear voices and crying. Later the guards began to take people out in small groups of ten and twelve. They pushed them onto planks set over the pit. Then you could hear the machine guns—a continuous *rat-ta-ta-tat*.'

In September 1976 an official request was made to send a Dutch investigation team to Podhorodze and Urych, now part of the USSR. Simultaneously, Hans Knoop of *Accent* requested visas for himself and a photographer: because of *Accent*'s fierce anti-Communism, he expected nothing, but in fact his visas came through in October, while the official party had heard nothing.

The two journalists were conveyed to Lvov, capital of Eastern Galicia under the old Polish regime, and from there to Podhorodze, where a team of pathologists was examining the freshly-exhumed remains of 180 people. They were invited to attend exhumations also at Urych, Dogve and Kropivnik, but decided after a week's investigating, tape-recording and photography that they had had enough.

A Fact-finding Mission to the Soviet Union by the Dutch Journalist Hans Knoop[302]

Figure 31: Hans Knoop

'The trip in that taxi was pleasant (although it smelled alarmingly of gasoline) and it took us all the way from Moscow's international airport to the national airport, Vnukova, past the other side of town, a distance of about 60 miles, which took a little more than two hours. Moscow, in that October of 1976, was already under a blanket of snow. It was cold. The people were wearing their heavy winter clothing.

Vnukova, the jumping-off place for our trip to Lvov some 1,400 kilometres (800 miles) west, was a grim and dreary place. And cold as it was outside, the airport building itself was stifling inside. (Something, by the way, which I hear is true all over the Soviet Union.) There wasn't really any proper waiting room, and no restaurant. There was nothing to do for four hours but hang around staircases and sit on rickety wooden benches, killing time by playing cards, waiting for the old-fashioned propeller plane which was going to take us to Lvov.

The plane was full of soldiers, and there was almost no room for anyone else. Since we were the only two non-Russians, we were expected to get on the plane first and leave it last. What a trip! Two and a half hours of sudden shuddering dropping and rising, to the accompaniment of motors which alternately angrily screamed and feebly whined. The only thing served to the passengers was one thimbleful of mineral water Aeroflot thought should sustain us! Tired and famished (we hadn't had anything since midday) we finally landed at one a.m. local time at the airport of Lvov, which as far as the eye could see was full of military planes.

As I've said, our interpreter, Vladimir Molchanov, wasn't there. Although we'd never met, we should have recognized each other quite easily. I knew what Molchanov looked like because he had worked with the Dutch television crew who made the trip earlier. And the Soviet Embassy in the Netherlands had sent him several copies of *Accent* which carried my picture. However, no one approached us, and there was no one even roughly resembling our missing translator. When all the Moscow passengers had left what was called the "arrivals hall," and not a soul had paid any attention to us, we decided to go outside and try to get a cab. We found a driver who could speak a few words of German, with which he addressed us because he assumed we were from East Germany. Since my hotel voucher mentioned that we were to stay in one of the town's two big hotels, the Lvov, I told the driver to take us there.

The reception desk inside that pompous building was deserted. After we had paced up and down for a half-hour, whistling and banging on doors and counters, an old woman appeared. Answering our questions in broken German, she kept telling us that there were no reservations made in our names. She had never heard of Molchanov either, and said we were probably booked at the Intourist Hotel some 100 yards up the street. There were no cabs, of course, so the photographer and I had to walk it, each of us lugging two heavy suitcases.

We were more successful at the Intourist. First of all, there was someone at the desk who spoke fluent German, and secondly there was indeed a reservation for us. And Molchanov, too, was staying there, we were told by the receptionist. But he wasn't in at the moment; he had left the hotel around ten o'clock and hadn't returned yet. Although the tiredness had reached my bones, and my eyes were at half-mast, we decided to wait for him in the lobby area and not go to bed before we had introduced ourselves to him.

Thirty minutes later Molchanov stood before us dressed in a raincoat, making a sort of qualified apology. It hadn't been possible for him to be at the airport because the wrong arrival time had been called through from The Hague, and there had been other circumstances involved too, he said. Molchanov spoke surprisingly good Dutch, only a slight accent betraying him as Russian. (It was not an exaggeration; several months later, during the Parliament debates concerning Van Agt's role in the Menten affair, I answered Van Agt's sleighting references to my interpreter's ability that the Dutch Molchanov spoke was much more understandable than the bureaucratic Dutch in which the minister of justice was expressing himself at that time.) Molchanov told me he had studied the language for several years at the University of Moscow, and that he'd written a thesis on the important Dutch novelist Louis Couperus.

We decided to continue our conversation in our hotel room, which had a great supply of heat but very little air. Molchanov ordered a bottle of mineral water from the female floor guard at the top of the stairs—every floor has one! Molchanov told us that we had come to the Soviet Union at just the right time, for a few days before, at the command of the district attorney of Lvov Province, Russian soldiers had opened the mass graves at Podhorodze. The remains of the victims were being carefully and elaborately studied on the spot by experts from the University of Lvov.

Next morning at ten-thirty, Popov, Novosti director in Lvov, a small, dark, energetic man, welcomed us with outstretched arms on the second floor of his Novosti office building. The man spoke nothing but Russian and Ukrainian; Molchanov translated for us. Popov offered us a chauffeured car for almost the entire length of our stay. He'd already telephoned Podhorodze and been told we could come the following morning. A representative of the Communist Party from the neighbouring village of Skole would accompany us for the last stretch from Skole to Podhorodze because it was difficult to find. I'd had a long telephone conversation with Chaviv Kanaan the evening before my departure to the Soviet Union, and asked him then if he could give me the names of any people to look up contacts who might be of importance for the investigation into Menten's crimes. Kanaan didn't have to think for long, rattling off the names of three Jews still living in Lvov who, according to him, should have full knowledge of the executions. If I succeeded in locating them, I should start off with a story he told me, and send them the regards of individuals in Israel in order to gain their confidence. Kanaan pointed out I might expect them to clam up when a Western stranger came knocking on their door unexpectedly. He emphasized that I should play it subtly, draw them out, and slowly try to win their confidence. One of them was a hard-core party man, an engineer for the city of Lvov, and I'd have to be especially careful to watch my words when I spoke to him.

The addresses for the three people given to me by Kanaan proved to be incorrect. They must have moved since the war. Popov promised to find them through the Lvov registry, and told us that he hoped to have them for us when we returned a few hours later.

My photographer and I, with Molchanov, spent the time driving around the beautiful city of Lvov. I could see why it was formerly called "Little Vienna." Before the war the total population of Lvov was 300,000, of whom more than a third were Jews. There is no longer any organized Jewish life as such in Lvov. Of course, that is to be found practically nowhere in the Soviet Union. The city has no synagogue, and religious services, when they are held at all, are conducted in the most discreetly private, almost clandestine manner. Lvov still maintains its large Jewish cemetery with a great deal of care.

Our tour carried us past the house of Dr Ostrowsky, the Lvov surgeon and art collector who had been killed in June 1941 during the so-called "professor murders." According to a number of depositions, Pieter Menten had moved into the famous physician's house the very night of the murder, appropriating the art collection. Menten's rushing in there to "take care of" Ostrowsky's valuable collection was brought to the attention of the Dutch press in 1951 by the bulletin of the Polish legation to the Netherlands, which was attempting to publicize Poland's request for the extradition of Menten. According to Wiesenthal, it's not at all unlikely that Menten played some role in those "professor murders." However, I wish to emphasize that I have no specific proof linking him to them. But Lvov neighbours of Ostrowsky's confirmed that Menten became their neighbour hours after the murder, and immediately had men working to remove the collection to a warehouse near the railroad station.

I questioned Menten about the whole Ostrowsky business, and so has Commissioner Peters. Menten stubbornly denies ever having heard the name, let alone living in the professor's house and stealing his collection. Neighbours of the professor, however (contrary to many press references, by the way, Ostrowksy wasn't a Jew), remember all too well Menten's nameplate nailed to the door. The same fact was communicated soon after the war to the former examining magistrate of the Special Court in Amsterdam, Mr. Rohling, later to be accused by Menten of having committed perjury and falsified evidence against him.

Rohling vividly remembers hearing Ostrowsky's stepdaughter give evidence as a witness in Amsterdam. Jadwina Roswadovska, one of the few remaining members of the Ostrowsky family after the war, testified to having seen Menten's nameplate on the door of her dead stepfather's house. Although its actual value was never assessed, Ostrowsky's collection was said to be worth millions. The house on what is now called Saskasangsko Street also contained many precious paintings and artefacts that had been brought to him for safekeeping by the Polish nobility of eastern Galicia. Many a Polish count and baron feared his art treasures would be devoured by the Russians (who were the ruling power in eastern Poland till they were chased out by the Germans in 1941). They believed that because Ostrowsky was a doctor and a professor, the Russians would let him be and their treasures would be safe with him. When the Germans attacked Russia, this collection fell into Menten's lap like a ripe golden apple.

In our ride through Lvov we also found Isaac Pistiner's last house. He had been trucked off to the Lvov ghetto from this place by the Germans sometime before Menten allegedly came looking for him, eager for revenge. And it was in front of this house that Menten had, according to witnesses, sent a bullet into Hirsch's head and succeeded in the cold-blooded murder of others in the Pistiner family. The present Ukrainian occupants knew nothing of the story, although they did say they'd heard that before the war the house had been lived in by a rich Jewish family. But they had no knowledge of Menten or of the execution of the members of that family in front of their door. Not so strange when one considers that the new occupants must have been children back then.

When we returned to the offices of Novosti, the helpful Popov had some good news for us—he'd found the addresses of the three people Kanaan had given me to contact. Together with Molchanov and Popov (Molchanov doesn't speak Ukrainian, but Popov does) we visited them in the afternoon. The engineer was indeed a good friend of someone living in Israel, just as Kanaan had said, and he spoke seven languages fluently—but he had very little to say to us in any of them. He had never heard of any massacres in Podhorodze and Urycz. He himself had always lived in Lvov, although it was true that in the old days he had had some good friends in Podhorodze. He didn't know exactly what had happened to them; he'd always assumed that they'd been killed by the Germans in a concentration camp during the war, just like so many members of his own family. One thing of which there was no shortage in eastern Galicia was death camps. Not more than two miles from Lvov was an immense concentration camp, Janowska. Hundreds of thousands of Jews had died there in that hell, fed into the place from Lvov and its surroundings.

We didn't find anything new about Menten on our second stop either. The man we were looking for wasn't in and his wife told us she didn't expect him back from Moscow for several days.

We did not come away empty-handed, however, at the third and final address: that of a man named Halpern (not to be confused with the Halpern from Stryj mentioned earlier). Kanaan had told me that after the war the monument to the Jewish dead had gone up in Urycz at the site of the executions largely because Halpern himself was a native of Urycz, and one of the few Jewish inhabitants of this village to survive Menten's mass executions. Halpern wasn't at home when we came, but his wife knew everything. Yes, her husband was indeed from Urycz, and his entire family was said to have been wiped out by a Dutchman named Menten. She wasn't Jewish herself, but had married Halpern after the war and knew the whole horrible story. But she'd let her husband tell us. She suggested we come back later that evening at around six when he was expected back.

When we returned we were met by a small, grey-haired man in his sixties. Halpern was most eager to answer all our questions. We had to set up a somewhat complicated assembly-line procedure: I asked my questions in Dutch, Molchanov repeated them in Russian, and then Popov translated them into Ukrainian. The line went into reverse for the answers. (Cassettes of this and all other taped interviews I conducted with witnesses in East Galicia were later handed over to the Dutch judiciary.)

Halpern could not recognize and identify Pieter Nicolaas Menten from the pictures we showed because he had never actually met the man. The name, however, was more than familiar. As a boy of ten or eleven, he'd often heard it mentioned in pre-war Podhorodze and it kept coming back after the war in connection with the Podhorodze and Urycz executions. Halpern told us he'd often played in Pistiner's back yard in Podhorodze only a few miles away from Urycz. He recalled the local gossip about a business argument between Pistiner and Menten, and also that Pistiner had lost a great deal of money to Menten.

Sometime during the war, Halpern had joined the Red Army. As soon as Lvov and surroundings were liberated in 1944 he had returned to Urycz to search out his family and acquaintances. One of the first people he met was a certain Cyglarova, a farmer's wife who'd known his family very well. This woman, now living in Poland, broke out in tears when she saw Halpern. She told him what had happened. On a summer's day in 1941, at ten in the morning, she had seen a German car enter the village. In the car were a young officer, a driver, and a German soldier. The car pulled up at the house of a certain Mr Nordligt, which stood on a little hill. The officer gave an order to the Ukrainian nationalists, who were gathered in some force there that morning, to round up all the two hundred Jews living in the town and corral them in that house. The nationalists (who had been recruited from neighbouring villages) then went on a house-to-house search, telling the Jews to come to Nordligt's house because someone wanted to address them there.

Of course, all knew what was going on, because they had heard what had happened in Podhorodze earlier that summer. Weeping and praying, the Jews were led into Nordligt's house. Halpern's mother, going by the farmer's wife, said: "I feel so glad Misja isn't here today." "Misja" was Halpern's nickname. Only one Jew refused to go along, a man by the name of Lev Roth who locked himself in his room. The Ukrainians forced the door and pulled him out, tied a rope around his feet, and had a horse drag him along the ground to Nordligt's house. The two hundred Jews locked up in those three rooms (the house was small, with a total area of about 1,000 square feet) must have been unbearably hot, Cyglarova told Halpern; they had to wait three hours before the Ukrainians finished preparing the great hole. The Ukrainians had initially ordered the Jews to dig their own grave, but they had refused.

Halpern told me that he was sure Menten had been in command, and it was all a ghastly repeat of his performance in Podhorodze. According to Halpern, only three Jews of Urycz escaped death that day: Michael Hauptmann, Nordligt's son Saul, and one other. The Ukrainians didn't completely close the grave full of dying and wounded as well as the dead, a grisly detail Halpern gave us which tallied with Hauptmann's description. Halpern lost his parents, his four sisters, his daughter, and his wife. He was sobbing by the time he finished Cyglarova's story.

Two weeks before I visited Halpern, he had journeyed to Urycz and had again stood at the place where on that 27th of August they all had stood. Again he saw it happening, heard the wailing and the bursting shouts of gunfire. While his wife got a photo album out of the closet and showed us pictures of his murdered family, Halpern put a nitro-glycerine tablet under his tongue. He had suffered a heart attack several months earlier.

While we drank down our vodkas Russian-style (emptying the glass at one toss), Halpern told us how peaceful life had once been in Urycz. It was a unique village, its population flourishing and prosperous, and the relations between Jew and non-Jew exceptionally harmonious. Although many other Jewish villages in Poland were plagued by a virulent anti-Semitism, this was not so in Urycz. Halpern gave a resonantly bitter laugh when I told him that according to Menten there weren't any Jews either in Podhorodze or in Urycz; they used to live in the big cities. Halpern said the Jews themselves always referred to their village as 'Little Israel' because there were so many of them there. In Urycz there were three prayer houses. Zionists among the Jewish population of Urycz had been laughed at by their fellow villagers. Why should a Jew want to emigrate from the paradise of Urycz to the desert of Palestine? Halpern was shaking his head slowly from side to side. How dare a vile criminal like Menten, with his record, say such a thing that there weren't any Jews in Urycz and Podhorodze? The insolent scoundrel! Now there weren't any Jews in Urycz and Podhorodze and only one man was responsible for that: Pieter Nicolaas Menten.

Halpern said that, of course, he knew the two chief witnesses for the prosecution, Hauptmann and Pollack. But after he had joined the Red Army he had lost sight of them, and it was news to him that one was living in Sweden now and the other in New York. Would we please give his regards to them?

Halpern was also of help in our locating another valuable witness, Hennek Schleiffer. On the eve of my departure for the Soviet Union, Commissioner Peters had told me that Schleiffer could possibly be the key to several unsolved unclarified points. Peters had put out a search for him throughout the world, with no results. Before the war Schleiffer had briefly been married to Michael Hauptmann's sister, but Hauptmann had lost all contact with his former brother-in-law. Halpern almost knocked over the vodka glass his wife was filling when I mentioned Schleiffer's name. "Well," he said, "you are certainly very well informed." Where had I found that name? He knew Schleiffer very well; he was an old boyhood chum from Urycz and he still saw him regularly. He lived in a place about 60 miles from Lvov, Drohobycz, not far from Podhorodze and Urycz. Halpern said, however, that there would be no point in our visiting Schleiffer; he wouldn't talk to us unless we were in Halpern's presence and since Halpern had to go on a business trip to Moscow the following day, we might as well forget about Schleiffer this time round. (After returning to Holland, the CID in Amsterdam was delighted to hear I'd located Hennek Schleiffer, and that he'd survived the war. The same CID, by the way, was still awaiting official permission to go on its fact-finding trip and would continue to wait until February 1, 1977.)

The following day we made the long and tiring journey from Lvov to Podhorodze. The chauffeur-driven car put at our disposal by Novosti was waiting promptly for us at six in the morning in front of the

Intourist Hotel (formerly called 'The George,' where Menten had conducted many of his business conferences). Popov was supposed to come along, but an acute backache kept him in bed, so we had to make out with one interpreter, Molchanov. In Skole, about 20 miles from Podhorodze, a functionary of the local Communist Party was supposed to join us. He'd show us the way, and in case any witnesses could only speak Ukrainian, he would fill in as interpreter. The two-lane highway from Lvov to Skole ran on with an endless sameness, a thick morning mist hung over the steppes, and all was grim and desolate as one imagines when reading about the landscape in many Russian novels. Only after the town of Stryi (Menten made his home there for a while before the war) did the landscape get richer and more pleasant as we were approaching the foothills of the Carpathians. We got to Skole in one and a half hours.

In the town hall (which was also the seat of the Communist Party) Molchanov made our introductions to the local dignitaries. We were to follow one of these officials, who would lead the way to Podhorodze in a jeep, and if necessary he'd assist us when we were there. The last stretch took us through a beautiful landscape, thick woods marching over hill-mountains while the dark, sliding Stryj River ran companionably along. Women in black wearing babushkas were toiling in the fields. Within half an hour we reached the village of Podhorodze and minutes later Molchanov was pointing to Pistiner's big farmhouse on top of a hill. Molchanov recognized it, because months earlier he'd gone the same road with our TV colleagues. When we drew close to the sign that said "Podhorodze" we decided to take a picture of it, a whim which seemed totally unimportant at the time, but which could play a role in Menten's trial. (When Menten was questioned by the CID after his arrest, he insinuated that the Russians had led us astray to another village with a more or less similar name and not to Podhorodze.)

The village was one big mud pool, impossible to drive into. We walked the last 50 yards to Pistiner's farm with pants' legs rolled up, sinking up to our ankles in the mud. What we saw next, I will never forget. The whole area was littered with children's shoes, braids, skulls, vertebrae, everything chaotically mixed together, and the grave staring at us like a great open eye. Some fifteen Russian soldiers were busy cleaning these remains on a large table off to the side, performing this macabre task in a sort of haughty, dreaming silence, supervised by an officer.

Figure: 32 Post-War reburial of the bodies from the Podhorodze executions

Podhorodze is a village where time seems to have stopped: small wooden houses, children playing in front of them in rubber boots; old, bent women bringing in wood for their stoves with cart and horse. This is the way Podhorodze looked, and this is the way it must have looked years ago when Pieter Menten owned his vast forests here before the war, and this is much the way Menten must have found it when on July 7, 1941, wearing his SS uniform, he returned to the village to take his revenge. The same road which led us to that small and peaceful village in the hills had carried him there.

While the Russian soldiers were scraping the bones clean with knives, I realized suddenly that this must have been the peaceful place where Chaviv Kanaan had played. Now, wherever one looked, there were skulls, ribs, shoulder blades, children's shoes, and other mute witnesses of the 1941 massacre. Several pathologists were sitting cross-legged on the ground, fitting together hundreds of vertebrae pieces, while others put the skulls in long, long rows on sheets of plastic.

The photographer was taking pictures, and while I followed behind him I stepped on some bones and was overcome by a sense of shame. But it was almost inevitable; one couldn't walk anywhere in Isaac Pistiner's garden without a horrible reminder that thirty-five years before scores of people had died there.

The chief pathologist was a middle-aged man wearing a white doctor's coat and a fur hat against the cold. When I was introduced to him he stood up and led me to a pile of bones. Picking up some of the shoulder blades, he showed me the bullet holes in them. He told me they had unearthed remains of about 180 people from the two separate graves in Pistiner's garden. The first held only men, and the second (which had been found the day before we arrived) was full of the remains of women and children. I walked behind the head pathologist, Vladimir Zelengoerov, and we stopped at a small table on which lay plastic bags containing the jewellery they had found in the grave. There were earrings, necklaces, and all sorts of other objects, among them several silver stars of David.

Dr Zelengoerov picked up a braid of hair, all intact. According to him, the human remains had been preserved reasonably well because the soil was so swampy. As far as possible they were trying to identify the victims through teeth and bridgework. Assistants were numbering every bone, and then putting the pieces together on a large canvas cloth, trying to build up skeletons.

There in that garden, warming myself before a blazing fire, I also met the Lvov district attorney, Mr Antonenko, who was in charge of everything. He told me that the Soviet judiciary had already questioned more than five hundred people living in the surroundings of Podhorodze who were born before 1926, and so were at least fifteen-years-old at the time of the murders. More than thirty people had declared they had seen Menten present at the executions and that he had been in command at the executions they had seen.

Antonenko was the first to tell me that Menten's murders were not limited to Podhorodze and Urycz. In at least two other villages not far away, he said, Menten had been equally active. According to the prosecutor, the total number of victims could be close to a thousand. This was the first time the name of Pieter Nicolaas Menten was mentioned to me there in Podhorodze. That morning, near the open grave, we were to hear it many more times, from the mouths of eyewitnesses who said they had been forced by Menten to attend the executions, often of their relatives. We didn't have to look for these witnesses; there were already three people present who had been there in 1941, at the executions. They would walk among the bones as if in a daze, staring into that hole for minutes at a time, while I registered their shocking stories on my tape recorder. It was the tape recordings of these interviews which were finally to lead to Menten's arrest in 1976.

One of these witnesses, Meron Wascielevitsj Pistolak, at the site of the open grave, told me how his brother Vladimir was murdered by Menten at the first Podhorodze execution on July 7, 1941. He was eleven years old then, and had watched from a tree. His eighteen-year-old brother was selected by Menten to be the first to walk the plank, the first to be shot, falling into the hole.

Pistolak, now forty-six, told me, "All the people of the village had to come to the grave to watch the mass execution—children too. The older people would form a semicircle around the grave so the children couldn't see anything. So we took to climbing the trees. I saw everything, and will never forget it for the rest of my life. My brother was first because he was the leader of the local Komsomol, the communist youth movement. Menten also had a special hatred for the communists because they took his land in 1939. So when he returned in 1941, the first ones he settled scores with were the Jews and communists. Menten gave the orders to shoot. There is no doubt whatsoever it was him. Everybody knew him. I estimate that more than a hundred people were shot at that first execution, by five or six soldiers under Menten's command. He even had a Nazi officer under him, who transferred his orders to the nationalists:

> "Not all the people who fell into the pit were dead; there were many wounded among them. When the pit was being covered with soil I could still hear them scream, from the grave. The ground was still breathing. I cannot say anything about the second execution because I wasn't present then."

I had hardly switched off the tape recorder when a second witness announced herself, Karolina Michailona Semelak, also forty six. She told me she was born in Podhorodze and lived there all her life. She'd known Isaac Pistiner, very slightly. Her mother, however, had known Pistiner and Pieter Menten very well. Mrs Semelak told me that her mother often mentioned that Menten and Pistiner had transacted a lot of business with each other, and that Pistiner had sold Menten some woods. Both were very well known, as important figures in the village. Mrs Semelak continued:

"When the executions happened here in 1941 I was eleven years old, but I still remember it as if it were only yesterday. Menten was in command and ordered all the people of the village to come watch the executions, children also. He himself didn't shoot, but each time the order was given by him. It was shortly after the German invasion of 1941. Menten came back here to Podhorodze ordering his soldiers to assemble all Jews and communist activists in the garden of Isaac Pistiner's house. Pistiner didn't live there anymore. I saw it all with my own eyes. Everybody, the whole village, was there. All the victims were brought together in Pistiner's house. And next they had to come out in groups of three and five and walk across a plank which had been placed across the grave. When they'd get to a point in the middle they were shot. I can still very vividly see Pistolak walk the plank; first the local leader of the communists fell, shot, into the hole. The commands were given by Menten. On that day, the seventh of July, only men were killed. But on August twenty-eighth, it was the turn of the women and children. Their grave is right next to the first. Yet there was one woman murdered at the first execution—she was called Novicka. When her husband, Novicky, had to walk on that board, she wouldn't stop her frenzied screaming at Menten, upon which he ordered his soldiers to shoot her, too. The second execution also, I saw it with my own eyes, and again Menten was in command. He must have been a very high-ranking man, for he gave his orders to a German officer, who then ordered the soldiers to shoot. It is impossible that I should be mistaken that this man was really Menten. When Menten, before the war, came to Podhorodze he was a very well-known man in our village, and when he returned in 1941 wearing a German uniform, people of course recognized him. They all said: 'That is Menten, Petro Menten.'"

A remarkable detail was that none of the witnesses there in Pistiner's garden stated that Menten fired a shot at the executions. They all said he gave the orders. According to them, Menten was present, he was in command, but he hadn't fired a single shot himself. He did do that in several other places, however.

One of the witnesses actually present at one of Menten's alleged personal murder actions was Stanislav Moechinsky. He told me that in 1941 he'd seen Menten cold-bloodedly order his former forest-keeper, Alfred Stepan, killed. Stepan had quarrelled with Menten before the war because Menten had refused to pay his wages:

> "When Menten came to our village as SS Sonderfuehrer in 1941, he tracked down Stepan and said, 'I've come to pay you now.' Then he ordered Stepan shot in front of his own house. His wife could not control her furious grief. Menten said to her: 'Shut up or you'll get it too,' and then said to the Ukrainian nationalist with him, 'Shoot her.'"

Another friend of Vladimir Pistolak who is still living, a certain Dimitri Federowitsj, was compelled by Menten on that 7th July in Podhorodze to watch the execution. Federowitsj was the second most important man in the Komsomol. When he saw his friend Pistolak die, the first to fall at Menten's orders, Federowitsj feared that his turn would come, too. But he slipped away through the crowd and fled to the surrounding hills to Borislav, where he stayed hidden for two weeks. Later he heard that indeed the Ukrainians had been looking for him, and that he'd been on Menten's list.

Altogether, I have fifteen of these eyewitness statements in my possession, recorded on the spot. By far the most shocking account, because it so strikingly demonstrates the behaviour and mentality of Menten, I recorded from a certain Dimitri Antoniak:

> "It happened in July 1941," he said. He was twenty years old then, and remembers how the invaders drove the people into the village centre, rounding them up inside a small Jewish prayer house. About 120 men, women, and children were brought together there. A little farther on the mass grave was being dug. The Germans took the victims out of that house in groups of three and five, and brought them to the big hole in the earth. There was an officer sitting in an armchair: Pieter Nicolaas Menten, dressed in Nazi uniform. The people of Dovge instantly recognized Menten, for they often used to see him in Podhorodze and Sopot. And now there he was in the chair, legs crossed, puffing casually on a cigar, and from time to time giving the orders to have more people come across the wooden board and be shot.

Antoniak remembered vividly a particularly horrible detail:

> "A tall thin SS man, a certain Horst, grabbed a woman's baby, threw it up in the air, and shot it as if it were a clay pigeon. When the mother of the child started screaming, he shot her too. Menten stayed in the chair, gave the orders, till there was no one else to be killed. Not all the people were dead immediately; some of them were given another shot while in the pit."

Antoniak ran away after seeing this spectacle, and some minutes later fainted out of sheer emotion. He estimates that about 120 Jewish inhabitants of that village were murdered at Menten's orders. Afterward, the Germans plundered the empty shops and houses of the Jews. When some of the villagers protested, the Germans yelled that they were claiming back Menten's possessions, seized from him by the communists. They were robbing everything in sight, according to Antoniak, including things which never could have been Menten's, and belonging to the workers of the village.

It is noteworthy that the statements by the witnesses from Podhorodze, Urycz, Dovge, as well as Kropovnyk, agree in the particulars of the method. All mention the long plank, set across a great hole dug in the ground, and the victims being compelled to step onto that board and start walking. In all cases, too, the graves were, more or less, closed without ensuring that all the victims were dead. And finally, in none of the four places did anyone see Menten do any of the shooting himself, although in each one he was recognized by scores of witnesses as the man who gave the orders.

After several hours of walking in the piercing cold among the bones in Isaac Pistiner's garden, the photographer and I had seen about as much as we could take. There was one more horrible sight. Passing through Pistiner's deserted house, we were shown the intact shrivelled mummified corpse of a woman in the basement. The district attorney told us it was going to be reburied elsewhere in the village the following Sunday together with all the other remains, in a special ceremony we were invited to attend. He asked again if we would be present in Urycz the next Monday when they planned to open the grave there, and we told him we were not sure yet.

I asked the district attorney why the Soviet authorities, so many years after the crimes, had suddenly decided to have the graves opened. He answered that the chief prosecutor of the Soviet Union, Rudenko (the same man who prosecuted for the Russians at Nuremberg), had received a request from the Dutch judiciary to be allowed to conduct an inquiry in East Galicia into the crimes of Pieter Menten. Therefore, after having discussed it with the prosecutor of Lvov, Rudenko decided to have the graves opened in order to try to determine how many victims had been there altogether, and to identify them if possible.

We took our leave from the place of slaughter and returned to Skole. The chairman of the town council was awaiting us with an elaborate meal, most liberal doses of vodka, and many speeches. Later that day, with the horror we had seen still vividly before us, we drove back via Stryj to darkening Lvov.

Molchanov, the photographer, and I were so powerfully affected that the return journey was almost silent; it was very difficult to put anything into words. We were not too eager to go to Urycz and the other places the next day. Still, I decided to visit Urycz, Kropovnyk, Dovge, and Drohobycz albeit before the graves in those towns were to be opened.

Two days later we were on our way again to that same fateful area along that lonesome road. Urycz, a village built on the edge of a fast-moving stream, looks even more peaceful than Podhorodze. The local headmaster was to be our guide there. His School lay in that part of the village which had held no Jews in pre-war years. Urycz had been composed of two sections, Jewish and non-Jewish. The Jewish part was about a mile from where we were, up in the hills and surrounded by thick pine woods. The headmaster led us a short distance upstream to a place simply but powerfully marked by the white obelisk Halpern had set up as a memorial. About 15 yards from that place at the edge of the stream, Nordligt's house still stands.

The present owners, a farmer and his wife, gave me permission to enter. It was horrible to realize that in the hot summer of 1941, on an August day, some two hundred men, women, and children awaited their turn for death, terrified in that small space. The farmer said he didn't know anything about what had happened some 15 yards in front of his house during the war, and he didn't know that the house had once belonged to a Jewish family. When he had come to Urycz in 1954, the house stood empty and they had been able to buy it from the village for very little money.

I couldn't find a single soul in Urycz who had been a witness to the slaughter in 1941. Because the village consisted of two separate sections, the massacre could occur out of sight of the non-Jewish villagers. A number of people, however, told me they had heard shots that day and there were plenty of hearsay witnesses whose statements weren't at variance with the eyewitness testimonies of Hauptmann and Pollak. One man told us he'd heard shooting that day, but did not go up to investigate until one month had passed. Then he was appalled to see how the land in front of Hauptmann's hiding place and the stream there too were still red with blood. A horrible and gruesome story, which was unquestionably true because of the following special circumstances: Right after the execution on August 27, a big storm had suddenly broken loose (Hauptmann had mentioned that) and heavy rains had come down on Urycz. At that point the Ukrainian collaborators and the few German soldiers had given the grave only a thin covering of earth. They rushed off when the storm began. As a result of the rainstorm, which continued for days, the stream became swollen and flooded the scarcely covered grave. Then a huge blood pool filled the field.

In one of the other villages I met a woman, Katarina Barnatska, who used to live in Sopot (which is in fact a continuation of Podhorodze and the place where Menten owned an estate). She told me that Menten and his men had had a bad reputation in her village. They were always very harsh in guarding against the villagers' making off with logs from Menten's woods for their household fires. In the war, she said, Menten came back, uniformed. And she also told me that he led the executions. He murdered, she said, her brother, Joseph. She also remembers her nephews and nieces, Joseph's children, dying of hunger.

All the witnesses I spoke to in Russia recognized Menten's picture without any reservations. I carried about ten photographs of different people in my pocket; one of them was Pieter Menten. Every witness pushed aside the rest of the pictures and picked his, without fail. That was him, that was Petro Petro Menten; or, as they pronounced it in the accusative, Menten.

After travelling in East Galicia for almost a week with our guide and interpreter Molchanov, the photographer and I decided to return to the Netherlands. We wanted to get back as soon as possible to report our findings and confront the Dutch judiciary and the CID with the shocking material. From my hotel room in Lvov, via a telephone conversation with my wife, I'd already informed Commissioner Peters of the main thrust of what we found. He was eager for me to get in touch as soon as we got back, and make an appointment to see our material.

After a journey of almost twenty hours, we touched down in London late Sunday night. Flying on to Amsterdam was impossible because all the flights were fully booked to the very last seat, filled with good Dutch citizens whose idea of adventure was to go on a bargain-shopping weekend trip to London. So we spent the night in a London hotel, and although we would much rather have been in our own beds, this wasn't too bad, actually. In Russia we had had to do without any kind of creature comforts or service. And now it seemed a tiny miracle to push a button and be able to order anything we felt like having; after six days of Ukrainian beet soup, finally a good big steak and a bottle of wine!

The material we brought back with us from Russia almost led to a crisis of the Dutch government. Less than three weeks later, during a spectacular Parliament debate on November 18, the minister of justice, Van Agt, was going to get his vaguely fluttering protesting hands rapped with copies of *Accent*.

I believe I may permit myself to point out that when, in November 1976, the decision was finally made to arrest Pieter Menten, it could hardly have been on the basis of the material gathered much later by the CID, but because of the evidence my photographer and I brought back from Russia. If we hadn't gone to Russia, then surely Menten wouldn't have gone anywhere either—he'd still be enjoying a hideously earned luxury and freedom.

Why two journalists were given the opportunity to attend the opening of a mass grave in East Galicia and the Dutch judiciary was not given visas till much later, I cannot say. It will remain one of the many unsolved riddles in the Menten affair. But I am prepared to state under oath my belief that there couldn't have been any form of staging by the Soviet authorities. It is true that the mass grave in Isaac Pistiner's back yard had already been opened by the time we got there. But the fact remains that other mass graves were still to be opened, and we could have been present at those. We were in Podhorodze on a Thursday, and four days later the great grave in Urycz was going to be opened. The prosecutor of the district of Lvov, whom we'd met in Podhorodze, invited both of us to attend the Urycz "opening." Even if it could be true (as some spiteful tongues keep saying) that the whole operation in Podhorodze was especially rigged up for us, such a thing was impossible for Urycz. And the same holds true for the villages of Kropovnyk and Dovge, where more mass graves were scheduled to be opened at spots located by relatives of other victims.

The only thing I'm willing to admit is that the Russians gave us our visas only when they knew graves were to be opened. But I myself would call this a good kind of "staging." If they let us come as witnesses only when there was something to see, I have more reason to be grateful than to blame them. We got all the cooperation a journalist could hope for while we were in the Soviet Union. For the purpose of fact-finding we were allowed to talk freely with everybody and see everything, and in theory nothing was impossible. One might wonder (and, of course, I have) what moved the Russians to be so generously helpful to two Western journalists, one of them a notorious anti-communist. They must have had their reasons for that, but I see no point in endlessly trying to figure them out.

We were out for facts, and facts were what we got in the Soviet Union. While some people said they didn't know anything, and others seemed close-mouthed, others knew a great deal. And told us!'

The Dutchman Runs![303]

Back in Amsterdam, Knoop showed the photographs to the Menten prosecution team, playing tapes of the statements of witnesses. They all agreed that if the material were to be published in *Accent*, Menten would attempt to abscond, and that they were aware that the Ministry of Justice would resist preventive detention, begged Knoop to wait until official evidence could be brought back from the USSR (due to Soviet delays, it was to be months before this happened).

Knoop, with some sympathy from the police, maintained that it was his duty to publish, and theirs to apprehend Menten. The story, he said, would appear in

Accent and in the Hamburg magazine *Stern* on the 20th November 1976. On the 11th November the police fixed the 15th November as the day that they would arrest Pieter Menten.

But on the night of the 14th November, warned by some still-unknown official in the Ministry of Justice, Menten and his wife got into their Simca estate car, drove away from their mansion at Blaricum and disappeared, leaving frustration by one and all.

Menten's escape led to a savage debate in the Dutch Parliament, lasting 14 hours and conducted before television cameras. The Prime Minister promised an inquiry to discover the source of Menten's tip-off, and a police search to bring him back to justice. Neither promise was redeemed.

Capture!

Menten was recaptured through the efforts of the journalist Hans Knoop and the German Magazine *Stern* who offered Knoop the use of their foreign network. On 6 December 1976 a freelance correspondent in Switzerland telephoned *Stern* and said that for 5,000 Deutschmarks he could reveal Menten's hiding place.

That evening Knoop and three Dutch police officers flew to Zurich, where a few hours later the Swiss authorities arrested Menten in his suite at the Hotel Muster.

The Swiss-Dutch extradition treaty does not mention war criminals, and the expensive lawyers hired by Meta Menten portraying their client as a victim of Jewish vengeance and KGB intrigue suggested that the Swiss should expel him to a country of his choice, such as Ireland.

That campaign collapsed when Hans Knoop and Haviv Canaan (his first Israeli informant) revealed to the Swiss press the available evidence against Menten. Swiss embarrassment was not lessened by wartime memories of how the country had excluded Jewish refugees and on the 24th December Menten was returned to Holland, with the condition that he must be tried there and not extradited to Poland.

Menten instantly claimed that he had lost his Polish naturalisation without regaining his Dutch citizenship: he was thus stateless, and couldn't be tried in Holland. The fact that this made Menten's previous accounts of his citizenship into perjury did not stop *De Telegraaf*, the most important Dutch newspaper, from leaping to his support and predicting that a trial would find him innocent.

When proceedings began the defence, led by a prominent member of the neo-Nazi Ritter van Rappard party, tried to repeat the 'Jewish conspiracy' ploy, with suggestions that Menten resembled Solzienitsyn as a victim of the KGB. But when the evidence of mass-murder became overwhelming, there was a startling tactical shift. The prisoner alleged that in 1952 the Socialist Minister for Justice had promised him immunity.

Chapter 9

Himmler Purges the Rabka Four... and their demise

ROBBERY ACCOMPANIED SLAUGHTER, but not without danger: Himmler's own favourite, SS-Col Karl Otto Korch, first commandant of Majdanek, was one of those executed for converting Jewish property to his own use. Schoengarth therefore was glad to employ Menten as his *homme d'affaires* in the business of looting the Jews. However, the SS Special Investigators were examining and targeting the inner sanctum of Einsatzgruppen personnel with positive results.

In April, 1943, there was a big upheaval of security personnel in Krakow and Lvov districts. The Reichsfuehrer SS Himmler, disciplined a number of Sipo-SD officers: Higher SS and Policefuehrer Fredrich Wilhelm Krueger (not our Krueger) was transferred to Berlin, Dr Schoengarth was transferred to Greece and later Holland; Hans Krueger moved to Paris; Rosenbaum, by the skin of his teeth, escaped charges, but not without serious condemnation from his superiors as to his actions in Rabka and implication in theft of Jewish property and black marketing activities. He was relieved from his duties at the Sipo-SD School to desk duties in Krakow. Pieter Menten was arrested and detained in the cellars of the Stycznia SS Headquarters where he remained in custody. Menten had overstayed his residence permit and was about to be expelled from Krakow. From his cell he wrote to Himmler pleading his case but any further indulgence was quickly dismissed and he was deported back to Holland on 31st January 1943, and allowed to take with him several box cars of objet d'art and other movables.

Rosenbaum Appeal and End-Game

Dr Schoengarth celebrated his transfer by holding a farewell party in Krakow which was attended by all the senior command of the Sipo-SD in Krakow district. It was at this party that Rosenbaum broke down and confessed and attempted to justify his actions, particularly to past executions, the shooting of the Jew Beck, and his involvement with others. Dr Kurt Neidling:

'I occupied a small flat in Dr Schoengarth's house in Krakow. One evening, maybe in the spring 1943, Dr Schoengarth held a party with many guests. The celebrations went on through the night and were very loud. I had stayed in my room and didn't join the party. When I got up the next morning at about 6 a.m., I met Rosenbaum in the hallway. He had been at the party and had consumed a lot of alcohol. He followed me to my room and sat down in a chair. He put his head on the table. Suddenly he started sobbing, his whole body shook. He looked at me helplessly and said, "I'm not guilty, I only carried out orders."'[304]

A few months after this episode with Dr Neidling (probably engineered by him as a sympathetic favour), Rosenbaum was transferred to the KdS (admin) in Salzburg as Polizei Inspector (SS-aligned rank 2nd Lieutenant) and adjutant to Ober Inspector (SS-aligned rank of Captain) Wilhelm Teege, arranging conferences and making provisions for those attending. On 7 August 1943, he married his fiancée Annemarie Bachus. Rosenbaum had come full circle, starting out with similar responsibilities of manager in the SD School Zakopane, 1939, to organiser and manager of conferences in Salzburg in mid-1943.

As a result of the massive clear-out of all personnel with past-related activities in Rabka, the SD School was totally cleansed and re-structured with new staff from outside and from the BdS in Krakow. There was a new emphasis on training. Rosenbaum had been replaced by a well seasoned desk-Nazi SS- Captain Fritz Herrmann, with SS-Captain Wilhelm Teege (recently transferred from Salzburg) as deputy for course construction. Courses continued for Civil servants of the government, Sipo-SD, and Polish police officers (Ukrainians had been dropped). Ethnic Germans and Poles continued to guard the premises. Oddly enough, the School driver, Bandura, was kept on and went about his business with the secrets of the School locked away in his head.[305]

Ober Inspector Wilhelm Teege arrived at the School in August 1943, a few weeks after the main deportation of Jews to KZ Plaszow. However, a small number (10-15) Jews were held back from this deportation to look after the animals on the School farm. Teege confirmed that there were 'Jew hunts' still going on in the area. All past deeds were 'swept under the carpet' of all that went before. It was a masterpiece of obliteration by deception.

It was about this time that attention was directed to the mass graves in the woods behind the School. The 'Blobel Commando 1005' were digging up mass graves and destroying the evidence in nearby KZ Plaszow and thoughts were now turned to solving the mass graves in Rabka, where it is thought over 2,000 bodies lay beneath the soil.[306] In any event 1005 bypassed the Rabka Sipo-SD School to more pressing appointments. For what reasons the Rabka graves were not exhumed is not known. [307]

In mid-1944, due to the heavy bombing in Berlin, all in-training courses from the city were transferred to Bad Rabka. The courses and curriculum at the now re-vamped Sipo-SD School were geared to Police Officers and Civil Servants who had been selected and earmarked for promotion. The courses were of 6-months duration and, by all accounts (as 1939), were very selective but with a high rate of failure. Candidates were tested every few weeks and those failing to pass the tests were removed. On June 1944 intake of 68 students: 24 left after the first test, 20 left after the second test, of the 24 students left who took the final exam, 3 failed. Running parallel to this course was a course of 62 Policefuehrers, all recruited from the elite of the civil service.[308]

At this time (June 1944), the war was still being heavily contested on all fronts. The Jewish Question had all but subsided, but the furnaces of Auschwitz were still filled with the Jews from Hungary, Lodz and elsewhere. The curriculum at the School had not quite reverted to civil proportions. There was a continued high emphasis on firearms training on Rosenbaum's shooting range, and it is interesting to note that, of these past students who were interviewed for the Rosenbaum trial, the majority had no idea that shootings had taken place there, or that there had been a significant Jewish presence at the School, or in the camps nearby.[309] For the teaching staff that was more established, it was known but never spoken of.[310] Other subjects covered general war conditions and regulations and their world view.[311] The School continued to function until January 1945 as an SD educational establishment, devoid of Jews and devoid of murder.[312]

Another curious twist in all this was, on 2 January 1945, whilst organising conferences in Salzburg Rosenbaum was selected for an Ober-Inspector's course to be held at his old School. He returned to Bad Rabka, to his former place of activity, as a participant in a Chief of Staff course on 3 January 1945, but due to the advancing Russians the course had to be abandoned on 17 January.[313]

Now operating under emergency orders from Berlin, the whole class of candidates led by Wilhelm Teege were directed to Krakow to assist the Volkssturm, Ordnungspolizei, Waffen SS, and Air force Officers to prepare for a counter attack against the advancing Russians. The overall commander of this '*Verbindungsfuehrer*'(intermediary) group was SS-Major General Dr Bierkamp.

Parts of their duties were the rounding up of German deserters and stringing them up on lamp-posts and planting a notice on them: 'I hang here because I left my unit without permission.' In another twist to events, Rosenbaum was to meet in Krakow, the Jew Henryk Ettinger, who had previously serviced the School vehicles in Rabka and had been on the deportation list to KZ Plaszow. Rosenbaum survived further investigation and was ordered back to Salzburg, where on 20 April, 1945, he was promoted to SS-2nd Lieutenant.[314]

When the war drew to a close in April, 1945, Rosenbaum moved from Salzburg to Simmling where he saw out the war. On the disbandment of the German military forces, Rosenbaum was employed as a transport manager for a farm co-operative in the eastern zone, but after a few months moved to Hamburg where he was employed as an Insurance Agent, Private Detective and Travelling Salesman. In 1949, he settled to taking a sweet shop in Hamburg, and then moved into wholesale confectionery where he was very successful. The Rosenbaum business had a total annual turnover of approximately 1.3 million DM. His marriage was childless, but adopted a nephew of his wife.[315]

Wilhelm Rosenbaum was almost hypnotised by Dr Schoengarth, like a rabbit caught in the headlights of a car. Of all the men who admired and feared Dr Schoengarth and obeyed him unquestioningly, all the evidence shows that Rosenbaum was the one most strongly under his spell.

Wilhelm Rosenbaum killed his victims based upon low motives, namely racial hatred and pure despotism to enjoy personal power. He regarded the Jews to be creatures of the lowest moral kind, 'Untermenschen' (Unworthy of life).

Rosenbaum fully and uncritically adopted the opinion of the Sipo-SD and the conviction of his model Dr Schoengarth that the inferior race of Jews had to be exterminated. He believed he had to prove his suitability as Sipo-SD-Fuehrer of the Commander-in-Chief of the Security Police by co-operating with or without the actual order to deal with these 'tasks'. This approach and not the security considerations persuaded him to carry out the killings. It was clear to Rosenbaum that Jews—as far as they were working in the School—had no legitimate claim to receive the same justified treatments as the German or Polish workers; he regarded them as 'people material', which he did not demolish out of a practical point of view when he needed them for work. This did not belong to the weak or unsuitable and therefore superfluous creatures were reminded with lashes of the whip and humiliations that the world in Bad Rabka was separated into the master race and inferior race.

Not only the surviving Jews, but also the Germans recognised that Rosenbaum had been a 'very small light' all his life and had to bear humiliations and disdain and whose unimportant social position as well as his miserable human powers of expression were based upon his aggressive instinct. It is ironic, perhaps, that he saw himself as powerful in Bad Rabka, the decision-maker about life and death, a veritable 'god'.

The product of this overwhelming lust for power was the barbaric tortures to which he subjected his victims; the climax of this voluntary power lust was the selections and executions. This also counts as much as Rosenbaum was covering himself for his killings by the general orders of the Commander-in-Chief of the Security Police. The feeling of the subaltern and anxious Rosenbaum to carry out the will of the leadership and receive the favour of Dr Schoengarth constituted the 'green light' to act. Within the wide framework that Dr Schoengarth's order gave him, he could enjoy and exercise his OWN power.

The killings of Jews also represent the horrifying execution and other surrounding circumstances of murder: In all the cases, the victims were locked for a while before the execution and left there without food or water, waiting death; the executions took place in a disgraceful way as the victims were forced to undress or they were undressed and then were shot naked. This did not apply to the Rosenbaum family four, who were dispatched around the corner of the School building fully clothed; the way the execution and other described modalities meet the sign of atrocity.

For the rest, there are circumstances in separate cases adding horrifying signs to the facts, such as the shooting of entire families where one member of the family had to experience the liquidation of the other ones, the killing of children before the eyes of their mothers, the insult and blasphemy of victims at the sight of the grave. It is in all probability that the Rabka Jews had accepted the notion of what was awaiting them when they were called to the School.

It was certain that the 'The Final Solution' embarked on by the Nazis were overpowering as far as the shooting of the picked up Jewish men and women, in the Generalgouvernement, were concerned. Since the Barbarossa Campaign, it was the rule to punish with death those people that tried to escape and sabotage in order to frighten the others: Rosenbaum cited in his defence, in respect of the shooting cases, the following instances where it was considered appropriate for Jews to be killed:

1. That a dreadful state of affairs regarding gangs in the East had taken an unbearable cost and threatened to become a serious danger where Jews were considered running around as potential opponents and supporters of the so-called gangs combat.[316]

2. That civilians that were found without any identification (ID) on the country roads and did not belong to the next village, were to be shot.[317]

3. The Court in Nuremberg also had stated that several thousands of partisans were shot and hanged in public and that the death by hanging was particularly off-putting; above that, many elements walking around without any ID were put to an end.[318]

4. Several examples were given of Jews, so-called supporters and aids in combat gangs, who were shot in co-operation with the local commander's office, military police station and Einsatzgruppen.[319]

As to the hanging action, Rosenbaum claimed 'justification in war' and based his defence on three documents. He had claimed that the execution of the picked-up Jews in the Generalgouvenement was encouraged and executed from a military point of view regarding the tight security situation in the area—namely because of the increasing partisan activity, gang developments, communist activities supported by the Jews. He believed that this situation was put very clearly in the three documents:

1. Document of the 'Oberfeld' Commander's Office (Oberfeld-Kommandantur) of Lublin dated 19th December 1941 with orders to shoot unidentified suspects.

2. Document of the Commander's Office in Warsaw dated 20.11.1941, stating that 26 Russian POW's were picked up and shot during the period from 15th October until 1st November 1941.

3. Document of the 'Oberfeld' Commander's Office (Oberfeld-Kommandantur) of Warsaw dated 22nd June 1943, stating that escaped Jews formed an integral part of all the communist gangs and that gang attacks in the countryside were mainly related to communist elements.

The Appeal Court denied these defences stating that even existing anti-Jewish decrees in those days—whose validity need not be disclosed—did not allow Rosenbaum to kill Jews; that Rosenbaum was condemned as sole offender of murder and not as an assistant; that he had acted without any general order or authority.   Rosenbaum is entirely responsible under criminal law for the committed crimes. The Appeal Court determined:

Rosenbaum was a ruler over life and death in the School; he ordered—and not the far-off Dr Schoengarth—what needed to be done. The accused decided which victims were unfit for work and which picked up Jews were to be liquidated, whether and which investigations regarding working suitability of the workers and 'law offences' of the picked-up Jews were to be determined. He determined how the killings were to take place from a local, temporal or other point of view and which measure needed to be taken to wipe away the traces of these crimes.

Eventually, certain dependability on the Commander-in-Chief of the Security Police was based upon the fact—as noted by Rosenbaum himself—that the far-off Dr Schoengarth gave instructions to the accused. After that, the accused is an offender in all cases for which he has been charged. He is the sole offender.

The Court could not determine whether other SS-people and Ukrainians who took part in the killings were accomplices to the crimes; according to the circumstances, only complicity is a possibility.

A complicity of the superior and the accused, especially the Brigadier General Dr Schoengarth, cannot be determined. It is doubtful whether the conferral of a general order by Dr Schoengarth could be the basis for complicity in specified cases; this need not be decided upon because if it is imagined that such a directive had existed in certain cases, it relates to an insinuation in favour of the accused which does not allow to determine the complicity of Dr Schoengarth in a positive way.[320]

The Appeal Court doubted whether Rosenbaum would have endangered his life by not executing the orders of Dr Schoengarth. I am not sure about this and the contrary may well have been a consideration. We already know of Schoengarth's attitude to his SD for refusing to carry out his execution orders. It is even more surprising as Hans Krueger gave evidence at the trial and it is mainly from his deposition that we learned initially of the Schoengarth 'kill or be killed' policy. I think the point is, that Rosenbaum acted on his own responsibility and this was recognised by the court.

The overview of this whole miserable episode is that moral values were turned around as such that it was a holy duty—although difficult to fulfil—to wipe the

'Jewish race' off the earth. The normal feelings of morality and right were turned into 'one's baser instincts' and into cowardice; instead of compassion with the victims, the complaint being made as to the weight of the historical task.

Rosenbaum was taught and indoctrinated by the SS and Sipo-SD, and this influenced his conduct, which was clearly expressed by Himmler in his Posnan speech on the 4th October, 1943. [321]

It is difficult to understand how this inadequate individual, Wilhelm Rosenbaum, came to go down in history as a cruel, sadistic murderer who had few equals.

Downfall of SS-Captain Hans Krueger[322]

Krueger's era in Stanislawow had now also come to an end. Already in the autumn of 1942, he had encountered problems when an audit of his office by the Reich Auditor's Office (RAO) had turned up certain surprising discoveries: An especially extreme case had been uncovered in the branch at Stanislasow in Galicia. Large amounts of confiscated money and jewels were retained there.

During a local inspection of the rooms of the responsible administrative official, Police Secretary B., officials of the Reich Auditor's Office discovered large amounts of cash, including gold coins, and all sorts of currency—even $6,000— as well as entire chests full of extremely valuable jewels. These were stored in all manner of boxes and containers, desks, etc. None of this had been listed or registered. In some containers, there was a slip with the original amount; but in most, there was no written record of any kind. It was no longer possible to determine how much had originally been there. The RAO had to limit it to establishing the exact contents of what was found there in order to prevent further valuables from disappearing. The cash alone amounted to 584,195,28 Zloty. Added to this were the jewels uncovered there; their precise value could not be determined, but is likely to be in the range of several hundred thousand Reichmarks. Several days after intervention by the RAO, the Political Sec. B., who had chief responsibility for these matters, shot himself.

Krueger himself ultimately brought about his own transfer and demotion by disclosing his murderous deeds to a Polish noblewoman under arrest. Following an intercession, the countess was released, and after she had made known what Krueger had confided to her, proceedings were initiated against him. He was formally charged with betraying secret information and was later transferred from his 'kingdom' in Stanislawow to Paris.

At the conclusion of the war Hans Krueger was detained by the Dutch authorities suspected of war crimes but no evidence was forthcoming. He was released in 1948, and returned to his native Germany where he worked as a salesman until 1950, when he started his own company. He attempted to be re-instated into the Civil Service but this was denied probably due to his past in the SD. Krueger made further attempts to gain respectability and acceptance in the 'New Germany' by applying to join the State Internal Security Agency (Verfassungsschutz) in North Rhine-Westphalia, but again he was unsuccessful.

Hans Krueger, instead of burying himself in obscurity where he would have been safer from subsequent investigation, turned to politics and became the district managing director of the Free People's Party (FVP) in Munster, later switching to the German Party (DP). From 1949 to 1956, he was state chairman of the Association of Former Germans from Berlin and Brandenburg (Landsmannschaft Berlin-Mark Brandenburg), where he served as spokesman, a high powered appointment which was his undoing. In 1954, Krueger attempted to be elected to the NRW state assembly campaigning on behalf of the League of Eastern Expellees and Victims of Justice (*Bund der Heimatvertrieben und Entrechteten*), but again was unsuccessful.[323]

Hans Krueger had also been on the periphery of the 'ODESSA' ('Organisation *Der Ehlemaligen SS-Angehorigen*'-Organisation of Former Members of the SS/Sipo-SD). Better known through the writers of spy thrillers, Krueger was a supporter of this organisation but preferred to stay within the New Germany. One of Krueger's Komrades, who did use this facility and escaped to Argentine via Spain, was Dr Walther Kutschmann, the alleged murderer of the Lvov professors. He was also the officer who had terminated Krueger's career over the Caroline Lanckoronska affair. Kutschmann, alias Pedro Ricardo Olmo, was eventually tracked down and arrested in the Argentine in November 1984, on extradition charges relating to murder of Jews in Brzezany, and the single murder of a Jewish girl in Drohobycz. Up until his death he was a regular contributor to the Kammeraden of the Death's head insignia, attending anniversary meetings in the beer halls of Munich.[324]

In 1959, Hans Krueger was eventually tracked down and arrested for alleged war crimes. No doubt his high profile over the preceding years had contributed to his demise. The State Prosecutor of Dortmund finally issued a formal indictment in October, 1965. The subsequent trial, known as the 'Stanislawow trial', opened in April 1967, when he was indicted with the murder of 120,000 Jews. The trial lasted two years, during which he had not lost any of his anti-Semitism which he displayed openly to the court. Facing him across the court were a few Jewish survivors, and Dr Carolina Lanckoronska. He was convicted, and later sentenced on the 6th May, 1968, to life imprisonment.[325]

Assistant professor Karolina Lanckoronska, arrested in 1943 by Hans Krueger, the Gestapo Chief at Stanislawow, learned from him that he took part in arresting the Lvov professors during the night on July 3 to 4, 1941. Lanckoronska was sure she would be executed together with his 250 victims: teachers, lawyers, judges, doctors, and with tens of thousands of Jews, known to have been victim of that massacre. Mrs Lanckoronska, due to the intervention of the Italian Royal Court, was at the last moment snatched out of Krueger's hands by the Lvov Gestapo. There she met Walther Kutschmann, Krueger's personal enemy, to whom she disclosed her knowledge about the execution of the Lvov professors. Kutschmann initiated in Berlin a trial against Krueger, at which the latter was sentenced for revealing official secrets. Mrs Lanckoronska was sent to the concentration camp at Ravensbrueck from which she was released thanks to the efforts of her friend Professor Burckhardt, President of the International Red Cross in Geneva. [326] A very interesting account of these events was published by Lanckoronska in the London issues of *Orzel Bialy* (*The White Eagle*), Nos. 46-48.

The Hans Krueger Case is Re-opened

After the war, Mrs Lanckoronska, living abroad, read in a newspaper about the trial against Krueger held in Muenster. He was charged with murdering thousands of Jews in Stanislawow. She went there as a witness and accused him with the murder of the Lvov professors. The court, however, concluded that there was no evidence proving his participation in the murder of the professors and implied that this may have been only boasts and attempts to intimidate the arrested woman. For his crimes committed in Stanislawow Krueger was nonetheless sentenced to imprisonment for life.

Consistent with the West German law, a person receiving capital punishment cannot be called to account for other even most serious crimes. This made it impossible to judge Krueger for the murder of the professors. On the request of Wladyslaw Zelenski, the prosecutor interrogated Krueger but he denied taking part in the Lvov crimes. The prosecutor suspended additional investigations implying that further details were of concern only to historians. All attempts of Mrs Lanckoronska, Mrs Krukowska, Wladyslaw Zelenski (Tadeusz Boy-Zelenski's nephew) and others failed to advance the case and to bring to justice the perpetrators of the bloody July night. Wladyslaw Zelenski published several articles in the London *Wiadomosci* (*News*) about the Lvov crime. He rectified in *Die Welt* the erroneous information suggesting that the murder of the professors was committed on racial grounds, because those killed were supposed to be Jews. Zelenski stated that there was no one who could be considered Jew in a religious sense among the 22 professors shot on July 4. Only Henryk Korowicz, killed on 11th July, was of Jewish descent, but he had a Polish name and was certainly not arrested by the Gestapo as a Jew but as a Polish scholar, just as the other 22, including Ruziewicz and Bartel.

Many Poles asked themselves who supplied the Germans with the '88 list' containing the professors' names. This is of little substance to the case, because the names and addresses could have been copied from the pages of a pre-war telephone book. But Walther Kutschmann had told Mrs Lanckoronska that Ukrainians prepared the list for the Gestapo. Luckily there were only 25 names on it, although the University itself had 158 members of the Faculty; among Lvov Institutions of Higher Learning, there was also the large Institute of Technology, the School of Veterinary Medicine and the School of Foreign Trade.

Taking into consideration that Gestapo searched during that July night also for persons who recently died, for instance for the ophthalmologist Professor Adam Bednarski and the dermatologist Professor Roman Leszczynski, we may assume that the list was prepared already earlier in Krakow. Since Lvov was then separated for 22 months by the German-Soviet border by the Krakow authorities who did not know about those details, it seems most probable that the Krakow Gestapo asked—prior to the German-Soviet war—the Ukrainian students or graduates from Lvov academic institutions to supply a list of names and addresses of professors known to them; hence the relatively short list. In my view the following were instrumental in the arrest and murder of the Lvov Professors: Hans Krueger, Walther Kutschmann, Kurt Stawizki, police officer, non-commissioned officers Hacke and Kohler and the Dutch collaborator Pieter Menten.

In 1976, Krueger, whilst in prison, was to receive unexpected visitors. Detectives investigating the Menten case which was at a crucial stage, requested to interview him regarding his association with Dr Schoengarth, Rosenbaum and particularly Menten, concerning their activities in Galicia during the war. Krueger refused to see the detectives and stated that he had no interest in meeting them until the question of the 'Breda Three' had been resolved.[327] The detectives came away empty handed.

(Breda was the site of one of the first panopticon prison establishments. This prison housed the only German war criminals ever to be imprisoned in the Netherlands for their war crimes during the Second World War. They were known as the 'Breda Four (and later three)'. They were Willy Paul Franz Lages who was released in 1966 due to serious illness, Joseph Johann Kotälla who died in prison in 1979, Ferdinand Hugo aus der Fünten and Franz Fischer who were both released in 1989.)

In 1986, Hans Krueger was released from prison and retired to the Bavarian town of Wasserburg am Inn, where he died in 1988.[328]

Figure 33: Countess Karolina Lanckoronska

A Brief Biographical Note

Countess Karolina Maria Adelajda Franciszka Ksawera Malgorzata Edina Lanckoronska (born August 11, 1898, Gars am Kamp, Lower Austria—Died August 25, 2002, Rome, Italy).

Karolina Lanckoronska was the daughter of Count Karol Lanckoronski, a Polish nobleman from a Galician family, and his third wife, Princess Margaret von Lichnovsky, daughter of Karl Max, Prince Lichnowsky. Karolina was reared and attended university in Vienna (capital of the Austro-Hungarian Empire, of which much of Galicia was then part), living at her family's palace, the Palais Lanckoronski.

After Poland regained independence in 1918, Lanckoronska taught at Lvov University. Following the invasion of Lvov by the Soviet Red Army and later the rest of Poland by Nazi Germany in September 1939, she witnessed at first hand the terror and atrocities committed by the Soviets and Nazis, which she later described in her *War Memoirs*.

Lanckoronska was active in the Polish resistance and was arrested, interrogated, tortured, tried and sentenced to death at Stanislawow prison. During her stay there, the local Gestapo chief, Hans Krueger, confessed to her that he had murdered 23 Lvov University professors, a war crime that she made it her mission to publicize.

Thanks to her family connections, Lanckoronska was not executed but was instead sent to the Ravensbrueck concentration camp for women. She somehow survived and, immediately after release in 1945, wrote her war memoirs. After the war, she left Poland and lived in Fribourg, Switzerland, and later, until her death, in Rome.

A patriot all her life, Lanckoronska bequeathed her family's enormous art collection to her beloved Poland only after her homeland became free from communism and Soviet occupation. The Lanckoronski Collection may now for the most part be seen in Warsaw's Royal Castle and Krakow's Wawel Castle. Countess Karolina Lanckoronska died aged 104.[329]

Pieter Menten is Protected by the Reichsfuehrer-SS[330]

As the Germans conquered Poland, all Jewish property was seized in operations enabling Menten to serve both Hitler and himself. He became *Treuhander* (administrator) for Jewish antiques and art-collections under SS Brigadiergeneral Schoengarth.

Just before the Wehrmacht invaded the USSR on 22 June 1941, Menten enabled Stieglitz to escape to Hungary from which he reached Palestine, returning many years later to help Menten stave off prosecution. Like all friendships that are based on greed and betrayal, there were to be serious repercussions, not only in respect of the 'Rabka Four', but for the general criminal factions that had spread throughout the Generalgouvnement.

In 1943, when the 'Rabka Four' were dispersed to other regions, Pieter Menten was escorted out of the Generalgouvernement with some pomp, heavily loaded with stolen property of the murdered Lvov professors and elsewhere. With the authorisation of the Reichsfuehrer SS and connivance of Dr Schoengarth, a special train was placed at his disposal for his journey out of Poland to Holland at the most critical time in the war. On arrival in Holland, Menten resided in the wealthy Aerdenhout where he maintained a low profile as an art dealer.

However, the Dutch Underground's attention was now focused on Menten and they recorded visits by Schoengarth to his residence.

Shortly after the liberation Menten was high on the agenda as a Nazi collaborator and as a result was arrested and held in custody for trial. The trial concluded in 1949 and Menten was sentenced to an eight-month term for having worked in uniform as a Nazi interpreter. In 1951 the Dutch government refused a Polish request for Menten's extradition to Poland to face war crimes charges. Menten lived an untroubled life until, on the 22 May 1976, Holland's most popular newspaper, *De Telegraf*, described a remarkable venture planned by the art-auctioneers Sotherby-Mak van Way:

Pieter Nicolaas Menten, one of the richest men in Holland was selling his Amsterdam apartment. He had to dispose of 425 pictures and other *objects d'art* for which there was no room in his country house at Blaricum, already crammed with other treasures. [331] Menten was quoted as saying that his fortune had first been acquired in pre-war Poland; he had been ruined by the Nazi occupation, but he had restored his finances, and his art collection. What Menten failed to mention was his service in the Abwehr (German Military Intelligence) pre-war, and his wartime service as an SS Sonderfuehrer, and that he was personally responsible for the slaughter of hundreds of Jews and communists in the villages of the Stryj valley. He also failed to mention that his coveted art collection was the proceeds of theft from the residences of the Murdered Professors of Lvov and elsewhere in the Galician District. Following investigations by Hans Knoop, the editor of the Dutch magazine *Accent*, in collaboration with Chaviv Kanaan from Israel, Menten was brought to trial after being extradited from Switzeland, where he had fled with his wife on 14th November 1976.

Chapter 10

The Menten Murder Trial

WE NOW MOVE FORWARD to 4 April, 1977, to the Amsterdam court concerning the Podhorodze murder Trial and refer to certain extracts from the trial.

For the first time, witnesses identified Menten and testified about the happenings in Podhorodze on Sunday the 7th July, 1941. The tellers of the tale were four Polish women (Mrs K. Tuzimek, Paulina Tycznska, Sabina Jaworska, and Ludwina Szuster), three of them sisters. The sisters had seen Menten come into the village with the executioners; they had seen him lead the slaughter of many Jews and three non-Jewish Poles. Menten himself, they said, had shot his former estate manager, Novicky, and Novicky's wife, and her brother, Alfred Stepan.

Forced to stand by the execution pit, they saw Menten dressed in a dark uniform. Mrs Tuzimek said: 'Menten stood on my left, he wore a uniform and a peak cap, he aimed at Novicky and at the same time I heard a shot. The man fell, and then another shot rang out. I could hear Mrs Novicky call out to the police chief Phillip Mueller, "Phillip, help me." The young girls cringed when they heard the first shots in Pistiner's yard, but were not allowed to turn away, and so saw how the German uniformed Dutchman performed his murders in cold blood.' Sabina and Paulina even remembered that before Menten fired his fatal shot at his ex-employee he snarled: 'Here's one for Hitler!' The image of Borislaw Novicka a few moments before her death is a disturbing memory for the four women: 'I can still see her babushka fluttering...sort of helplessly, in the wind,' said K. Tuzimek, the eldest sister. They all remembered how Mrs Noviska kept standing after the first shot, refusing to fall into the pit. Menten walked up to her and viciously kicked the woman into the grave, still alive.

Surprise Witnesses

On the third day, a surprise witness appeared for the prosecution. A simple lampshade maker from Arnsberg, West Germany, Hans Geisler had read about

165

the trial in his local newspaper. It was his duty, he told the court, to clear up a misunderstanding. Menten testified that he had never been a member of Schoengarth's Einsatzgruppe. But Geisler had been a member, and he knew. He even brought along a couple of interesting old photographs. One showed a group of military officers surrounding one civilian, like students around a teacher in a graduation pose. At the time, before he sent the photograph home to his parents, Geisler had written on the back, 'The man with the glass in his hand, that's me, because war makes one thirsty.' The civilian, he had written, was 'van Menten, a Dutchman who has a great deal of possessions.' 'Yes, (pointing in the court) that is Menten sitting there,' he said. 'That's not me,' Menten said, examining the photograph. Ignoring him, Geisler said, 'I had a lot of contact with him. I used to sit next to him at the table. One day I went for a drive with him and a few others to see his possessions around Lvov.'

Menten had always denied having worn a German uniform and alleged the photographs were faked. In the much later trial, the arresting office was able to rebut Menten's version:

'As detective, I was at the time active in the case of P.N. Menten in Aerdenhout. In the course of performing my duties in making his arrest, I came upon several pictures of P.N. Menten himself, which I pocketed. When I left the PRA-Haarlem to join the national police I kept those photographs in my possession. At your request now, I deliver these pictures.'

Further corroboration as to the veracity of the photographic evidence was offered by a chief witness for the prosecution, the former Dutch consul in Krakow, Dr Bruin. He confirmed that the person in the picture (above) is P.N. Menten. He went on to say that the picture was in fact taken in 1941 in the garden of his house in Krakow: Alega Grottera No. 12.[332] Further corroboration came from two other sources: a former Polish antique dealer who stated that he could give the names of witnesses who had seen Menten in German uniform and Dr Schoengarth who was biding his time in prison after the war as we shall see.

In those days, executions of Jews were beginning on the edge of Lvov, near the electricity plant. When Geisler was asked by the court if he knew of the Professors' murders, he replied '*I am not aware of the Professors' murders* (of the Ostrowskis, and others on the night of July 3, 1941), *but Menten did seem enthusiastic about the executions*'. He said to the ambitious Holz Apfel, who killed a lot of Jews, that he (Apfel) deserved the Iron Cross. '*If I said that, I meant it ironically,'* Menten said. Geisler replied, *'Yes, maybe you meant it ironically.'* Geisler turned to the judge, *'But he considered Holz Apfel a hero. He also had a friend from the Einsatzgruppen named Kipka. Kipka was a bad person. He had a girlfriend who played the piano. When he didn't like it any longer he shot the piano to pieces.'*[333]

In the early 1960s Rosenbaum had been arrested for War Crimes and in 1965 so he wasn't difficult to find as he was in Hamburg prison serving sixteen life sentences where he was interviewed. Rosenbaum was forthcoming to the detectives about Menten with his recollections of their plundering expeditions in and around Krakow and East Galicia in the 1940s where they had stored their illegal gains in the cellars of the Rabka SD-Sipo School. However, Rosenbaum had unfinished business with Menten over failure to get his share of the profits in 1951 and was now getting payment in kind: In 1951, Rosenbaum and his wife had travelled to Holland to seek out Pieter Menten who owed him a share of the looted property from East Galicia in the 'Good Old Days'. Not finding Menten at home, Rosenbaum returned to Germany.

More surprises:

Further corroboration comes from Dorothea Schoengarth (wife of Dr Schoengarth), who after the war in the trials of both Menten and Rosenbaum gave evidence that her husband had taken Menten along because he had an antiques shop in Lvov. Her husband had given him a uniform to perform his duties as interpreter for the commando and that Menten and her husband's deputy SS-Obersturmfuehrer Heim were mixed up in shady antiques deals. And, that Pieter Menten had honoured a promise to her husband by paying their daughter's school fees which had been agreed shortly before he was hanged for war crimes.

The Menten Verdict

After a 46-day trial the verdict was announced by Judge Schroder:

> 'Mr. Menten, at the preceding sessions you have frequently voiced the expectation that you would be acquitted. You are only acquitted partially. The charges involving the Urycz massacre are dismissed. But in the case of Podhorodze we have found you guilty. The verdict is guilty, and a sentence will follow. The reading of our entire verdict and sentence will take two hours. I can imagine that you may not feel up to

hearing out the whole thing. So, if you wish, you may now leave the courtroom. You may also stay. But you must refrain from interrupting. If you don't, I shall have to have you removed.'

Menten: *'No, Your Honour I stay.'*[334]

The Judge read the court's decision: Urycz indictment—*'Not guilty.'*

Evidence in the Urycz case was found to be insufficient for a conclusive guilty verdict. None of the witnesses saw Menten actually shoot anyone. Nor had any of them been able to determine definitively what role exactly had been played by Menten at Urycz. In addition, statements to the effect that Menten had been seen there were less convincing, since the people of Urycz had been forewarned, expected him to come, after what had happened in Podhorodze. So the element of 'spontaneous recognition' could not be said to exist in the Urycz case. However, Judge Schroeder made a point of adding that the court 'is of the opinion that it is very likely that the defendant also participated in the Urycz executions.' And he continued:

'This acquittal does in no way imply that the court has found that the witnesses of Urycz have spoken untruths, as was repeatedly suggested by defendant and counsel. On the contrary, they probably did say what they had observed, exactly and truthfully. But those observations in themselves amount to insufficient evidence for a conviction.'[335]

In the Podhorodze indictments—*'Guilty.'* Judge Schroeder continued:

'The court believes that a sentence of punishment should also be preventive, functioning partly as a warning, in order that the crime it is applied to will be less likely to occur again in the future. However, after ample and careful consideration, the court did not deem it appropriate to impose the maximum sentence. Administering justice in the name of Her Majesty the Queen, we sentence you to fifteen years in prison.'

According to Hans Knoop, who was present, Menten replied: *'For so cleverly abusing the fact that I cannot appeal for another trial.'* Menten knew well that his trial was brought under specially constituted war-crimes procedures and that only the sentence could be appealed.

Two days after the conviction, Menten's lawyer announced he would appeal on behalf of his client and bring the case to the Supreme Court in The Hague. The next day Prosecutor Counsel announced that he too would appeal, on the grounds that he did not agree with the relatively mild verdict.

According to Hans Knoop the Supreme Court decided differently. It unexpectedly annulled the Amsterdam court's verdict and announced that a new court in The Hague would reopen the case. All the twenty-eight grounds brought up by the defence counsel were rejected by the Supreme Court, but the Court itself discovered other grounds on which it decided the verdict had to be annulled. In the official records of the Amsterdam trial, the Supreme Court discovered that Menten had told the Court that in 1951 the late Minister of Justice, Dr Donker, had promised him that he would never be brought to trial. It was in that year that the minister had had to answer the Polish government's request for Menten's extradition to Warsaw. The Polish government already had sufficient evidence to put Menten on trial for war crimes and crimes against humanity, but the so-called 'Cold War' was then at its height and the minister turned down the Polish request and according to Menten promised him in a private conversation that he would never allow him to be extradited or to be prosecuted in Holland.

The Supreme Court held that the lower court should have investigated Menten's claim, either verifying or refuting it: it should not have ignored it. The Supreme Court indicated clearly that even if it had been established that such a promise had been given to Menten, the Amsterdam court could still have convicted him provided it had explained in its verdict why it had ignored the promise. Thus the verdict was annulled, and a new court in The Hague was appointed to investigate and clarify these points.

The Supreme Court had not acquitted him, nor had it declared that the prosecution had no legal right to prosecute him. So Menten remained in the hospital section of Scheveningen prison while an investigative judge was appointed by the court in The Hague to hear as many witnesses as possible and to clarify once and for all whether or not Menten had indeed been promised immunity from trial by the late Minister of justice.

It was about this time that the twenty-room house in the wealthy Amsterdam suburb which had contained Menten's $7-million art collection caught fire and was reduced to rubble. It was suspected that an arsonist had firebombed the premises.

At the end of 1978 the Menten trial reopened in The Hague. In his plea, Defence Counsel insisted that his client had been given a promise that he would not be prosecuted for collaboration (re the Donker affair above) and that any legal body including an independent court had to honour such a promise. In his view the evidence that such a promise had been given was sufficient. Furthermore, defence counsel referred to the Declaration of Human Rights which stipulated that a legal case against an accused person should be ended within a 'reasonable' period of time, arguing that twenty-six years was far from being a 'reasonable' period.

The prosecution stated that the crimes Menten was accused of were so serious that they had to be brought to the attention of the court and that the court should pronounce upon them. However, the court was not considering the crimes, only the question of the alleged immunity promise. For the moment it was up to the prosecution to convince the court that the evidence was hearsay and insufficient.

According to Knoop, Menten was given a last word, a 'word' that lasted for two hours and was once again full of allegations against Police Commissioner Peters, against me and against all those others who had contributed to his conviction. Once again he stated over and over again that the late minister Donker had given him that promise. Or to be more precise, that he, Menten, had managed to extort such a promise from the minister:

> 'In the early 1950s,' he said, 'I managed to buy for an awful lot of money a secret report from somebody that contained shocking revelations concerning high ranking Dutch officials who all collaborated with the Germans during the war. The minister knew that I had that report and was dead scared that I would publish it. That's why he gave me the promise that I would not be prosecuted if I kept my mouth shut and did not reveal the contents of that dossier. I made a deal with him,' he said, and then continued: 'I am willing to make a "deal" with you as well.'

Menten said that he was afraid that the court in The Hague would not decide in his favour because if he were freed it would mean that he could ask millions of guilders' compensation from the government as well as from individuals. 'If you release me from prison and leave me alone I am willing to refrain from any lawsuits for compensation,' Menten bluntly proposed to the court.

After his last word, the President of the court closed the session:

> 'The accused,' he said, 'has made very serious and insulting allegations directed against many people present here. The fact that we did not stop him from doing so does not mean that the court agrees with the accused, but only that we did not want to restrict his defence. The court will announce its verdict on Monday, December 4.'[336]

Finally, on 4th December 1978, the court in The Hague announced its verdict. They had decided that the prosecution had no grounds on which to prosecute Menten because of the promise given to him by the late Minister of Justice. The court had accepted Van Heijningen's 'hearsay' evidence that such a promise had been given and in its verdict declared that 'the prosecution had to respect the expectations that were aroused in Menten after he'd received such a promise.' Furthermore it accepted the Universal Declaration of Human Rights issue that 'a case against an accused should be ended within a reasonable period of time' and that this period had been greatly exceeded. Although he had been released on a technicality, his guilt remained. That same day the Prosecution appealed against the verdict. [337]

In March 1979 the advocate-general addressed the Supreme Court for the second time. 'The verdict,' he said, 'cannot be confirmed by the Supreme Court.' It did not indicate, he said, why the accusations against Menten had been ignored, and the reference to the Declaration of Human Rights was baseless. 'This refers only to the duration of a prosecution. A prosecution should be finished within a reasonable period of time. Well, the prosecution against Menten only began at the beginning of 1977. The time should be measured from 1977, and not from 1951. If we were measuring from 1951, or even from the time he committed the crimes [1941] this would mean that we respected a Statute of Limitation. As there is no Statute of Limitation, the Declaration of Human Rights cannot be applied to Menten,' the advocate-general concluded. Menten himself was not present but still in hiding somewhere in Holland. The hearing was adjourned until May 22nd 1979.[338]

On that day the presiding judge took twelve minutes to read the judgment, but the verdict was clear from the very first paragraph. In fact, the Supreme Court rejected all the grounds on which Menten's appeal had been granted the previous December, and ordered that he should stand trial again before a special court in Rotterdam.

On May 31, 1979 the Rotterdam court met in camera to consider the application for Menten's arrest. After hearing the defence counsel's submission (which dwelt chiefly on the poor state of his client's health), and the forceful counter-arguments of the prosecution, the president adjourned the session. The court announced its decision the following day: Menten was to be arrested but because of his ill-health, would be allowed to remain in his own home under guard. An Amsterdam police officer was instructed to notify Menten of the verdict and to read him the warrant. That same day the police went to Menten's residence and when they read the warrant to him Menten collapsed. An ambulance was immediately called and Menten was rushed, with a police escort, to the university hospital at Utrecht. Once again, with the retrial scheduled for the autumn of 1979, drama and uncertainty hung over the future of the Menten Affair.[339]

In between his court appearances, Menten was busy making claims to the Dutch government for his alleged losses at the hands of the Dutch Resistance in 1945. He collected 700,000 guilders for missing family property but failed to share the proceeds with his brother Dirk. His next endeavour was to sue the West German government, by claiming that in Poland he had been the victim of the Nazis. In this he was aided and abetted by one former SS-Lt. Wilhelm Rosenbaum, who testified to the court that he had known Menten in Krakow, and knew him to have been imprisoned and robbed by the German security forces in 1943. Menten received 500,000 Deutschmarks. [340] It is not known if Rosenbaum ever received a share of this bounty or any of the other valuables that Rosenbaum had been chasing Menton for over the years.

Trial Time Line: The Menten Affair

1. July 1979: Trial Opens
2. 17 May 1980: It is announced that brother Dirk Menten will give evidence for the prosecution
3. 10 July 1980: Pieter Menten found guilty and sentenced to 10 years imprisonment and fined 100,000 Guilders
4. 23 Oct 1980: Plea from Menten to be released on the grounds of ill health—Denied
5. 28 Oct 1980: Appeal Starts
6. 14 Jan 1981: Appeal Dismissed
7. 15 Mar 1988: Menten applies for early release due to ill health, aged 85 years
8. 19 May 1981: Irish Jewish residents protest to keep Menten out of Ireland

9. 23 May 1985: Pieter Menten released from prison
10. 23 June 1981: Menten's art collection is sold and raises 2.8 million Guilders. But due to claims by the West German government and the Dutch branch of Southerb-Mak van Way, he is now penniless.
11. Pieter Menten dies at an old people's home in Loosdrecht, Holland on the 15th November 1987, aged 88 years.

In that summer of 1979 the trial re-opened at the Rotterdam court which was one last gasp by Pieter Menten to bamboozle the court and witnesses into so much confusion that no other verdict than 'Not Guilty' was likely. Whereas the prosecution were content to rely on written evidence given to the court in previous sessions, Menten's defence spread their net wide issuing witness summonses to the judiciary, police, politicians, and former SS Officers et al. One final arrogant and contemptuous act was to dismiss his legal team and seek to represent himself and claim to the court that this whole prosecution was a conspiracy thought up by the establishment, and further, that the evidence presented by the prosecution was directed at the wrong man. They should be looking for no other than his brother Dirk who was the real executioner of the Pohorodze murders. The courtroom gasped at this incredulous statement and it seemed that Menten, by his uncontrollable conduct, had had a breakdown in the dock. The court adjourned directing a medical report of the defendant's mental suitability to stand trial. Pieter Menten left the court to seek professional help in one last bid to beat the verdict.

This final twist was indeed the last throw of the dice as the court, the Psychiatrists and 'uncle tom cobley' were not fooled and the court reconvened in the spring of 1980, thirty-nine years after the villagers of Podhorodze had been shot into the pit.   Days of examination and cross-examination passed with the same allegations by the accused. One final twist which shocked the court to its foundations was the appearance as a witness of his brother, Dirk Menten. Dirk had been devastated that he had been brought into his brother's murderous activities in 1941. Entering the court not looking left or right, Dirk entered the witness box. He had not seen or corresponded with his brother for twenty years:

'Unfortunately, I am Pieter's brother. I have known about what happened in Podhorodze for quite a long time... Pieter signed the contracts with the Pistiners. The lawsuits concerned themselves with wood from maple trees. There was a lot of chicanery in the contract. But Pieter, an incomprehensible human being, does not know the concept of 'mine' and 'yours'—only 'mine'. We always felt that because of his greed, he was not accountable for his actions. For my own security, we drew up a statement, my wife and I, and we promised my mother (before she died) that we would only use the statement if our personal honour or good name were ever threatened by him. His accusations have given me good reason to use it now.'

Dirk Menten produced a document from his briefcase dated 1953, signed and notarized. It would appear that in the winter of 1943, Pieter had visited Dirk in Paris.

'He was worried about how the war was going to end. It was there that he told us how he had been at the execution in 1941. He said that Jews had dug their own grave, and he had warned two people, Schiff and Altmann. It was the first time he told us of this.'[341]

Now eighty-one years old, Menten stood silent with head bowed; he was finished and had lost all his composure with little fight left.

In 1980 Menten was sentenced to 10 years in prison and was fined 100,000 guilders for war crimes, including being accessory to the murder of Jewish villagers in 1941, Poland.

Upon his release he believed he would settle in his County Waterford mansion in Ireland, only to find out Garret Fitzgerald, the Taoiseach at the time, had barred him from the country.

Figure 34: Pieter Menten c. 1985

The Barbarossa campaign had sparked Menten's deep commitment to something altogether darker than legalised art-robbery and treachery to his adopted country—namely, to Hitler's 'Final Solution'.

Chapter 11

The Murder of Lt Americo S. Galle: Dr Schoengarth's Final Contribution[342]

Figure 35b: Dr Schoengarth

'When these things are known, world opinion will not allow the criminals to escape just punishment for their crimes. The facts are being put on record so that in due time the world may pronounce its judgment. With victory will come retribution!'

Anthony Eden Foreign Office, October 8, 1941

Preparations for Defeat

ALTHOUGH DR SCHOENGARTH became enmeshed in a serious war with his superiors—especially with his Higher SS-and Police Fuehrer Friederich Wilhelm Krueger (not to be confused with Hans Krueger), and with the 'Reichsfuehrer' SS Himmler, who personally took care of Dr Schoengarth's degradation and transfer to Greece and finally to Holland where he was the Commander of the Sipo-SD, and deputy to General Rauter.

Dr Schoengarth's demise had already been sealed when on the 10th August, 1943, RFSS Himmler issued his directive concerning the fate of English and

American captured airman: *'It is not the task of the police to interfere in clashes between German, English, and American fliers who have baled out.'*[343]   This order was transmitted on the same day by SS-Obersturmbannfuehrer Brandt of Himmler's personal staff, to all Senior Executives SS and Police Officers with the following directions:

> 'I am sending you the enclosed order with the request that the Chief of the Regular Police and of the Security Police be informed. They are to make this instruction known to their subordinate officers verbally.'[344]

The whole question of prisoner of war status was taken out of control of the army and placed in the hands of Himmler and his SS by a short directive to all Security Police personnel on 6th March 1944:[345]

War Crimes: Kugel Erlass ('Bullet Decree')

TRANSLATION OF DOCUMENT 1650-PS
Source: Nazi Conspiracy and Aggression, Vol. IV. USGPO, Washington, 1946, pp.158-160

SECRET STATE POLICE—STATE POLICE OFFICE COLOGNE.
Branch Office, Aachen.
To be transmitted in secret—To be handled as a secret government matter: To all State Police Directorates except PRAGUE and BRUNN-Inspectors of the Security Police and of the Security Service.

Subject: Measures to be taken against captured escaped prisoners of war who are officers or not working non-commissioned officers, except British and American prisoners of war.

The Supreme Command of the Army has ordered as follows:

1. Every captured escaped prisoner of war who is an officer or a not working non-commissioned officer, except British and American prisoners of war, is to be turned over to the Chief of the Security Police and of the Security Service under the classification 'Step III' regardless of whether the escape occurred during a transport, whether it was a mass escape or an individual one.

2. Since the transfer of the prisoners of war to the security police and security service may not become officially known to the outside under

any circumstances, other prisoners of war may by no means be informed of the capture. The captured prisoners are to be reported to the Army Information Bureau as 'escaped and not captured'. Their mail is to be handled accordingly. Inquiries of representatives of the Protective Power of the International Red Cross, and of other aid societies will be given the same answer.

3. If escaped British and American prisoners of war who are officers or not working non-commissioned officers, respectively, are captured, they are to be detained at first outside the prisoner of war camps and out of sight of prisoners of war; if Army-owned buildings are unavailable they are to be placed in police custody. In every instance the Corps Area Command will request speedily the Supreme Command of the Army (Chief, Prisoner of War Section) for a decision as to whether they are to be turned over to the Chief of the Security Police and of the Security Service.

In reference to this, I order as follows:

1. The State Police Directorates will accept the captured escaped officer prisoners of war from the prisoner of war camp commandants and will transport them to the Concentration Camp Mauthausen following the procedure previously used, unless the circumstances render a special transport imperative. The prisoners of war are to be put in irons on the transport—not on the station if it is subject to view by the public. The camp commandant at Mauthausen is to be notified that the transfer occurs within the scope of the action 'Kugel' [*translator's note: the literal translation of 'Kugel' is 'bullet'*]. The State Police Directorates will submit semi-yearly reports on these transfers giving merely the figures, the first report being due on 5 July 1944 (sharp). The report is to be made under the reference 'Treatment of Captured Escaped Prisoners of War who are officers within the Scope of the Action "Kugel".' In the case of special events, reports are to be submitted immediately. The State Police Directorates will maintain exact records.

2. For the sake of secrecy, the Supreme Command of the Armed Force has been requested to inform the prisoner of war camps to turn the captured prisoners over to the local State Police Office and not to send them directly to Mauthausen.

3. Captured escaped British and American officers and not working non-commissioned officers are to be 'detained in police custody in a city in which a State Police office is located provided the Army has no suitable quarters'. In view of the existing crowding of police prisons, the State Police officer will accept captured prisoners only if the Army actually does not dispose of any suitable space. The prisoner of war camp commandants are to be contacted in reference to their quarters immediately after the receipt of this order. In the interest of the secrecy of this order, confinement outside of police jails, e. g. in Labour Education Camps is not permissible.

4. If escaped prisoners of war who are officers and not working non-commissioned officers except British and American prisoners of war are captured by police authorities, reasons of practicability render it unnecessary to return the prisoner to the prisoner of war camp commandant once the facts have been clarified adequately. The prisoner of war camp is to be informed of the capture and is to be requested for a transfer under the classification 'Step III'. Captured escaped British and American prisoners of war who are officers and non-commissioned officers are always to be turned over to the Army.

5. The city and county police authorities are not to be informed of this order. Chief of the Security Police and of the Security Service, IV D5d-B NR 61/ 44 GRS.—For the Chief.

(Signed) Mueller. SS General.
Branch Office Aachen.
Aachen 6 March 1944

Overview of War Crimes Violations and Nazi policy

War crimes: namely, violations of the laws or customs of war shall include, but not be limited to, murder, ill-treatment or deportation to slave labour or for any other purpose of civilian population of or in occupied territory, murder or ill-treatment of prisoners of war or persons on the seas, killing of hostages, plunder of public or private property, wanton destruction of cities, towns, or villages, or devastation not justified by military necessity.

Top L – R: Lew Baxter; Americo S. Galle; Dick Edgar; Bill Cox
Front L – R: Dick Sipes; Merle Auerbach; Jenkins; Bill Massy; Herman
Schroeder; Marvin Cooper

Top L: Lt Galle with crew

Far left is Merle Auerbach The centre figure is unknown. Far right is Lt Galle

In the course of the war, many Allied soldiers who had surrendered to the Germans were shot immediately, often as a matter of deliberate, calculated policy. On the 18th October, 1942, the OKW circulated a directive authorised by Hitler, which ordered that all members of Allied 'Commando' units, often when in uniform and whether armed or not, were to be 'slaughtered to the last man' even if they attempted to surrender. It was further provided that if such Allied troops came into the hands of the military authorities after being first captured by the local police or in any other way they should be handed over immediately to the SD. This order was supplemented from time to time, and was effective throughout the remainder of the war. This order was distributed by the SIPO-SD to their regional offices. These escaped officers and NCO's were to be sent to the concentration camp at Mauthausen, to be executed upon arrival, by means of a bullet shot in the neck.

In June 1944, there were a number of conferences attended by the Nazi top order which had been initiated by Goebbels, and endorsed by Hitler. These meetings of the principal leaders of the Nazi Party proposed to legalise the lynching of captured allied bomber crews in the occupied zones. This was not only the basis for the indictment against Dr Schoengarth after the war, but was also the damming evidence that was used at Nurenberg.[346]

Further, it was also about this time that the entire Security Services of the Reich were advised from the centre to prepare false identity papers in the event of the government collapsing under military pressure from the Allies and that poison capsules for personal use be issued should they be arrested and feel the need.[347]

The Mission 21st November 1944:

On 21st November 1944, thirty four aircraft from the 493rd Bomb Group, plus two pathfinder aircraft from the 34th Bomb Group left their bases in Suffolk on a bombing mission to the Synthetic Oil Plant at Merseberg, Germany. Our subject: 2nd Lieutenant Americo S. Galle was co-piloting Aircraft 107, Piloted by Lieutenant Llewelleyn Baxter. See below:

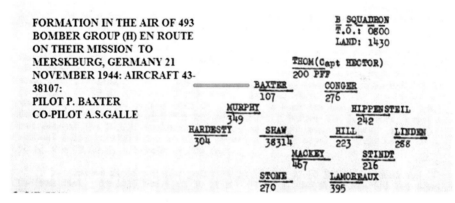

Figure36: Mission 'Merseberg'; Flight Plan Formation over the countryside of Suffolk 21st November 1944

One Aircraft was Lost: Aircraft 43-38107 was damaged by flak while passing over Zwelle and crashed. The aircraft was last seen under control heading west. No open chutes were noted: Report by Major L. Dwyer, Group S-3: The aircraft referred to: B-17G; AAF S/N 43-38107; Group 493; Sqdn 861.

'Aircraft 43-38107 was damaged while passing over Zwelle at about 1100 hours. It slid out of formation about five minutes later and dropped bombs, then made a 180-degree turn under perfect control with number four prop feathered. When aircraft was last seen, it was under control heading West. No chutes were noted.'

The crew of nine bailed out Northeast of Enschede, Holland: the officers escaped from the front escape hatch; the enlisted personnel left the aircraft through the rear door. Eight of the nine were captured and dispatched to interrogation centres. The three officers: Baxter, Edgar and Cox were transferred to Stalag-Luft 1. Enlisted men were sent elsewhere. All were well treated and subsequently released when war ended. They had flown 27 missions.

1. Pilot: Lieutenant Llewellyn Hunter. Baxter, service number 0-818812, born Jan 20, 1924

2. Co Pilot, 2nd, Lieutenant Americo S. Galle, service number 0-886490. Next of kin listed as his mother Mrs Margaret Galle of 12, Montague Street, Yonkers, NY

3. 2nd Lieutenant Richard Edgar, Navigator, service number 0-886467, born June 1, 1919

4. 2nd Lieutenant William Biggs. Cox, service number 0-886637, born June 28, 1920

5. Sergeant Richard L. Sipes, service number 6896232

6. Sergeant William Carrington Massey, service number 20937609

7. Sergeant William Brake Jenkins, service number 6552038 born December 12. 1913.

8. Sergeant Merle Auerbach, service number 36730072 born Apr 2, 1925.

9. Sergeant Herman Adam Schroeder Jr, service number 37623121, born Jan 21, 1924

On their release and de-briefed as to the whereabouts and subsequent fate of 2nd Lieutenant Galle, the following responses were recorded in the individual casualty questionnaire:

a. 'While being interrogated I heard a German guard say that one man was killed or shot. The German officer then turned to me and said that I had a brave pilot. I knew that Lt Baxter was alive so I presumed that he was speaking about Lt. Galle.'

b. 'Lt. Galle was the only crew member who carried a firearm, a .45 calibre sidearm and may have used it to offer resistance.'

c. 'The enlisted men left the ship (B17) via the rear door at about 2,000 ft. Cox, Edgar Galle and myself left via the front escape hatch at about 500 ft.'

d. 'I saw all members of the crew in good condition at one time or another after being captured, with the exception of the Co-pilot.'

e. 'Lt. Galle was a devout Catholic and a Latin scholar and maybe he sought help from the church and community.'

f. 'He was in good spirits and laughed when I told him I would see him in London.'

g. 'My personal opinion is that he was shot during the descent as the gun-fire was directed to the front of the ship.'

h. 'German interrogators at Frankfort had said that German Intelligence had failed to find him.'

The Facts on that Day: 21st November, 1944.

Figure 37: SD Headquarters: Villa Hoge Boekel at Enschede, Holland 1944

The scene of the events in question was the Villa Hoge Boekel at Enschede, Holland, which was occupied from September 1944 to April 1945 by a detachment of the Sicherheitsdienst, that is to say the German Security Service, under the immediate command of SS-Obersturmfuehrer Beeck. This detachment was primarily concerned with economic matters, requisitioning agricultural supplies. In addition to the members of the detachment there were some twelve Dutch political prisoners employed there. There was also a Dutch forester who had worked at the Villa since before the war. There were also a few Germans there who described themselves as Kommand-diensten (voluntary members of the SS). (Several of these Kommand-diensten and Dutch politicals were later called to give evidence at the subsequent trial of the seven accused.)

Brigadier and Major General of the Police Dr Schoengarth was in command of the whole German Security Services in Holland. On the night of the 20th/21st

November he had stayed at the Villa, where a party took place following a conference. The following morning at about 12.30 hours, some airmen were seen to bale out of an Allied bomber. One airman dropped into the Villa grounds. The airman was apparently unhurt and was taken into the Villa where he was kept under guard while arrangements were made by Brigadier Schoengarth for a locally based Einsatzgruppe commando (execution squad) to attend the Villa and deal with the airman. (We must remind ourselves that Dr Schoengarth was well versed in organising executions as he had supervised the executions of the Lvov Professors and had trained his own zbV personnel in the art of execution.)

The principal SS/SD officers engaged at the Villa to deal with the airman were as follows:

1. Dr Schoengarth – Brigadierfuehrer.
2. Beeck – SS Obersturmfuehrer officer in charge at the Villa.
3. Knop – Kriminal Kommissar, Einsatzgruppe commando
4. Hadler, Wilhelm – Kriminal Sekretaer, Einsatzgruppe
5. Gernoth Herbert Fritz Willi – Kriminal Sekretaer, Einsatzgruppe.
6. Lebing Erich – SS Scharfuehrer, Villa Security Police.
7. Boehm Fritz. SS Scharfuehrer, Villa Security Police.

The Crime Unravels

After the war several witnesses came forward and volunteered statements to the War Crimes Commission. Their observations were the substance of charges initiated against Dr Schoengarth and his SD men. These edited accounts by the author set the scene to events on that day:

Prosecution Witnesses:

Figure 38: Entrance to Sipo-SD Headquarters Villa Hoge Boekel

Local forester from Enschede Sybrand Lefers (author's brackets):[348]

'On 21st November 1944, two airmen baled out from a three-engine aeroplane (number four propeller was feathered) which had colour circles on the side. The colours were red and blue. One airman landed about 150 metres from the Villa Hoge Boekel. The other airman landed somewhere in the neighbourhood of the airfield at Twente. I did not go to his assistance because the Villa was occupied by Germans. This occurred between 1200 hrs and 1230 hrs.

At about 1530 hours I was standing about 300 metres from the house when I heard a single shot from a small bore weapon coming from the direction of the grave of the unknown airman. I have been told that Oberscharfuehrer Beeck wore felt-lined airman's boots after the 21st November, 1944, and that a tunic, coloured blue-grey, and a brown overall suit were seen in a cart used by the troops occupying the Villa.'

Political prisoner Jacobus Rippers:[349]

'At about midday I heard a bomber come over very low and people shouting, 'They've baled out!' I later saw an Allied airman brought to the

Villa by SS-Obersturmfuehrer Blankenagel. The airman was in uniform and wore a cap and large Jack-boots. At the time the Brigadierfuehrer (Schoengarth) was present at the Villa. Sometime later I saw the airman being taken to the cellar where he was guarded by two SS men.

Later in the afternoon I went to the cellar where I saw the airman sitting on a bag wearing white pants, without shoes and barefooted. I did not see any civilian clothes. Some minutes afterwards I heard a shot. I was told that the airman had been taken away in a car.'

Workman Heinrich Albert de Haar: [350]

'When the airman was in the cellar, four soldiers of the Wehrmacht came to the Villa and demanded that the airman be handed over to them. SS-Rottenfuehrer Kampf denied that there was any airman and the soldiers went away. When I first saw the airman he was wearing grey-green trousers of a rough material, the ends if which were tucked into his dark coloured boots. On the left leg of the trousers was roughly painted in white the following marks:

B 83 / B

At about 3.30 p.m. I saw the airman coming from the house and enter an open car. His hands were bound behind his back. He had no shoes, very light socks, dark grey civilian trousers and a light coloured shirt. The following persons accompanied the airman into the car: I did not recognise the driver, Scharfuehrer Liebing, SS-Hauptsturmfuehrer-Kommissar Knop who had an automatic rifle on his right shoulder, and Scharfuehrer Boehm. Two minutes later I heard a shot from the direction of the grave.

Some days later I saw in a room at the Villa a parachute and a pair of trousers which had the same markings as described earlier. I also saw boots similar to those that the airman wore. These boots were later used by the men in bad weather. I saw Beeck wearing felt slippers which I believe airmen wear inside their boots. The boot-maker named Fokkens removed electrical heating elements from these slippers. Also present that day was a Brigadierfuehrer whose name I do not know. He was there when the airman was captured but left before the airman was killed.'

Workman Hugo Reul:[351]

In November 1944, during an air attack, an Allied plane was shot down. One member of the crew was brought to the office where I was working at the time. He came for a short spell into the storeroom. There, I myself brought him dinner which he did not accept. I was then relieved after dinner, and when I came downstairs from my room, the prisoner was in the corridor. He had received a civilian suit from SS-Sturmscharfuehrer Blankenhagel. He did not wear shoes. Later I was told by SS Oberschafuehrer Boehm that the prisoner was taken away for execution. We showed our disapproval by stating between ourselves that it would not be just to treat a prisoner of war in that way.

Requisitioned Civilian Clothing

Shortly after the war, when the War Crimes Investigators searched the Villa a number of civilian suits were found which, it was established, had been seized by the SS from the local neighbourhood. The significance of this, I would suggest, is that it was a common occurrence that when aircrews baled out over the occupied area many were murdered by the SD, but before execution the individual was stripped of his uniform and dressed in civilian clothing. This no doubt, was to conceal the identity of the victim should their remains be recovered at a later date. It didn't go unnoticed by the Nazis that the war was not quite going according to plan.

Post-War Exhumation: September 1946.

Major William M. Davidson, R.A.M.C, a medical Practitioner attached as Pathologist to the War Crimes Investigation unit, was present at the exhumation of one grave found in a wood behind the Villa Hoge Boekel. Major Davidson was also present at further exhumations when three further graves were found. The graves were numbered 1—4. From all four graves the contents were examined and photographed with forensic samples taken from the bodies in situ.[352]

Major Davidson particularly examined grave number four which had been identified as the grave where the Allied airman had been interned. He came to the following conclusions:

Grave Number Four: Pathology Report.

1. No headgear was found in this grave.

2. The hair was of medium brown colour and was straight. The composition was more advanced about the face and neck, with particular separation of the vertebrae. A ragged exit wound was found in the region of the inner end of the right supra-orbital ridge, and the bullet was traced through the dorsum seller and the supro-internal wall of the right orbit. The bullet appeared, by the line of the track and the more advanced state of decomposition at the back of the neck, to have entered the skull from slightly to the left of the middle line, by passing between the atlas and the base of the skull, or to the edge of the foramen magna.

3. The dental state was as follows: upper right, 87654321/ 8 metal filling in crown, 7 and 6 large metal fillings in the crown; upper left, /12345678 6 had a metal filling in the crown, 7 had two small metal filling in the crown and 8 had metal fillings in the crown, and two on the outer side, 7 had a metal filling in the crown, 8 had small metal filling in the crown. Lower right 87654321/, 8 had metal fillings in the crown, 6 had metal fillings in the crown and outer side; lower left /12345678, 6 had a large metal filling in the crown and back, 7 had a metal filling in the crown and 8 had a small metal filling in the crown. The cervical vertebrae were intact, but were separating from decomposition.

4. There was not any sign of injury to the trunk or limbs, and no tattoo marks could be found.

5. **IDENTIFICATION:** No identity discs or documents were found. The teeth were in excellent condition. The body was of a slim build and measured 165 cms in length, making the height in life 5' 5'. The body was dressed in a blue waistcoat with four outer pockets—the upper one on the right side, which had a flap, contained two pieces of good quality thin string. There were no markings on the waistcoat apart from the buttons being marked 'Hengelo' A long sleeved, thin woollen under-vest without markings and long woollen underpants buttoned at the top and having a lace behind were marked 'Size 32 S—Wool NORWICH KNITTING COY....Phila. Q.M. Depot' and stamped G1938 and, on the front, L214 L80 (identified as USAF issued clothing by the author), black thin cloth trousers with pleated tops and turn-up foots had, in the

right hand pocket, one .22 bullet and three air-gun slugs as well as some pieces of corn. White or grey woollen socks, the right one being worn inside out—no shoes were found. (Note: It was the practice that before execution to re-dress the victim with spare clothing held at the base.)

6.   No incongruous tissues were found in the grave.

Summary

A young man of slim build, dressed in civilian clothes, some allied origin (probably American) with a bullet wound through the head. Teeth were in good repair.

It is my opinion—

1.   That the bodies found in graves one, two and three had been hanged, while that in grave four had been shot through the head from the back of the neck.
2.   That from the post mortem findings, despite the identification, the body in grave four may be that of the airman.

In the wood north of Villa Hoge Boekel four graves were found, containing four male bodies. The body found in grave **four** was the most decomposed and that in grave **one** the least decomposed. The body in grave **one** appeared to be the youngest and that in grave **four** only slightly older. All were in civilian clothes with, in the cases of bodies in graves **two (three)** and **four**, garments of British or American origin. The body in grave **one** was of a short stocky build, that in grave three of a large heavy build while the other two were slim. The bodies in graves **two** and **three** had elaborate dental repair work, that in grave **one** had neglected teeth and that in grave **four** had teeth in excellent condition. The body in grave **four** had been shot through the head.

General Conclusions:

It is my opinion:

1.   That the bodies found in graves **one**, **two** and **three** had been hanged (see the statement of Wilhelm Hadler above), while that in grave **four** had been shot through the head from the back of the neck, and

2. That from the post-mortem findings, despite the identification, the body in grave **four** may be that of the airman, as I do not consider it likely that an airman would have been permitted to go on operational duties with completely neglected teeth

Signed: Major William M. Davidson, Major, R.A.M.C War Crimes Investigation Unit, British Army of the Rhine.

The Law Takes its Course

After the interrogation of six former SS suspects by Harold Johnston, formerly Lieutenant-Colonel, R.A., recommended the following: This appears to be a clear case of murder of a prisoner of war. It is considered that the evidence contained in the statements will be sufficient to convict all the accused.[353]

Number and description of the crime alleged: **No. 1 - Murder**

The relevant provisions under which all the defendants were being investigated was as follows: Breaches of the Laws and Usages of War and in particular Article 2 of the Geneva Convention 1929 relating to the treatment of prisoners of war.

All the defendants named:

1. **Karl Eberhard Schoengarth** - Doctor at Laws and Brigadierfuehrer. In custody
2. **Frederick Beeck** – SS Obersturmfuehrer. Not in custody
3. **Erwin Knop** – Kriminal Kommissar. In custody
4. **Wilhelm Hadler** – Kriminal Sekretaer. In custody
5. **Herbert Fritz Willi Gernoth** – Kriminal Sekretaer. In custody
6. **Erich Lebing** – SS Scharfuehrer. In custody
7. **Fritz Boehm** – SS Scharfuehrer. In custody.

Charge Against all Seven:

Murder: on the 21st November, 1944, of an unknown member of the crew of an Allied aircraft. The deceased landed from an aircraft by parachute and was immediately apprehended and made a prisoner of war by the first named accused. After some hours in custody a grave was dug, on the orders of the second named accused, and shortly after its completion the deceased was ordered to get into a vehicle accompanied by the third, sixth and seventh named accused and was driven to the location of the grave where he was shot by the fifth named accused in the presence of the third, fourth, fifth, sixth and seventh named accused.

A wealth of detail is supplied by the statements made by the various accused when interrogated, and by the evidence at their trial:

Karl Eberhard Schoengarth, aged 42 years, Doctor of Laws and Brigadierfuehrer in the Security Police (Gestapo) which he commanded in Holland. He remembered being at the Villa about that date, when an Allied plane flew low, but has no recollection of an airman baling out in the grounds, nor was such incident reported to him. He blamed the other defendants for concocting their defence by blaming him.

The 'Einsatzgruppenkommado Knop' was an execution squad consisting of the accused: Knop, Hadler, and Gernoth, brought in from outside by Brigadier Schoengarth to deal with the airman's execution. At the Villa they liaised with the office in charge, SS Obersturmfuehrer Beeck, to carry out Schoengarth's order.

Continued cross examination of Dr Karl Eberhard Schoengarth: on the fourth day of the trial, Monday 11th February, 1946. Defence Counsel for the other accused directs his questions to the defendant:

After preliminary opening questions of identity the line of questioning was a follows:[354]

Q. What were your duties while in Holland?
A. I was Commander of the Sichereitspolizei. My task was to command the Sichereitspolizei, to carry out the central power of command, to keep open the communications with higher SS commanders and to the duty officer of the Reich Kommissar and to the commander of the Wehrmacht and also with other commanders of the Wehrmacht

Q. Did you have many men under you?
A. Yes.

Q. Did you often go to the Villa Hoge Boekel?
A. Until the end of the war I have been there about five or six times.

Q. Do you know what happened when you went there on the 21st November?
A. I cannot remember the 21st November, I cannot remember the date, but I was present at the meeting in the autumn when a plane with a loud noise of its engines came in the direction of the house.

Q. For what purpose had you gone there the night before?
A. I had a conversation about duties.

Q. Where were you when you heard the aeroplane?
A. In a room inside the Villa.

Q. What did you do when you heard the plane?
A. I was having a conversation with Standartenfuehrer Albart.

Q. What was the conversation about?
A. About the evacuation of the population who were still on the right side of the Maas to the north and to the east of Holland. Against these measures I had been opposed before. This part of the country had already been taken away from my command and put in the hands of Albart, and the evacuation would take place into the region of the Rhine.

Q Did you mention in the discussion about the treatment of prisoners of war who had been captured?
A. No, we had no reason to speak about, that.

Q. What happened after your conversation?
A. The conversation was over and Albart wanted to go away, and then we heard the plane.

Q. Did you notice anything about the plane?
A. No, I only heard a very loud noise of engines, and I thought they were going to dive-bomb the house.

Q. Did you notice anything else?
A. Then I went outside.

Q. What did you do then?
A. I walked to the front of the house with Albart and I saw a plane whose nationality I could not discern at a distance of about 400 metres. I saw it disappear above the woods, and I saw several white parcels coming down, and I

thought they would be airman who baled out. I did not see the parachute unfold because at the same moment everything was hidden from my eyes by the wood.

Q What did you do then?
A. Then I entered the house again.

Q And then?
A. After the conversation I wanted to drive away, I wanted to fix up some technical difficulties about this evacuation and I wanted to speak about this to the chief of my staff, and I went back to finish my second breakfast which had been served to me.

Q. Was anybody with you while you were having your meal?
A. Yes, my adjutant was also with me; and when I have no guests also present at my meals.

Q What was the name of your driver at that time?
A. My driver is Heinz Grotjahn.

Q He was your driver at the Villa on that day?
A. Yes, as far as I can remember he was my driver that day because shortly afterwards he left for Bremen; I think it was in the beginning of December.

Q. Did you see any captured airmen?
A. No, I saw nobody.

Q. Did you give any orders about any prisoner of war?
A. No, I never gave an order about a prisoner of war.

Further cross-examination of Dr Schoengarth:

Q. You have heard your two officers, Knop and Beecks and the four NCOs describing their various parts in the murder of a prisoner of war on the 21st November?
A. Yes.

Q And you are agreed that that day, the 21st November, when you and Dr Alban had been in conference at the Villa, was the day that the parachutist landed?
A. I do not quite know that it was the 21st November, but it was on the day when I had the conference with Dr Albert when the plane appeared.

Q. Was the discipline in the SS strict?
A. Yes.

Q. Can you imagine an SS detachment murdering a prisoner within half an hour of their Major-General's departure without his orders?
A. As I have heard of this here I must assume this was so. I had been away for several hours already.

Q What was your pre-war occupation?
A. I was in command of a detachment of the State Police.

Q Are you a Doctor of Laws?
A. Yes, I am of the legal profession.

Q Were you at the University of Leipzig?
A. Yes.

Q Was Leipzig the seat of the German Supreme: Court?
A. Yes.

Q Did you make any studies of international law?
A. I know in general those laws.

Q Do you agree that during a war no one power can repudiate conventions such as the Hague Convention to which all powers were parties before the war?
A. Yes, I agree.

Q Do you agree that if any officer or soldier was ordered by his superior to murder a prisoner of war and did so, the subordinate would himself be guilty as an accomplice of his superior who ordered that breach of international law?
A. Yes.

Q Did you ever hear of an order issued during the latter part of the war from the highest authority in Berlin to the effect that! *Terrorfliegell* were not to be protected from the anger of the population?
A. I have heard for the first time of this order during my captivity. During my time of service, until the capitulation I have never received such an order, either verbally or written and I have never at any time to any of my commands given such an order.

Q What newspapers did you read during the war?

A. I arrived in Holland in June, 1944. Up to the time of the strike of the railways I read the German newspaper of Holland and other papers which I got there from the line.

Q Where were you in May 1944?
A. I was in Greece; I was fetched back at the end of May.

Q Did you know that that order was quoted in all the Berlin papers in an article by Dr Gobbels in May 1944?
A. No.

Q If such an order had reached you, what would you yourself have done about it in your commands?
A. May I ask from which source this order is supposed to originate?

Q If you received an order from Hitler or from Himmler that you were to disregard the rights of prisoners of war, would you, as a Doctor of Laws, have felt bound to obey that or not?
A. I would have had to carry out this order, because an order of the Reichbelung (?) has to be carried out even if it cancels any existing laws.

Q So your fellow Accused were correct when they told us that the SS and the Sichereitspolizei stood outside the law?
A. No, they are just the same subject to the same ordinary criminal law as any other German.

Q How is it that they all believe that if they had handed over this captured airman to the Luftwaffe or the Wehrmacht they would have been summoned before an SS court for disobeying your orders?
A. This is an assumption of the Accused, which is wrong. There is no special SS police court; SS police courts are equivalent to the normal courts. The SS police court convicts on the same basis as any ordinary court, according to the law. It is correct, however, that these sentences are much severer than those of any normal court

Q Would the SS then be bound by the regulations made during the war by Marshall Keitel of the Wehrmacht regarding the proper manner of carrying out executions?
A. No, we have received all our orders via the Chief Security Office.

Q You said in answer to your Defending Officer that you had certain responsibilities to the Wehrmacht as well as to the Police in Holland?
A. I did not have responsibilities, merely liaison between all parts of the Wehrmacht.

Q Will you as a lawyer agree with me that under German military law a sentence of death should only be executed by a firing party commanded by a staff officer, with another officer 'representing the tribunal present, to read out the sentence, a priest of the condemned man's religion and a medical officer?'
A. The German regulations were not so comprehensive.

Q I put it to you that that regulation was signed by Field Marshall Keitel in October 1939.
A. I do not know this regulation.

Q Tell us the SS regulations for carrying out executions?
A. I can quote the regulations of the police.

Q Did they apply to the SS?
A. I do not know whether they applied to the Waffen SS, I assume so.

Q I am not referring to the Waffen SS, I am referring to the SS of the Sicheitsdienst (SD) and the Sichereitspolizei?
A. Yes, they were applicable.

Q Tell us what those regulations were.
A. The firing squad was supplied by the normal police force; an officer was in charge; a medical officer had to be present; for every man to be executed there had to be at least three rifles; the aim was to be taken at the head and the chest of the man; the presence of a priest was not necessary during the war because of the lack of manpower; in the ordinary police force executions have been carried out by the SS police.

Q Where did they learn this technique of shooting a man in the back of the neck?
A. There were no orders that executions were to be carried out in this manner. If these cases have occurred I know that this has come from the east.

Q Do you remember saying when you were interrogated on the 24th January: 'I never had any complaints about the staff of the Villa Hoge Boekel or Enschede Einsatzcommando'?
A. Yes.

Q You have heard the things that your staff have been saying about you in this Court?
A. Yes.

Q You heard, for instance, Blankenagel saying: 'I myself heard Schoengrath ordering Knop to shoot the airmen?'
A. I heard that.

Q And you heard Boehm say that he himself was told by Reul that you captured the airman?
A. Yes.

Q And you heard Knop, say: 'I received my orders from Schoengrath'?
A. Yes.

Q And you heard Beeck say: 'Schoengrath told me personally that Dr Albart had suggested airmen were treated as terrorists in the Reich', and you had decided to do the same at the Villa Hoge Boekel?
A. No.

Q Look at your former and once loyal staff and tell one why they should say this about you, their commander whom they once trusted.
A. I do not know why. I can only think that because I was there when the plane came down they wanted to put the blame on me.

Q To put the blame for the murder on you?
A. Yes, one of these men has taken this decision to put the blame on me.

Q Did you hear what Boehm and Lebing told us on Saturday about the shooting?
A. This is the first time I have heard about it.

The Legal Member of the court and who acted as 'referee' for and behalf of the accused allowed further questioning to Dr Schoengarth:

Q. During your period in Holland, how many executions in all did you have to order or sanction?
A. At the time of that interrogation I thought it would be about 150 to 200 cases, but they were all executions after proper sentences; they were only civilians who were sentenced to death on account of their disturbing order; and that was an order from the Reichkomnissar.

Q Am I right that those sentences had to be confirmed by your superior, Obergruppenfuehrer Rauter?

A. At the end of the war the Polizeigericht were summary courts, and these sentences were afterwards examined by a lawyer on my staff, and this lawyer had the power of a judge. After that they were given to the higher SS Polizeifuehrer Rauter. This only concerns the cases in which the evidence was clear. If there were cases in which the evidence took a long time to be proved, then the cases were handed over to the normal courts.

Q After the attempt on Rauter's life, whose duty was it to confirm sentences?

A. I was his deputy, but after I took on my duties we did not have any other cases, after we had a meeting with the leaders of the Resistance Movement that they would stop their terrorist activities.

Q Do you think it is possible that just as one man was shot, as you say, without your knowledge at the Villa Hoge Boekel, and six without your knowledge at Gorssel, 150 hostages could be shot without your knowledge by people such as the Accused, similar Commandos, after Rauter was shot?

A. After the attack on Rauter we did not shoot hostages, but we shot people who were already condemned to death.

Q Was that the 100 shot on the road between Apeldoorn and Arnhem and in the town of Schevengen?

A. About those at Schevengen I do not know, but the 100 on the road from Apeldoorn to Arnhem were shot on account of the attempt on Rauter's life; but they were not hostages but people who had already been condemned to death, and they were condemned to be shot at that place.

Final remarks to Dr Schoengarth by defence counsel for the other accused:

Q. I put it to you that the real truth of what happened on the 21st November is this: a British or American airman landed in the grounds of the Villa and was captured by your men. You yourself decided that he was to be shot. You yourself ordered Knop to have him shot. You then went away in your car leaving your men to take the responsibility, and now that they stand in peril you, their commander, are trying to save your life at their expense.

A. No.

The other accused:

Friederich Beeck, aged 60 years, Kriminal Sekretser (Sicherheitspolizei) and Commander of Villa Hoge Boekel, chose the burial site and gave orders for the grave to be dug, and waited for the report that all was ready, before the airman was brought out of the Villa. He superintended the execution from start to finish at a discreet distance.

Erwin Knop, aged 40 years, a Commissar in the Security Police (Sicherheitspolizei), was in charge of the Detachment at Enschede. Knop stated under cross-examination that he made the arrangements for the execution and supervised it, but he did so under the orders of Schoengarth and with the assistance of Beeck, who was the senior police officer at the Villa. Knop agreed that he spoke to the airman in English when he was escorting the handcuffed airman to the grave site: ' *"I said to the airman, I have orders by the General to shoot you. I can do nothing for you, but would you be so kind and give me your name and home address."* The airman was very downhearted.'

When asked by defence counsel at the trial if the execution team had refused to carry out the Brigadierfuehrer's order, Knop replied: '*We could say Yes or No to this question, but because we belonged and were under the jurisdiction of the SS Polizei we did not act under normal laws. If we had refused to obey this order we would, after a very short trial, be sentenced to death. The SS Polizeigericht have their own procedures and courts.*'

(In addition to the airman's body found in a grave, three other bodies of SS men were also found in graves nearby having been hanged.)

Figure 39: The track where Lt. Galle was driven to the execution site

Wilhelm Hadler, aged 47 years, Kriminal Sekretser and SS Untersturmfuehrer and member of the Einsatzcommando. He was told by Knop that the airman was a 'terror-airman' *('Knop gae dem Gernoth den Befehl; Das ist ein Terrorflieger, der ist zir erschiessen')* and was to be shot, and we (Knop, Beeck, Gernoth, and Hadler) were to carry it out. After searching for a suitable spot in the woods Hadler and Gernoth dug a shallow grave. When the rest of the team arrived with the airman Hadler and Gernoth escorted the airman from the car towards the grave. Gernoth then dropped back behind the airman and then shot him in the back of the neck. Hadler agreed that he was present when an SS man called Bell was hanged and brought to the wood to be buried. Hadler also confirmed that it was Dr Schoengarth who had ordered Bell's hanging.

Herbert Fritz Willi Gernoth, Kriminal Sekretser (Sicherheitspolizei), SS Unterschafuehrer aged 39 years. Part of the Einsatzgruppencommando (execution squad). Gernoth admitted that he carried out the 'execution' under the orders of Knop: *'After a conversation with Knop, with Hadler, we escorted the airman in the direction of the grave. I did not know whether the man was aware that he was about to be shot. I came to the conclusion that I should do it in such a way that he would not be aware of what was going to happen to him. I stayed back for two or three paces, and without warning I shot him.'* In cross examination Gernoth was asked what would have happened if he had not shot the airman and replied: *'I myself would have been shot or hanged. Two of my comrades were already lying buried nearby.'* When asked by defence counsel: *'What was the German for shot in the nape of the neck or the base of the skull?'*, he replied: *'Genickschuss—the recognised method of the Security Services for executing people.'*

Erich Liebing, SS Scharfuehrer aged 56 years, was on duty at the Villa Hooge Boekal under the orders of SS Obersturmfuehrer Beeck. Liebing went with Beeck to the woods where he witnessed Hadler and Gernoth digging a grave. He was told by Beeck to keep watch and inform him when the grave had been completed, which he did as ordered.

Fritz Boehm, aged 28 years, SS Unterscharfuehrer, Waffen SS, attached to the Polizei. Boehm was told by his commanding officer, Beeck, that he had received orders to shoot the airman who was under guard in the cellar and to assist the others in preparation of the execution.

The Allied Airman Trial and Sentence: Military Court at Burgsteinfurt 11th February 1946: All the accused were found guilty:

Karl Eberhard Schoengarth was sentenced to death but claimed total denial of complicity. Schoengarth had taken refuge in The Hague and transferred to Germany for his trial before he was returned to Holland for interrogation as to his activities there. Other SD/SS personnel arrested and tried by the British Military Court were:

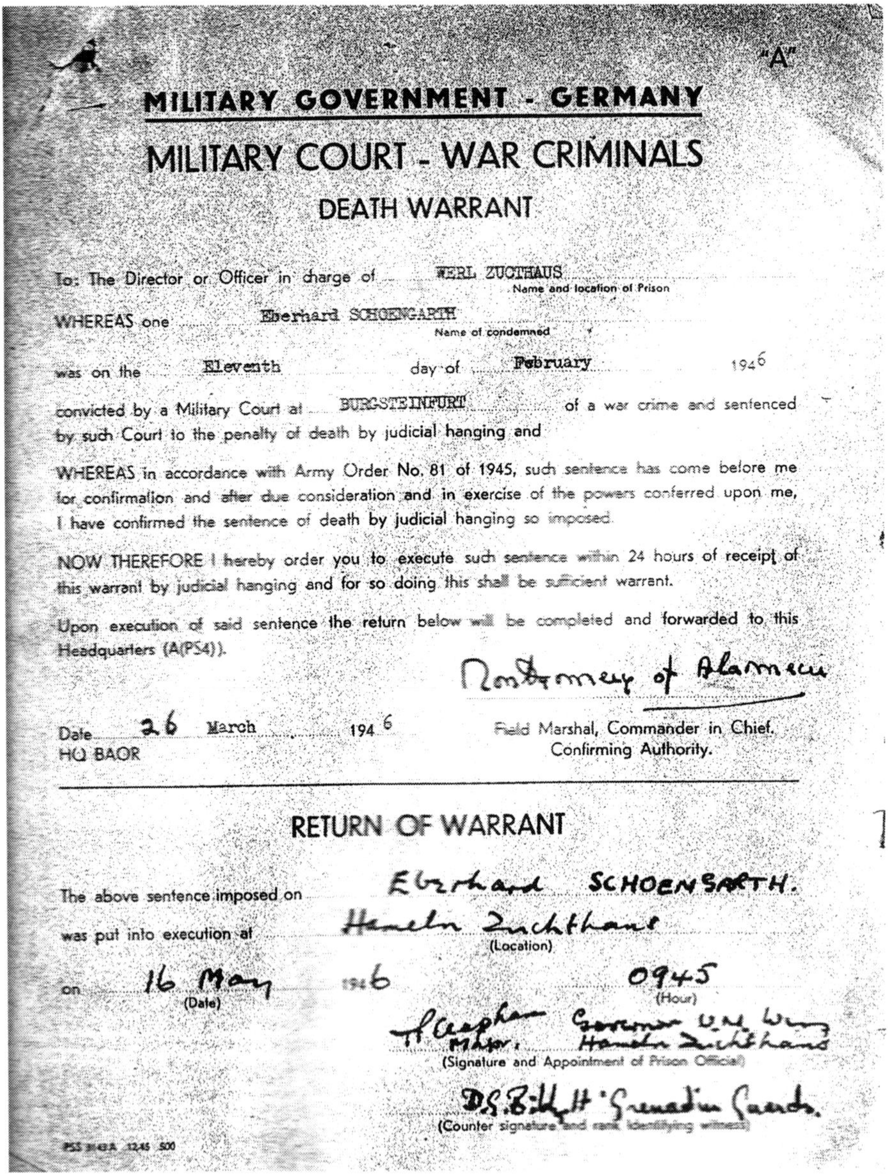

"A"

MILITARY GOVERNMENT - GERMANY

MILITARY COURT - WAR CRIMINALS

DEATH WARRANT

To: The Director or Officer in charge of WERL ZUCTHAUS
Name and location of Prison

WHEREAS one Eberhard SCHOENGARTH
Name of condemned

was on the Eleventh day of February 1946

convicted by a Military Court at BURGSTEINFURT of a war crime and sentenced by such Court to the penalty of death by judicial hanging and

WHEREAS in accordance with Army Order No. 81 of 1945, such sentence has come before me for confirmation and after due consideration and in exercise of the powers conferred upon me, I have confirmed the sentence of death by judicial hanging so imposed.

NOW THEREFORE I hereby order you to execute such sentence within 24 hours of receipt of this warrant by judicial hanging and for so doing this shall be sufficient warrant.

Upon execution of said sentence the return below will be completed and forwarded to this Headquarters (A(PS4)).

Montgomery of Alamein

Date 26 March 1946
HQ BAOR

Field Marshal, Commander in Chief.
Confirming Authority.

RETURN OF WARRANT

The above sentence imposed on Eberhard SCHOENGARTH.

was put into execution at Hameln Zuchthaus
(Location)

on 16 May 1946 0945
(Date) (Hour)

Major. Governor ... Hameln Zuchthaus
(Signature and Appointment of Prison Official)

Grenadier Guards.
(Counter signature and rank identifying witness)

PSS 3143A 12/45 500

Figure 40*:* **Death Warrant signed by Montgomery of Allemane against Karl Eberhard Schoengarth.**

Frederick Beeck (death), claimed superior orders.
Erwin Knop (death), Claimed superior orders.

Wilhelm Hadler (death) claimed superior orders carried out in the presence of the superior.

Herbert Fritz Wille Gernoth (death) claimed superior orders disobedience would have been fatal.

Erich Liebing (15 yrs imp.), claimed he did not know that the victim was a POW until too late.

    Fritz Boehm (10 yrs imp), claimed ignorance and disgust at the shooting. I protested to the uttermost of my power.

Pieter Menten Resurfaces

At about this time Pieter Menten surfaced as he now resided in Holland and had been in regular contact with Dr Schoengarth.[355]

In a letter to his wife written by Schoengarth before his execution, there was a request that Pieter Menten be informed and reminded that he (Schoengarth) had done him many favours in the past. There was a request from Schoengarth that Menten now repay this debt by looking to the welfare of Mrs Schoengarth and his 5-year old-daughter Ermuth.[356]

The Army investigators were anxious to identify the subject Pieter Menten, as to his possible implication in war crimes. Enquiries were made with the result that he was traced and identified as a man of Dutch nationality, engaged in art dealing and residing in Aardenhout, Holland. It was established that Menten had previously been arrested for 'collaboration' and sentenced to 8 months imprisonment (the time in custody) and then released. There were no other charges pending. The report also confirmed that Pieter Menten had previously resided in Eastern Poland where he had a large forest estate, and that he had resided in Krakow where he had become friendly with Dr Schoengarth. This purported personal friendship continued during Schoengarth's service in Holland. Otherwise there was nothing to report.[357] However, shortly after liberation, Dutch investigators acted on other information and arrested Menten. When they searched his house the investigators found incrimination evidence of collaboration with the Nazis, together with a photograph showing Menten in the uniform of an SS-Unterscharfuehrer. This was enough to detain him in custody. Now the investigators were anxious to interview Dr Schoengarth.

After sentence, Schoengarth was returned to Holland to assist with other enquiries that were gathering pace at that time, particularly in respect of Pieter Menten who was also languishing in jail.

A Dutch war crimes investigator interviewed Schoengarth in the Dutch prison where he produced a photograph of Pieter Menten in SD uniform and asked him if he recognized the subject of the photograph. Schoengarth, without hesitation, identified Pieter Menten: 'That is Pieter Menten—how is he?'

Schoengarth confirmed that Menten had been a *Trehaunder* (caretaking Jewish properties) in Krakow and had been part of his zbV unit as an art consultant and interpreter. He further confirmed that he had associated with him in 1944 when they were both in Holland and had often discussed 'old times'.

Then, as he was about to leave the cell, Inspector van Izendorn asked Schoengarth to sign the back of the photograph of Menten and the pages of notes van Izendorn had written. Schoengarth replied, 'You know, I have only three weeks to live. That's the whole truth.'

A few days later Schoengarth welcomed another visitor to his cell: Pieter Menten had arrived to say his farewells. Because of these circumstances the meeting between the two men suggested some urgency; the content of what they discussed went well beyond the grave. With the guards and prison officials respecting their privacy, this was the most important discussion either man would have in his life.

Back in their days in the Generalgouvernement, as close friends, Menten and Schoengarth had promised to take care of each other, no matter how it turned out. Drink had stimulated a lot of that Casino talk, but for some reason, perhaps friendship, they had kept their word. Schoengarth had asked Himmler for Menten's private train transport from Krakow to Holland. He had seen that Menten received priceless artefacts of great value. Now in return for those favours he wanted a promise that Menten would keep no matter what. The discussion was about Schoengarth's immediate family. With only a few weeks to live before facing the hangman, he wanted to put his affairs in order, and Pieter Menten at that time was his closest friend. Schoengarth's family— Dorothea his wife, Ermuth his beloved daughter aged 5 years, and his two sons who had both died as officers on the Eastern Front—presented a dim future without financial support.

Straight out, Schoengarth asked Menten to 'watch over' Ermuth and ensure that she did not suffer for his crimes. If that meant paying her school fees or, later, her university tuition, then would Menten do that? Would he become Ermuth's 'uncle'? Menten responded, 'Yes, of course.' In return, Schoengarth advised

Menten to the line of defence he should adopt when his time came to face the Allies' retribution. Despite the horrendous past of both men, at this very moment was a moment of sadness.

The matter was finally concluded when on 16th May 1946, the official UK Legal Executioner, Albert Pierrepoint, visited Schoengarth and his fellow accused and carried out the sentences according to the warrant.

It is of note, that Schoengarth was charged and executed for the one single act of murdering the airman on the 21st November, 1944. For all his other crimes, committed in Galicia, which are too numerous to account, and including the ordering of the execution of 260 Dutch hostages after an unsuccessful attempt on the life of his immediate chief, SS Gruppenfuehrer Hans Albin Rauter that same year,[358] justice was seen to be done.[359]

Reference has been made to the uncompromising stance that Dr Schoengarth took when it came to the execution of the Jews in Lvov by officers under his command—that any SS officer would be shot for failing to carry out an order of execution, and that he would support any officer who shot his comrade for this failure. It is also interesting to note, and in some way corroborates this attitude, that when the grave of the airman was exhumed, three other corpses were found in graves nearby. All these three corpses had been hanged as opposed to the airman who had a bullet wound in the head. The three corpses, in SS uniform, were identified as SS/SD officers, one of them named as SS Hauptscharfuehrer Peter Bell.[360] We may assume, with some certainty, that these corpses had been the subject of an SS hanging party, but for what offences it has not been ascertained.

These actions corroborate the defence suggestion by the Einsatzgruppe that had they refused to carry-out the execution of the airman they too would suffer a similar fate.

Rosenbaum, Krueger, Schoengarth and Menten had teamed up to play a dangerous game in their rampage of condoned murder and theft. Krueger would make history in the killing fields of Galicia. The Rabka School under Rosenbaum became the centre for murder and the instruction of murder. With the help of Menten, the School would be used for storage of their loot and their investments. Schoengarth was their leader and willing supervisor of this unobtrusive training establishment. For the Jews that survived Bad Rabka and surrounding communities, their end was in sight.

The one that got away:
SS-Colonel Dr Bruno Walter Hugo Albath, Doctor of Laws, Gottingen University.

In connection with the American airman investigation one man escaped the due process of law: SS-Colonel Dr Walter Albath, who had been present with Dr Schoengarth at the time the decision was made to execute airman Galle.

Bruno Walter Hugo Albath, born in Strasburg, West Prussia, in 1904. He was a German lawyer, SS officer and official of the Gestapo. He studied law and graduated to Dr. jur. In 1939 he was the head of the State Police, Central Dusseldorf, and at the beginning of the Polish campaign was leader of Einsatzcommando 3 in Olsztyn. In 1941 Albath was Chief of Security Police and Security Service and was appointed head of the Gestapo at Konigsberg. His responsibilities saw the infamous detention camp Soldau. In November 1943 he was promoted to SS Colonel and Government Director.

On Albath's arrest he was found to have in his bedroom eight tablets of poison. He stated that he obtained the poison in January 1945 at the same time as his false papers had been prepared stating, 'Everyone in the SD Headquarters was ordered to do this.' He tried to have his teeth drilled for a capsule, but this had been impossible. His wife at the time of his arrest was living with family at Heslingen. When she was questioned after her husband's arrest she was convinced she would never see him again. They had arranged mutually that should he be arrested he would send his gold ring to her—a sign that he had committed suicide. His wife was also in possession of letters from her husband to his children to be read when they became of age in the event of his demise. Mrs Albath knew nothing of her husband's SS lady friend who was residing in the Russian Zone.

On the 23rd February, 1946, Albath was in custody when he was interrogated by the War Crimes Investigation Unit:

Dr Albath agreed with the interrogating officer's opening suggestion that he must have found his duties as an official of the Gestapo somewhat out of keeping with his legal conscience as a Doctor of Laws at the Gottingen University. Albarth replied that he had not joined the Gestapo of his own free choice—he was detailed there [sic]. It was pointed out to him that he had been continuously serving in the Gestapo ever since its formation about six years before the war. Albath stated that he had just completed his university studies and entered the police administration shortly before the Nazis came to power, and when first detailed to the Gestapo he was so reluctant to undertake this class of work that he applied to be released on the pretext of wishing to pursue further university studies, and was, in fact released but was recalled eight months later.

Albath had completed a Questionnaire where he gave details of visits abroad during the war to various occupied countries including Holland, but had not included in those dates his visits to Holland in November 1944. He had been circulated by the Allies as wanted for inciting Schoengarth and others to the murder of an Allied airman at Enschede (for which the others had already been convicted).

Questioned about this visit, he first purported not to remember it and then, when he realised that all the details were already known he said that in the course of a number of visits to posts on the Dutch frontier, he happened to learn at Gronau that Schoengarth whom he wished to see had been spending the previous night at the Villa Hoge Boekel near Enschede and that he might just catch him there which he did at lunchtime (a likely story—author). Albath was obviously reluctant to volunteer any information about this excursion but when it was put to him, he agreed that he saw an Allied bomber crashing near the Villa and parachutists jumping out, but he told the same story as Schoengarth—namely that they saw personnel going into the woods but did not see any of them captured and denied that he had said to Schoengarth, 'In the Reich we treat these bomber-pilots as terrorists' or that he had encouraged the shooting of the airman.

When it was pointed out to Albath that he was, throughout the latter half of the war, Regional Director and Inspektor of the Sipo in District 6 which included the Ruhr, where more murders of allied airmen are known to have occurred than anywhere else, Albath replied that he had received s copy of Himmler's order that Allied airman were not to be protected from the populace but denied having passed the order on though he admitted knowing that it had in fact been passed down to all Gestapo and ordinary police in the District. Albath firmly placed the issuing of this order on SS-Major General Guttenberger, his immediate superior. He said that Guttenberger ordered him to furnish a periodic return of airmen killed in accordance with Himmler's order, and was annoyed because the only return he was ever able to make reported the killing of only two airmen by the Populace of Wuppethal. Albath professed complete ignorance of other such crimes, and expressed the belief that members of the German populace who give evidence of their commission by the Gestapo had really committed the crimes themselves.

Questioned about the murder of at least 1089 victims of nine different nationalities by the Cologne Gestapo—many already identified in Cologne cemeteries or from the Gestapo's own records—Albath professed ignorance although he willingly furnished particulars of Gestapo chief Kulzer and other associates of the Cologne Gestapo Office.

(There is no doubt that Albath was reiterating a well rehearsed script which he had thought over for some months whilst in custody.)

The questioning continues:

Albath stated that units of the Sipo in towns the size of Cologne received their orders direct from Berlin and not through himself, as his duties being of an administrative character were concerned with such matters as location of Gestapo billets for officers and workers, routine inspections, internal discipline, etc., and with no executive authority (a Chief of the Gestapo—a likely story—another ruse to avoid responsibility). However, it is true that the Sipo-SD came directly under the Chief of the RSHA Security Office, Kaltenbrunner (who replaced Heydrich when he was assassinated). Albath knew full well that there was an order authorising the Sipo-SD units to shoot foreigners who looted during air-raid alerts or the black-outs.

He denied having had any training in Special Intelligence sabotage, subversive and fifth column activity of Security for which kind of work he professed that the Sipo-SD drew exclusively on trained detective personnel of the Kripo. He denied that he was granted a delay in his military service in order to carry on with certain lectures at the Sipo-SD School in 1938. He also denied that he had served in the army at all. These were all lies as the interrogating officer had his military file in front of him showing that he served as a gunner in 1937 and 1940 and further, that he had been an 'Assessor' at the Sipo-SD Training School in 1936-7 in examinations for the rank of Kriminal Kommissar. This information is very relevant when we consider the association he must have had with SS-Major Rosenbaum and Dr Schoengarth who served at the training School about this time.

Asked why he had made such complete arrangements for suicide to avert capture if he had nothing on his conscience, Albath said that he recognised he was in the category liable to be arrested and such was his love of liberty that he did not feel his physical or mental health equal to enduring captivity. He agreed that he and his office had all been issued with false identity papers should they be overrun by the Allied Forces.

Finally, the remarks by the interrogating officer:

'Albath is probably a degenerate but not unintelligent type of rat and is unlikely to incriminate himself willingly in war crimes, although it is to be estimated that once Guttenberger, Kuzler and others are located and arrested thanks to information provided by Albath. He also volunteered information that a mixed party of 32 airborne troops who had apparently landed in the wrong place during the battle of Arnhem were handed over to him by Guttenberger with instructions that they were to be 'sonderbehandelt' (receive special treatment). He quite understood that "special treatment" might mean that the prisoners were to be killed but on this occasion to have whom he believes to have deliberately misinterpreted his orders by assuming the "special treatment" to mean that the search of the prisoner's identity papers, etc., was to be specially thorough. Albath states that after being inspected he passed these prisoners (including a Lieutenant and some Americans) to the Wehrmacht. The depravity of Nazi standards is perhaps illustrated as well not by the direct evidence of their crimes but by the fact that the equivalent of a full Colonel or Brigade Commander, a Doctor of Laws, should claim special credit for the fact that he refrained from murdering 32 POWs when he had the opportunity to do so, as if such self-restraint possessed the merit of positive virtue. I have cautioned him that he is liable to be charged as a party to the murder of the airman at Enschede.'

Subsequently, several investigations were initiated against him by the War Crimes Commission resulting in a British Military Court trial when Albath was sentenced to 15 years in prison from which he was released in 1955. He died in 1990.

AMERICAN BATTLE MONUMENTS COMMISSION

THE WORLD WAR II HONOR ROLL

Americo S. Galle Second Lieutenant, U.S. Army Air Forces Service # O-886490
861st Bomber Squadron, 493rd Bomber Group: Died: 21st-November 1944.
Awards:
Air Medal with 3 Oak Leaf Clusters, Purple Heart

**Figure41: Buried at: Plot B Row 38 Grave 34,
Ardennes American Cemetery Neupre, Belgium**

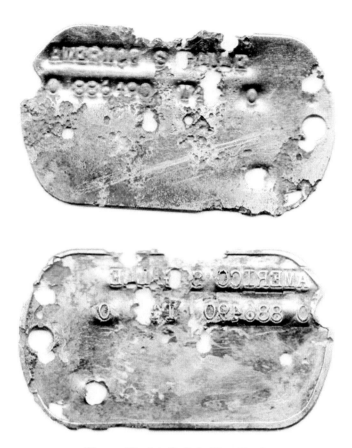

Figure 42: Lt. Galle's 'Dog Tag'.

The dog tag was one of several recovered from the 'dump site' which is not far from the airfield, by Mr & Mrs Roger Blunt. There would have been duplicates held by the administration office should the owner 'lose' his originals. When the 8th AF moved out of Debach the tags were sent to the dump to be burned but for some reason they survived. On a recent trip to the USA to attend a 493rd BG association reunion, Mr Blunt, along with his wife, was able to return several tags to their original owners.

APPENDIX 1

The Werner Oder and Mark Goldfinger Meeting

OVER 60 YEARS LATER, in the author's home town, an extraordinary article appeared in the local newspaper. Mark Goldfinger, who had lived near the Rabka School as an 11-year-old boy, met up with Werner Oder, the son of SS-Unterscharfuehrer Wilhelm Oder.

Figure: 43 Werner Oder (L) and Mark Goldfinger 2009

The Salisbury Journal: **'Bringing hope after Holocaust', Thursday 29th January 2009.**

'A TELEPHONE call two years ago sparked an extraordinary friendship that has its origins in the horrors of the Holocaust. The call brought together a survivor of the concentration camps and the son of a Nazi war criminal who, this evening at Salisbury City Hall, will tell their remarkable stories and how their paths crossed.

Werner Oder was born in Hitler's Austrian home town of Linz five years after the war ended and spent his formative years in a household that still cleaved to its Nazi past. *"I grew up in a home I thought was normal but I grew up with anti-Semitism, I grew up hating the Jews,'* he says. *"There was this post-war insanity of blaming the Jews, regretting that Germany didn't win the war and that they weren't all killed."* His father was absent from home and it was some years before he was told that Wilhelm Oder was in prison, sentenced for war crimes committed as a member of the German SS. Even before the war he had been pro-German and, in 1940, Wilhelm Oder resigned from the Catholic Church and joined the SS.

In March 1942 he arrived in the small Polish town of Rabka, halfway between Krakow and Zakopane, where he was to be a deputy commandant of the Sipo-SD Police School, the only one of its kind in Poland. *"They requisitioned the girls school, which they changed into a school where they trained German, Ukrainian and Austrian soldiers to become executioners, teaching them killing technique—my father was an expert in that,"* says Werner. *"You must understand that you can't get an ordinary person to just start killing women and children. It was a prestigious thing to get into the SS, but many of them didn't know what they would be commanded to do, so they had to be hardened first. This was my father's job."*

Rabka's purpose was to desensitise the men who would carry out Hitler's Final Solution. *"They were using children as target practice. They were observed while they were doing it and if they showed any emotions, they would have to do it again,"* Werner says. The atrocities committed at Rabka make unbearable reading as Jewish families in the village and then from further afield were rounded up and used as practice for hangings, shootings, beatings, and religious vilification. The Nazis used the Jewish population of Rabka first as workers then simply as fodder for their training sessions.

Born in Krakow, Mark (or Marek) Goldfinger was an 11-year-old Jewish boy, living just a few hundred yards from the school in Rabka when Werner's father arrived there. His own father was a POW in Siberia and his sister, some ten years older than Mark, worked as a nanny and housemaid at the school:

> *"I lived a few yards from the school,"* Mark tells me. *"I could hear what was going on—terrible things—I could hear the screaming. Our family knew exactly what was going on in the school, that Jews were being systematically killed by shooting. We all lived in fear of the happenings*

in Rabka. Our home was so close that we could hear the gunfire, and when the wind was in the right direction we could hear the screams and distress of the prisoners."

In May 1942, his grandmother was among those rounded up and executed. One day, the commandant's mistress quietly warned Mark's sister that she and her family should disappear that night. *"We did,"* says Mark (now 78). *"I was one of four people who escaped in the middle of the night—me, my mother and my sister—and my sister took a girl friend of hers."* The following day, all Jews who remained in Rabka were rounded up and sent to the concentration camp at Belzec. Mark and his family travelled to Krakow and endured the harsh conditions of life in the ghetto, before escaping the horror briefly to stay with an uncle outside the city. His mother was murdered by the Nazis as they returned to the ghetto and Mark was sent first to Plaszow, the factory camp where Oskar Schindler's 'list' saved many Jewish lives, and thence to Buchenwald. *"I travelled on these cattle trucks that you must have seen to Buchenwald. There were difficult times, dangerous times but not final times,"* he says. *"I was just nine years old when the war broke out and when it finished, on April 11, 1945 (the day they liberated Buchenwald), I was not quite 15 years old."* His sister (Lucia Schon), narrowly escaping transportation to Auschwitz, had crossed Europe to Palestine and now lives in Tel Aviv. She returned to Hamburg to testify at the war crimes trial of Rabka's commandant Wilhelm Rosenbaum. Mark's father survived the Siberian prison camp and through the Red Cross arranged for Mark to be taken to England where he has lived ever since. A great grandfather, his home is in Bournemouth—astonishingly, not three miles from where Werner Oder now lives.

Werner's childhood had been troubled. Surrounded by hate, he admits he went badly off the rails, constantly in trouble with the police, but an encounter with a church minister when he was 15 changed his life. He underwent a spiritual conversion that he says is difficult to explain or understand. *"I gave my life to Christ and asked him to forgive me,"* says Werner, who is now a minister at Tuckton Christian Fellowship. *"From that day onwards, a change took place. The hatred and insanity disappeared—I suddenly had an interest in the Jews and I wanted to find out more. I started to research and discovered my father's history and I was absolutely aghast."*

His research also revealed that his uncle Herman, had never been associated with Rabka, or at any time a member of ODESSA, the organisation that helped prominent Nazis escape prosecution by spiriting them away to South America.

Alienated from his family, Werner came to England to study at bible school but continued his research. *"I found out about Rabka, the war crime trial that my father was in, and I kept reading a name Goldfinger—a woman who was giving evidence in the trial—and I was curious to know whether these people were still alive."* It was then that he read an article about Mark in the *Bournemouth Echo* and managed to make contact with him.

Mark takes up the story: *"I had no idea what it was about, just that someone called Werner wanted to talk to me. When I asked: 'What is your name?' and he said: 'Oder O-D-E-R,' I said: 'I think I know that name.' Initially, when I heard the name Oder, I went silent—it was as if curtains opened up, memories came back."* Mark says he ran errands in Rabka and knew all of the officers by sight. It's almost certain Werner's father was one of them. Does he still harbour animosity, I ask? *"Of course I hated the Nazis but I could not bring myself to hate the generations that followed. You can never forget what happened. I have been helped by Germans, even saved by Germans; there were Germans who selected me to be killed, not once, not twice, but three times in one day, but it did not happen. I believe in God and am religious in a quiet way, but what is definite is that I am extremely lucky—I must have been guarded by a regiment of angels. My existence is living proof that somebody, if not the angels, was protecting me."'*

APPENDIX 2

Wilhelm Rosenbaum is let out on bail to public dismay:

Newspaper of the Association of Jewish refugees, **Volume XXXII No. 3rd March, 1977.**

Ref: Wilhelm Rosenbaum and others...

THE PAROLE COMMITTEE of the Hamburg Senate has provoked a spate of protests by releasing four Nazi criminals, sentenced to life imprisonment for mass murder, for periods of six months. Wilhelm Rosenbaum, 61, was sentenced to hard labour for life in 1968 for the murder of 168 Jews in the Bad Rabka area of Poland. Max Krahner, 72, received the same sentence for complicity in the murder of more than 500 Jews in Poland and Russia. He headed a special operations unit which destroyed evidence of wartime atrocities and subsequently killed Jewish prisoners who were forced to assist him in this task. Otto Drews and Otto Goldapp, both 78, were punished for the same offence. Drews committed suicide when he was due to return to jail after six months.

The action of the Parole Committee was attacked by members of all parties in the Senate, but Justice Senator Professor Klug said that Nazi criminals should not be treated differently from other life prisoners. The Christian Democratic Union proposed a vote of no confidence and demanded the resignation of Senator Klug, but the Socialist Free Democratic Coalition Government did not support them. The leader of the C.D.U., Jurgen Echternach, said the outcome was an insult to the survivors of Rosenbaum's victims. Hamburg's Lord Mayor Klose had been in Israel when this happened, but on his return said that he, too, was of the opinion that even Nazi prisoners were eligible for parole.

APPENDIX 3

Rabka Zdroj—Cemetery

Figure: 44: <u>Rabka - Zdroj</u> – Cemetery: The Resting Place for the Rabka Jews murdered within the School premises.

THE AUTHOR HAS VISITED THIS LOCATION many times. Sometimes alone, and sometimes taking small groups from many different countries. This is the place where Mojzesz and Rachel Künstlich, the subjects of this book's dedication, were murdered.

The cemetery in Rabka particularly distinguishes itself in the history of local Jewish people due to the fact that it became the symbol of martyrdom and innocent deaths of hundreds of people. Situated on the hillside of the Grzebien Mountain, on a small forest glade near the Gorzki Stream, it occupies an area of around five hectares. The place is closely attached to the 'Tereska' building, situated on Sloneczna Street. It is in this building that during the war, the infamous School for the Commanders of the Security Police and Security Service was located. The course participants from this school along with Commandant Wilhelm Rosenbaum were responsible for the persecution and extermination of the Jewish population in Rabka. The wood near 'Tereska' was chosen as the murder place.

According to various sources, there are 400-500 victims buried in the mass graves. Most of them are Jews, though, according to some sources, not all of them. Also, the inhabitants of Rabka were among the victims; those that either resembled Jews or, for other reasons, were sentenced to death. Between May and July 1942, mass executions of Jewish people coincided with the arrival of transports from Nowy Sacz. The area of the current cemetery, which is a monument to Jewish martyrdom, is a symbolic place. It includes 16 concrete slabs which indicate the places of mass graves. There are also unmarked graves scattered around the local wood. After the war, it was made sure that the place would be saved from oblivion. It is surrounded with a metal fence. On the gate there is the symbol of the Star of David along with a plaque giving information about the solemn nature of this place.

A commemorative plaque was set up with the following inscription carved on it: *'Let's honour the martyrs who died from the hands of the Nazi perpetrators of genocide 1941-1942'*. It also includes an inscription in Yiddish. From the plaques found in the wood, a Jewish Martyrdom Monument was formed. The plaques probably come from the cemetery in Jordanow. They were used during the war to regulate the Gorzki Stream. An interesting fact is the presence of the only Catholic gravestone in this place. It is the gravestone of Dr Olga Rubinow-Horoszkiewicz and it includes the date of her death: 17th May 1942. In the cemetery, there are also two plaques which belong to the sponsors of the renovation works in this area. One is from 1989. It tells about the establishment of 11 new gravestones and it comes from the Peller Sisters' Foundation. It has an inscription saying: *'Peace for the innocently murdered.'* The other plaque has information in three languages, including Polish. It says that the cemetery of Jewish victims was renovated by Mr Leo Gaterer from Dobra with the help of the Municipal Council. According to the accounts of the inhabitants, the cemetery is often visited by foreign pilgrims, which is reflected in the eternal lights on the cemetery that were brought from Israel. The cemetery is taken care of by the Municipal Council as well as students from the local high school. There is a small problem connected with the location of the place because the path leading to it is not marked.

APPENDIX 4

The Menten Case

Historical Research as an Answer to Critical Political Questions:
The Example of the Menten Case[361]

Introduction

POLITICIANS OCCASIONALLY REQUEST that historians conduct investigations in order to solve problems which are essentially political in character; political, because among other things the credibility and reputation of past and present politicians, indeed the careers of these politicians and of other public figures, are at stake. In the Netherlands during the period from 1966 to 1980, leading politicians made several such requests. Three times historical investigations were required into real or alleged wrongdoings during World War II, and, occasionally, into the post-war reaction to such wrongdoings. (It was this post-war reaction that led to the challenging research task to be discussed here.) Each time, the political boat was severely rocked, and great pressure was brought to bear upon the cabinet to order an investigation. Because the government of the day had a direct stake in the findings, it was imperative that the investigation be conducted not by civil servants, but by independent researchers or a research committee specially set up for this purpose.

I will focus here on the research demands placed upon the shoulders of scholars engaged in 'applied' or 'public' history. As an example I will provide an account of the investigation of the so-called 'Menten case', which I undertook with some colleagues. (I might add that the case has already become nearly forgotten history, perhaps as a result of the success—from historiography's point of view—of our research.)

The Menten Affair, 1976 -1981

The political upheaval and public outcry which surrounded the Menten case in the summer of 1976 had a rather inconspicuous beginning. On May 22nd the largest-selling Dutch newspaper *De Telegraaf* published a full-page article about

219

the then seventy-six-year-old Pieter Nicolaas Menten and his art collection, part of which was to be sold at a public auction because he was 'cramped for space.' The rather obvious purpose of the article was to draw attention to the auction, thereby raising the bidding prices. By coincidence, however, this article provided leads for journalist Hans Knoop, who at the time was working for the then struggling weekly magazine *Accent*, which has since folded. Knoop was investigating Menten at the suggestion of his Israeli colleague Chaviv Kandan, who was convinced that Menten was a war criminal but who had been unable in the late forties and early fifties to persuade the Dutch Department of Justice to take action. Kandan, in turn, had been tipped off by Henrietta Boas, a Dutch correspondent. Very soon Knoop was able to supply ample evidence which, though incomplete, was nevertheless very incriminating for Menten. Knoop's articles and his direct involvement with a broadcasting organization, which produced television programs about this case, drew national attention. Perhaps in poor taste, the scandal nevertheless appealed very much to the public imagination. Menten himself, in fact, welcomed the publicity and attempted to apply it to his advantage. He flatly rejected all accusations and argued that, as long ago as 1950, his case had been investigated and that he had been cleared of all charges. He frequently referred to public officials from those days by name. Most prominent of these was the former Speaker of the House, Dr. L. J. Kortenhorst. This Catholic politician had at the time been Menten's lawyer and had supposedly demonstrated his innocence of the charges.

In the public debate at least two distinct matters were confused. First, was Menten indeed a war criminal, and if so, how serious were the crimes which he committed? Was he actually a mass-murderer or an accessory to such acts? If so, should he still be prosecuted? Secondly, did Menten avoid prosecution or at least conviction after the war by bribing the judicial and political officials or by blackmailing them? If any of these charges were indeed true, wasn't it time that the facts about them were finally made public?

At first the Ministry of Justice opposed taking action. They considered the issue overblown, merely a passing public mood. They also wondered how strong the prosecutor's case would be, whether there would be sufficient reliable witnesses, and whether the case had not already been dealt with at an earlier date and then dismissed. The press displayed little sympathy for such arguments. To them this hesitation appeared in fact as heel-dragging. It seemed as if the Minister of Justice, A. A. M. Van Agt, preferred to turn a blind eye on the whole matter. After all, he had been in political hot water before when handling affairs involving war criminals. At that time he had wanted to pardon three German war criminals still in prison, the so-called 'Three of Breda'. After many very emotional protests on the part of war victims, however, Van Agt withdrew his proposal. Now once again he appeared to be over-lenient and insensitive to the feelings of those who had suffered at the hands of the Nazis. Moreover, he was suspected of conspiring to protect those who twenty-five to thirty years earlier had been members of his own political party from possible revelations about corruption or political wrongdoings. Best known perhaps is the case of Dr Kortenhorst, who had been accused of having used the influence of his position as speaker of the house on behalf of Menten in return for the (at that time) a staggering sum of Hfl. 200,000—in other words, to have received bribes.

The Ministry soon changed its attitude about prosecuting Menten, due not to the influence of the press or Parliament, but to the strength of the evidence. The Ministry made a preliminary legal investigation in July 1976. It would take too long to discuss in detail the course of these legal proceedings. Suffice to say that it was very complicated, offering great excitement for the public, with many court sessions resulting in various differing verdicts. Not until 1981, after a long juridical struggle, was an irreversible verdict reached whereby Menten was declared guilty of war crimes in Poland. He was sentenced to ten years' imprisonment and fined one hundred thousand guilders.

At first Minister of justice Van Agt remained opposed to a special inquiry about the possibility that Menten had obtained protection during the immediate post-war years. However, extensive material relevant to the case emerged from the post-war years 1945 to 1955. In those early years Menten's name had repeatedly cropped up in the press and in official inquiries. One could even say that at that time there were several Menten cases. In addition, Menten exacerbated the embarrassment of the Department of Justice, and especially Minister Van Agt, by making a successful escape from the country, an escape cut short only by journalist Hans Knoop, who doggedly tracked him down. Suspicion of Menten, and also of Van Agt, increased steadily. Finally it became clear that the minister was no longer able to stave off public and parliamentary pressure. A number of fierce debates in Parliament followed. These forced the hand of Van Agt to initiate an official investigation into the proceedings surrounding the prosecution of Menten from the period immediately after the war until the summer of 1976, and into the role and effect of possible means of influence which affected the outcome of these prosecutions. This investigation was to be carried out by a specially appointed investigator or a group of investigators.

For several reasons Van Agt was initially unable to find a qualified and prestigious investigator willing to take charge of such research. At last Dr I. Schoeffer, who holds the chair of Dutch history at Leyden University, said he was willing to form such an investigative committee, which he presented to the public at the beginning of 1977. Schoeffer requested the cooperation of Dr A. C.'t Hart, professor of criminal law at the Catholic University of Tilburg, and the author. Our official title was 'The Committee of Investigation Concerning Menten.' At the end of January we began our proceedings, with the initial expectation that it would not take very long to complete our work. Schoeffer was thinking on the order of three months, but in fact this timetable was grossly overoptimistic. After having worked nearly full-time for 18 months, and then half-time for another year, we were able to present the final report, The Menten Case 1945-1976, in September 1979.

The so-called 'Menten case' involved several extremely complicated affairs which could perhaps be examined as a set of separate cases, but which in fact are very much interconnected. Menten himself was not even directly involved in a number of these, including several court cases dealing with wartime behaviour, crimes committed after the war, business transactions, and claims for payment of compensation, perjury, and slander. The committee also had to investigate press manipulations and political manipulations, or at least attempts toward the latter. In our report we examined each of these cases separately in as detailed a manner as possible, and we tried to describe the various interlinkages.

We paid explicit attention to all suspicions and accusations related to these cases which had been raised up to 1976 and thereafter, even if there were no reasonable grounds to substantiate them. In addition we demonstrated that a convincing explanatory interpretation required careful examination of three main aspects. First, the exact chronological sequence of the events. Second, the fluctuations in the political moods which took place after the war in the Netherlands, especially with respect to the desirable treatment of political delinquents. (Later on the Cold War influenced the concept of what constituted desirable treatment.) Third, the very aggressive manner in which Menten, his lawyers, and other advisers defended his interests.

Following this approach we attempted to do more than merely research the scandals in which Dutch judicial and political officials had allegedly been involved. These officials certainly made mistakes. Often they had been slow in acting, and they handled a number of matters very clumsily. Moreover a number of their activities were questionable and deserving of condemnation. But on the whole no evidence turned up which demonstrated that the more serious and scandalous allegations were justified. In this respect the report was anticlimactic. Much more importantly, however, the report lived up to its main requirement, the reconstruction of the facts and this reconstruction has not been challenged. The committee's interpretations elicited only a few negative comments. The reactions in the public media and professional circles were very complimentary to the activities of the committee. The publication of the report brought to an end this aspect of the Menten case which was formally wrapped up with a short parliamentary debate in February 1980.

Research Problems

Although the committee's research did not essentially deviate from the approach of the historical research, we encountered some problems and circumstances characteristic of this type of research. First of all there is the matter of tracing documents. A government's promise to cooperate is not in itself sufficient, since the documents that one would like to examine need to be located. This turned out not always to be possible. In some cases the archives had been destroyed in line with official guidelines, while other archives had been lost for other reasons (especially in the chaos of the first months following the Second World War). Fortunately it was sometimes possible to locate particular materials, either the original documents or copies of them, by calling in the assistance of specialized archivists.

Nevertheless, in the end there remained a list of documents which could neither be located nor accounted for. This provided fuel for rumours that evidence which incriminated either Menten or certain public officials had been destroyed deliberately, and in fact such suspicions were voiced in the public media. This deliberate destruction of evidence had allegedly taken place between 1945 and 1955, although later dates were suggested, such as summer and autumn 1976, when the Menten case had received renewed attention but the investigation had not yet started. For our purposes, the alleged destruction of documents did not matter very much, since the missing documents were not needed to complete the overall picture. Moreover, nothing suggested any deliberate destruction or removal of evidence. Nevertheless, the absence of these documents might have reduced the credibility of the final report. Fortunately, we found some very important dossiers, purely by coincidence.

These dossiers, which incidentally also proved to be very important later on in the court case against Menten, contained the files of the most important lawsuits against Menten during the period 1945-1955. According to the public media, these files had been lost deliberately. They were found together with several other documents hidden behind a file case in the attic of the Palace of Justice in Amsterdam. In 1955 the attorney general in Amsterdam (in the Netherlands a high-ranking public prosecutor) had kept these and other documents separate from the regular archives because of their delicate nature. Since then they were moved a few times and in 1976 and 1977 only one person remained who knew of the documents which were hidden among various kinds of rubbish. He had not made the connection with the Menten case, but when some other names were mentioned he remembered the existence of these documents. So the Menten files eventually re-emerged, discrediting those who argued that the documents had been stolen.

Our research was hampered, however, in other ways. Only a few private archives provided us with additional information. And most lawyers maintained that, regardless of the age of the files in question, examination of them would constitute a threat to the confidential character of their relation with their clients. They therefore refused to have them examined—quite rightly so, in our opinion.

Altogether different was the issue with respect to the files held in the family archives of Menten's former lawyer, the aforementioned Dr Kortenhorst. There were at least several reasons why in this case 'confidentiality' could not be invoked as a persuasive excuse to refuse access to them, and initially the family did not use this argument. The fact was that they considered the committee to be their acknowledged enemy. Their lack of cooperation did not hamper our research to a large extent, but the fact remains that others, notably the lawyer representing Menten in a fresh war criminal case, were permitted to examine these files. Significantly, they revealed nothing new or startling. In fact, they even failed to produce those documents which existed according to Menten and which were supposedly very favourable to his defence, though incriminating to several politicians who had served as ministers of justice during the early 1950s. The committee doubted that these documents ever existed at all. Nevertheless, when the committee had completed its research and presented it publicly, we were challenged and were forced to concede that we had not been allowed to examine the Kortenhorst archives. Such files would normally have constituted an important component of the kind of research conducted by the committee. This (imposed) omission, therefore, was very unfortunate indeed. In the evaluations of the report this omission has been mentioned frequently.

Another problem concerns contact with 'witnesses' and their testimonials. The committee wanted to talk to as many of those people who had been involved with the Menten case(s) as possible. We contacted about 150 people, on the whole with very disappointing results. The explanation for this is rather simple: most of these people were civil servants who had been involved in some capacity with one of the many cases which the committee was researching. Most of the information we wanted concerned the details of cases which had taken place twenty-five years ago. Understandably, memories from so long ago were dim, and on balance, the information obtained from the files proved considerably more reliable. Moreover, several people who were at the time closely associated with Menten refused to cooperate. Menten himself broke off all contacts with the committee after a few interviews. During these conversations he made some rather obvious attempts to get the committee entangled in the current court case against him. It is a pity that we had so little cooperation from these circles, because otherwise we could have explained some aspects of the behaviour of Menten and his consorts more satisfactorily. During the period from 1945 to 1955, however, Menten and his 'party' had produced such an abundance of material that information highlighting their point of view was readily available.

The conclusion must be that the oral history method is not particularly suitable for this type of research. Only in a few cases was useful information obtained as a result of the personal contact with the people involved in these cases. I hasten to add that this observation is not intended as a general evaluation of the methodology of oral history per se. This method can be applied very successfully, but to research of a different nature. In retrospect it was perhaps predictable that this method yielded limited results. Details were of prime importance for our research, and several of the people interviewed still had direct interests at stake. However, the credibility of our research would have suffered if we had omitted such interviews.

Another complication was brought about by the fact that the court case pertaining to Menten's behaviour during the war took place at the same time as our research. Thus there was the constant danger that the committee would become entangled in the court case. (Menten, in fact, wanted this to happen.) Despite the careful defining of the issues and the separation of cases concerning Menten's behaviour during the war from cases dealing with post-war developments, it proved to be impossible to separate clearly the respective investigations. In the court case the judicial developments after the war were relevant in connection with the judicial procedure of '*ne bis in idem*', which states that a person cannot be brought to trial twice for the same offense. As a consequence, the committee and the judges not only had to study the same documents, but they also had to come up with an interpretation of the same problems.

Several problems arose due to this entanglement of investigations. At the start of its research the committee made an unfortunate and rather naive mistake when it let the examining magistrate look at a very provisional draft of a list of dates, which ended up in the actual dossiers of the court case. Later on it became clear that this list contained several errors. Menten's lawyer used one of these errors as part of his defence case, and naturally this aroused undesirable publicity for the committee

The committee faced another thorny problem when in the court proceedings a particular issue became very important. Once the committee had completed its 'reconstruction' of this issue it decided that, given the developments in court, it should not withhold the results of its research. So the committee published an 'interim report,' thereby risking the possibility of standing accused of interference in the proceedings of a criminal investigation. The court's reconstruction differed, unfortunately, from the one by the committee. Although the verdict was annulled in appeal, the committee felt obliged to discuss this question in the final report, because it considered the court's reconstruction to be based on false grounds. This course of events attracted a lot of unfavourable public attention. Although inevitable, proceedings of this nature can hardly be considered a showcase of judicial elegance. Fortunately, these developments did not tarnish all of the committee's work, especially since its interpretation was not convincingly challenged.

The eager interest of the press also presented some problems. To some extent the very existence of the committee was brought about by the activities of the press. After all, newspaper publications provided the momentum which built up sufficient parliamentary pressure upon the cabinet to set up an inquiry. Moreover, the discoveries of several journalists had provided a basis from which the research could proceed. So there was in fact every reason to have a positive attitude toward the press. However, this very same eagerness of the press was potentially disturbing to our research activities. Shortly after beginning its research the committee attempted to court the press by inviting all those journalists who had produced valuable publications about the Menten case to discuss their work. The committee inquired extensively into the journalists' sources and interpretations. Because the committee had just begun its research, it was unable to provide anything in exchange at that time. We explained to the journalists that we were going to make a careful and original inquiry into these cases, strongly resisting any outside influence. Only after completion of our task would we publish a final report, and no interim information would be provided to the press. The committee pleaded for understanding regarding this position and on the whole, our request was honoured. With few exceptions, such as the one mentioned above, relatively little publicity about our research appeared at that time. The fact that the journalists themselves did not come up with anything of real significance after the committee was established was helpful, because it meant that the journalists did not have any incentive for further publications besides reporting on the developments in court. After the committee had completed its research and published the final report we stated our willingness to respond to any questions which the press wished to direct to us, though in fact all relevant information could be found in this final report.

Final Report

Several important decisions preceded the determination of what should be included in the committee's final report. Foremost was the question of how detailed the report should be. On the one hand it was desirable to be brief and to prevent wasting energy on relatively unimportant aspects, while on the other hand so much excitement had been aroused that a detailed account seemed desirable. After careful consideration the committee decided on a detailed report. Since the research had been intended to calm the waters by providing reliable information, it was imperative that no questions be left hanging in the air.

Another exception was the journalist N. Polak, who published about the Menten case in 'Het Vrije Volk' in *De Haagsche Post*. For his views and the comments of the committee on them see the report of the committee.

Each and every open question and every fact which third parties (such as the press) might legitimately argue had been omitted by the committee would provide a basis for undermining the conclusions of the research. This is the main reason for the length of the report (922 pages). (In relation to Dutch history as a whole, this case was much less important than the size of the report would suggest.) The committee presented the report in a format which made the central issues stand out, while the more peripheral ones were presented either in footnotes or printed in small lettering, enabling the reader to skip those parts without losing the thread of the argument.

The committee also had to decide whether to publish the most important documents and accompany them with a limited amount of 'commentary,' or whether to write an extensive report providing references to the original documents in footnotes. For two primary reasons, the committee decided to follow the latter course. First, the number of documents which would have to be published to enable the reader to reconstruct the case would be so large that the resulting publication would have been much more voluminous than the existing (already very sizeable) report. (In fact, readers would not have been able to find their way through such a maze without spending several months.) This consideration would have sufficed in itself. Moreover, while it may seem that the publication of the actual documents is more objective than a story produced by historians, this is not really so. After all, the very selection of the documents would have reflected the subjective interpretation of the historians. As a matter of principle, therefore, it is more legitimate for investigators to present their findings in a narrative fashion. The committee's publication contained, first of all, a chronological and thematic history followed by a number of concluding remarks which link up the main interpretative elements; secondly, an account of the sources used; and finally, an illustrative sample of the most important documents.

Closely related is one last issue, value judgments on the part of historians. On the whole I feel it is preferable for historians to restrain themselves, expressing as few moral and political judgments about the people whose actions they describe as possible. The objective of historical research is the reconstruction of events and the accompanying analytical explanatory evaluations (the interpretation). The latter have to be clearly and explicitly stated. In this case, however, issues of a political and moral character brought about the research in the first place. Consequently, their omission would have seemed contrived. This is why, in addition to the analytic explanatory judgments, the committee at times expresses approval or disapproval of the behaviour of various parties. The committee did attempt to restrain its tone and to display an understanding of the situation at the time that these acts took place. After all, it was not the committee's task to serve as hangman, and the committee had the benefit of hindsight and the necessary time to weigh the arguments after examining the case from all angles. The public officials who dealt with such cases at the time were handling many cases simultaneously and their time was quite limited. The committee took these considerations into account when formulating its concluding opinions. Readers of the report must decide whether the committee was fair. However, we maintain that on the whole we succeeded in reaching our main objective, which was to clear up all questions concerning the Menten case(s).

In closing, I would like to point to a side effect of research like ours. Although our project originated from the desire to contribute to the solving of an immediate political problem, it turned out to have wider significance. As some professional historians reacting to our work have claimed, our report also makes a useful contribution to the scholarly historiography of the post-war period.

APPENDIX 5

Rudolf Reder's *Bełzec:*[362]

The End Product of '**The Rabka Four's'**
Activities in Distrikt Galicia.

Figure 45: Book Cover

Introduction

ORIGINALLY PUBLISHED in Polin: 'Studies in Polish Jewry', Volume 13: *The Holocaust and its Aftermath*, edited by Antony Polonsky and published by the Littman Library of Jewish Civilization for the Institute for Polish-Jewish Studies and the American Association for Polish-Jewish Studies (Oxford and Portland, Oregon, 2000). Translated by the respected historian Margaret Rubel.

In 1946 a slim volume entitled *Belzec* came out in Krakow. It was published by the Jewish Regional Historical Commission, which collected the testimonies of Holocaust survivors. The booklet included an introduction by Nella Rost, who was on the committee's editorial board, and Rudolf Reder, a former soap manufacturer from Lvov who managed to escape from the camp and lived long enough to tell his story. He was one of only two known survivors of Belzec death camp. The other, Chaim Hirszman, was murdered in Lublin in 1946 by two youth members of a Polish underground organization the day he began to testify about the camp to the Lublin branch of the Jewish Historical Commission. Thus, Reder's booklet remains to this day the only document written by a victim concerning this most obscure murder camp.[363]

Belzec murder camp was the first camp set up by Action Reinhardt, an operation whose purpose was to dispose, in the least obtrusive manner, of the Jewish population of the Generalgouvernement and adjacent countries under Nazi rule. The other two camps were Treblinka and Sobibor. The building of Belzec started towards the end of November 1941, and at the beginning of March 1942 the camp was ready. On 17 March the first transport arrived; about 10 December that year saw the last. Between those two dates, with a break for 'modernization' which lasted six weeks, Belzec murder camp claimed between 500,000 and 650,000 victims, of whom over three-quarters came from the provinces of Krakow and Lublin, and the Distrikt Galizien.[364] The remaining 150,000 or so consisted of Jews expelled from those parts of pre-war Poland which had been incorporated into the Third Reich, Austria, and Czechoslovakia.

Like the other two camps of Action Reinhardt, Belzec had no attached labour camp and no ordinary prisoners. It consisted of rudimentary murder facilities: an undressing barracks for men, another for women to have their hair cut, and yet another with the gas chambers, about thirty pits of different sizes for burying corpses, a couple of barracks for the Jewish death brigade, and living quarters for the Ukrainian guards, or askers, who numbered about 100. Its SS garrison was small: about twenty all told.

Into this camp Rudolf Reder was brought with one of the first transports of Jews from Lvov caught during the great Action, which lasted for two weeks in August 1942 and which netted about 50,000 victims. He came alone: his son, Bronislaw, had been apprehended in Lvov on 10 August and was never seen again. His daughter, Sophia, managed to survive the war in Krakow; she emigrated to England, where she married. It is not known what happened to his wife. Although Reder was then 61, he was one of the lucky few to be selected on arrival at the unloading ramp to join the Jewish death brigade and to become the camp's odd-job man. He remained in the camp for a little over three months. Towards the end of November he was taken to Lvov, where he managed to escape. He survived the war in Lvov, hidden by his former housekeeper.

Reder arrived in Belzec at the height of the camp's activity. Because of his position as odd-job man he was allowed considerable freedom of movement. He was used as a spare pair of hands to dig pits, he was called upon to help repair the machinery which produced the carbon monoxide pumped into the gas chambers, and he also worked as a bricklayer. He was therefore able to describe the camp, its installations, and its functioning in considerable detail. But his story is also the deeply harrowing account of someone who witnessed with horror the slaughter of innocents which went on day after day. And this, together with the relevant details which, without his description, might have remained for ever obscure, make Reder's booklet a unique document of this terrible but little-known chapter in the history of the Holocaust.

Reder was born on 4 April 1881 in Debica, in the voivodeship of Krakow. From the 1910s he lived in Lvov. Soon after the end of the war he must have left the town (which was then incorporated into the Soviet Union) for Krakow, where he testified about the camp three times in 1945, twice for the Jewish Historical Commission, and the third time for Jan Sehn, a district attorney who collected evidence on behalf of the regional commission investigating German crimes in Poland. In 1946 Reder collaborated with Nella Rost on the booklet about Belzec, which appeared under his name, but was probably written by her. He emigrated to Canada perhaps in the early 1950s under the assumed name of Roman Robak, the name of his former housekeeper, whom he married. In August 1960 he was in Munich, where he made a deposition at the office of the public prosecutor concerning Belzec ('The Case against Josef Oberhauser et al.') in preparation for the Belzec trial, which took place in Munich in January 1965. He died in the late 1960s or early 1970s in Canada.

M. M. Rubel

REDER'S *BELZEC*

I

In August 1942 there still wasn't a walled ghetto in Lvov. Instead there were several streets where we were forced to live: nowhere else. These together became known as the Jewish quarter. It consisted of the following streets: Panienska, Waska, Ogrodnicka, Sloneczna, and a few others, which had once been a part of the third quarter of Lvov. There we lived in constant anxiety and torment.

Nearly two weeks before deportation everyone was talking about it as an imminent disaster. We were in despair, since we all already knew well what the word *Aussiedlung* (Jewish resettlement) meant. We were being told the story of a worker who had once belonged to a death commando in Belzec, but then eventually managed to escape. While still there he was employed in building chambers disguised as baths which in fact were intended for gassing people. He forecast that none of those who had gone there would ever return. We had also heard the story of a Ukrainian guard employed there in murdering Jews recounting his experiences to his Polish girlfriend. The woman was so terrified by what she had heard that she decided to pass the news round in order to forewarn prospective victims. That is how we got to know about Belzec.

Belzec's legend thus became a reality, which we all knew and dreaded. That is why, for several days before 10 August, the streets of the Jewish quarter were filled with frightened and helpless people repeatedly asking each other the same question: what should they do and where should they go? Early in the morning of 10 August all exits leading out of the Jewish quarter were sealed by German patrols. The Gestapo, SS, and in groups of five or six patrolled the streets a few paces apart. They were enthusiastically assisted by the Ukrainian police.

Two weeks earlier Generalmajor Katzman, the chief butcher of Lvov and eastern Galicia, had distributed permits among some of the ghetto workshops. Other workshops got theirs from a police station at Smolka Square. The lucky ones were not very numerous. The vast majority of Jews, overcome by mortal fear, tried all sorts of rescues or escapes, but no one really knew what to do or how to save himself.

Meanwhile, for a few consecutive days, German patrols combed one house after another, looking into every nook and cranny. Some of those caught by the Gestapo had their permits honoured, others did not. All those without permits, or whose permits the Germans did not honour, were driven out of their houses without food or clothing. Next the Germans herded people into large groups. Those who resisted were shot on the spot. I myself was in my workshop working. I did not have a permit. I locked the front door and did not open up, even though I heard them banging outside. Eventually the Gestapo forced their way in. They found me hiding in a corner, beat me on the head with a stick, and took me away.[365] They squeezed us like sardines into trams and transported us to the Janowska camp. We could neither move nor breathe.

Night was already falling. All 6,000 of us were squeezed into a meadow. We were ordered to sit down, and forbidden to move, raise an arm, stretch a leg, or get up. A watchtower directed its blinding light at us. It became as light as if it were day. We sat there, packed tightly together, young and old, women and children alike. A few well-aimed shots were fired in our direction. Someone got up and was shot on the spot. Perhaps he wished to die a quick death.

And so we passed the night. The crowd was deathly silent. Not even women or children dared to cry. At six o'clock in the morning we were told to get up off the wet grass, on which we had been sitting all night, and to arrange ourselves in a column, four in a row. The long line of condemned was then made to march in the direction of Kleparowski railway station. Our column was guarded on both sides by the Gestapo and Ukrainian police. There was not the slightest chance of escape. Our column was driven to the railway station and onto a ramp, where a long train of cattle-trucks was waiting. The Germans began to load the train. They opened the doors to each truck. On both sides of the doors stood the Gestapo men, two on each side, whips in hand, slashing each of us on our faces and heads. All the Gestapo men were alike. They all beat us so badly that each of us had marks on our faces or bumps on our heads. Women sobbed; children in arms cried. Thus driven along and beaten mercilessly, we climbed on top of one another. The doors to the trucks were high above the ground. In the general scramble we trampled those who were below. We were all in a hurry, wanting to have all this behind us. On the roof of each truck sat a Gestapo man with a machine-gun. Others beat us while counting 100 people to each car. It all went so fast that loading a few thousand people took no more than an hour. Our transport contained many men, including some who had the so-called 'secure' work permits, young girls, and women. Finally they sealed all the trucks. Squeezed into one trembling mass we stood so close to each other that we were almost on top of one another. Stifling heat was driving us mad. We had not a drop of water or a crumb of bread. The train started to move at eight o'clock. I knew that the train-driver and fire-stoker were Germans. The train went fast, although it seemed to us that it moved at a snail's pace. It stopped three times, at Kulikowo, Zolkiew, and Rawa Ruska. I suppose it was giving way to other railway traffic. During those stops Gestapo thugs got down from the roofs in order to stop anyone coming near the trucks. They were there to prevent anyone from the outside from showing us a little mercy and giving water through the small window secured by barbed wire to those who were dying of thirst inside.

We went on and nobody spoke, completely apathetic and silent. We knew that we were being taken to our deaths and that we couldn't do anything about it. Although all our thoughts were occupied with escape, we saw no possibility of success. Our truck was a new one; its windows were so narrow that I would not have been able to squeeze through. In other trucks it was possible to smash doors. Every few minutes we heard shots being fired after breakaways. No one said a word to anyone else; no one tried to console lamenting women or to calm crying children. We all knew one thing: that we were going towards a certain and terrible death. What we all wished for was that it would be quick. Perhaps somebody managed to escape, but I do not know. Escape was possible only from the train.

About midday the train pulled into Belzec. It was a small station surrounded by little houses occupied by the Gestapo. Next to the station stood a post office and the lodgings of the Ukrainian railwaymen. Belzec is on the line between Lublin and Tomaszow, 15 kilometres from Rawa Ruska. At Belzec our train left the main line and moved onto sidings about a kilometre long, which led directly into the camp. At the main station in Belzec an old German with a thick black moustache mounted the engine. I do not know his name, but I would recognize him at a glance. He looked like a butcher. He took charge of the train, bringing it into the camp. The journey lasted no more than two minutes. During my four months in Belzec I saw no one but this thug doing the job.[366]

The sidings led through empty fields: not one habitable building in sight. The German who brought the train climbed down from the engine in order to 'help'. With shouts and kicks he drove people out of the trucks. Then he went to inspect each truck personally, in case someone was trying to hide. He took care of everything. When the whole train was empty and checked, he signalled with a flag and moved the train away from the camp.

The camp was under the total control of the SS. No one was allowed to come near. Those who found themselves in the area by mistake were shot at. The train would come into a courtyard 1 square kilometre in size enclosed on all sides by barbed wire and wire netting to a height of 2 metres. This fencing was not electrified. The entrance to the courtyard was through a large wooden gate covered with barbed wire. Beside this gate was a guardhouse with a telephone. By the guardhouse stood a few SS men with dogs. When the train had been brought into the courtyard, one of the men would come out of the guardhouse, shut the gate, and then go back in. At this moment the reception of the transport began. Several dozen SS men yelling 'Los' opened the trucks, chasing people out with whips and rifle-butts. The doors were about a metre from the ground, and the people, young and old alike, had to jump down, often breaking arms or legs. Children were injured and all tumbled down exhausted, terrified, and filthy. The SS men were assisted by the so-called Zugsfuehrers,[367] who supervised the Jewish death commando. They were dressed in everyday clothing without any distinctive marking. The sick, the old and small children in other words, all those who could not walk on their own were thrown onto stretchers and taken to pits. There they were made to sit on the edge, while Irrmann, one of the Gestapo, shot them and pushed their bodies into the pit with a rifle-butt.

This Irrmann, who specialized in murdering old men and small children, was a tall, dark, handsome man, quite normal-looking.[368] Like the others, he lived in a small house next to the railway station in Belzec. Alone like the rest, without women or family. He used to turn up at the camp early in the morning and stay the whole day receiving death transports. As soon as the train was empty, all the victims were assembled in the courtyard and surrounded by the askers. It was then that Irrmann would give a speech. There was deathly silence. Irrmann stood close to the crowd. Everybody wanted to hear him. We all suddenly hoped that, if we were spoken to, then perhaps it meant that there would be work to do, that we would live after all, Irrmann spoke loudly and clearly: '*Ihr geht jetzt baden, nachher werden Ihr zur Arbeit geschickt.*'[369] That was all.

The crowd rejoiced; the people were relieved that they would be going to work. They applauded. I remember his words, repeated day after day three times a day on average, during the time I was there. It was a moment of hope, of illusion. The crowd was peaceful. And in silence they all went forward: men straight across the courtyard to a building bearing the inscription '*Bade und Inhalationsraume*' In large letters, the women, some 20 metres further on to a large barracks, 15 by 30 metres. They were led there not knowing why. For a few minutes more there was peace and quiet. I saw that when they were handed wooden stools and ordered first to stand in a line and then to sit down, and when eight Jewish barbers, silent as death, came in to shave their hair to the bare skin, it was at this moment that they were struck by the terrible truth. It was then that neither the women nor the men already on their way to the gas could have had any illusions about their fate.

With the exception of a few men chosen for their trade, which could be handy in the camp, all the rest, young and old, women and children went to certain death. Little girls with long hair had it shaved; others with short hair went to the gas chambers directly, together with the men. And all of a sudden, without any transition from hope, they were overcome by despair. There were cries and shrieking. Some women went mad. Others, however, went to their death calmly, young girls in particular. Our transport consisted largely of the intelligentsia. There were also many young men, but, as in every other transport I saw, women were in the majority.

I stood to one side with others left to dig pits, watching my brothers, sisters, friends, and acquaintances being driven to their deaths. While the women, naked and shaved, were rounded up with whips like cattle to the slaughter, without even being counted 'Faster, faster' the men were already dying. Shaving the women took approximately two hours. Two hours was the time it took to prepare for murder and for the murder itself.

A dozen or so SS men drove the women along with whips and fixed bayonets all the way to the building and from there up three steps to a hall. There the askers counted 750 people for each gas chamber.[370] Those women who tried to resist were bayoneted until the blood was running. Eventually all the women were forced into the chambers. I heard the doors being shut; I heard shrieks and cries; I heard desperate calls for help in Polish and in Yiddish. I heard the blood-curdling wails of women and the squeals of children, which after a short time became one long, horrifying scream. This went on for fifteen minutes. The engine worked for twenty minutes. Afterwards there was total silence. Then the askers pushed open the doors that led outside. It was then that those of us who had been selected from different transports, in unmarked clothing and without tattoos, began our work.

We pulled out the corpses of the people so recently alive. We dragged them to pits with the help of leather straps while an orchestra played from morning until night.

II

After a while I came to know the whole area well. The camp was surrounded by dense forest of young pine. Although the forestation was thick, extra branches were cut and interwoven with the existing ones over the gas chambers to allow a minimum of light to penetrate. Behind the gas chambers was a sandy lane along which we dragged the corpses. Overhead the Germans had put wire netting interwoven with more branches. This part of the camp was covered by a sort of roof of greenery and was darker than elsewhere. I suppose the Germans wanted to conceal the area from aerial observation. The main gate led to a sizeable courtyard. There was a substantial shed where the women had their hair shaved. Next to the shed was another small courtyard, surrounded on all sides by a fence 3 metre high. It was made of close-fitting wooden boards, greyish in colour. The courtyard led directly to the gas chambers. Thus no one on the outside would have been able to see what was happening within.

The building containing the gas chambers was not high, but long and wide. It was made of grey cement blocks, and was covered by a flat roof made of asbestos sheets. Immediately above it stretched wire netting covered with branches. The door to the building was approached by three steps a metre wide and without railings. In front stood a large flower-pot filled with plants. There was an inscription in large letters on the front: '*Bade und Inhalationsräume*'. The steps led to a completely empty and unlit corridor: just four cement walls. It was very long, though only about a metre and a half wide. On both sides of it were doors to the gas chambers. These were sliding doors made of wood, with wooden handles. The gas chambers had no windows. They were dark and empty. In each gas chamber there was a round hole the size of an electric socket.[371] All the walls and floors were made of cement. Both the corridor and the gas chambers were no more than 2 metres high. On a wall opposite the entrance to each gas chamber were more sliding doors 2 metres wide. Through these the corpses of the gassed were thrown outside. On one side of the building was an adjoining shed no bigger than 2 metres square. This housed the engine, which was petrol-driven. The gas chambers were about a metre and a half above ground level. The doors leading to the ramp, onto which the bodies of the victims were thrown, were on a level with the gas chambers.[372]

There were also barracks for the camp's death commando. The first served the workers doing miscellaneous jobs; the other was for the so-called 'professionals'. They were identical. Each had space for 250 people. There were bunks on two levels, consisting of bare wooden boards with one small angled board as a headrest. Not far from the barracks was a kitchen, the camp's store, an office, a laundry, a tailor's shop, and, finally, comfortable barracks for the askers.

There were mass graves on both sides of the building housing gas chambers. Some were already full; others were still empty. I saw many graves filled to capacity and covered high with sand. It took quite a while for them to level down. There always had to be one empty pit, just in case.

III

I stayed in Belzec death camp from August until the end of November. This was a period which saw the gassing of Jews on a massive scale. I was told by some of the inmates who had managed to survive from earlier transports that the vast majority of the death convoys came during this precise period.[373] They were coming each and every day without respite. Usually they arrived three times a day. Each convoy was composed of fifty cattle-trucks, each truck containing 100 people. If a transport happened to come during the night, the victims were kept in locked cars until six in the morning. The average death toll was 10,000 people a day. Some days the transports were not only larger, but even more frequent. Jews were brought in from everywhere: no one else, only Jews. I never saw anybody else. Belzec served no other purpose but that of murdering Jews. All the transports were unloaded by the Gestapo, askers, and Zugfuehrers. Further on, in the courtyard where the people undressed, there were also Jewish workers. We would ask in a whisper, 'Where are you from?' In a whisper they would answer, 'From Lvov', 'From Krakow', 'From Zamosc´', 'Wieliczka', 'Jaslo', 'Tarnow', and so on. I witnessed this once, twice, even three times every day.

Each transport received the same treatment. People were ordered to undress and to leave their belongings in the courtyard. Each time there was the same deceptive speech. And each time people rejoiced. I saw the spark of hope in their eyes, hope that they may be going to work. But a minute later, and with extreme brutality, babies were torn from their mothers, old and sick were thrown on stretchers, while men and little girls were driven with rifle-butts further on to a fenced path leading directly to the gas chambers. At the same time, and with the same brutality, the already naked women were ordered to the barracks, where they had their hair shaved. I knew exactly the moment when they all suddenly realized what was in store. Cries of fear and anguish, terrible moans, mingled with the music played by the orchestra. Hustled along and wounded by bayonets, first the men were made to run to the gas chambers. The askers counted 750 people to each chamber. Before all six chambers were filled to capacity, those in the first had already been suffering for nearly two hours. It was only when all six chambers were packed with people, when the doors were locked into position that the engine was set in motion.

The engine was large, about a metre by a metre and a half. It consisted of a motor and wheels. The engine whirred at intervals and worked so fast that one could not see the spokes turning. It worked for twenty minutes. Afterwards it was turned off. The doors leading from the gas chambers onto the ramp were then opened. Bodies were thrown out onto the ground in one enormous pile a few metres high. The askers who opened the doors took no precautionary measures. We did not smell any particular odour; I saw no balloons filled with gas, or any powder thrown in. What I saw were petrol canisters. The machine was manned by two askers.[374] But once, when the engine went wrong, I was called in to put it right. In the camp they called me an *Ofenkünstler* (stove-setter). That's why they selected me. I looked it over and saw glass tubes connected to metal pipes, which led to each gas chamber. We thought that the engine worked either by producing high pressure, or by sucking air away, or that the petrol produced exhaust fumes, which suffocated the people. The calls for help, shrieks, and terrible moans of people locked in and slowly asphyxiated lasted between ten and fifteen minutes. Horribly loud at first, they grew weaker and weaker, until there was complete silence. I heard desperate cries in many different languages. Apart from Polish Jews there were also transports of Jews from other countries. The majority of foreign transports came from France. There were also Jews from Holland, Greece, and even Norway. I do not recall seeing German Jews.[375] On the other hand, I do remember Jews from Czechoslovakia. They were brought in cattle-trucks like the Polish Jews, although they were permitted to take their personal luggage and food. Transports from Poland were full of women and children. In contrast, transports from abroad consisted mostly of men. Children were few. Evidently their parents were able to leave them in the care of goyim in their respective countries, so they were able to save them from a terrible fate. The foreign Jews had no idea of their future. They were sure that they were being brought to Belzec to work: they were well dressed and carefully prepared for the journey. Once there, they were treated by the German thugs in the same way as the Jews from other transports And they were murdered by the same method, perishing in an equally horrible manner. About 100,000 foreign Jews might have been brought to the camp while I was there. They were all gassed.

When, after twenty minutes of gassing, the askers pushed open the tightly shut doors, the dead were in an upright position. Their faces were not blue. They looked almost unchanged, as if asleep. There was a bit of blood here and there from bayonet wounds. Their mouths were slightly open, hands rigid, often pressed against their chests. Those who were nearest to the now wide-open doors fell out by themselves. Like marionettes.

IV

Before they were murdered, all the women were shaved. While the first group was rushed to the barracks, others waited their turn, naked and barefoot even in winter and snow. Lamenting and nearly mad mothers pressed their children close. Each time I watched them with a bleeding heart. I could not really stand the sight of them. A group of women already shaved was hustled along, while those who followed waded through the hair of many shades which covered the entire floor of the barracks like some soft and silky carpet. When all the women had been shaved, four workers using brooms made from the branches of lime trees swept the floor and collected the hair into a large pile the size of nearly half a room. Then with bare hands they put this multicoloured pile into jute sacks, which they carried to a store.

The store where the hair, undergarments, and outer clothing of the victims were collected was in a small barracks not larger than 7 by 8 metres. Hair and personal possessions were kept there for ten days. After this time the hair in sacks was put on one side and personal possessions on the other, both ready to be loaded onto a goods train, which came to take away the spoils. Those who worked in the camp's offices told us that the hair went to Budapest. One Jew in particular told us all he knew. His name was Schreiber, a lawyer from the Sudetenland. Schreiber was an honest man. Irrmann had promised to take him on holiday. One day Irrmann took a short break. I heard Schreiber asking, '*Nehmen Sie mich mit?*' ('Are you going to take me with you?') Irrmann answered, '*Noch nicht*' ('Not yet'). And so he kept Schreiber hoping. But I am sure that he perished, just like all others. It was he who told me that every few days a railway truck full of hair went to Budapest.

Apart from hair, the Germans also sent away baskets filled with gold teeth. In those few hundred metres separating the gas chambers from the pits stood some dentists with pliers. They stopped everyone as they dragged the corpses away. They opened the mouths of the dead and yanked out the gold teeth, which they then threw into baskets ready for the purpose. There were eight dentists, usually young men specially selected to do the work.[376] I knew one of them well. He was called Zucker and came from Rzeszow. The dentists occupied a small separate barracks, which they shared with a doctor and a chemist. At dusk they went back to the barracks with baskets full of teeth, gold crowns, and bridges. There they separated the gold, which they melted into ingots. They were supervised by a Gestapo man called Schmidt, who beat them when he thought they were not working fast enough.[377] The gold was turned into ingots 1 centimetre thick, 50 millimetres wide and 20 centimetres long.

Every day the SS men collected jewellery, money, and dollars from the store. They loaded them into suitcases, which a Jewish worker carried to the camp's main office in Belzec. A Gestapo man went ahead, while the suitcases were carried by Jewish workers. The main office was a short distance away, no more than twenty minutes on foot. Belzec murder camp was run from this office. Jews who worked in the administration told us that a whole transport of gold and precious objects was dispatched to the headquarters in Lublin, of which the camp in Belzec was a branch.[378]

Clothing torn from the Jewish victims was carried by workers to the store, where another ten workers took each garment apart in search of gold and money. These workers were supervised by SS men, who beat them frequently. The SS men divided the money found in clothing between them. These SS supervisors were specially chosen for the job; they never changed. The Jews who worked there never took anything for themselves. Nor did they want to. For what could we do with money or jewellery? We could not buy anything. We had no hope of staying alive. No one believed in miracles. But although each worker was searched very thoroughly, it often happened that we trod on dollar bills which nobody had noticed. But we did not even try to pick them up. They served no useful purpose. One day a shoemaker took a five-dollar note. He did it deliberately and openly. He was shot together with his son. He went to his death quite obviously glad of the fact that soon he would leave all this behind him. Death was a certainty, anyway. There was no reason to prolong this agony. In Belzec dollars helped us to die an easier death.

V

I was a member of the permanent death commando. We were 500 men all told. The 'professionals' accounted for half of the total, but even they were employed where no special skills were required, like digging pits and dragging corpses. We dug pits, enormous mass graves, and pulled bodies along. After they had done their own work, all the professionals had to take part in this job. We dug with spades, but there was also a machine which loaded sand, brought it to the surface, and emptied it beside the pits. There was a mountain of sand which we used to cover the pits when they were filled to overflowing. On average 450 people worked round the pits on a daily basis. What I found most horrible was that we were ordered to pile bodies to a height of about a metre above ground-level, and only then to cover them with sand. Thick, black blood ran from the mounds and covered the whole area like a sea. In order to get to the next empty grave we had to cross from one side of an already full pit to another. Ankle deep we waded through the blood of our brothers. We walked over mounds of bodies. And this was most dreadful, most horrible.

We were supervised on this job by Schmidt,[379] a complete thug, who punched and kicked. If somebody was not working fast enough in his opinion, he ordered the man to lie on the ground to receive twenty-five lashes with a riding-crop. The poor fellow had to count the lashes. If he made a mistake, he was given fifty. The mangled victim had no chance of survival. He was hardly able to crawl back to the barracks, where he was usually found dead the next morning. The same thing went on several times a day.

No fewer than thirty or forty workers were shot each day. Usually it was a camp doctor who prepared a list of those too weak to work, but sometimes it was a kapo with the function of Oberzugsfuehrer who submitted names of so-called criminals. At least thirty to forty men from the death commando were shot daily. They were taken to the pits during the lunch break and shot. The death commando was supplemented daily by other men from the incoming transports. One of the jobs of the camp's administration was to keep records of all the workers of the death commando, both past and present, in order to make sure that the figure of 500 was always kept up. But there were no records concerning the number of transports or victims.[380] We knew, for example, that Jews built this camp and set the death machine in motion. Not one of those who worked on the original installations survived until my arrival there. It was a miracle if anyone survived for longer than five or six months at the most.

The gassing machine was serviced by two Askers, always the same two murderers. When I came to Belzec they were on the job, and they were still at it when I left. The Jewish workers had no contact with either of those two, or with any other askers for that matter.[381] When the people in the transports begged for a drop of water, the askers shot those Jewish workers who tried to bring some.

Besides digging graves the commando was also employed in emptying the gas chambers, piling the bodies on a ramp, and dragging them all the way to the pits.

The ground was sandy. Two workers dragged one body. We had leather straps with metal braces, which we put round the hands of a corpse. Then we pulled, while the head of the dead man often dug deep into the sand. As regards small children, we were ordered to carry them in pairs on our backs. If we dragged the dead, we did not dig graves. When we dug graves we knew that thousands of our brothers were being murdered at the same time. And on those jobs we spent our days, from morning until night. Dusk signalled the end of a day. This 'work' was done only in full daylight.

At half past three in the morning an asker-posten (guard on duty) who kept watch of our barracks during the night would bang at the door shouting 'Auf! Heraus!' ('Up! Out!') We were barely up when this thug Schmidt would burst in, chasing us outside with his riding-crop. We would run out, often barefoot, holding our shoes in our hands. We seldom undressed for the night. Often we also lay down in our shoes, since we rarely had enough time in the morning to put them on. It was still dark when we were woken up. Schmidt would run through the barracks like a madman, slashing his riding-crop left and right. We got up as exhausted and desperate as we had been the night before. We were given one thin blanket, either to lie down on or to use as a cover. They always chose for us old and worn rags to dress in. If anyone so much as sighed, he was hit about the face. We were allowed a light on for half an hour in the evening; then it was switched off. An Oberzugsfuehrer went round the barracks, whip in hand. He did not allow us to talk. We communicated in whispers with our neighbours.

The death commando consisted mostly of men, who had seen their wives, children, and parents gassed. Many of us managed to smuggle a tallit and tefillin from the store. After our barracks had been secured for the night, a murmur of Kaddish could be heard from the bunks. We prayed for our dead. Later there was silence. We were so benumbed that we never complained. Perhaps those fifteen Zugsfuehrers still cherished some hope. We didn't.

We moved around like people without a will of their own: like one body. I remember some names, but not too many. It was of no importance in the camp who-was-who before, or what name he bore. I recall that one camp medic was a young doctor called Jakubowicz. He came from the vicinity of Rzeszow. I also knew a merchant and his son, both from Krakow. Their name was Schlüssl. Also a Czech Jew called Ellbogen. He said he had once owned a bicycle shop. There was also a Goldschmidt, once a well-known cook from the Brüder Hanicka restaurant in Carlsbad. No one was really interested in anyone else. We were just carrying on this dreadful existence mechanically.

We got our lunch at midday. At the first window we got a bowl, at the other a pint of watery soup with a potato thrown in if we were lucky. Before lunch and also before the evening meal we were forced to sing songs. At the same time we heard the moans of those who were being gassed, an orchestra played, and opposite the kitchen stood the gallows.

VI

The SS men lived without women both in Belzec and in the camp. Even their drinking parties took place in male company only. All the work in the camp was done by men alone. But this changed in October.[382] In that month a transport came from Zamosc carrying Jewish women from Czechoslovakia. Among them were several dozen women whose husbands worked in the death commando. We decided to save some. Forty were assigned jobs in the kitchen, laundry, and tailor's shop. They were forbidden to communicate with their husbands. In the kitchen they peeled potatoes, washed up pots and pans, and carried water from a well. I do not know what happened to them. Presumably they went the same way as the others. These were educated women, belonging to the intelligentsia. They brought their personal possessions to Belzec. Some even carried butter. They gave us all they had. They also helped those who worked either in the kitchen itself or in the vicinity. They lived in a small separate barracks supervised by a female Zugsfuehrer. I often saw them talking (my job of stove-repairer gave me an opportunity to move around freely). They did not seem to have been as maltreated as we were. They finished their work at dusk and stood in pairs waiting for their portion of soup and coffee. Like us, they had kept their original clothing: no striped uniforms in Belzec. I suppose it did not pay the Germans to introduce uniforms for a crew which was to stay alive for a very short period.

Straight from a transport, dressed in their own clothes and with their hair intact, these women were sent to workshops and the kitchen. Through the windows of their workplaces they could see the death convoys arriving daily.

VII

The camp heaved with mass murder. The days were full of mortal fear and death. But there were also cases of individual butchery. I saw some of those. There was no roll-call in Belzec. Nor was it needed. Spectacles of horror were played out to a gallery without any special announcement. I must tell you about a transport from Zamosc. It arrived some time about 15 November.[383] It was already cold. Snow and mud covered the ground. The transport from Zamosc came in a snowstorm. It was one of many. It carried the entire Judenrat. When, in accordance with the usual procedure, the victims were all naked, the men driven to the gas chambers and the women into the barracks to have their hair shaved, the president of the Judenrat was ordered to stay back in the courtyard. Then, while they were driving everybody to their deaths, the SS men paraded round the man. No, I do not know his name. I saw a middle-aged man, deathly white and very still. The SS men ordered an orchestra to come to the courtyard and await further orders. The orchestra, composed of six musicians, was in its usual place on the path between the gas chambers and the pits. The musicians played on instruments which had belonged to the victims. I was working in the vicinity, doing some brickwork, and so I saw it all. The SS men ordered the orchestra to play *'Es geht alles vorüber, es geht alles vorbei'* and *'Drei Lilien, kommt ein Reiter, gefahren, bringt die Lilien'* ('Everything passes, everything goes by' and 'Three lilies, comes a rider bringing lilies'). And the orchestra played those tunes on violins, flutes, and an accordion. This went on for quite a while. Afterwards they ordered the man to stand against a wall and lashed him about the head and face with riding-crops tipped with lead until the blood ran. Irrmann participated in this savagery, and also that fat pig Schwarz,[384] and Schmidt and some askers. While he was being beaten, the victim was ordered to dance and jump to the rhythm of the music. After a few hours he was given a chunk of bread and beaten again in order to force him to eat it. Covered in blood he stood there, indifferent and solemn, without as much as a moan. For seven hours he was tortured. The SS men stood there laughing. *'Dasist eine höhere Person, Präsident des Judenrates'* ('What a distinguished person, the president of the Judenrat'), they called in harsh voices. It was not until six o'clock in the evening that Schmidt drove the man to a pit, shot him in the head, and kicked the body onto a pile of other corpses.

There were other singular events. Soon after my arrival at Belzec the Germans picked out from a transport (we did not always know the name of the locality a transport came from) several young men, including a young boy. He was the picture of youth, health, and strength. He also amazed us by his good humour. He looked round and asked almost playfully, 'Did anyone ever sneak out of here?' And that was that. He was overheard by some Germans. As a result this young boy, practically a child, was tortured to death. They stripped him naked and hung him upside-down on the gallows. He was there for three hours and he was still alive. So they took him down, threw him onto the ground, and pushed sand down his throat with sticks. He died.

From time to time a transport larger than usual arrived; instead of fifty cattle-trucks, there could be sixty or more. Not long before my escape one such transport arrived. The Germans calculated that they had to keep aside 100 men already naked to help with burying the murdered, who were too numerous for the death commando to manage in one day. They chose young boys only. Whipped and bludgeoned, the boys dragged corpses to the pits, naked in the snow and cold, without even a drop of water. In the evening Schmidt took them to the pits and shot them one by one with a pistol. He ran short of bullets for the last few, so he killed them with the handle of a pickaxe. I did not hear them moaning, but I saw them trying desperately to jump the death queue, tragic and helpless relics of youth and life.

VIII

The camp was under the constant surveillance of armed askers and several dozen SS men, but only a few were particularly active. Some of them stood out for their cruelty. They were real animals. Few murdered in cold blood. Others clearly enjoyed it. I saw their happy and contented faces at the sight of naked and wounded people driven to the gas chambers at bayonet point. They took evident pleasure in the sight of the resignation and despair of the young people, who were shadows of their former selves.

We knew that the nicest house next to the railway station in Belzec was occupied by the commandant of the camp. He held the rank of Obersturmfuehrer.[385]

No matter how hard I try, I cannot remember his name. It was short. He did not come often to the camp, except on special occasions. He was tall and thick-set, over 40 years old, and with a boorish air, a real bully and a complete pig. One day the death-machine went out of order. [386] When he was informed, he came on horseback and ordered an immediate repair. He did not allow the gas chambers to be opened to let the people out: let them asphyxiate slowly and die in agony for a few hours longer. He crouched beside the engine, yelling and shaking with fury. Although he seldom came to the camp, for the other SS men he was a terror. He lived alone, attended by an asker who did all sorts of work and brought daily records from the camp.

Neither the commandant nor the other Gestapo had personal daily contact with the camp. They had their own canteen and a cook from Germany, who prepared meals for all the Germans. No family ever came on a visit. None of them lived with a woman. They kept large flocks of ducks and geese. People said that early in the summer they received whole baskets of cherries. Deliveries of wine and other alcohol arrived daily. I repaired an oven there once and saw two young Jewish women plucking geese. They threw me an onion and some beetroot. I also saw a village girl working there. There was no one else besides them, except orderlies. Every Sunday they took an orchestra from the camp and had a drinking orgy. The Gestapo drank and stuffed themselves like pigs. No one else was there. They threw scraps of food to the musicians. When the commandant visited the camp, I saw the Gestapo and askers shake with fear and apprehension.

Besides them, the Belzec slaughterhouse was run and controlled by four other thugs. It is difficult to imagine anyone more depraved than those four criminals. The first was Franz Irrmann. About 30 years old, with the rank of Stabscharfuehrer, he was responsible for the camp's supplies.[387] His little sideline was shooting old people and small children. He performed his murderous tasks coolly. Not talkative, he liked to give the impression of inscrutability. Every day he reassured people about to be murdered that they were going to work, having bathed first: a conscientious murderer.

An altogether different sort of murderer was Oberscharfuehrer Reinhold Feix.[388] It was said that he came from Gablonz, on the Nissa, and was married and the father of two children. He spoke like an educated man, but fast. If someone failed to get his meaning first time, he punched and yelled like mad. One day he ordered the repainting of a kitchen. The person doing the job was a Jew with a degree in chemistry. He was high up a ladder when Feix came in. Every few minutes he ordered him to come down and beat him about the face with a riding-crop until the man was covered with blood and swollen all over. This is how Reinhold did his work. He gave the impression of being abnormal. Feix played the violin and ordered the orchestra to pay endlessly the tune '*Goralu czy ciniezal?*' ('Mountaineer, do you not feel sad? (That you have to leave your own land)'), forcing people to dance and sing while he laughed and beat them. A mad dog.

I do not know which of them was more diabolical and cruel: Feix or the fat, squat, dark-haired Schwarz.

He came from somewhere deep in Germany. He took care that the askers did not show us any sympathy. He also supervised us when we were digging pits. Whipping and yelling, he drove us to the gas chambers, where piles of bodies awaited their final journey to the mass graves. Once he had driven us to the gas chambers, he ran back to the pits again. There, staring blankly into the depths, with a lunatic gaze in their eyes, stood old people, children and the sick, all waiting to be shot. They had been given plenty of time to see the corpses, to breathe the smell of blood and putrefaction, before they were shot by Irrmann. Schwarz beat everyone constantly. He did not allow anyone to protect his face against the blows. *'Hände ab!'* ('Take your hands away!'), he yelled. Tormenting was his pleasure and joy.

Even more beastly was a young officer called Heni Schmidt. Probably a Latvian, Schmidt spoke German with a strange accent. He pronounced 's' as 't' (not 'was' but 'wat'). And he spoke Russian. He was in the camp every day. Agile, thin, and quick—looking like a real cut-throat and constantly drunk, Schmidt rushed around the camp from four o'clock in the morning until night. He beat whomever he could find with evident pleasure. 'This one is the worst,' we whispered among ourselves, adding immediately: 'They are all equally bestial.' Schmidt always turned up where harassment was at its worst. He never missed an opportunity to see victims being driven to the gas chambers. He stood there listening to the terrible piercing cries of women being gassed. He was the real soul of the camp, bloodthirsty, monstrous, and degenerate. It gave him real pleasure to observe the expressionless features of the death commando returning exhausted to the barracks at night. On the way back each one of us received a blow on the head from his riding-crop. If anyone tried to evade it Schmidt would run after him.

There were also others perhaps less memorable, but they were all inhuman monsters. Not for a moment did any of them show any human feelings. They tormented and tortured thousands of people from morning until night. At dusk they went back to their little houses by the railway station in Belzec. During the night the camp was guarded by the askers, who manned the machine guns. During the day it was the Gestapo who 'welcomed' the death transports.

The biggest event for those thugs was Himmler's visit. It took place sometime towards the middle of October.[389] That day we knew that something unusual was afoot. There was an air of secrecy all around. Everything was done with great speed. Even the process of murder took a much shorter time that day. Irrmann announced that because *'Es kommt eine höhere Person, Ordnung muss sein'* ('A distinguished guest is coming; everything must be in order'). He did not elaborate, but we all knew from the whispered exchanges of the askers.

About three o'clock in the afternoon Himmler arrived, escorted by Generalmajor Katzman (the butcher of Lvov and eastern Galicia), an aide-de-camp, and ten Gestapo. Irrmann and others conducted him to the gas chambers just in time for him to see corpses falling out: a terrible pile of bodies of very young people, small children, and babies. The Jewish death commando dragged the corpses along while Himmler stood there watching. He stayed and watched for half an hour and then left the camp. I saw how pleased and uplifted the Gestapo felt. I saw their joy and I heard them laughing. I also heard them talking of promotions.

IX

Words are inadequate to describe our state of mind and what we felt when we heard the terrible moans of those people and the cries of the children being murdered. Three times a day we saw people going nearly mad. Nor were we far from madness either. How we survived from one day to the next I cannot say, for we had no illusions. Little by little we too were dying, together with those thousands of people who, for a short while, went through an agony of hope. Apathetic and resigned to our fate, we felt neither hunger nor cold. We all waited our turn to die an inhuman death. Only when we heard the heart-rending cries of small children 'Mummy, mummy, but I have been a good boy' and 'Dark, dark' did we feel something. And then nothing again.

I had been in this nightmare for nearly four months[390] when, towards the end of November, Irrmann told me that the camp would need metal sheets, and a lot of them. I was swollen and blue all over. Pus ran from open wounds. Schmidt bludgeoned me about the face with a truncheon. With an ironic smile Irrmann told me that I would go to Lvov under escort to fetch the sheets, adding '*Sollst nicht durchgehen*' ('don't try to escape'). Off I went in a lorry with one guard and four Gestapo. After loading the whole day, I stayed in the lorry guarded by one of the thugs, while the others went away looking for fun. I sat there for a few hours without moving or thinking. Then, quite by chance, I noticed that my guard was asleep and snoring. Instinctively and without a thought, I slipped down from the lorry and stood on the pavement pretending to adjust the load. Then I slowly backed away. Legionowa Street was full of people. There was a blackout. I pushed my cap down lower and no one noticed me. I remembered the address of my Polish housekeeper and went straight to her flat. She hid me. It took twenty months for the physical injuries to heal. But what of the mental wounds? I was haunted by images of past horror, hearing the moans of the murdered and the children crying, and the throb of a running engine. Nor could I wipe from my memory the faces of those German thugs. And in such a state of continuous nightmare I survived until the liberation.

When the Red Army expelled the Germans from Lvov and I was finally able to come out of hiding without fear, to breathe fresh air and to begin to feel and think again, I was seized by a desire to go back to this place where two and a half million of our people met their terrible death. [391] I went there soon and spoke at length with the locals. They told me that in 1943 a much smaller number of transports came to the camp.[392] The murder centre for the Jews moved further west, to the gas chambers of Auschwitz.

In 1944 the Germans opened up the pits and burned the bodies with petrol.[393] Dark, heavy smoke rising from the enormous open-air pyres hung over an area of several dozen square miles. The wind carried the stench still further, for many long days, nights, and weeks. [394]

And later, the locals told me, the Germans pounded the remaining bones to powder, which the wind blew away over the fields and forests.

The machine for pounding the bones had been put together by someone named Spilke, a prisoner from Janowska camp brought to Belzec for the purpose. He told me that he found nothing in the camp except mounds of bones. All the buildings had already gone. (Spilke managed to escape, and survived the war. He now lives in Hungary. He told me all this in Lvov, where we met after the liberation.) When the production of 'artificial fertilizer' from human bones came to a halt, the open pits were filled with soil and the blood-soaked earth scrupulously levelled.[395] The German murderers covered this graveyard for millions of murdered Jews with fresh greenery.

I said goodbye to my informants and went along the familiar siding. The railway line was gone.[396] Through a field I reached a young and sweet-smelling pine forest. It was very still. In the middle of it was a large, sunny clearing.

****

Bibliography

Berenstein, T, 'Eksterminacja *ludnosci zydowskiej w dystrykcie Galicja 1941-43,*' in: Biuletyn Zydowskiego Instytutu Historycznego, No 61, Warsaw, January - March 1967.

Gilbert, Martin. *Atlas of the Holocaust*, London 1993.

————, *Holocaust Journey*: Travelling in Search of the Past, London, 1997.

————, *The Holocaust: The Jewish Tragedy*, London 1987.

Hilberg, Raul, *The Destruction of the European Jews* (3 vols.), Chicago 1961 (rev. Ed), New York 1985.

————, *Documents of Destruction*. Germany and Jewry 1933 -1945, London 1977.

Klee, Ernst. Dressen, Willi. Riess, Volker (eds.), *Those were the Days*: *The Holocaust as seen by the Perpetrators and Bystanders*, London 1991.

O'Neil, Robin, *'Belzec: A Reassessment of the Number of Victims,'* in: East European Jewish Affairs, vol. 29, Nos -1-2 (Summer-Winter) 1999.

————, *'Belzec—the Forgotten Death Camp,'* in: East European Jewish Affairs, vol. 28, No. 2 (Winter) 1998-9.

————, *The Belzec Death Camp and the Origins of Jewish Genocide in Galicia* (unpublished PhD Thesis).

————, *Oskar Schindler: Stepping Stone to Life*, NY, 2009.

————, *Belzec: Stepping Stone to Geno*cide, NY, 1998.

'*Opening and Closing Speeches of the Chief Prosecutors Sitting at Nuremberg 1945-1946,*' in: International Military Tribunal: *The Trial of German War Criminals*. (2 vols.), London 1946.

Paechter, Heinz, *Nazi Deutsch*, New York 1944.

Pohl, Dieter, *Nationalsozialistische Judenverfolgung in Ostgalizien 1941-1944*. Munich 1996.

————, *Von der 'Judenpolitik' zum Judenmord: Der Distrikt Lublin des Generalgouvernments 1939- Goekel 1944*, Frankfurt-am-Main 1993.

————, *Nationalsozialistische Juden verfogung in Ostgalizien. Organisation und Durchfuehrung eines staatlichen Massenverbrechens*, Munich 1996.

251

————, 'Hans Krueger and the Murder of the Jews in the Stanislawow Region (Galicia),' in: Yad Vashem Studies XXVI, Jerusalem 1997.

Reder, Rudolf, '*Belzec*,' Zydowski Instytut Historyczny, Krakow 1945, English transl. in: Polin – Studies in Polish Jewry, vol. 13, London 2000.

Redner, Mark, *Recollections on the life and Martyrdom of Jewish Medical Doctors in the Lvov Ghetto*: Translated from Polish by: A.S. Redner. Edited by: Isabel Alcoff. Yad Vashem, file 03/430.

Sereny, Gitta, *Into the Darkness*: *An Examination of Conscience*, London 1974.

Wells, Leon W., *The Death Brigade*: *The Janowska Road*, New York 1978.

Secondary Sources

Berenstein, Tatiana, '*Eksterminacja zydowskiej w tzw, dystrykcie Galicja*,' in: BZIH, H. 61, Warsaw 1967.

Bullock, Alan, *Hitler: A Study in Tyranny* (rev. ed.), New York 1962.

Dabrowska, D.; Wein, A.; Weiss, A. (eds.), *Pinkas Hakehillo: 'Eastern Galicia'* – Encyclopaedia of Jewish Communities in Poland, vol. 3, New York 1980.

Dawidowicz, Lucy, S., *The War against the Jews 1933-1945*, London 1987.

Fleming, Gerald, *Hitler and the Final Solution*, London 1985.

Garrard, John, '*The Nazi Holocaust in the Soviet Union*: *Interpreting Newly-Opened Russian Archives*,' in: East European Jewish Affairs, vol. 25, 2, London 1995.

Gellately, Robert, *The Gestapo and German Society*, Oxford 1988.

Gilbert, Martin, *Auschwitz and the Allies*: *How the Allies responded to the news of Hitler's Final Solution*, London 1981.

Kahane, David, *Lviv Ghetto Diary*, Massachusetts 1990.

Klemperer, Victor, *The Language of the Third Reich*: LTI, lingua tertii imperii : *A Philologist's Notebook*, London 1999.

Knoop, Hans, *The Menten Affair*, London 1979.

MacPherson, Malcolm, *The Last Victim*, London 1984.

Musmanno, Michael A., *The Eichmann Commandos*, London 1969.

————, Western Galicia and Silesia, vol. 4, London 1984.

Reitlinger, Gerald, *The Final Solution*: *The Attempt to Exterminate the Jews of Europe, 1939-1945*, London 1953.

Russell of Liverpool, *Scourge of the Swastika*, London 1954.

Salsitz, Amalie, *Against All Odds*, New York 1990.

Sword, Keith, *The Soviet Take-Over of Polish Eastern Provinces 1939-1941*, London 1991.

Trunk, Isaiah, *Judenrat: The Jewish Councils in Eastern Europe Under Nazi Occupation*, New York 1972.

Vern, Thomas Larry, '*Friedrich-Wilhelm Krueger*', Höherer SS-und

Wistrich, Robert S., *Who's Who in Nazi Germany*, London 1982.

Yahil, Leni, *The Holocaust: The Fate of European Jewry 1932-1945*, Oxford 1990.

Zygmunt, Albert, *The Murder of the Lvov Professors – July 1941*, Wroclaw 1989.

Glossary

Action Reinhardt: Code name used by the Nazi for their Jewish genocidal policies.

T4: The centre for state sponsored murder of so-called 'incurables' – T4 is a shortened title taken from the address of the central office in Berlin, Tiergartenstrasse 4.

BDC: Berlin Document Centre – Personnel files of members of the SS. [397]

BdO: Befehshaber der Ordnungspolizei (Commander of Orpo – Order Police).

BdS: Befehlshaber der Sicherheitspolizei und des SD (Commander-in-Chief of the Sipo-SD).

Einsatz/Einsatzgruppen: Groups/Security Police and SD.[398]

Gauleiter: The supreme territorial or regional Nazi Party authority, used in Germany and some annexed territories. The geographical units were termed Baue, headed by Gauleiter (the term is singular and plural).

GDG: Gouverneur des Distrikts Galizien (Governor of Galicia).

GDL: Ibid (Governor of Lublin District).

GedOb: Generaldirektion der Ostbahn (Director of Eastern Rail).

Gestapo:[399] **Gestapo** is a portmanteau contraction of the name of the official secret police force of Nazi Germany, **Geheime Staatspolizei**, (German for 'secret state police'). During the reign of Nazi Germany, the Gestapo was the central intelligence agency of Germany, under the overall administration of the SS. It was administrated by the Reichssicherheitshauptamt and was considered a dual organization of the Sicherheitsdienst and also a sub-office of the Sicherheitspolizei.

GG: Generalgouvernment. Main part of occupied Poland made up of four districts (later five, including Galicia).

GPK: Grenzpolizei – Kommissariat: A regional frontier HQ of the Grenzpolizei-controlled Grenzposten (border posts).

Hilfspolizei: Auxiliary Police, recruited from Nazi Party formations and sympathisers in occupied territories that assisted the regular police and security services in various functions but were not part of the Ordnungspolizei (Orpo).

HHE: Himmler-Heydrich-Executive Used to identify the main protagonists of genocide within the RSHA (Reich Security Main Office).

HSSPF: Höhere SS- und Polizeifuehrer (Senior SS and Police Commander): Himmler's personal representative in each district and liaison officer with the military district commander and regional authorities (Nominally the commander of all SS and police units in the occupied territories).

KdF: Hitler's Chancellery.

KdO: Kommandeur der Ordnungspolizei (See Ordnungspolizei).

KdS: Kommandeur der Sicherheitspolizei und des SD (See Sipo-SD). Hans Krueger was the KdS Regional Commander in Stanisławow. Krueger's immediate superior was Dr Schoengarth, the KdS commander of the SD in Krakow. The KdS was the cadre responsible for mass executions and resettlement. The KdO (units) were on the periphery of events and only utilised when requested by the KdS commanders.

KdSch: Kommandeur der Shutzpolizei (Commander of the City Police).

Kreishauptleute/Kreishauptman: City Governors during the occupation in Galicia. Many were with the SD and very active in the Jewish resettlement programme.

Kriminalassistent: Lowest grade of criminal police (Criminal Investigation Department).

Kriminalkommissar: The lowest rank in the upper officer class of the CID (Obersturmfuehrer). Promotion to Kriminalrat (Hauptsturmfuehrer). For the outsider, the rank alignment is complicated: An officer could hold the rank of Kriminalkommissar but also hold a higher rank in the SS as SS-Hauptsturmfuehrer. In many of the Security offices, the lower grade CID officer could out-rank his boss with SS rank, and although this situation should not have presented any problems, sometimes it led to an awkward awareness within the office.

Kripo: Kriminalpolizei; Detective Police.

NSDAP: Nazi Party. National Socialist German Workers Party.[400]

OKW: Obercommando der Wehrmacht – the high Command of the Third Reich armed forces.

Orpo: Ordnungspolizei (Order Police): Separate from the Gestapo and Criminal police. The Orpo within Germany handled civilian matters such as traffic patrols and routine police business. However, in the occupied territories or regions – notably Poland and Russia – Orpo often had Einsatzgruppen roles, including carrying out mass killings. Since 1933, the Ordnungspolizei and Shutzpolizei had become the foot soldiers of the Nazi Security Service.

Reichsleiter: Member(s) of an executive board of the Nazi Party.

RFSS: Reichsfuehrer-SS (Chief of all police cadres – Himmler).

RSHA: Reichssicherheitshauptamt (Reich Security Main Office), formed in 1939 under Reinhardt Heydrich. The department included the Gestapo, the Criminal Police and the SD.[401]

SA: Sturmabteilung (Brown Shirts, Storm Troopers).[402]

Schupo: Shutzpolizei. Auxiliary police recruited in the eastern occupied territories from the local population.

Sipo-SD: SD Sicherheitsdienst:(+ Sicherheitspolizei = Sipo-SD of the RSHA).

Selbstschutz: A militia as used by Globocnik in the early stages of Jewish oppression in the Lublin area.

Sonderdienst: A militia that replaced the *Selbstschutz* in name only.[403]

SS-Schutzstaffel: (Lit. 'Defence echelon').

SSPF: SS-und Polizeifuehrer (commander of a police district e.g. Globocnik in Lublin).

Volksdeutsche: ethnic Germans, that is, people of German origin whose families had lived outside Germany for generations. Reichsdeutsche refers to German nationals living within the pre-1939 boundaries of the Third Reich.

WVHA: Wirtschaftsverwaltungshauptamt der SS: Economic Division RSHA, which administered and supervised the vast web of concentration camps (but not the 'Reinhardt' camps).[404]

zbV: Einsatzgruppen zur besonderen Verwendung (Einsatzcommando, zbV for special purposes).

Every Jew carried one - just in case: 'It was a passport to life'

This 500 Zloty currency note dated 1940 (to-days value £100) came into the author's possession in 1990, having been given to him by a former Polish police officer who had served in Rabka, June 1942. Wishing to remain anonymous, the former officer stated that he had taken the money as a bribe to release a Jewish male in his custody on Zaryte Street, Rabka during the deportation round-up for the Belzec death camp.

The author has donated the currency note as a gift to Pastor Werner Oder (the son of former SS Scharfuehrer Wilhelm Oder) and to his church: the Tuckton Christian Centre.

End Notes

[1] In December 1941, during the evacuation of the Riga ghetto, the 81-year-old historian Simon Dubnow was shot. The story is told that Dubnow's last words were an admonition to his fellow Jews: 'Write and record!' (*Yidn, shreibt un farschreib*'). It was a phrase written on walls and scraps of paper in a last desperate act of defiance when the victims saw their immediate demise. These 'last gasps' can be found in many thousands of locations, including Fort IX, Kovno, the Sipo-SD School Rabka and in the last transport bringing the Jewish workers of the 'death brigade' from Belzec to Sobibor where they were all shot on arrival.

[2] Where possible I have written or contacted photographic sources. Some have replied, some have not. Acknowledgement is shown where possible.

[3] Raol Hilberg, *The Destruction of the European Jews*, 3 vols (vol. 1).

[4] Heinz Paechter, *Nazi Deutsch:* New York 1944, 1-128.

[5] See: Viktor Klemperer, *Language of the Third Reich,* (trans. by Martin Brady), London, 1999.

[6] In a Nazi circular issued by Martin Bormann (No. 33/43), one finds the following: 'By order of the Fuehrer. In public discussions on the Jewish Question any mention of a future total solution must be avoided. However, one may discuss the fact that all Jews are being interned and detained to purposeful compulsory labour forces.'

[7] See Claud Lanzmann, *Shoah*, London 1985, 103-4.

[8] Orth, *KZs*, 310.

[9] Mark Mazower, *Dark Continent*, London 1998, 174.

[10] Hilberg, *Destruction*, vol. 3, 1205.

[11] Ibid, 1009.

[12] See Sandküler *Endlosung,*71-76.

[13] One of the plusses of going direct to the High Court records was that I found material not generally kept in police prosecution files, i.e., psychological assessment reports obtained by Court Medical psychologists, namely Dr Gercke of the Hamburg Court. Dr Gercke must have spent many hours interviewing Rosenbaum prior to sentencing.

[14] Hans Krueger Sipo-SD Fuehrer In Krakow Just before he was to taken up duties in the Zakopane and Rabka Sipo-SD School.

[15] Ibid. Statement of Dr Gercke, psychiatric expert witness for the prosecution. 'I remember Rosenbaum as a young, witty Unterfuehrer. He was the type of young inexperienced Unterfuehrer who froze with respect before a superior.'

[16] Ibid.

[17] Dieter Pohl: *Hans Krueger and the Murder of the Jews in the Stanislawow Region (Galicia)*

[18] IMT. HMSO, Part 3, 184. The set-up and administration certified by Dr Otto Ohlendorf, Chief of Amt 1V of the RSHA (prisoner indicted), and by Walter Schellenberg, Chief of Amt V1 of the RSHA (prisoner indicted). Himmler's decree of 27.9.1939 amalgamated Sipo and the SD into one organisation under Heydrich, (Reichssicherheitshauptamt) Reich Security Main Office. (RSHA), which had now grown from the original 280 men, to nearly a quarter of a million men – the instrument for the Security of the State and the annihilation of the Jews.

[19] Hitler never bothered to abolish the Weimar Constitution and resisted all attempts by Reich Interior Minister Frick to give the Reich a constitution.

[20] Heinz Paechter, *Nazi-Deutsch* (New York, 1943), 114, 119. Hereafter Paechter. In Nazi speak – Nation, National: these terms were replaced by Volk, Volkisch of Reich. The Nazis distinguished Volksnation – the nation identical with a race – from Staatsnation – a nation created by the State (such as Italian Fascism).

[21] 'Volkischer Beobachter', 30th January, 1936.

[22] Paechter, 73. Nothing exceptional in this remark, as it is a fundamental basic principle of any rank structure.

[23] Ibid. Decree: 4/14/33, giving the NSDAP status of a corporation under public law (12/1/33), purging civil service from republicans (4/7/33, making Hitler Fuehrer and Chancellor (8/1/1934), giving the NSDAP control of civil service nominations (1/26/1937). Abolition Equality before law and of Independent Justice (suspension of civil liberties 2/28/1933) etc.

[24] E.J. Feutwanger, 'Nuremberg Laws', unpublished paper.

[25] Paechter, 114.

[26] Raol Hilberg, *Destruction of the European Jews* (3 vols), Vol. 1, 35. Hereafter 'The Destruction'. See also, Martin Gilbert, *History of 20th Century* (Harper-Collins 1996), 835.

[27] Feuchtwanger.

[28] The Euthanasia program was rationalised along the lines of Karl Binding and Alfred Hoche's book, *Life Unworthy of Living*, published sometime in 1920. The Hoche thesis suggested that Euthanasia was a kindness to the patient. This was followed up by the research analysis of psychiatrist Ewald Meltzer, who published a paper on the subject in 1925, hoping to prove them, misguided, but to his astonishment was forced to agree and enhance their theories. He discovered that 73% of parents were in favour of killing their children provided that they were not presented with the facts. See Mini Gelbard, 'An Aspect of the Holocaust – A Master Psychologist', unpublished document, 3.

[29] Paechter, 83.

[30] Feutwanger.

[31] The Trial of German Major War Criminals, HMSO, London 1946. IMT, Speeches, 19.

[32] Sipo-SD training academies were established in 1935 when they came under Zentralamt II (Personnel Office), Hauptabteilung III (Training, education and recruitment of the Sicherheitshauptamt). With the amalgamation of all security services in 1936, they crossed the corridor to the RSHA.

[33] Dr Schoengarth was a regular attendee of the Evangelist church before he joined the HHE.

[34] Paechter, 127

[35] Ibid. 128. Teutonic Creed Movement, German Race Church (spiritualistic circle).

[36] Ibid.

[37] Effective power resided with three men of 'The Triumvirate': Goring, Himmler and Bormann who controlled the SS and police, and the NSDAP. Hermann Goring, 'Reichsmarschall', the highest economic authority and of home administration, Heinrich Himmler, 'Reichsminister des Inneren, Reichsfuehrer SS und Chef der deutschen Polizei', and Martin Bormann, 'Chef des Stabes des Stellvertreters des Fuehrers', who could veto any nomination of civil servants and labour service leaders. His agreement was required for discussions on regional administrative authorities regarding laws.

[38] George C. Browder, *Hitler's Enforcers* (Oxford University Press, London, 1996), 103.

[39] In most Holocaust literature there is an overuse of the word 'Gestapo' (Geheime Staatspolizei = Secret State Police). The early Prussian version under Goering was the Gestapa – Geheime Staats Polizeamt. The later Gestapo had offices all over the Reich. In popular parlance, however, it is applied to all police institutions created since 1933. See: Paechter, *Nazi Usage*, 79. The organisation of the Sipo-SD in Galicia, of the BdS and KdS, which replicated the five departments of the RSHA: Personnel, Administration, Intelligence, Secret State Police, and Criminal Police. Department IV dealt with Jewish matters.

[40] Rupert Butler: *The Gestapo*, London, 1992, 51. Typewriters always seemed to be in short supply and during 'operations' officers left their posts, not to join in, but to seize any typewriters that may have been available.

[41] In recent times, police forces outside Germany have sought radical solutions to solve policing problems: leadership by means of direct entry to supervisory positions, amalgamations, police academies of excellence, senior command courses, special squads to deal with particular issues, such as terrorism and drugs, major crime and the special branch.

[83] The HHE organised and supervised these changes from the newly-established RSHA Amt V, under the direction of Arthur Nebe.

[43] Rupert Butler, *The Gestapo*, Allen, London, 1992, 51.

[44] Sereny, Stangl, 30-37. The author suggests one treats Stangl's explanations with scepticism.

[45] Ibid.

[46] Browder, Enforcers, 57. Among the earliest members of the Sipo und SD, 20% came from the lower ranks of the civil service.

[47] 'Carrying' a uniform is a police phrase which, in this meaning, reflects a professional, hard working, officer. It can however also mean 'uniform carrier', an officer who wears a uniform and draws his pay, but does little work.

[48] After ignoring the Concordat with the Holy See, signed in July 1933 in Rome, the Nazi Party carried out a long and persistent persecution of the Catholic Church, its priesthood and congregation members, including police officers.

[49] Sereny, Stangl, 37.

[50] Browder, Enforcers, 212.

[51] Andrew Ezergalis, *The Holocaust in Latvia*, Washington, DC, 1996, 146.

[52] Martin Gilbert, 20th Century, 841.

[53] Acknowledgement to Krystyna Kynst: See Zoe Zajdlerowa, *The Dark Side of the Moon*, London, 1989, 55. Over one million were deported by the Soviets during their occupation. Mass deportations occurred: February, April and June 1940, June 1941.

[54] Some of the educational courses at the Rabka School can be gleaned from the School curriculum in *Befehlsblatt des Chefs der Sicherheitspolizei und des SD*, No. 41, Berlin, 15th September, 1942. See also KGB Trials Archive, Delo No. 292, and Archive No. 28446.

[55] Polish intelligentsia, particularly those Poles who had taken part in the referendum held in Silesia after the First World War and voted against Germany. Strechenbach and his EG then turned their attention to the Jews before moving on to the town of Jaroslav. (Bruno Strechenbach later served on the Russian front where he was captured. He was tried by the Russians after the war and sentenced to a period of imprisonment. On his release, well after the war, he was closely questioned on the Nazi leader's orders for the implementation of the 'Final Solution of the Jewish Question'.) Nowy Targ was assigned to the Third Company of EG, commanded by Dr E. Hasselberger. See *Rabka and District Memorial Book*, HMM, Washington, DC. (RO November, 1997)

[56] Ibid.

[57] *Memorial Book of Rabka and District*, (including the Ben-Ami Documentation) The Holocaust Memorial Museum, Washington. DC.

[58] Alexander Ben-Ami, *The Zakopane Judenrat* (known as the Ben-Ami Documentation), HMM, Washington .DC.

[59] After the war, both Weissmann and Samish were tried for war crimes in the town of Frieburg, Germany. The trial lasted for 5 months. Many of the prosecution witnesses fainted in the course of giving detailed evidence of the murders and other crimes. Weissmann was sentenced to 7 years imprisonment for having taken part in the murder of 111 Jews.

[60] *Memorial Book.*

[61] The Mauer brothers were to serve with Hans Kruger in Stanilslawow for the murder of over 20.000 Jews.

[62] *Nowy Targ Memorial Book.*

[63] Ibid.

[64] Ibid.

[65] Ibid.

[66] Ibid. See Adolf Hutler?

[67] Ibid.

[68] One of the training priorities was the 'V'-Agents.

[69] It was very common for Jews in Eastern and Central Europe to speak many languages – Yiddish, German, Polish, Russian and Ukrainian etc.

[70] In the District of Neumarkt (Nowy Targ) Krakow. Shown on present day maps as Nowy Sachs.

[71] The earliest blueprints for the Russian campaign were known as '*Aufbau Ost*', or Eastern Build. This directive, which set out the basic strategy and the date of the 15th May, 1941, for the attack, was submitted to Hitler on December 17, 1940. Hitler made two changes, 1; the direction of the attack, and 2, the name of the operation would be 'Barbarossa'.

[72] At the end of July/early August. 1941.

[73] Our understanding of the Holocaust in Galicia is indebted to the work of Dieter Pohl, especially his *Nationalsozialistische Judenverfolgung in Ostgalizien 1941-1944* (Munich, 1996). In 1998, Pohl published a study for Yad Vashem entitled *Hans Krueger and the Murder of the Jews in the Stanislawow Region (Galicia)*, which is now available on-line in English (See http//www1.yadvashem.org.il/ odot_pdf/Microsoft Word – 2292.pdf). Pohl's research, combined with the well-known report from Brigadier Katzmann to Krueger (Nuremberg doc L-18), enables us to identify conclusive sources that demonstrate the co-ordinated genocide carried out by the Nazis in the region.

[74] See Zoe Zajdlerowa, *The Dark Side of the Moon*, London, 1989, 55. Over one million were deported by the Soviets during their occupation. Mass deportations occurred: February, April and June 1940, June 1941.

[75] ZbV – units by definition (special group) were used elsewhere, particularly in the opening phases of the invasion of Poland in September 1939. E.g., SS-Obergruppenfuehrer Udo von Woyrsch at Kattowice whose zbV unit was responsible for murdering many thousands.

[76] Confirmation of Schoengarth's zbV appointment can be seen: Affidavit Dr Otto Ohlendorf, 5th November 1945, IMT 2620 PS.

[77] Krueger Verdict: Hans Krueger statement 8 January 1962: See the composition of zbV and the named Sipo-SD officers, are shown in a number of sources: Dieter Pohl. Berlin Document Centre Personnel Files of the SS (Yad Vashem) – BDC, Stellebbesetzung des KdS Krakow (Abschrift): Dienstelle; Kommandeur der Sicherheitspolizei und der SD fur den Distrikt Krakow (1940-1943), Zentralkartel erganz am: 23rd October 1962, hereafter Krakow KdS (Yad Vashem). The personnel 'cards' clearly show the progress of these officers from Krakow to their postings in East Galicia.

[78] Yehoshua Buechler, '*Kommandostab Reichsfuehrer-SS*', 13 (Holocaust and Genocide Studies. Vol. 1. No. 1, 11-25.

[79] PRO: WO 2890 IMT No. 2890, statement of Ohlendorf.

[80] Krueger Verdict: statement of Hans Krueger.

[81] Hilberg, *Destruction*, vol. 11, 406.

[82] Krueger *Verdict*. See also PRO: WO 3644. Document No. 3644, statement of Erwin Schulz who describes the Sipo-SD actions in Lvov.

[83] Christopher Diekmann, *The War and the Killing of the Lithuanian Jews* (National Socialist Extermination Policies, Ed. Ulrich Herbert, Oxford, 2000, 240).

[84] Ralf Ogorreck, Die *Einsatzgruppen der Sicherheitspolizei und des SD im Rahmen der 'Genesis der Endlosung,* Berlin, 1996, as cited by Dr Dieter Pohl in correspondence to RO.

[85] PRO: NTD 2620-PS. Affidavit Otto Ohlendorf. (My underline). See also University of Southampton Archives (Ohlendorf) NMT/9/14/1) r.21.

[86] See Garrard, *East European Jewish Affairs*, vol. 28, number 2, winter 1998/9, 22.).

[87] B. F. Sabrin, *Alliance for Murder*, NY, 1991, 64.

[88] Christopher Browning, *Ordinary Men* 241.

[89] Hilberg, *Documents of Destruction*, London, 1972, 88.

[90] Goetz Aly, *Political Prehistory*, (National Socialist Extermination Policies, ed. Ulrich Herbert, Oxford, 2000, 71).

[91] Krueger Verdict: statement of Hans Krueger 8 January 1962 (my brackets).

[92] Thomas Sandkühler, *Galicia*, Oxford, 2000, 113.

[93] Menten Verdict.

[94] Ibid.

[95] See Browning, *Path to Genocide*, Cambridge U.P. 1992, 105.

[96] Ibid. 107.

[97] Dieckmann, 246.

[98] Hans Frank must have been tearing his hair out. All efforts to get rid of his Jews were now compounded by events.

[99] See *Recollections on the life and Martyrdom of Jewish Medical Doctors in the Lvov Ghetto* by: Dr. Marek Redner, Translated from Polish by: A.S. Redner Edited by: Isabel Alcoff. I met A.S. Redner on a journey to the official opening of a memorial service at the site of the former Belzec death camp in 2004.

[100] The composition of zbV and the named Sipo-SD officers are shown in a number of sources: Dieter Pohl, 'Nationalsozialistische Judenverfolgung in Ostgalizien 1941-1944', Munich, 1996, 411-423. Berlin Document Centre Personnel Files of the SS (Yad Vashem)-BDC, Stellebbesetzung des KdS Krakow (Abschrift): 'Dienstelle; Kommandeur der Sicherheitspolizei und des SD fur den District Krakow (1940-1943)', Zentralkartel erganz am: 23 October 1962, hereafter Krakow KdS (Yad Vashem).

[101] Hilberg, *The Destruction*, vol. 1, 296.

[102] The Redner Papers.

[103] The form of murder was based not on any individual trait but simply on membership of a certain group: the murder of the Polish intelligentsia had been a priority objective of German policy ever since they occupied Polish territories in 1939. Under the heading 'AB' (Allgemeine Befriedung: general pacification) SS Gruppenfuehrer Bruno Streckenbach (Schoengarth's predecessor) had since the spring of 1940 organised the murder of 5000 university people, artists and intellectuals. At the time a colonel in the NKVD was attached to the Soviet liaison officer to Dr Hans Frank (GG); he can scarcely have been unaware of Operation AB.

[104] Dr Otto Rasch (EG 'C') with the OUN and Wehrmacht, whose actions were approved by the High Command of the 17th Army, shot all Jewish males of military age. See also Operation Station Report USSR No. 10, 2nd July, 1941 (Arad, EG Reports, 2).

[105] Thomas Sandkühler, *Anti-Jewish Policy and the Murder of the Jews in the District of Galicia*, 1941/2 (National Socialist Extermination Policies, Oxford, 2000, 109).

[106] The rank of Sonderfuehrer may be described as a specialist officer functioning above his rank. In Krakow, Schoengarth and Menten were on first name terms and may be described as friends. Menten was thieving Jewish art for the benefit of the SS. When zbV was being put together, Schoengarth invited Menten to join zbV for the Lvov venture. Menten was never trained (like other Sonderfuehrers) for this duty, but when in East Galicia, committed theft and atrocity, as we shall see. The information about Menten mainly comes from his trial notes (Menten Verdict), and from Mrs Dorothea Schoengarth in correspondence to the trial investigators to seek a pension after her husband had been convicted for the murder of Americo S. Galle, the American airman who had baled out over Holland and shot by Schoengarth's security department.

The personnel 'cards' clearly show the progress of these officers from Krakow to their postings in East Galicia. Another interesting point: a number of these men were involved in the massacres committed in Poland late 1939 and further atrocities in May 1940. They were trained killers. Many on this list appear in the list of Sipo-SD stationed in East Galicia.

[107] BDC 806.

[108] Krueger Verdict.

[109] PRO WO235/631. Helm and Menten teamed up together in the plunder of Jewish art in Lvov (statement of Dorothea Schoengarth).

[110] In late August 1941, Rosesbbaum returned with Dr Schoengarth to Krakow where he was the Head of the Sipo-SD Training School at Bad Rabka. Dr Schoengarth remained in Krakow to administer and supervise the Jewish destruction. He was the main perpetrator in the Krakow District consolidating 'AR', liaison with the HSSPF F.W. Krueger, SSPF Globocnik (Lublin), and the HHE in Berlin.

[111] Ministry of Justice trial transcripts, 'The Netherlands v Pieter Menten 1977-1980' (hereafter Menten Verdict). A surprise witness at the Menten trial after the war was Hans Geisle who had been a member of zbV, and remembered Menten being added to the Commando as 'guest and interpreter.' There is further corroboration, surprisingly as it may seem, from Dorothea Schoengarth (wife of Dr Schoengarth), who after the war in the trials of both Menten and Rosenbaum gave evidence that her husband had taken Menten along because he had an antiques shop in Lvov. Her husband had given him a uniform to perform his duties as interpreter for the commando. She also stated which the court interpreted as a defensive line, which Menten was sent back to Krakow without his uniform as he and SS-Obersturmfuehrer Heim were mixed up in shady antiques deals. (See Rosenbaum trial statement of Mrs Schoengarth RAD Az.1 141 Js 856/61, 141 Js 61/65), 2436-2444. See also PRO WO235/631.

[112] Menten Verdict. Malcolm MacPherson, *The Last Victim*, 1984, 98. (This faction/fictional account by MacPherson has been well researched. Where I have sourced this material it has been corroborated, usually by trial references. Through Kiptka, Menten met Wilhelm Rosenbaum at the Magrabianka SS Club in Rabka. Menten, Kiptka and Dr Schoengarth had stayed at the residence in the winter of 1941.

[113] A number of SS-officers of Scharfuehrer rank were either in the first transport, or joined up with the team later. Several were transferred in to the Sipo-SD offices when they were established. We are able to identify a number of them from the Stanislawow Office of Sipo-SD: Heinrich Schott (Jewish Affairs), Josef Daus, Kurt Giese, Hans Greve, Wilhelm Hehemann, Walther Lange, Otto Ruckerich, Kurt Wulkau, and the Mauer brothers, ethnic Germans who had served with Hans Krueger when he was commandant of the Sipo-SD Training School at Bad Rabka (Rosenbaum had replaced Krueger as commandant). These non-commissioned officers held the principal decisions over 'life or death' in the coming actions.

[114] The Sipo-SD arrested: Professor Tadeuz Boj-Zelenski, a member of the Union of Soviet Writers, and author of numerous literary works, Professor Roman Recki of the Medical Institute, Vladimir Seradski, Dean of the University and Professor of Forensic Medicine, Roman Longchamp Deberrier, Doctor of Law, together with his three sons, Professor Tadeusz Ostrovski, Professor Jan Grek, Professor Henryk Gilarowicz the surgeon, Professor Anton Tesziaski the Stomatologist, Witfold Nowicki, Professor of Pathological Anatomy, Vladimir Stozhek and Anton Lomnicki, Doctors of Physico-Mathematical Sciences, Academician Solovi, Kazimir Bartel, an honorary member of many academies of science, Stanislav Pilat, Doctor of Chemical Science, Kaspar Vaisel, Roman Witkiewicz and Vladimir Rukowskin, Doctors of Technical Science, Professor Stanislaw Progulski, Professor

Mendzewski, Adam Fiszer the ethnographer, Kazimir Vetulyani, Doctor of
Technical Science, the prominent lawyer Professor Mauricius Arerhand, a member
of Poland's Codification Committee, the Lvov authoress Galina Glyska, the critic
Ostap Ortvin, the university lecturers Auerbach and Piasiecki, Vander the physicist,
Simon Blumental the engineer, Ruff the surgeon, Czortrover, a university lecturer
and other professors and teachers employed in local educational establishments. It is
interesting to note that this elite 'men of letters' survived under Soviet rule that was a
contradiction to Soviet policy. See *The Soviet Take-over of the Polish Eastern
Provinces, 1939-41*, London 1991, edited by Keith Sword. See also Bogdan
Czaykowski, 'Soviet Policies in the Literary Sphere: Their Effects and Implications',
102-130. These intellectuals collaborated and were protected to play the 'Polish
Card'.

[115] Albert Zygmunt, *Murder of the Lvov Professors* in July 1941, Wroclaw' Poland
1989, 69-99. Bartel had been earmarked by General Sikorski to take over as
Ambassador to Moscow should the Soviets denounce the two treaties with Germany
of August and September 1939. See also *Soviet Polish Relations*, Vol. 1. No.93,
118.

[116] The Hamlyn Marcus Collection, *Soviet Government Statements on Nazi Atrocities,*
London, nd). – Communiqués issued by the Soviet Extraordinary State Commission
for ascertaining and investigating crimes committed by the German-Fascist invaders
and their accomplices: 242-255. NB: These reports must be treated with care. See
report concerning the 'Katyn' shootings (107-135) that is complete fabrication of the
facts. However, the Lvov murders have been corroborated elsewhere and I am
reasonably confident of their findings.

[117] Ibid.

[118] These 'Murders' were so secret that nothing leaked out until after the war.
However, direct corroboration of the Lvov professor murders was being enacted on
about the 8th October 1943. The notorious Blobel Commando 1005 was active in
the Lvov area. A surviving Jew of that Commando, Leon Weliczker (Wells), *The
Janowska Road*, London, 1966), 197: 'I was chosen to go with an "elite" group. It
was all hush, and we cannot Figure: out why. We go to a sector of the town called
Wulka. We are put to digging in a small area of ground. In fifteen minutes bodies
become visible. We could tell they were very important people by their clothes and
their jewellery. Some of them had been buried in tuxedos. We remove all the bodies
and load them into an, including the professors, (Abbreviated) insulated truck, and
then the pyre to be burnt. The documents show that among these dead are Professor
Kazimierz Bartel, Dr Ostrowski, Professor Stozek, T. Boy Zelenski, and others.
There were 38 bodies – the very cream of Poland's social and intellectual life. On
the 9th October we burn over 2,000 bodies.'

[119] Ibid.

[120] In June 1942, Himmler ordered Colonel Paul Blobel to dig up and burn all corpses from locations where massacres had occurred.

[121] Leon Wells, *The Janowska Road*, London, 1979.

[122] Soviet Special Commission report, 244. Two witnesses are named, but which one made the statement is not recorded. The Commission resolved that 70 of the most prominent representatives of science, technology and art were murdered.

[123] Wells, 201.

[124] Krueger Verdict: final remarks, of Prosecuting Counsel, 1167-1174. After the war, Hans Krueger was interviewed whilst in detention in Munster. He was asked to name his fellow culprits in the Professors' murder but he refused. Another witness to the Professors' murder, and a witness in the Oberlander trial in East Germany, was Max Draheim, a senior police officer who was present at the execution of the professors. All Draheim could say was that the officer had the rank of SS-Untersturmfuehrer – he couldn't recall his name. Many years later when Wiesenthal had obtained a photograph of Kutschmann, the witness Draheim was dead.

[125] Correspondence author-Wiesenthal 1997.

[126] Knoop, 59.

[127] Menten also sealed 6 other apartments and seized valuable art property. This included the apartment of Professor Jan Grek. Menten posted an official bonding order (in Polish and German), a decree that made the premises Reich property. Jadwina Roswadovska, one of the few remaining members of the Ostrowsky family after the war, testified to having seen Menten's nameplate on the door of her dead stepfather's house, Knoop, 59.

[128] Rosenbaum Verdict: Jewish witnesses, Ettinger and Schon who were both retained during this time at the School. See also Malcom MacPherson, *The Last Victim*, London, 1984, 108.

[129] This is an interesting point and the nearest explanation I have found is in an article written by Bogdan Czaykowski (See *The Soviet Take-over of the Polish Eastern Provinces, 1939-41*, edited by Keith Sword, London, 1991), 102-130.

[130] Zygmunt Albert, *The Extermination of the Lvov Professors in July 1941*, in idem (ed.), Kazn profesorow Lvovskich, lipiec 1941. Studia oraz relacje i dokumenty (Wroclaw: Wydawnictwo Uniwersytetu Wroclawskiego, 1989), pp. 69-99 (Albert, Kazn profesorow); Slawomir Kalbarczyk, 'Okolicznosci smierci profesora Kazimierza Bartla we Lvovie w lipcu 1941 r.,' Biuletyn Glownej Komisji Badania Zbrodni przeciwko Narodowi Polskiemu, 34 (1922), 112-123.

[131] Dr Redner, Papers to the author: Original Memoirs (in Polish) written between 1944 and 1949.
The manuscript is preserved by Yad Vashem, file 03/430 in Jerusalem, Israel.

[132] Ibid.

[133] Ibid.

[134] Ibid

[135] Arad, Krakowski, Spector, *The Einsatzgruppen Reports*, London 1989, 2. The NKVD on the 25.6.41 in Lvov bloodily suppressed Ukrainian insurrection movements. About 3000 were shot by NKVD. EK 4a and EK 4b have arrived in Lvov'. Operation Report USSR No.10. There were three prisons in Lvov: Brygdik at Kazimierzowska Street, the prison at the former police headquarters on Lecki Street; and the prison at the former military headquarters on Zamarstynowska Street. Their population consisted mostly of criminals and political prisoners from the Lvov area. Many of them had been murdered by the NKVD and buried in the prison courtyard. The Lvov Jews were made to dig up the corpses and photographed in the process for propaganda purposes – 'look at the Jewish-Bolshevik murderers whom we have just caught red-handed!' (See David Kahane, *The Lvov Ghetto Diary*, 4).

[136] Krueger Verdict: Statement Hans Krueger, 8th January 1962.

[137] Ibid.

[138] The commander of EG 4a, Paul Blobel, delivered in Sokal on 27th June 1941, made similar demands. He gathered his men around him and explained that the Jews must be killed and that everybody must participate, as the order to do so was a 'Fuehrer Order'. See YVA TR-10/616, 137, 142. See also Helmut Krausnik, *Anatomy of the SS State*, London, 1968, 262. Dr Otto Rasch, commander of EG 'C', made similar demands.

[139] Ibid. The shooting of women and children was now taking place on a daily basis, although it would appear there was no authorisation for it. I would suggest that Himmler was influenced by zbV's actions that subsequently resulted in a directive to kill all genders of all ages. (I refer to this later.)

[140] Ibid. For many of the junior ranks this was their first introduction of what was expected of them. Some refused, some looked to more senior officers for help. On this aspect Schoengarth was not approachable.

[141] Ibid. I think the point to highlight here is that these SD commanders were acting on their responsibility (vide the Hitler-Himmler Directive). It is interesting to see how many writers have gone along with the excuse: 'Orders are orders' and their refusal or failure to pull the trigger was never the subject of reprisal by the senior officers. It is shown: J. and C. Garrard, *East European Jewish Affairs*, vol. 28, number 2, winter 1998/9, note 22, 19. See also Klee, Dressen, Riess, *Those were the days*, London 1988), 77. This subtle point, I would suggest, has been overlooked in both cases.

[142] Ibid.

[143] Krueger Verdict: statement of Hans Krueger, statement 8 January 1962. In the first paragraph I am not sure that this was the case and that it may have been a defensive lie on behalf of Krueger. The second paragraph seems more likely.

[144] See Klee, Dressen and Riess, xiii

[145] Belzec Verdict.

[146] The villages in the Stryj valley – see below.

[147] The Mauer brothers had previously done this job, but had left Bad Rabka to join Hans Krueger, as part of the SD team in Stanislawow and never returned.

[148] RAD: Statement of Rosenbaum, 11th January1962, 729-745.

[149] Ibid: Statement of Johann Bornholt, 19th September1962, 96-102.

[150] Ibid: Statement of Rosenbaum, 30th July 1963, 138-6. Oder, Wozdolowicz, Jaworski and Proch (all 'Zugfuehrer') were the expert killing instructors. Using Walther PPK, calibre 765 pistols, they would shoot Jews in the back of the neck at a distance of 10-20cm. Proch was very central to the murders in the School and in the town where he would shoot anyone he took a dislike to – Jew or non-Jew. Beck usually accompanied Proch when collecting the Jews from Nowy Sacz for labour. He shot many Jews, several at a time, before returning to the SD School. See RAD, statements of the Jews Grossbard and Blatt (Rosenbaum cross-examination statement, 20th September 1963, 1398-1411). See also Wiesenthal, *The Murderers Amongst Us,* London, 1987. Wiesenthal tracked down Proch (Austrian) in 1947 in Blomberg, a village near Salzburg. He was subsequently sentenced to 6 years imprisonment for his activities in the Rabka School.

[151] Yad Vashem Archives.

[152] RAD. Statement of Dr Kurt Neiding, Wiesbaden 1st January 1962, 765-776. SS-Hauptstumfuehrer Dr Neiding was a lawyer by profession and had been drafted into the SD-Sipo apparatus as legal adviser and interrogator to the BdS in Krakow in July 1942, where he prosecuted SS officers. He was a long-standing colleague and personal friend of Dr Schoengarth. He also knew Rosenbaum and the set-up in Bad Rabka.

[153] RAD. Statement of Schon (604-614). Helen Bauman was brought from Zakopane by Hans Krueger where she was his maid. She was awaiting orders to move with Hans Krueger to Stanislawow, but was shot by the SS when the Rabka Jews were killed, much against Krueger's wishes. Helen was a close friend of Sarah Schon. (Mark Goldfinger to the author, 1998).

[154] Rabka and District Memorial Book (National Archives, Washington, DC).

[155] See www.vineland.org. Edited by Mrs Genia Kuhnreich.

[156] RAD. Part of the Jewish workers in the School was finally transported to Belzec in August, 1942 and the rest in September, 1943, to Plaszow Concentration Camp.

[157] Ibid. The observations are based upon the statements of (non-Jews) – Dr Bath, Hans Krueger, Meta Kuck, Elfiede Bohnert, Dr Hann, Draheim, Oder, Dr Neiding and Alfred Kuck.

[158] Ibid: The behaviour of Rosenbaum towards friends and subordinates is described in statements of: (non-Jews) Alfred Kuck, Ilse Raemisch, Dittmar, Draheim, Muller, Czakainski and Bohnert.

See also Statement of Friedrich August Glienke, 16th June, 1961, 274-277.

[159] Ibid: Jewish witnesses stated that Rosenbaum wore an SS ring from which two spikes protruded as if they were large teeth, or maybe the eye-sockets.

[160] Ibid.

[161] Ibid. No German witness from the Rabka trials has ever referred to '*live training*', which is not surprising. The evidence comes mainly from Jewish witnesses (Ettinger, Goldfinger and Schon), all present at the School during the relevant period.

[162] Once the School was established it became the approved centre in west Galicia where small groups of prisoners were brought from outside areas for immediate execution. A phone call to the School reception was sufficient to organise an execution party.

[163] RAD: Statement of Rosenbaum cross-examination of 20th September, 1963, 1398-1411, refers to the witness Steiner's allegations of 19th June, 1962.

[164] Ibid: Ettinger, Schon and Goldfinger – Statements and interview with the author.

[165] Reuben Ainsztein, 'The Collector', *New Statesman* 27th February 1981, 9

[166] Photograph by kind permission of Krystyna Kynst sent to the author. During my visit in 1998, I found several mature trees that still bore the marks of bullet holes. The bark of these trees was still weeping after all this time. I confirmed this with the help of Jan Krakowski (Secretary of the present-day School for deaf and dumb children) and a metal detector which registered when placed against these locations.

[167] Lord Russell of Liverpool, *Scourge of the Swastika*, London, 1964, 58.

[168] Ibid.

[169] In answer to allegations by former employment Head in Neu Markt, Grimmlinger, Statement 4th July, 1962, 13. Grimmlinger opened a whole '*bag of worms*'.

[170] Ibid. The cellars and stables which were used for imprisonment are directly under present-day converted sleeping quarters.

[171] Ibid. Rosenbaum cross-examination, 3rd January, 1962, 675-681.

[172] Ibid.

[173] Ibid.

[174] Lord Russell of Liverpool, *The Scourge of the Swastika,* London, 1964, 212.

[175] Rabka and District Memorial Book for the town of Makov Podhalanski.

[176] '*Soviet Government Statements on Nazi Atrocities*', London 1946, 19-20. (Report signed by Molotov, People's Commissar for Foreign Affairs, Moscow, and 6th January, 42). See also Russell, '*Swastika*', 119.

[177] Ibid.

[178] Ibid.

[179] Klee, Dressen, Reiss, *Those were the Days,* 120.

[180] RAD. Statement of Ettinger and interview with the author Haifa 1997.

[181] Ibid.

[182] Ibid. Statements of the Jews – Derschowitz, Kolber and Dattner and Goodrich.

[183] Ibid

[184] Ibid. Statements of the Jews – Form, Goodrich, Derschowitz, Kolba, Mendel, Lustig, Kesterbaum, Gold. Frolich, Farber, Susskind, Statter, Steiner, Kalfus, Grossbard, Lonker and Zwi Schiffeldrin.

[185] Interview Mark Goldfinger and Sarah Schon (brother and sister) with the author, June, 1997, Israel and London. A few days after the murder of Mrs Kranz, Sarah Schon identified her grandmother's dress that had arrived in the laundry room for processing. She recognised the dress as the one worn by her grandmother on Shabbat.

[186] Ibid.

[187] Rosenbaum states that he made it his policy to obtain Schoengarth's approval for all his actions. This was not the conclusion of the court.

[188] Interview with Norman Salsitz, survivor of the Pustkow camp in Washington DC, November, 1997. There were thousands of camps, of all sizes and for many purposes in Poland and Ukraine. Many of the camps sound or are spelt very much the same. For reference purposes: *Hitlerowskie Obozy Na Ziemiach Polskich W Latach 1939 - 1945*, obtained from the Polish Underground Trust, West London.

[189] Rosenbaum Verdict: Mishana Dolne, nearer to Rabka but was under the jurisdiction of the Nowy Sacz Gestapo. Whereas Rosenbaum chose his execution place in the Rabka School, Hamann chose the village of Mishana Dolne for his executions. He demanded that the Judenrat collect an exorbitant amount of money to stop the deportations. When the Judenrat could not pay, Hamann gathered 800 Jews in the Square and murdered them. Hamann, after the war, was sentenced to life imprisonment for the Mishana-Dolne murders.

[190] Ibid.

[191] Ibid. Statement of Johann Bornholt, 19th September 1962, 96-102. Bornholt was a police officer with the Grenzpolizeikommissariat (Krakow District).

[192] Ibid. See also Klee, *Those Were The Days*, 76.

[193] Ibid. The Jews Grun and Regina Weiss.

[194] Several Jews were able to escape unnoticed with the help of the J.E.O. By marking up cards 'dead', these cards were destroyed by the German Authorities, along with the identity.

[195] RAD. On this transport from Nowy Targ were the Jews: Statter, Derschowitz, Henry Frolich, Joseph Grossbard, Alexander Lustig, Mendel Lustig, Kolber, Appel, Farber, Stammberger, Steiner, Lonker, Sammy Frolich (brother of Henry), Zwickler, Einhorn, Wenger, Wolkowitz, Kauffer, Buxbaum, Gutwirt, Kalman, Tiefenbrunner, Wildfeuer, Wildstein and Schermer.

[196] Ibid.

[197] Ibid.

[198] Ibid.

[199] Ibid. 410. 16,000 Jews deported from this region to Belzec.

[200] Ibid.

[201] Ibid.

[202] Ibid. Among them were the Jews Form (who had just arrived from Neu Markt), Susskind, Goodrich, Kalfus and others.

[203] Ibid. Statement of the Jew Form.

[204] Ibid.

[205] Ibid. Statement of Rosenbaum, 20. 9. 1963, 1398-1411, cross-examination of the Jews Steiner and Blatt. It is probable that this group, which numbered about 50 and may have been political executions as they were shot, were clothed, which was unusual.

[206] Ibid. Although denied by Rosenbaum, witnesses stated that over 2000 Jews were murdered in the School.

[207] Ibid. Statements: The Jews Form, Goodrich, Derschowitz, Kolber, M, Lustig, Kestenbaum, Dattner, Ettinger, Zollmann, Grossbard.

[208] Historia Rabka: Komendant szkoły *Wilhelm Rosenbaum* co jakiś czas odwiedzał biuro i nakazywał wymeldować rozstrzelanych z adnotacją zmarł na zawał serca.

[209] SPP-3.18.1. Polish Underground and Movement Study Trust, London, *German Reprisals*, 17, 25.10.1941.

[210] RAD. Statement of Frania Tiger. Interviewed by the author, Israel, 1997.

[211] Ibid. Statement of the Jew Goodrich.

[212] RAD. Statement of the Jew Form.

[213] Ibid. Statement of Fruederich August Glienke.

[214] Ibid. Statements of the Jews Goodrich, Bar-Sade, Ettinger, Zollmann, Zwi Schiffeldrin, Abraham Schiffeldrin, Alicja Nogala, Elfyd Trybowka, Schon, Blatt, Czarnowicki, Derschowitz, Steiner, Farber and Mendel Lustig.

[215] Mark Goldfinger, interview with the author.

[216] The witness Schon who gives an account of the Jordanow action obtained from residents brought to Rabka, and the atmosphere in the Rosenbaum household on the day of the action.

[217] Ibid.

[218] RAD. The practice of throwing young children in to the air (see notes re Janowska camp) and shooting them was demonstrated by the instructors to impress (and show off) to those present, and to convey the contempt of any value that was to be placed on the Jews; the pit and plank procedure was demonstrated, shooting in the back of the neck was demonstrated, torturing and interrogation techniques were demonstrated, hitting children with the butt of the rifle was demonstrated, and the '*sardine method*' (lining up children/adults one behind the other and shooting them with a single bullet) was demonstrated.

[219] Ibid. Statement of Dr. Neiding.

[220] Ibid. Statement of Rosenbaum.

[221] According to Mark Goldfinger, who knew the Ettinger brothers very well, the Ettinger brothers appear to have been cushioned from the normal harassment and were able to find comfortable jobs at Rabka, the kitchens in Plaszow and finally with the Madritsch and Schindler transport. 'You didn't get this sort of treatment without having to offer in return'?

[222] Michael Ettinger, shown on the Schindler list as number 69014.

[223] **Sources**: The testimonies of Julian Feuerman and Joachim Nachbar have been published: Julian Feuerman, 'Pamietnik ze Stanislawowa (1941-1943)' in: *Biuletyn Zydowskiego Instytutu Historycznego* 59 (1966), pp. 63-91; Joachim Nachbar, *Endure, Defy and Remember. Memoir of a Holocaust Survivor* (Southfield, Mich., 2003) [first published in 1977, by Joachim Nachbar]. There are many testimonies quoted in Elisabeth Freundlich: *Die Ermordung einer Stadt namens Stanislau*, (Vienna: Österreichischer Bundesverlag, 1986) and also Towiah Friedman (ed.), *Schupo und Gestapo Kriegsverbrecher von Stanislau vor dem Wiener Volksgericht: Dokumentensammlung* (Haifa: Institute of Documentation in Israel for the Investigation of Nazi War Crimes, 1957). There are two excellent German studies about the annihilation of the Jews in *Distrikt Galizien* that contain much information concerning the events in Stanislawow: Dieter Pohl, *Von der 'Judenpolitik' zum Judenmord. Der Distrikt Lublin des Generalgouvernements 1939-1944* (Frankfurt am Main: Peter Lang, 1993) and Thomas Sandkühler, *Endlösung' in Galizien. Der Judenmord in Ostpolen und die Rettungsinitiativen von Berthold Beitz 1941-1944* (Bonn: Dietz, 1996). Dieter Pohl has also published an article mainly focused on Stanislawow: 'Hans Krueger and the Murder of the Jews in the Stanislawow Region (Galicia)' in *Yad Vashem Studies* 26 (1997), pp. 239-264. In *Pinkas Hakehillot Polin: Encyclopedia of*

Jewish Communities, Poland, Volume II, Eastern Galicia (Jerusalem: Yad Vashem, 1980) on pages 359-67 there is an entry about Stanislawow. There are many survivor testimonies in the Jewish Historical Institute in Warsaw and in the Yad Vashem Archives in Jerusalem. Especially RG-302 (Diaries and Testimonies) at the JHI contains several very detailed and useful personal accounts. Contemporary German documentation on the administration of *Distrikt Galizien* can be found in Archive of the Institute for National Memory (IPN) in Warsaw, the Archive of New Documents (AAN) in Warsaw and documents from Stanislawow itself in the State Archive of the Ivano-Frankivsk Oblast (DAIFO). The documents from the Stanislau trial in Münster against Hans Krüger and others can be found in the Zentrale Stelle Dortmund (ZSt Dortmund), the Bundesarchiv-Aussenstelle Ludwigsburg (BA-L) and also in the Institut für Zeitgeschichte, Munich (IfZ).

[224] South-eastern Poland (Galicia) became the 5th District of the Generalgouvnement by enactment of a decree (signed by Hitler, Keitel, and Lammers), 17th July 1941, NG - 1280. See Hilberg, The Destruction Vol, 1, 349.

[225] Krueger Verdict/Pohl.

[226] My findings appear to be corroborated (independently) by Thomas Sandkühler, *National Socialist Extermination Policies*, edited Elrich Herbert, Oxford, 2000, 109.

[227] See Hans Mommsen, *The Realisation of the Unthinkable* Translated by Alan Kramer and Louise Willmot, from *Die Realisierung des Utopischen, functional analysis,* Yad Vashem, 1983, 381-420.

[228] (1906—1957), SS officer. Fritz Katzmann joined the Nazi Party in 1928 and the SS in 1930. From November 1939 to August 1941 he served as SS and Police Leader in the Radom district of the Generalgouvernement. Next, he was appointed SS and Police Leader in the Galicia region, a post he held until the fall of 1943. In this capacity, Katzmann was in charge of the implementation of the 'final solution' for the Jews of Galicia. Under his direction, most of the Jews of Eastern Galicia were exterminated. On 30th June, 1943 Katzmann submitted a report to his superiors, in which he described in great detail how he and his men had eliminated almost all of the Jews who lived in the region, either by shooting them on the spot, or by deporting them to their deaths at forced labour or extermination camps. His report also made mention of cases of Jewish resistance to his actions. In 1944 Katzmann was appointed SS and Police Leader in Military District XX, whose main offices were located in the city of Danzig. After the war, Katzmann falsified his name and went into hiding; he died in 1957. No other details are known about his post-war life.

[229] SD Jewish Department 11/112 (Surveillance of Ideological Opponents/Jewry) in the Berlin HQ, to emerge as RSHA 1VB4. The Judenreferate (section for Jewish affairs) was a mechanism in radicalising the persecution of the Jews, which since

1933 kept a watching brief on the numerous anti-Jewish legislation. Every citizen in Germany could refer to this legislation by referring to the Reichsgesetzblatt (Official Gazette).

[230] It is still not clear who – Schoengarth, Tanzmann, or Katzmann – issued the precise orders for the mass murders carried out in the eastern Galicia. Decisions on the '*Final Solution*' throughout Europe were being made at that time in Berlin, such as deportations of Jews to the East; such decisions were reached around the 18th September, 1941, with the agreement between Himmler and Globocnik (SSPF Lublin) to set up the first extermination camps. The question to ask: '*Why did they commence immediately with the mass murder of Jewish men, women and children in the Galician District, while in the other Generalgouvnement districts the authorities waited until the extermination camps had been completed?*'

[231] Ibid. A flour mill owned by Samuel Rudolf. A large red brick, unoccupied building, several stories high situated on Halitska Street. This building was to remain the central feature of the occupation which was to serve the Germans as a temporary prison and execution site guarded by Ukrainian and Jewish auxiliaries (police and fire brigade). With the influx of the Hungarian Jews there was a desperate effort by the local Jews to feed them. The Jewish baker, Yaakov Krigel, scavenged the town collecting food and clothing for these refugees. (See also Norman and Amalie Petranka Salsitz, *Against All Odds: A Tale of Two Survivors,* NY, 1990, and *Pinkas Hakehillot*, Vol. 11, 359 - 376). Hereafter PH.

[232] Amalie Salsitz (wife of Norman) who lived with her family in Stainslawow at the time and had a brief association with a Hungarian Count, who was privy by his position, to have some knowledge of the German intentions.

[233] Referred to by Amalie Salsitz as the '*stately courthouse*' on Bilinski Street.

[234] Official communication authorisation dated from Goring to Heydrich to prepare for the implementation of the Final Solution of the '*Jewish Question*'.

[235] Krueger Verdict/Pohl: Krueger had a staff of 25 made up of the various security sub-sections, i.e. Gestapo, Kripo and SD etc.; for the Grossationen, Krueger relied on augmenting his forces from outside, including railway police. This was a very common factor with the Security Forces and in particular the SS/SD engaged in the '*Operation Reinhardt*' Camps. Very few SS were actually engaged in the camps – 12-15 SS was not uncommon. The SD and their Jewish Departments were very small, even in the Action Reinhardt extermination camps, SD/SS staff was at a minimum. The '*workers*' were mainly the auxiliaries, and of course the Jews.

[236] Dieter Pohl – Krueger Verdict.

[237] Amalie Salsitz was assaulted and robbed of her purse by locals whom she knew.

[238] In November, 1938 Hungary joined Germany in the carving up of Czechoslovakia, annexing some Slovakian districts and a part of Ruthenia. In March, 1939, when

Slovakia declared itself an independent state, Hungary occupied the rest of Ruthenia. In August, 1940 Hungary received northern Transylvania from Rumania. On the 22nd June, 1941, Hungarian forces joined the Germans in invading Russia and acquired further territory in Eastern Galicia. The Hungarians placed the same restrictions on her newly acquired Jews but the Hungarian military did not countenance any pogroms against Jews or mass executions in the area under their control; they even prevented a number of such actions: 'Isolated operations against Jews carried out by militia. In the second half of August, 1941, Hungarians prevented a massacre of Jews in Kolomyja. This was on the initiative of Krueger, since the Gestapo detachment for Kolomyja did not arrive there until the first week in September, 1941' (see report: Tuvia Friedmann, 'Police Battalion 24/Company 7, to the Order Police in Galicia, September, 24, 1942.' Zentrale Stelle der Landesjustizverwaltugen, Collection UdSSR, vol. 410, 508-10. Hereafter Friedmann.

[239] Arad. RSHA 1V – A-1. Operation Report USSR No. 23 (32 copies) July 15, 1941.

[240] Dieter Pohl to author.

[241] Ibid. Also personal recollection by Amelia Saltsitz to RO. Among those Jews assembled included: Lawyers, engineers, physicians, pharmacists, teachers, Rabbis (including Rabbi Horowitz and the preacher Bartish), Mohels and many others. These men were kept for two days in the courtyard next to the jailhouse before taken away for execution.

[242] Gilbert, *The Holocaust*, London, 1987, 179.

[243] Krueger Verdict, Statement Hans Krueger 22. 5. 1963.

[244] Alfred Rosenberg (12th January 1893 – 16th October 1946) was an early and intellectually influential member of the Nazi Party. Rosenberg was first introduced to Adolf Hitler by Dietrich Eckart; he later held several important posts in the Nazi government. He is considered one of the main authors of key Nazi ideological creeds, including its racial theory, persecution of the Jews, *Lebensraum*, abrogation of the Treaty of Versailles, and opposition to 'degenerate' modern art. He is also known for his rejection of Christianity, having played an important role in the development of Positive Christianity, which he intended to be transitional to a new Nazi faith. At Nuremberg he was tried, sentenced to death and executed by hanging as a war criminal.

[245] Hilberg, 'The Destruction', vol.2, 812.

[246] Ibid.

[247] Ibid.

[248] Ibid. A local witness recalls that a grave was about to be covered when a man shouted from the dead: *'I am a Hungarian doctor, I live!'* (Statement of Marek Langer, 28th January, 1948, reported in T. Friedmann's collection of 'Stanislawow

reports', (Haifa, 1957), 37-39. Also statement of Marie Durr in same collection. Sent to RO by Friedmann December, 1997.

[249] Von Thaden to RSHA dated 6. 1. 43. In this report it was quoted, 'A Jew walked up to a German police sergeant and had declared in Yiddish-German jargon: "Sergeant, *I am a Jew, and you can't do anything to me because I am a Hungarian soldier.*"' See Hilberg, 'The Destruction', vol. 2, 810.

[250] Ibid. The Kursk reference escapes me. In Brest-Litovsk it was alleged that Jews from these battalions were stealing property in the presence of the Wehrmacht. See Hilberg, 'The Destruction', 811.

[251] The first '*Final Solution*' conference was held in Berlin. Frank sent his representative (Buhler) to find out the latest thinking on the '*Jewish Question*'. Buhler returned to brief the conference in Krakow on the 16th December, 1941. Those attending: Hans Frank; Health President Dr Walbaum; Labour President Dr Frauendorfer; Dr Schoengarth, Governor Kundt (Radom) and Amtschef Dr Hummel.

[252] Up until December, 1941, only 45 Jews had been sentenced to death and only 8 sentences had been carried out for contravention of Nazi Jewish regulations. This fact was the impetus that goaded Frank and his cohorts into action. From then on there was no looking back.

[253] Krueger Verdict/Pohl. Statement of Hans Krueger 22.5.1963.

[254] Ibid. The more one reads into the detail of how those responsible went about their business of murdering the Jews, the more one realises that an overall blueprint had been drawn up for the implementation of these actions. This blueprint was probably drawn up within the RSHA and circulated to the HSSPF. I am thinking of the promises, deceptions, ruses, lies, etc.

[255] Ibid. In Stanislawow there were a total of about 50 Security personnel with about 50% on duty at any one time. Krueger, Brandt and Erwin Linauer of the Gestapo, Heinrich Schott of the *judenreferent* (Jewish Department), the ethnic-German Mauer brothers who had served in the Rabka School, (Amelia Salsitz knew the Mauer brothers very well. She stated that the woman in charge of the domestics in the Gestapo building was Frau Z., who argued with her direct boss, Josef Daus (Gestapo) of the way he was treating the domestic staff. Daus slapped Frau Z across the face, not realising that Frau Z was the aunt of the two Gestapo men, the Mauer brothers. Amelia Salsitz not only cleaned the room of Daus, she also cleaned the room of Willi Mauer and therefore knew these men personally. She was to have further contact with Willi Mauer when her sister Celia was arrested and deported), Kurt Giese, Hans Greve, Wilhelm Hehemann, Walther Lange, Otto Ruckerich, and Kurt Wulkau, all who had seen service with the Krakow KdS. Also in the team were Werner Hagemann from Zamosc, and Franz Mause from Warsaw District. Werner

Sandowsky, KdS Galicia joined Krueger later. These were all non-commissioned officers, with the rank of *Scharfuehrer*, who had the power of life and death over tens of thousands in their hands. (KdS personnel cards-Krakow AGK. CA 375.) See also Pohl documentation and Amelia Saltsitz who particularly remembers Hans Krueger and Oscar Brandt.

[256] See Dieter Pohl. Krueger initiated the '*Grenzpolizei-Kommissariat*' for the purpose of securing the border passes on the borders with Hungarian-annexed Ruthenia.

[257] Ibid. Rudolf Muller (Wyszkow Pass) and Ernst Varchmin (Tartarow) were radical anti-Semites; there were also security detachments in Kalusz, Dolina, Nadworna, and Tlumacz, but these were manned by Polish and Ukrainian Police.

[258] The highest level of civilian administration in the Stanislowow District was the County Superintendent or Town Major (September, 1941) Heinz Albrecht, an official of the internal affairs department who had previously held a similar post in Konskie.

[259] Commanded by Paul Kleesattel. Kleesattel was the subject of a SS trial for his brutal treatment of Poles.

[260] Ibid.

[261] Trial Verdict: Zstl, 208 AR 967/69, 39. See also 'Browning, Ordinary Men', 132.

[262] Ibid. All the evidence suggests that this was the start of mass execution to the Jews.

[263] Ibid. The SS/SD were issued with the 9mm Parabellum pistol, model 08, or the Luger FIR 1411/2, FIR 6307/ According to the preference of the EG Commanders a number of machine guns and pistols were used. Krueger preferred the Russian machine gun, while other units preferred the German FWW.sub-machine guns MP 28 and 35. Most of the shell casings at mass murder sites were from these weapons (Nelson cartridges). We found similar cartridges at Belzec in 1998, at a location I believed was the Lazeret (bogus field hospital).

[264] The plank/pit device was introduced by Krueger to students of the Rabka School.

[265] At the Stanislawow cemetery in the presence of Hans Krueger, scores of Jews were standing in a long line at the open grave, waiting for their death. In the '*line-up*' one Jew, a butcher by trade, was openly inciting other Jews to attack the Germans. One of the Jews replied, '*Don't forget that there are still several thousand Jews left in the town. Are you prepared to have them on your conscience?*' The man lowered his head and gritted his teeth, and waited patiently for his death. See David Kahane, 'Lvov Ghetto Diary', 74. This is an interesting point and goes some way to explain the term 'led to their death, like sheep to the slaughter' (Ringelblum). This was not an act of cowardice, but an act of honour. What was the alternative?

[266] Correspondence sent to the author August 1999, by Renate Krakauer, daughter of Stanislawow survivor.

[267] David Kahane, 42.

[268] Hilberg, 'The Destruction', vol. 1 292.

[269] Ibid. Hilberg, 496.

[270] Again we have an instance where there was a subtle change of direction by the Nazis. This would have not gone unnoticed in RSHA, Berlin, and may well have influenced subsequent '*Actions*'. Not for the first time, particularly zbV under Schoengarth's direction, were making it up as they went along.

[271] Dieter Pohl to author 1996.

[272] Underground report, Ringelblum Archive, June, 1942. See also Krueger Verdict, fols. 294-306. Belzec was open for business from about the 17th March, 1942.

[273] See Hilberg, 'The Destruction', vol. 1.496.

[274] Ibid. This was the largest single transport to Belzec up until that time. Krueger Verdict.

[275] Ibid.

[276] PH. Amongst the Judenrat that were taken: Goldstein, Fogel, Horowitz and Akhoiz, only Goldstein returned to the ghetto.

[277] Krueger ordered all the Jews in the Mill to be liquidated. SS. Schott (Gestapo and Jewish Department), and Schupo Lieutenant Ludwig Grimm carried out the killings in Rudolf Mill.

[278] Ibid. Goldstein had attempted to escape to Hungary but this had failed. This new Judenrat consisted of 24 Jews, including: Have, Ziskind, Aaron Kaush, Shifer, Baumer, Mandler, Scmuel, Gotlieb, Herman, Halpern, Buchwald, Nachber, Wilhelm Zukerberg, Imanuel Weingarten, Kimmel, Reich, Bires, Drach, Avzeig, and Younis.

[279] Krueger Verdict. Statement and later recollections of Amalie Salsitz. Photograph produced of Jews hanging from lamp posts. The Officers identified in this action were Hauptmann Strege and Lieutenant Grim, both Schupo from Vienna.

[280] The Karaites were a sect of Jews who had broken away from the mainstream of Rabbinic Judaism in the eighth century. Followers refused to accept the authority of the Talmud or any oral tradition, adhering only to strict interpretations of the Bible, the written law. Only two towns in Poland had a Karaite community: Troki, near Vilnius (now Lithuania), and Halitz in southern Poland not far from Stanislawow. The German authorities decided that the Karaite communities were, in reality, Turks, not Jews, and left them alone.

[281] See Hilberg, 'The Destruction', vol.1. 496. Statement of Alois Mund, December, 5, 1947, and the statements by survivors and Order Police personnel of Stanislawow, 1947 and 1948, in the collection of T. Friedmann.

[282] PH. A Railway official saved 150 Jewish workers who were allowed to remain in the city.

[283] Very much like what Oskar Schindler and Julius Madritsch had done in Krakow. These employers in Stanislawow, many of which were German, have not had books or films recording their actions!

[284] Jewish resistance was centred in this factory in early 1942. Leading this small armed Jewish resistance unit of Stanislawow residents was the Jewess Anda Luff. She was killed on 11 May, 1942.

[285] The owner of this factory saved many Jews by hiding them in his basement at 54, Safeizinska Street.

[286] Some references to the Menten story hereafter are based on the book *The Menten Affair* first published by Robson Books in 1979, by the author Hans Knoop, and the book, *The Last Victim*, published by Weidenfeld and Nicolson, 1984, by the author Malcolm MacPherson. Hereafter 'Knoop' and 'MacPherson'.

[287] Ainsztein, R, 'The Collector', *New statesman*, 11.2.1981. The Jew Stieglitz stated in 1976, that a number of the paintings then in Menten's apartment had originated from Lvov where he had been engaged with Menten in the seizure of art from the Polish intelligencia between 1939-41. Stieglittz stated that he and Menten knew too much about each other and on no account would he (Stieglitz) return to Holland and give evidence. Knoop, 31. Dirk Menten corroborates that in his brother's Aerdenhout apartment there were many paintings that had been brought from Poland in 1943. Knoop, 28.

[288] The SD power and efficiency in Galicia was mainly due to the web of spies nurtured over several years before the war, especially during the opening phases of the war.

[289] Knoop 32-33. The Dutch Consul in Lvov was Jacob Jan Broen who remarked, 'He was really getting on thick with the Nazis and saluting them in the Nazi way... he told me that he had decided to stay in Krakow to get back his fortune that he had lost on Lvov.' In 1945 Broen was interviewed and confirmed that on Menten's arrival in Krakow in December, 1939, he had only a few possessions, which shows that his subsequent acquisitions were obtained between December, 1939 and when he was banished from Poland by the Nazis in 1943.

[290] Ainsztein, R, 'The Collector', *New Statesman*, 11.2.1981. The Jew Stieglitz stated in 1976, that a number of the paintings then in Menten's apartment had originated from Lvov where he had been engaged with Menten in the seizure of art from the Polish intelligencia between 1939-41. Stieglittz stated that he and Menten knew too much about each other and on no account would he (Stieglitz) return to Holland and give evidence. Knoop, p.31. Dirk Menten corroborates that in his brother's Aerdenhout apartment there were many paintings that had been brought from Poland in 1943. Knoop, p. 28.

[291] In 1977, when Menten was finally arrested he denied that he was a Dutch citizen and that the police had no jurisdiction over him. When it was suggested that he be sent to Poland where there was an arrest warrant out for him, he changed his mind.

[292] Knoop, 38.

[293] Knoop, 3

[294] Menten Verdict: The Podhorodse murders were not part of any organised Sipo-SD action. It was a personal vendetta instigated by the zbV Sonderfuehrer SS-Scharfuehrer Pieter Menten. Menten, before the war was an agent of the SD Abwehr and the landed agent of a small group of villages in the Stryj valley. Menten had made it his business to return to the area to take revenge of some blighted property disagreements.

[295] Ibid: This is absolute proof of Menten's independent actions and culpability in mass murder outside of his military attachment to zbV, however bogus. Menten lived in this village for many years before the war, and was now extracting revenge on past enemies. He had used the confusion in Lvov to slip away, taking with him SD personnel. According to the witnesses, although not the leader of this group, he was giving all the orders.

[296] Ibid: Menten's (zbV) entry in this district, at this time, was well before the official action by Hans Krueger on the 1st September 1941, when he targeted this area for clearance. Menten had already done it. I am not sure that Menten's action was ever authorised.

[297] Ibid.

[298] Menten Verdict: Statements of Tuzimek etc. as above. Some of the murdered Jews: Philip Wecker, (son-in-law of Isaac Pistiner) Benzion Neuman, Josel Nass, Moshe Halpern, Uzik, Shabtai Katz, Alfred Favel, Mendel Yeckel, Mordechai Londer, Voit Heeler, Pinchas Bernstein, Mr Greenberg, Geiwel Hellmar, Haim Jakov, Schlossberg and Schleiffer and Zuckerman.

[299] It is interesting to note that in the Tarnopol region, several hundred Women and children were killed out of a total of 5,000 Jews, between the 4th and 11th July, 1941).

[299] In Brest on 10 July 1941, over 6,000 Jews, men women and children were shot into pits by the 'EG'.

[300] Menten Verdict: In one of the Menten trials after the war, Menten had tried to establish that is was impossible for him to have been in the Podhorodse area at this time as the Wehrmacht was heavily engaged there and that battles were being waged all around. This defence was rebutted by Hans van der Leeuw, the researcher from the Rijks Institute for War Documentation who presented the Nazi Order of Battle from archives in Berlin, proving that Menten, as part of an SS-Einsatzgruppen, could easily have driven to Podhorodze on that day. However, I believe Menten must have

been authorised unless he was taking advantage of the turmoil in Lvov at that time. It was important enough for him to make this detour, with or without authorisation.

[301] Ibid. This technique was taught at the Rabka School in late 1941 (see Krueger verdict). Of four Jews who watched this execution in concealment from a nearby attic, Michael Hauptmann, and Henryk Schleiffer survived to testify at Menten's trial after the war.

[302] Knoop, see Chapter 4.

[303] Reuben Ainsztein, *New Statesman*, 8.

[304] Ibid. Statement of Dr Karl Neidling 24. 1. 1962, 765-776.

[305] Ibid. Statement of Teege, 19. 1. 1962, 751-2.

[306] Ibid. The whole question of using the services of Blobel 1005 was allegedly discussed between Teege and Rosenbaum. See Rosenbaum Statement 11. 1. 1962, 729-786. With the prospect of over 2, 000 bodies lying in the School graves there had been discussions on whether1005 should be used. However much the Nazis tried to destroy the evidence, they would have been unsuccessful as shown by our investigation at the Belzec death camp 97/99.

[307] In 1943, Paul Blobel, an SS colonel, is given the assignment of co-coordinating the destruction of the evidence of the grossest of Nazi atrocities, the systematic extermination of European Jews. As the summer of 1943 approached, Allied forces had begun making cracks in Axis strongholds, in the Pacific and in the Mediterranean specifically. Heinrich Himmler, leader of the SS, the elite corps of Nazi bodyguards that grew into a paramilitary terror force, began to consider the possibility of German defeat and worried that the mass murder of Jews and Soviet prisoners of war would be discovered. A plan was devised to dig up the buried dead and burn the corpses at each camp and extermination site. The man chosen to oversee this yearlong project was Paul Blobel. Blobel certainly had some of that blood on his hands himself, as he was in charge of SS killing squads in German-occupied areas of Russia. He now drew together another kind of squad, 'Special Commando Group 1005,' dedicated to this destruction of human evidence. Blobel began with 'death pits' near Lvov, in Poland, and forced hundreds of Jewish slave laborers from the nearby concentration camp to dig up the corpses and burn them—but not before extracting the gold from the teeth of the victims.

[308] Ibid. Statement of Kriminalkommissar Helmuth Armbrecht, Hannover, 19. 6. 1961, 243.

[309] Reading closely into these statements I am reasonably satisfied as to their accuracy.

[310] Ibid. Statement of Willy Teege, 19. 1. 1962, 751-2. Teege was an established teacher in the last phase of the School and a close friend of Rosenbaum, personally and professionally.

[311] Ibid.

[312] Ibid. Statement of Kriminalkommissar Heinz Bohm, Dusseldorf, 29. 6. 1961, at the School June - December 1944, 92. See also Paul Enders, Solingen, 26. 6. 1961, 210, who was the School between 15. 6. 44 and 15. 12. 1944, 210.

[313] Ibid. Rosenbaum.

[314] Ibid. Rosenbaum/Teege.

[315] Ibid.

[316] RAD. OKW law/WFSt Op.Nr. 00 2811/42 (directive nr. 46) d.d. 18.8.1942

[317] RAD. Law 'Behaviour of the troops in the East' in the version 12. Inf. Div.Abt.Ic/Ia Nr. 607/41 geh. Dd. 17.11.1941.

[318] RAD. Judgment X11 of the American Military Court in Nuremberg.

[319] RAD. List of shootings within the bounds of the 11th Army, June 22nd, 1941.

[320] RAD.

[321] On October 4, 1943, Reischsfuehrer-SS Heinrich Himmler gave a speech to a secret meeting of SS officers, in Poznan, Poland. In this speech, he spoke frankly about the ongoing extermination of the Jewish people.

[322] Acknowledgement to Dieter Pohl's assessment of Hans Krueger.

[323] Ibid.

[324] Simon Wiesenthal, 'Justice Not Vengeance': *The Reluctant Murderer*, Weidenfeld, London 1989, 164-173

[325] Krueger Verdict.

[326] Ibid. When Kaltenbrunner was on trial after the war at Nuremberg, in his defence he produced a copy of the letter he had sent to the Red Cross concerning the release of Countess Lanckoronska. Kaltenbrunner was hanged in Nuremberg prison on 16th October 1946.

[327] Ibid. 'Breda Three' – the remaining life-term Nazi war criminals in Dutch jails. For years the 'Breda Three' had been a *'cause-celebre'* in West Germany.

[328] Ibid.

[329] Lackoronska did not want her war memoirs published in her lifetime. After much persuasion, however, she consented to publication in Poland, by ZNAK Publishing of Krakow, in 2001, just a year before her death. The book, whose British version is titled *Those Who Trespass Against Us: One Woman's War Against the Nazis*, sold over 50,000 copies in the Polish original and is now selling well in English. The U.S. edition was published in hardback in spring 2007 by Da Capo Press (Perseus Publishing Group) under the new title, *Michelangelo in Ravensbrueck*. In 1967 Lanckoronska established the Lanckoronski Foundation, which promotes and supports Polish culture, awarding over a million *złotych* per annum (£208,000) for scholarships, publication of learned books, research into Polish archives in countries such as Lithuania, Belarus and Ukraine, and similar projects.

[330] Jonathan Petropoulos, based on his book *Art as Politics in the Third Reich*, London 1997.

[331] Ainsztein, R, 'The Collector', *New Statesman*, 11.2.1981. The Jew Stieglitz stated in 1976, that a number of the paintings then in Menten's apartment had originated from Lvov where he had been engaged with Menten in the seizure of art from the Polish intelligencia between 1939-41. Stieglittz stated that he and Menten knew too much about each other and on no account would he (Stieglitz) return to Holland and give evidence. Knoop, 31. Dirk Menten corroborates that in his brother's Aerdenhout apartment there were many paintings that had been brought from Poland in 1943, Knoop, 28.

[332] Ibid, 34

[333] Malcom MacPherson, *The Last Victim*, London 1984, 285.

[334] Knoop

[335] Ibid.

[336] Ibid

[337] Ibid

[338] Ibid

[339] Ibid.

[340] Ministry of Justice, Trial Transcripts , The Netherlands vs Pieter N. Menten, 1961 - 65, 1977-80.

[341] MacPherson, 296-299

[342] Schoengarth, Dr. jur. Eberhard (22.4.1903-15.5.1946) [*SS-Brigadeführer und Generalmajor der Polizei*] – NSDAP: 2848857; SS: 67174; commander, Secret State Police (*Geheime Staatspolizei – Gestapo*) Bielefeld 1937-1938; commander, Gestapo Dortmund Jan-Mar 1938; commander, Gestapo Muenster Mar 1938-Oct 1939; Inspector, German Security Police and Security Service (*Sicherheitspolizei und Sicherheitsdienst - Sipo/SD*) Dresden Oct 1939-Mar 1941; commander, Sipo/SD Cracow Mar 1941-Jun 1943; commander, Action Group (*Einsatzgruppe*) for Special Tasks Jul-Aug 1941; service, 4th SS Division 'Polizei' Jul 1943-Jul 1944; commander, Sipo/SD the Hague (Den Haag) Jul 1944-May 1945; Senior SS and Police Commander 'Northwest' (*HSSPF 'Nordwest'*) (Netherlands) 10 Mar 1945-Apr 1945 as Hans-Albin Rauter's substitute {arrested and put on trial by a British military tribunal at Burgsteinfurt for the murder of an RAF air crew member POW at Schede, Netherlands on 21 Nov 1944; convicted and sentenced to death by hanging 11 Feb 1946 (History of the United Nations War Crimes Commission and the Development of the Laws of War p. 532, United Nations War Crimes Commission, London: HMSO, 1948) or 3 Apr 1946 (LT 13 Feb 1946:3d); executed at Hameln 15 May 1946 (Allgemeine-SS p. 87; Hilberg 713; Ency Holo 1592; 'Hameln 1945-

49,'http://home.c2i.net/sudeten/Seite_1/194 ... 5-49.html; Dienstaltersliste der Schutzstaffel der NSDAP [9 Nov 1944]).}

[343] Ibid. A similar order by Hitler, dated 18th October, 1942, referred to the slaughter of *Commandos* to the last man after capture (498-PS)

[344] IMT (HMSO) – R-110.) 'Opening Speeches', 32.

[345] Ibid 058-PS

[346] See Michael Bloch, *Ribbentrop*, Bantam Press, London, 1992, 402.

[347] WO 311 1304 Interrogation of Walther Albarth. When Joachim von Ribbentrop was arrested on the 14th June, 1945 and examined by a doctor he was found to have a small tin of poison attached to his lower parts (*The Times* 16 June 1945). Herman Goering managed to use his poison the evening before he was due to be hanged.

[348] Statement 11th August 1945. See WO 311/1304.

[349] Ibid 15th August.

[350] Ibid 16th August.

[351] Ibid 16th August.

[352] Ibid 12th September.

[353] Ibid 22th August.

[354] WO, 3544. 235 / 102A, 35-44.

[355] This was to be a recurring factor in the War Crimes Trials of the 'Rabka Four'. Each would support the other in some way or other. In my opinion, Menten was the most dangerous and devious, and his actions resulted in the destruction of many careers in the process.

[356] Corroboration of fact re the agreement of the 'Rabka Four'. See PRO, WO/235 – report from War Crimes Section (Gr.Capt. Legal Staff, requesting information as to the identity of this man Menten, dated 14.6.1946, to the War Crimes Investigation Unit, ref. BAOR/15228/2/c.7.JAG.)

[357] Ibid, reply to request for information vide report dated 17.10.46, ref. BAOR/WC/CMisc C.19.

[358] Rijks Institute for War Documentation. On the 6th March, 1944 the Dutch Resistance mounted an attack on Rauter's chauffeur-driven BMW staff car in the village of Woeste Hoeve (between Arnhem and Apeldoorn) in an attempted assassination on Rauter (Kommissar-General fur das Sicherheitsdienst in den Niederlanden).

[359] Ibid.

[360] Ibid. Post-mortem report of the bodies found.

[361] J. C. H. Blom: *The Public Historian.* Vol. 6, No. 4 (autumn, 1984), 37 - 48 (edited by author).

[362] Originally published in *Polin: Studies in Polish Jewry, Volume 13: The Holocaust and its Aftermath*, edited by Antony Polonsky and published by the Littman Library

of Jewish Civilization for the Institute for Polish-Jewish Studies and the American Association for Polish-Jewish Studies (Oxford and Portland, Oregon, 2000).

[363] There are two other documents written by eyewitnesses. Both were SS visitors to the camp. The first was Kurt Gerstein, a disinfection expert. Deeply shaken by what he saw, he tried unsuccessfully to pass his knowledge on to the neutral parties, the Swedish and Vatican legations in Berlin. In French custody after the war he wrote a harrowing account of his visit, which included a 'show gassing'. The other was Wilhelm Pfannenstiel, a professor of hygiene. He went to Belzec with Gerstein and also accompanied Himmler on a visit in Nov. 1942. He did not come forward voluntarily to testify about Belzec, but was interrogated about it after the war, first by the Allies and then twice by German legal authorities.

[364] The name Distrikt Galizien refers to a fifth province of the Generalgouvernement created by the Nazis in July 1941 with Lvov (Lwow L'viv) as its provincial capital. It consisted of three pre-war voivodeships situated in south-eastern Poland: Lvov, Tarnopol, and Stanislawow.

[365] In a deposition taken down in Krakow in 1945 by the Regional Jewish Historical Commission (Collection of Testimonies of Jewish Survivors, Zydowski Instytut Historyczny, Warsaw, file 302/162) Reder says that he was betrayed to the Germans by two Ukrainians: Edward and Marjan Kobzdej. The information was omitted from the book. (All notes in this chapter are mine—M. M. Rubel.)

[366] The German in question was a German career railway official by the name of Rudolf Goekel (1883? – 21 Aug. 1960). In 1941 he was posted to Belzec as a station-master. When Jewish transports began to arrive at Belzec in the middle of Mar. 1942, he was relieved of his post and became a liaison officer between the station and the camp. In 1946 Goekel was arrested in Berlin and in May 1947 deported to Poland, where he was kept in protective custody in Zamosc. There, on 19 Nov. 1948, he was interrogated by Hieronim Rolle, the district attorney. In the course of the inquiry Goekel stated that: 'I stayed in Belzec from July 1941 until January 1943. During that period I worked as a station-master. If I remember well, transports with Jews were coming to Belzec from about Pentecost 1942 until September that year. I cannot be sure, but not all trucks were always full: only five to six trucks on average. I was not allowed to look inside the trucks, nor had I the right to inspect them in any way. Trucks that were empty were open. I did not count Jewish transports arriving in Belzec. Therefore, I cannot say how many came. I also do not know the number of victims, but I could see that most of them were already dead on arrival... I did not have permission to enter the camp, and therefore know nothing about what was going on inside. But, on the basis of hearsay and talks with the locals, I imagined the camp in Belzec to be like other concentration camps of isolation which received and dispatched transports. I believed that only bodies of

those already dead were burnt there, and not of those who had arrived alive.' In 1950 Rudolf Goekel was released from protective custody without charge. He returned to Germany a free man. (See Coll. OB, 2 pt. 11, Archiwum Glownej Komisji Badania Zbrodni przeciwko Narodowi Polskiemu, Warsaw.)

[367] In normal circumstances Zugsfuehrer meant 'train master'. In the camp's usage the term referred to fifteen or so Jews selected from the death brigade, led by an Oberzugsfuehrer, with the task of being present at the ramp to meet each transport as it arrived.

[368] SS Hauptscharfuehrer Fritz Irrmann (11 Oct. 1914 – 1942) was in charge of a platoon of Ukrainian guards. He was accidentally shot dead in Belzec sometime in the autumn of 1942 by his colleague Heinrich Gley in a scuffle during an escape attempt by two Ukrainian guards. (See Dr Janusz Peter'Kordian', W Belz cu podczas Okupacji, Diaries, no. 221, Z.ydowski Instytut Historyczny, Warsaw.)

[369] 'You are going to take a bath now. Afterwards you will be sent to work.' The text of the speech varied, according to different testimonies. But it contained two basic elements: an instruction to undress in order to take a bath, and a vague promise of work. It was not always delivered by Irrmann, but by any member of the SS garrison who was at the ramp on duty.

[370] The building with the gas chambers had six cubicles, each about 25 sq. m. It is almost impossible to squeeze such a large crowd into such a small space. The figure of 750 people was provided by Christian Wirth, the camp's first commandant, to a company of high-ranking SS officers who visited the camp in the middle of Aug. 1942. Wirth's purpose was to impress them with the efficiency of his methods of murder, which they had come to improve. The figure must then have become official, although highly unrealistic, and the source of the wild overestimate made by Reder after the war of 2.5 million victims. See n. 32.

[371] This was the outlet of a gas pipe.

[372] The first building housing the gas chambers, which was constructed some time towards the end of 1941, was made of double wooden planks with the spaces in between filled with sand. It was only half the size of the second gassing installation described by Reder, and had only three gas chambers. This building was taken down some time in June or July 1942, during the camp's extensive modernization.

[373] Between 20 July, the date when the camp was reopened after modernization, and 11 Dec. 1942, the date of arrival of the last transport from Rawa Ruska, no fewer than c.520, 000 Jews were murdered in Belzec, of which c.38, 000 died between 20 and 31 July, c.172, 000 in Aug., c.132, 000 in Sept., c.110, 000 in Oct., c.61, 000 in Nov., and c.10, 000 in Dec.

[374] The engine, said to have come from a captured Russian tank, was installed and supervised by SS Scharfuehrer Lorenz Hackenholt (b. 25 June 1914), a mechanic

responsible for the gassing installations constructed first in Belzec and then in Sobibor and Treblinka. Apart from the two askers, the engine was switched on and off by a Jew called Moniek, a taxi-driver from Krakow. This incriminating information comes from Reder's interrogation by Jan Sehn. The interrogation took place in Krakow on 29 Dec. 1945 (Collection of Testimonies of Jewish Survivors, Zydowski Instytut Historyczny, Warsaw, file no. 102/46). The information was omitted from the printed edition of Reder's booklet.

[375] Reder is wrong. No French Jews were deported to Belzec. Some Dutch Jews were deported to Sobibor. Some Greek Jews were taken to Treblinka. But there were German Jews in Belzec; most came from different ghettos in Lublin district, where they had been taken after deportation from Germany sometime in the early months of 1941.

[376] A Jew named Sanio Ferber employed in one of the SS workshops in Lvov testified after the war that 'Towards the end of December 1942 there came to our workshop once a young dentist whose name I do not recall. He told us that he escaped from Belzec. This dentist was in Belzec for three months. Because of his profession he was detailed to a dentist brigade, which numbered, if I remember correctly, fifteen men. Their job was to pull out gold teeth and bridges from corpses yanked out from the gas chambers.' What happened to this dentist afterwards is not known. (See Collection of Testimonies of Jewish Survivors, Zydowski Instytut Historyczny, Warsaw, file no. 4732.)

[377] See n. 18.

[378] Lublin was the headquarters of Action Reinhardt, the operation consisting of the organized murder and plunder of the Jews in the specially designated murder camps of Belzec, Sobibor, and Treblinka. In charge of Action Reinhardt was Brigadefuehrer Odilo Globocnik, SS- und Polizeifuehrer for Lublin district. From 1 Aug. 1942 the responsibility for economic plunder was entrusted into the most capable hands of Christian Wirth (24 Nov. 1885 – 26 May 1944), Kriminalrat from the criminal police in Stuttgart, who became an inspector of SS garrisons in all three camps of Action Reinhardt after relinquishing the post of first commandant of Belzec. Part of his new job consisted in preparing for further use the mountains of clothing and personal items belonging to victims murdered in the Action Reinhardt camps. The spoils were collected in hangars at a disused airport in Lublin, where 500 Jewish workers did the job of sorting, checking, and preparing items for dispatch. Money and precious metals were sent to Hitler's chancellery via Globocnik's headquarters. A final report of the financial gains of Action Reinhardt was submitted to Himmler by Globocnik in 1944 for approval. It was approved.

[379] Heni, or Christian, Schmidt was a Volksdeutsch from Latvia with the rank of Zugwachtmann. He was one of the former Soviet prisoners of war trained in the

camp at Trawniki for service in the murder camps of Action Reinhardt. These people were known to the Poles who lived in the vicinity of the camp as Ukrainian guards (prisoners of war of Ukrainian origin were in the majority), or askers. In German they were called either Trawniki Männer or Hilfswillige, Hiwis for short.

[380] Reder is wrong. Bills of lading were delivered to the German station-master. They contained not personal names, but average numbers and the names of the localities where the Judenzüge (Jewish deportation trains) originated. Belzec railway station was set on fire by a bomb dropped from a Soviet plane in 1944, and the documents did not survive. Documents from the other murder camps of Action Reinhardt were destroyed on Himmler's specific orders after the termination of the murder operations, to obliterate all traces—written and material—of the massacre.

[381] Reder contradicts here his earlier and later testimonies. During an interrogation by Jan Sehn (see n. 13) he gave a list of four names of askers (Schmidt, Schneiner, Kunz, and Trottwein) and only three names of the members of the SS garrison (Irrmann, Schwarz, and Feix), which suggests that members of the Jewish death brigade had at least some contact with the Ukrainian guards and very limited contact with the Germans. This is confirmed by the fact that, during an interrogation in the office of a public prosecutor in Munich in Aug. 1960, Reder stated that he had never heard the names of Oberhauser, Fichtner, Floss, Hering, Schwarz, Dubois, Girtzig, Dachsel, Barbl, Groh (Groth), Kamm, Schluch, Zirke (Zierke), and Gley, although most of them had been members of the SS garrison in Belzec murder camp. (The name of Schwarz crops up in Reder's booklet on numerous occasions.)

[382] Between 16 and 19 Oct. three transports came to Belzec from Zamosc via the transit camp in Izbica carrying between 12,000 and 16,000 victims, the majority of whom were foreign Jews.

[383] The transport, which went via the transit camp in Izbica, carried 4,000 victims, among whom were the last Jews of Zamosc.

[384] SS Oberscharfuehrer Gottfried Schwarz (3 May 1913 – 19 June 1944) held the post of deputy commandant of Belzec from the end of 1941 until May 1943, when the camp was dismantled under his supervision. In 1943 he was promoted by Himmler to the rank of SS Untersturmfuehrer.

[385] Neither the first nor the second commandant of the camp held the rank of Obersturmfuehrer. Christian Wirth (see n. 15) was responsible for the construction of Belzec; he held the rank of SS Sturmbannfuehrer after promotion by Himmler in 1943. From 1 Aug. 1942 he was replaced by Gottlieb Hering (2 June 1887 □ 9 Oct. 1945), Kriminalkommissar in the criminal police in Stuttgart, promoted to the rank of SS Hauptsturmfuehrer by Himmler in 1943. The description by Reder fits both Wirth and Hering. Both were known and feared for their extreme brutality.

[386] As is known from other sources, the gassing engine broke down on numerous occasions. One such breakdown occurred in the middle of Aug. 1942 during the 'show' gassing witnessed by Kurt Gerstein and Wilhelm Pfannenstiel, two SS experts on disinfection (see n. 1). The breakdown, timed by Gerstein, lasted for over two hours, with the victims locked inside.

[387] Not SS Stabscharfuehrer but SS Hauptscharfuehrer; see n. 5.

[388] SS Scharfuehrer (not Oberscharfuehrer) Reinhold Feix (3 July 1909 ☐ 30 May 1969) was a supervisor of the Jewish death brigade (those who emptied gas chambers, dragged bodies, and dug pits). Reder spelt his name wrongly as 'Faix'.

[389] See n. 23

[390] See n. 18.

[391] According to Yitzhak Arad (Belzec, Sobibor, Treblinka: *The Operation Reinhardt Death Camps* (Bloomington, Ind., 1987), 165☐9, Himmler never went to Belzec but visited Sobibor and Treblinka in 1943. However, according to the post-war testimonies of Polish inhabitants of Belzec and Tomaszow Lubelski, Himmler visited Belzec twice: once in Aug. then in Oct. or Nov. 1942.

[392] Reder was brought to the camp on either 18 or 19 Aug. 1942. He escaped towards the end of Nov. that year, which makes it a little over three months—not four months, as he wrote earlier.

[393] The figure given by Reder is a gross overestimate. Post-war estimates by Polish railway workers from Belzec give a figure of about 1 million. Polish commissions investigating Nazi crimes cut this figure by half. Arad (Belzec, Sobibor, Treblinka) estimates c.518, 000 victims. My own estimate comes close to Arad's: c.520, 000 (see n. 12). Latest estimates based on digs carried out on the site of the camp during 1997☐8 raise the figure to 550,000 and even 650,000.

[394] In the 1960s, Waclaw Kolodziejczyk, a former worker at the Belżec railway station, created 6 paintings showing Belzec during the German occupation. In the years 1939-1944 Kolodziejczyk supervised repairs to the rail tracks, and lived with his family in buildings close to Belzec station. Because he spoke and understood German well, the Germans used him as an interpreter for contact with the Polish railway staff. According to some testimonies by local inhabitants from Belzec, he was even temporarily employed in the *Kommandant*'s house as the person responsible for the SS store. There he had contact with the Jewish prisoners from the death camp who worked in the SS houses, and he probably learned some details about the camp from them. He never personally entered the death camp.

[395] No transports arrived at the camp after 11 Dec. 1942, but it is quite possible that Jews caught during the so-called Judenjagd (Jew hunt) were brought to the camp and shot there. The opening of pits and burning of bodies began immediately after the transports stopped.

[396] The opening of pits and burning of bodies began immediately after the transports stopped. The burning continued for three months. By May 1943 the camp had been dismantled, the buildings taken down, and the ground levelled and planted with young conifers. Members of the Jewish brigade were loaded onto a train, which took them straight to Sobibor, where they were murdered on arrival after refusing to disembark.

[397] Berlin Document Centre (*jetzt: Bundesarchiv, Aussenstelle Zehlendorf*) is the central archive for research concerning former members of the SS. In this thesis, the author has referred to copies held in Yad Vashem, Israel. Further references have also relied on the comprehensive bibliography as shown in the publications of Dieter Pohl (*OSTGALIZIEN*) and Thomas Sandkühlrer (*ENDLÖSUNG*).

[398] The *Einsatz* groups – and it is important that the full title be held in mind at all times – were the Offices of the Sipo-SD operating in the field behind the armies (*Einsatzgruppen*). When police control had been established in the newly occupied territory, the mobile *Einsatz* groups were disbanded and became regional offices under the commanders of the Sipo-SD in the occupied territories.

[399] Gestapo (State) and SD (Party) are inextricably linked due to their indistinguishable criminal enterprises.

[400] No one was compelled to join the Nazi Party, much less to become one of the leaders. Many joined for business, social or selfish reasons. There was no legal compulsion to join.

[401] R.S.H.A. A department of the SS; substantially all of its personnel belonged to the SS. It was under the command of Heydrich (later Kaltenbrunner). In addition to the SD, which was always an SS formation, it included the Gestapo and the Reich Criminal Police both of which were State agencies. For this reason the R.S.H.A was also recognised as a department of the Reich Ministry of the Interior.

[402] The SA should not be underestimated as to their contribution to the Nazi war effort, particularly as a combat unit for defence of the Party. They were used extensively as guards in Danzig, Posen, Silesia and the Baltic Provinces. Particular attention is drawn to their actions in the Kovno and Vilna ghettos in the guarding of Jews when digging up and burning corpses: See IMT Speeches, 45. Affidavit of Szloma Gol: International Military Tribunal: '*SPEECHES OF THE PROSECUTORS*': The Trials of German Major War Criminals (London, 1946), 45. Hereafter IMT Speeches.

[403] See for formation and daily duties of the *Sonderdienst: Zygmunt Klukowski, DIARY FROM THE YEARS OF OCCUPATION 1939-1944*, translated from the Polish by George Klukowski, ed. Andrew Klukowski and Helen Klukowski May (Chicago, 1993).

[404] The W.V.H.A. was under the leadership of *SS-Obergruppenfuehrer* Pohl who was charged with the administration of concentration camps (KZs), and the exploitation of labour.

Lightning Source UK Ltd.
Milton Keynes UK
UKOW032043111012

200468UK00001B/40/P